# Shadow over Shangri-la

# Shadow over Shangri-la

## A Woman's Quest for Freedom

·

## Durga Pokhrel

### with Anthony Willett

Brassey's
Washington · London

Library of Congress Cataloging-in-Publication Data
Pokhrel, Durga.
Shadow over Shangri-la: a woman's quest for freedom/Durga Pokhrel
with Anthony Willett.—1st ed.
p. cm.
Includes index.
ISBN 1-57488-061-6
1. Pokhrel, Durga. 2. Nepal—Politics and government.
3. Political prisoners—Nepal—Biography. 4. Women—Nepal—
Biography. I. Willett, Anthony. II. Title.
DS495.592.P65A3 1996
954.96—dc20
[B] 95-44455

Names and distinguishing characteristics of several individuals in this book
have been changed to protect their identities.

Designed by Tanya M. Pérez

First Edition
10 9 8 7 6 5 4 3 2 1
Printed in the United States of America

# Contents

# Acknowledgments

The only spirit that kept me sane and alive during my incarceration was my personal deity, Ganesh. I bow down humbly before him.

My gratitude to Amnesty International for adopting me as a Prisoner of Conscience goes beyond words. I wish especially to acknowledge Amnesty USA's California chapter, whose members worked constantly until I was released. While I was missing for several months, of all the members of my family, only my father, Kaviraj Narapati Pokhrel, and my fourth elder sister, Subhadra Devi Dhakal, took the risk of investigating my whereabouts and filing a *habeas corpus* writ in Nepal's Supreme Court. My appreciation for them is beyond expression. I also owe thanks to others that I was finally released. My work partner, Shrish Rana, the sole witness to my abduction by the police, helped in a crucial way until the last moment. As a result of Shrish's efforts, the youngest prince, Dhirendra Bir Bikram Shah, opened the essential line of communication about my case with the king. I am deeply grateful to him. I remain thankful to King Birendra Bir Bikram Shah Dev for authorizing my release.

One policewoman, who shall be left nameless, became a ray of hope for me while I remained in Central Women's Prison. So did a veteran of Nepali social service work, the late Manjoor World, who never failed to put a positive spin on events. I appreciate them. Above all, I wish to thank my fellow inmates in the prisons. Their humor, trust, and courage, and the way they strengthened me, are etched eternally in my memory.

Most of all, I thank my husband, Anthony, for using his savings and giving up his job for over two years to write this book with me. My love for him and my appreciation for his intelligence, sensitivity, and devotion know no bounds. He is the one who skillfully and carefully organized and word-processed our long conversations and my rough drafts into manuscript and contributed innumerable insights, details, and descriptive passages from his own experience. The book is truly half his work. I am equally thankful to my three sons, Samyog, Shristi, and Tapasya, who have been so understanding and patient waiting for the day we would finish the book and could go outside and enjoy some fun.

I gratefully acknowledge the J. Roderick MacArthur Foundation for an award toward writing this book that provided us a great moral boost during our time in Iowa without other income. Also Sidney Jones of Asia Watch for her enthusiasm and support. I would also like to sincerely thank our close friends from Harvard days, Gerry Bodeker and Sara Taber, and also Lynn Franklin and Muriel Nellis, for reading and offering their valuable suggestions on our earlier manuscripts.

Finally, although she did not live to see the book in print, my mother-in-law, Barbara Mary Willett, took the trouble to read an early manuscript and then expressed great appreciation for who I was. I thank her for her understanding.

# Foreword

Many brave individuals and dedicated organizations have kept alive the hope that human beings could someday be afforded the dignity that all men, women, and childen deserve. The author of *Shadow over Shangri-la*, Durga Pokhrel of Nepal, is one of these heroes. Fortunately for all of us, she survived her dreadful political imprisonment and lived to tell her remarkable story.

I visited Nepal in 1993. It is such a beautiful, peaceful country—an ancient land of majestic mountains and green valleys graced with a gentle people of deep spirituality. It truly is the lengendary Shangri-la.

But a country's surface appearance can be very deceiving. Reading Durga Pokhrel's *Shadow over Shangri-la: A Woman's Quest for Freedom*, I was struck by how Durga's story parallels my own. I, too, was imprisoned for voicing my beliefs in democracy and human rights in my native country before I was able to escape to the United States. However, when I recently returned to China, I was again jailed. Accounts like mine and Durga's, and countless others around the world, show that the campaign for universal human rights is far from over.

A great many victims of human rights abuses suffer alone, and survivors are rarely able to tell their stories in such an eloquent way as *Shadow over Shangri-la*. As much as any warrior, Durga proves herself a hero. She endured humiliating torment, but still helped her fellow inmates. She has not wavered in her convictions and continues to voice her opinions (and prudent advice) about the political situation in Nepal.

Compared to the past thirty years, Nepal's human rights situation today is much improved, thanks largely to courageous leaders like Durga Pokhrel. I highly recommend her inspirational book. *Shadow over Shangri-la* is unique: an uplifting account of human and women's rights, an adventure tale, and a heart-warming love story. As someone who has been deeply concerned about human rights issues, I believe that the world is better today because of the sacrifices Ms. Pokhrel was willing to make. Everyone who cares about freedom should be interested in her story.

HONGDA HARRY WU
January 1996

# Shadow over Shangri-la

# 1

·

# End of Best Day

May 31, 1981, was to be the day of reckoning for our small publishing business. It was a Sunday, the first day of the work week in Nepal. We had made a bid to the government for a major contract and that was the day when tenders were going to be opened at the national telecommunications office in Kathmandu. At four-thirty A.M. I was fully awake, and decided to make an early-morning visit to the temples to start the day with every positive influence. I began my morning rituals by taking a cold shower, then worship, yoga, and meditation.

The morning felt quite beautiful, and I chose a fresh green chiffon sari to wear. Then I told Ram Bahadur Lama, my houseboy, that I would drink tea after returning from the temples. I left the apartment, following an alley winding between the fruit, vegetable, and flower gardens of old residential estates. Several passersby offered their greetings. The raucous throttle of a motor-rickshaw announced the main street, interrupting the quiet of the early morning. A taxi blared its horn as it passed a cow lying across the road. I stopped the taxi and asked the driver to go to the temple of Pashupatinath, a name for Lord Shiva. Taxis were not allowed to drive right up to the temple precinct, so I had a walk of about ten minutes through a thin pine forest and then down some ancient cobbled streets to reach the temple. Worshippers were already on the road. As I passed a Vedic school, the high clear voices of young boys rang out, rhythmically chanting a series of Sanskrit verses from the Vedas, the ancient Hindu texts. I took off my shoes outside the golden doors of the temple's main entrance and bought a basket of flowers, garlands, and incense as an offering to Pashupatinath. A policeman was already on duty at the gate, watchful in case any non-Hindu should try to enter the temple—one of the Hindu world's holiest places of pilgrimage. Lightly touching the floor with my fingers and bringing them to my forehead in a customary gesture of reverence, I walked into the temple compound. Inside, the air was already laden with the heavy sweet smell of incense and flowers, and every now and then the temple bells clanged as a worshipper finished prayer. I allowed my mind to settle and become aware of God as I silently repeated and reflected on the sacred set of words of the Shiva mantra that are believed to embody the divine influence of this deity.

Devotees had been chanting *bhajan* prayers throughout the night in a side temple. One by one they rose to their feet and, palms pressed together, turned to face the east and saluted the rising sun. Without pause, other devotees took over the sacred chanting in an unbroken, centuries-old vigil in this Himalayan seat of Shiva. Down some steps from the temple was the Arya cremation ghat on the banks of Kathmandu's holy Bagmati River. By a smoldering funeral pyre, ash-smeared yogis sat motionless in the lotus position, detached from the world. A pious widow, dressed in accordance with custom in a white sari, and wearing no ornament or red mark on her forehead, made her way along the riverbank toward the temple for her morning devotion.

After receiving the *darshan*, or presence, of Pashupatinath, I crossed a short stone bridge over the Bagmati and climbed the hill that leads to Guhyashwori, a shrine commemorating Shiva's consort. As is the Hindu custom, I wanted to offer worship to the female as well as the male aspect of the Divine. Having completed this ritual, I made my way back to the taxi stand beyond Pashupatinath in order to take a taxi to a temple of Ganesh. The elephant-headed Lord Ganesh, the child of Shiva and Parvati, is the cheerful, bountiful deity who removes obstacles and brings good fortune. Since childhood I had been his devotee. At a nearby shop, I bought eight *laddu* sweets, which are believed to be Ganesh's favorite, and a little basket of flowers to offer him. After finishing this worship ritual, I returned home, drank my morning tea, and went to my office—the press and newspaper business that my partners and I managed. Two members of the office staff were already busy in the back room preparing for the next day's edition of our newspaper.

१२

Poles apart politically, my two partners and I had come together for the sole objective of running our printing press and newspapers professionally and commercially. One partner, Upendra Rana, was a paternal uncle of the Queen of Nepal and taught commerce at the university. Associated with leftist university teachers and journalists, he was perceived by the public as being "a royal communist." For seven years, until 1945, Upendra's grand-father had been one of the most powerful Rana prime ministers. The Ranas had ruled Nepal as *de facto* sovereigns for a period of 104 years, ending only in 1950. The real kings were the Shahs, whose rule over present-day Nepal began in the mid-1700s, when King Prithvi Narayan Shah of Gorkha unified neighboring principalities, including the three kingdoms of the Kathmandu valley. The Ranas' oligarchic rule began in 1846, when Jang Bahadur Rana, the second-favorite courtier of the regent queen, staged a palace coup known as the *kot parva* ("armory massacre"), in which he killed her first favorite along with his entire entourage. By siding with the then-more-powerful junior queen and becoming her first favorite, Jang gained access to unbounded political power. Appointed in due course to be prime minister, Jang took advantage of the queen's distance from day-to-day affairs and consolidated his position through her legal approval to the extent of having the premier position made hereditary within the Rana family. All other chief positions in the military and civil service of the government—from central to district levels—followed suit and became reserved for Ranas. To strengthen their position as a feudal class, they dis-tributed national land among themselves as rewards called *birta*—tax-free, inheritable land grants. Furthermore, they restricted the royalty's social in-tercourse by so arranging things that the Shah kings and princes should marry only Rana girls. In this way, the Ranas promoted themselves to the status of royalty. The then-regent queen, other queens, and even suc-ceeding kings apparently were slow to recognize that the Ranas were turn-ing the Shahs into powerless figureheads, prisoners within the royal palace.

My other partner, Shrish, was from the same Rana clan as Upendra. Shrish's grandfather had been the Rana governor of eastern Nepal, with his residential headquarters in my hometown, Dhankuta, and he and my father were close friends. One of Shrish's uncles, Damodar Shamsher Jang Bahadur, was widely known and feared for his role in maintaining the grip of the authoritarian regime headed by the absolute monarch who had ruled Nepal with an iron fist since taking over power in 1960. Shrish was very close to this uncle, and, worse still, in his student days had been one of the organizers of the *Mandale* student union, which was created and funded by the government to suppress oppositional student organizations. For a career, Shrish had gone on to become subeditor of *The Rising Nepal*, the state-run English-language daily newspaper that was the main official voice of the government. To everyone's surprise, Shrish resigned that position in order to work in our little publishing business.

Both Upendra and Shrish had been groomed by the Jesuit Fathers at Saint Xavier's in Kathmandu, and were thoroughly anglicized. Because of their polished education and lofty background they were considered sophisticated.

Unlike my two Rana partners, I was a most unsophisticated person from a remote mountain district. They used to call me *"parkote"* in Nepali—"rustic hillbilly." I had previously taught modern political history to undergraduate and graduate students, but had been expelled six years earlier by Tribhuvan University, in Kathmandu, for a series of political charges. I was also a journalist and held a law degree, which I had pursued in the event that it should ever be necessary to defend myself against any legal challenges that the government might bring. Above all, I was an active member of the Nepali Congress. This was a social democratic party, the largest of Nepal's political parties. Since December 15, 1960, the Nepali Congress, along with all other parties, had been banned by royal decree. From that time, to be known as a Nepali Congress member was like living on death row.

On that "Black Day," as we in the banned Nepali Congress referred to December 15, 1960, Nepal's first elected prime minister and the leader of the Nepali Congress party, Bisheshwor Prasad Koirala—popularly known as "B.P."—was arrested by soldiers sent by King Mahendra Bir Bikram Shah while he was addressing a huge conference of Nepal's youth in Kathmandu. The king then dismissed the popularly and democratically elected parliamentary government, restricted all fundamental rights of Nepali citizens, and imprisoned all members of the cabinet along with other democratic leaders. Neither Prime Minister Koirala nor the other cabinet ministers received any formal charge or explanation. The prime minister was kept in prison for almost eight years, and was adopted by Amnesty International at one point as their "Prisoner of the Year." His release on October 30, 1968, followed persistent pressure and advocacy by Amnesty International and other human rights organizations and individuals against the king's action. Immediately after his release, he exiled himself to India and declared the Nepali Congress party's "armed struggle" against the government system introduced by King Mahendra and for the restoration of democracy. From

1960 to 1990, thousands of party political workers disappeared, were arrested, or were brutally killed.

The irony was that the democratic leaders who were treated so inhumanely by King Mahendra were the very people who had struggled to restore his father, King Tribhuvan Bir Bikram Shah, to the throne in 1950 after he escaped from palace arrest under the Ranas. The Nepali Congress party—formed by B. P. Koirala in 1949, two years after India's independence—overthrew the Ranas in 1950 through an armed revolution. Koirala became Nepal's first democratically elected prime minister, and, following his ideals of democratic socialism, for the first time Nepal's government developed policies with the aim that all Nepalis should share equally in national development.

But the Nepali Congress's populist policies were perceived as threatening by the kingdom's hereditary feudal class and other reactionary elements. A coalition of vested interests—palace courtiers (power-broking secretaries and retainers from Rana days), hard-liner royalty, the king's in-laws, election losers, and landlords—formed to steal the king's trust away from the democratically elected leaders. To divert King Mahendra from his *dharma*—his right duty—of upholding justice was not a difficult task for these groups because he appeared jealous of his prime minister's popularity at home and abroad. Fresh, too, was the memory of his forefathers'— even his father's—palace imprisonment as puppet kings by the Ranas. For King Mahendra, the popular B.P. became the embodiment of all his fears.

The psychologically insecure, still-feudal King Mahendra listened to the reactionary group and, on "Black Day," dissolved the eighteen-month-old Nepali Congress government, replacing it with an authoritarian one-party state euphemistically termed "Panchayat," apparently alluding to the indigenous system of "rule by five elders" (*pancha* means "five"). Village governance by five respected elders was simple and effective, but now became distorted.

After the Panchayat king died, his Eton- and Harvard-educated son, Birendra, was crowned in January 1972, and many people hoped that this modern king would introduce significant constitutional changes to accommodate the democrats. Instead, the new king moved in an opposite, more totalitarian, direction, creating in 1975 an all-powerful extra-constitutional political organ called the "Back to the Village National Campaign." This screened all candidates for public office in order to prevent anyone affiliated in any way with party politics from entering the system unless they issued "statements" condemning their past affiliation and took the oath of allegiance to the "Partyless Panchayat system." Significantly, it was mostly communists who infiltrated the system in this way. The campaign's chairman was a Nepal Communist party politburo member, and its policy guide was published in the form of a little red book identical in color and shape to that of Maoist China.

The Nepali Congress's armed struggle lasted seven years. It ended after a futile attempt to capture a remote hill district capital by dispatching a small militia of exiled Nepali Congress activists in 1975. The king's military massacred them. After this tragedy, B.P. decided to end the armed resistance and his Indian exile, and in 1976 he returned to Nepal with a message of national reconciliation with the king. Predictably, he and his colleagues were met at the airport by the military and taken into custody, and those of us who were at the airport to welcome B.P. were met by *Mandale* thugs. A three-year reign of terror against the Nepali Congress followed, until the arbitrary execution of two Nepali Congress activists near the time of Prime Minister Bhutto's execution in Pakistan sparked a revolution in Nepal. This forced King Birendra to hold a national referendum in which he presented the electorate with a choice of a multiparty political system or "Panchayat with timely changes." After referendum day, December 16, 1979, the government delayed publishing the results for twelve days. Everybody guessed then that Panchayat would come up with a narrow victory. Indeed, the multiparty side was awarded 45 percent and Panchayat got 54 percent. A year later, King Birendra announced the 1980 constitution—in which he remained the absolute monarch and Panchayat remained partyless. The *Panchas* started parroting, "Now the king has opened the door for everybody to join the system." But the reality was that to contest an election one had to belong to one of the system's class organizations and swear the oath of loyalty. Any other politically oriented candidates were disqualified.

Perhaps King Birendra deceived his people in a nicer way than his father, but the outcome confirmed that *Panchas* were licensed to do what they wanted. And until 1990, when democracy was restored in Nepal for the second time, anyone belonging to or sympathizing with the Nepali Congress was subject to persecution by the state.

෴

Because of our political differences, writing editorials and deciding which news stories to emphasize was a tense game for me and my two Rana partners, particularly when political upheavals occurred in the nation. Shrish had a client group who used to gather regularly over the weekend for card sessions in Shrish's wing of the family palace. From the circle grouped around the cards his supporters would comment, to Shrish's annoyance, "It seems you are moving toward the Nepali Congress line." Similarly, my democratic supporters would criticize me, remarking, "Those two Ranas seem to be dragging you into the system." And Upendra's colleagues would question him, "What are you doing in between Shrish and Durga—two extremes?"

We were well aware of the tightrope we walked trying to run an independent newspaper in that dangerous and repressive political climate. The general role of a newspaper during Panchayat rule was either to serve as the mouthpiece of the government or to pander to the interests of some foreign embassy. Either way brought financial rewards. Until 1979, licensing had been very strict, with no chance for members of the Nepali Congress to obtain a press or newspaper permit. Even my Rana partners had to buy an existing fortnightly newspaper because the restricted licensing policy affected them as well. As the government liberalized licensing a little, I converted my literary magazine *Manas* into a weekly newspaper. *Horizon*—a quarterly on development issues—I kept as it was. Upendra and Shrish converted their English-language *National Star* into a weekly and, later, a daily. Then we merged all our publications and formed a company, Star Publications Ltd. In addition to our own publications we used to publish for others as well. Despite all odds, we survived for three years and our business had just started to take off.

೧೯೧

May 31 was indeed a great day. Early that morning, I bought a Kawasaki motorcycle from the Toyota dealer next to our press and Shrish drove it as I rode sidesaddle on the back. We were bound for the government's telecommunications office, where we had made our bid for a contract to publish Nepal's telephone directory. We needed the contract badly; beyond the profits from publishing, we would also be earning advertisers' fees from corporations and private businesses. Normally a tender from someone in the Nepali Congress would never have been entertained by the government. However, I had discovered a back-door approach to the section chief of the responsible department. His wife was related to the wife of one of our leaders, so he had some sympathy for me. Of course, if anyone in the government had known this, he could have lost his job. At the same time, our odd partnership at the press had an advantageous twist to it. Because of the two Rana partners, people in government would not suspect that this section chief was granting a favor outside the system. The bids were opened in our presence and ours was the lowest, which meant that it had a chance to win on its own merits. For the first time we had won the bet. Shrish and I left the office in a buoyant mood, building castles in the air—thinking about how, from this better financial position, we could start expanding our press.

Newly mobile and upbeat from our success, we went around town collecting money from various corporations for printing jobs we had done for them. We felt that this was absolutely our day. Wherever we went we met warm appreciation for our news coverage and commentaries. We returned to the press in high spirits at around three P.M. and let our staff know the good news. Naturally, they were all delighted, and someone proposed, "Let's celebrate this evening with *momos* and *aila*." *Momos* are boiled pastry balls filled, customarily, with meat. *Aila*, made from rice or finger millet, is a burning, homemade Newari alcoholic beverage whose vapor alone is enough to intoxicate. We all agreed on the celebration, even though I would not partake in the *aila* and would have vegetarian *momos*.

As my apartment was close by, Shrish and I went there for a light snack. By three-forty-five P.M., we were back at the press. I was deeply tired, having worked very late the previous night reading papers, writing news items, and working on my column. I had risen early and been busy around the city throughout the day, having eaten only an afternoon snack. This was not unusual for me, though.

Upendra was a little different, and this day was no exception. He had a habit of not being punctual. It was not necessarily intentional. He lived in the old Rana lifestyle to some extent. Whenever we phoned him at home his servants, using language reserved for the royalty, would reply, "*Raja* is sleeping" or "*Raja* is eating."

Shrish and I sat at the wooden desk in our front office anxiously waiting for him to arrive. Upendra had not yet heard the good news.

At four P.M. a large, official-looking black car pulled up outside in front of the press doorway. A short, stocky man walked in. In stature and appearance he was typical of the Gurkhas, the hill ethnic groups traditionally recruited by the British army. Although he was in civilian dress, I recognized him immediately as the deputy superintendent of police and chief of the Interrogation Department. "IGP wants to talk to Pokhrelji," he announced in a peremptory tone. The inspector general of police was the highest police rank in the kingdom and inside I felt a thrill of excitement. I thought, "Great! Maybe the IGP has a special news release for us." Since I was the editor, it seemed perfectly natural that he would call me.

Shrish offered the DSP a cup of tea.

"Yes, why not?" replied the interrogation chief. He took one of our chairs and sat down.

Right next door was Ringmo's, a modest, friendly Chinese restaurant managed by another Saint Xavier's man. Ringmo's served tea and other beverages virtually around the clock, and all we had to do was call out "Oh! Mahila" or "Chyangba! Tea!" and one of these devoted waiters would appear instantly to take our order.

Three cups of sweet milky tea were brought, and we sipped them without much conversation. "What is up then?" Shrish eventually asked the DSP.

"I don't know," he replied, adding, "After getting there it'll be easily known." He avoided looking at me as he made this remark.

At four-thirty P.M. I climbed into the back of the DSP's black car for the drive to meet the IGP.

"Come back soon!" Shrish called out.

"I will phone you if it is going to be late," I called back.

Then the DSP drove the car away. On the way I asked him, "Why do you think the IGP asked me to come? Why not Shrish or Upendra?"

Again the DSP offered a cryptic reply. "I don't know," he said. "You will know when we get there."

Everything had worked out so well that day, and although I was tired, I was still elated. As the DSP maneuvered through the familiar streets of Kathmandu, I busied myself imagining that the IGP was going to ask us to print a big notice for tender or to publish an important advertisement in our paper. Although my experience over the years had given me cause to have less than positive feelings for the police, I was buoyed by an old Nepali proverb: "On a good day even an ox can bear a calf."

The DSP took me straight to the so-called Police Club, where the IGP had his office. As we entered the compound I saw the theater on the right and the training center where the police learned judo and karate on the left. Straight ahead was a big building, several stories high, that housed the central offices of the Nepal police. At the back of the building were a number of rooms facing in the opposite direction. These were the notorious police custody cells. The DSP led me up the stairs and along a corridor to a second-floor room that faced the courtyard. He told me that it was the IGP's office. He pointed to a metal chair and asked me to sit down. I sat down to wait and looked around. The room was large, L-shaped, and carpeted with a jute floor covering. Although my chair was placed in the smaller section of the room near the end wall, I could see around the corner to a large desk with the usual arrangement of His Majesty's government equipment—the ornate pen and inkstand, a miniature Nepal flag flying incongruously like a child's toy, and the trays for correspondence. Looking down from the wall from behind the officer's chair were the standard pictures of the king and queen. Minutes went by. "The IGP must be busy doing something somewhere," I thought. "He should come soon."

I waited for almost two hours. I was feeling restless and thought of phoning Shrish to ask him to come and collect me. Even if the IGP was going to come eventually, I did not want to wait forever. I stood up and parted the curtains that hung across the doorway to see if there were any police nearby so I could request the use of their telephone. As I parted the curtains, a glint of steel caught my eye. Outside were two policemen, one on either side of the entrance, fully armed with bayonets pointing in my direction.

"Hey, *bhai* . . ." I started, addressing one of them as "younger brother," as we do when speaking to a younger man or boy.

But before I could complete my sentence the other replied, "We are on duty for you. We do not know anything. All we know is that you cannot move anywhere."

I felt suddenly grave and turned back into the room. I sat in my chair and took a deep breath. What was all this about?

What to do? I tried to meditate. But the hours were too long even for meditation. I began to experience an intuitive sense of foreboding, accompanied by involuntary flickering of the muscles around my left eye. I knew the experience well. It was an incessant warning, springing from the deepest level of my consciousness. I tried to focus my mind as if to receive a message. "What was my crime?" There was no answer.

I thought about a couple of critical news items we had written on the police recently. Could those have been the reason for my arrest? The usual legal procedure in such a case was for the local government to bring a case against the paper, or for the police themselves to take the newspaper to court. It could not be this. Then I remembered that, under law, a person could not be arrested without a warrant. But even while thinking this, an inner voice interjected, "As if their law means anything."

I sat on that metal chair for twenty-seven hours without food, drink, or use of a toilet.

Finally, footsteps and men's voices sounded in the corridor outside. The curtains were pulled back and into the room walked the IGP, the superintendent of police, and the same DSP of the previous day. They looked severe and unfriendly—evil. "Let's go!" I did not ask where. I just followed.

They took me along the corridor I had previously come through, then down a flight of steps and out the back door to another building. As we walked along the hallway inside this building we passed some horrifying rooms with wires and electrical equipment hanging from the ceiling. My heart raced. Many people in the Nepali Congress knew about those rooms. How many of our colleagues had been dragged into them and how few had returned? I became very frightened, feeling like a little goat being led to sacrifice. Finally, we reached a very small room that was bare except for a short, vinyl-covered bench. Two policewomen came into the room and the country's three most senior police chiefs left without saying anything.

"*Didi*, why are you arrested?" one policewoman asked me, addressing me with normal friendly respect as she would an older sister.

"You might know why," I replied. "I don't know anything."

"Oh, we are very small fry," they responded. "Only our chiefs know the reason why anybody is arrested. We just follow orders." However, I felt as though this was a well-scripted drama; everyone knew their part—with the exception of the subject.

I felt heavy with exhaustion and hunger. The policewomen said that the vinyl bench was my bed. As they talked I collapsed onto it.

In the middle of the night I was awakened by the pathetic cry of a male voice.

"Who is that?" I asked the policewomen.

"He has also been arrested—like you," one of them replied.

"Where is he?" I asked.

"On the ground floor of the building where you were yesterday," she answered.

"Why is he crying in that way?" I questioned.

"Anybody who is brought here is beaten," the policewoman explained, stating just the facts of life as she knew them. "Maybe the police are beating him right now. It is very common here. The more you stay here the more you will hear all sorts of cries and noise."

I tried to close my eyes and only then became conscious of the bright light from a powerful bulb hanging from the ceiling above my bench. The door leading into my room was not closed, and through the doorway I saw an empty pitch-darkness beyond. I complained about the light, but, shrugging, my female guards said that the whole police compound was lit up like my room. I just lay down again on the bench.

By the third day in captivity I fully understood the degree of the police officers' hostility. They had provided me with nothing to eat or drink since my capture and I had still not been served with an arrest letter, although I had demanded one several times. I had no power, even to find out the reason for my arrest. Then I thought of a way of protesting my illegal arrest. Now, at the mercy of the police, I decided to begin a hunger strike. It was not going to be easy. I was already weak and hungry. I also remembered that not so long before, in Belfast, Irish prisoners had gone on a hunger strike and the authorities had paid no attention. The hunger strikers had died. I steeled myself. "I am prepared for that. I am not afraid to be a martyr."

I announced to the guards that I was starting a hunger strike that would continue until I knew the reason for my detention. Later that evening they asked me if I was hungry. I said, "No." After a while I wondered, "Even if I had said yes, would they have given me food?"

"Tonight," I thought, "it is better that I lie down on this bench, facing the wall away from the guards at the door, and keep my resolve." Thoughts of the inevitable conclusion of my hunger strike kept recurring. My mind continually wanted to go off on its own course. To control the thoughts, I decided to live hour by hour. Before that determination the nights had been the most emotional time. I knew that if I allowed my mind to stray, I might start feeling weak and full of pity for myself. I had to toughen my mind and be prepared and ready to fight back if necessary. Some mental and physical energy returned to me. With this new realization of strength I must have fallen asleep.

The next day the DSP who had arrested me came to my room and announced, "We have to go to your house."

"What do you want from there?" I asked.

He only replied, "Let's just go."

Accompanied by a woman guard, he took me outside, where a police van was parked. The woman sat with me in the enclosed back of the van. Although I could not see out properly, it was possible to make out the places we were passing.

We drove through central Kathmandu, passing on our left the huge, dusty parade ground, where every year the regime would hold its rigid observances of Mahendra's Constitution Day (our "Black Day"). Royal birthdays were also celebrated there. Beyond the parade ground came New Road, its shops stuffed with smuggled, imported goods. Cut through the ruins of the 1934 earthquake, it was now the old city's only modern street, wide enough for two-way motor travel. Police always stood at intervals down the middle of the road as if still trying to get the disorderly tangle of traffic and cows used to the idea of two lanes.

The police van turned into Durbar Marg, a spacious street lined by airline offices, tour agencies, and gift shops that gives way to the south gate and perimeter of the king's palace. A stone's throw before the royal grounds, we passed Shrish's century-old family palace. Faded blue and slightly crumbling, it seemed to symbolize the waning power of the Ranas. At a small roundabout controlled by more police we entered Lazimpat Street, drove right past the press, and turned onto a rough dirt track between some residences. The van stopped. We got out and took the footpath the remaining few yards to the three-story building where I lived. My apartment was on the third floor. An Indian military man, his wife, and their two small sons lived on the second floor. On the ground floor lived a clerk from the Indian embassy with his wife and adult son and daughter. As the daughter had been my very good student in college, she was the chief reason for my deciding to live in this house. Otherwise I would have been hesitant to live alone there as the house was adjacent to the embassy and could be watched by intelligence people.

As we arrived, instinctively the first thing I did was to call for Lama, who sometimes used to stay while I was out, locking himself inside the apartment. No reply. The Indian daughter called from her ground-floor window, "I have not seen Lama for four days."

We went up the two flights of concrete stairs. From a passage at the top of the stairs, I opened the living room and study room doors and, beyond the study, my bedroom.

The DSP said that he wanted to read my diaries and whatever papers were in my bedroom. The floor was still strewn with the papers I had been reading the night before I was taken. There was no point in refusing. I had kept a diary for many years and the current volume was under the bed. The DSP systematically went through my bedroom, then the study and living room. He scrutinized all of my papers, read the diary and other notebooks, and searched through everything. I watched as my apartment was ransacked. Most painful was his intrusion into my private study and bedroom. He did not utter a word to indicate what he was looking for. At one point I said, "If you would tell me what you are searching for then I may be able to find it more quickly. After all, this is my place and I do know where things are." He did not respond.

I looked on, powerless. My apartment had been an ideal arrangement—perfect for living alone. There was seclusion and peace at the top of the house, security (or so I had assumed), and a roof garden terrace. My bedroom, light and sunny, was the most peaceful room, furnished only with a single bed and some pretty Tibetan-style Nepali carpets. I had arranged the room to do my meditation and yoga there; I felt more comfortable sitting and relaxing on the soft carpets than on a sofa or a chair.

Now I wished that I could lie in my bed; all my body needed was the caress of those soft sheets. Or make a cup of tea in my kitchen. My stomach was absolutely empty, but although there was plenty of food in the kitchen, I could not eat anything. Could there be a more paralyzed state of mind than this? A sense of outrage welled up within me. Who were these police to control someone even in her own house? No freedom even to lie on my own bed. It was those holding powers, and the system, that curtailed our fundamental rights. There were no individual rights in this country. No human rights. We the public were like sacrificial goats and they, the powerholders, were tigers, always hungry, voracious for ever greater helpings. And the goats kept on disappearing.

I remembered what one of India's renowned astrologers had forecast for me in 1974. "Nineteen seventy-five will be the beginning of your journey towards severe struggle," he had said. I remarked that as I was already struggling intensely, how could there be more struggle? He replied, "The struggle you have been through so far is nothing. In the near future you will reach the mouth of death, but with some good fortune, if you make your mind strong, you will survive. No matter how much struggle you have, keep restoring your strength and chant your mantras." He also warned me, "You will feel so lonely that it will seem as if you are the only person left in this world. Everybody around you will turn their back. Go ahead alone. Do not stop. If but once you stop you will be defeated."

Seated on my bedroom floor, I suppressed a knot of emotion that had formed in the center of my chest and made myself step outside of the frustration and wretchedness of the circumstances. Events of my life filed through my mind in a sort of timelessness. What an effort and a battle life had been. Whatever I had deeply aspired to or enjoyed had been blocked, either by my family or by hostile forces in the government. And whatever I would have avoided had been forced upon me. Some called me a revolutionary. Although I was not a rebel by nature, I had been made a rebel as my personal life had become an eddy against the great turbulence of national life. Life for me in Nepal's authoritarian state, with all the distortions that pervaded the society, was a complete riddle.

Like most in Nepal I lived amid arbitrariness and ambiguity. The ruling system was a mystery, a survival game in which the players competed with one another in keeping the palace happy—through sycophancy and deception. Honesty and loyalty counted for nothing, and it was my experience that the majority of officials and their patrons remained within the system to seek a shield for their misdeeds. And all misdeeds were carried out with the same excuse—*mathi bata*, "from above"—in an oblique reference to the king, as if he personally ordered each and every action that they carried out. There was no way of knowing the reality, because he would not come out to defend himself. Nepali life was one great charade.

It seemed that Nepal was really a cursed country. I recalled the fate of one of our greatest prime ministers, Bhim Sen Thapa. In the early eighteen hundreds, he served the country for thirty-four years, through three generations of kings. He was a man of reforms and development who modernized and trained the military, reformed the civil service and the court system, and built roads and bridges as well as many religious projects. Bhim Sen was also the man who saved Nepal from British colonial invasion in 1816.

Conspiratorial politics, however, brought him to an untimely end. In the intrigue-filled palace, a prince was assassinated and Bhim Sen Thapa was falsely accused of the crime and imprisoned. His enemies spread rumors that as part of his punishment his wife would be paraded around the city naked and that he would have to watch from his confinement. Bhim Sen preferred death before dishonor and committed suicide in 1839.

His devoted wife immolated herself on her husband's cremation pyre, and as she did so, she uttered a curse: "In this country, whomsoever should do good for the country will have misfortune befall them."

Misfortune seemed indeed to have been how our country's nationalists and democrats had been rewarded. I wondered, when would we be free from the power of her spell? Perhaps we should have redirected ourselves long ago from the course of conspiratorial politics and returned to our Vedic cultural heritage, under which, according to tradition, Nepal had enjoyed a Golden Age. Those were times when our monarchs were pious, benevolent, and impartial, overseeing a decentralized, people-oriented administration. Historically, from the third century until the mid-seventh century was the heyday of such superior governance, when the kings remained conscious of their duty as protective fathers or spiritual masters, seeing to the welfare of their citizens in every aspect—social, economic, and spiritual. All Nepal's antiquities—innumerable temples and shrines—can be credited to these spiritual kings for whom prime ministers, gurus, and ministers of worship were of equal status in helping to direct them toward the right path. Nepal's traditional kings inherited these qualities from the prehistoric kings, Rama, Yudhisthira, and others who, Hindus believe, were instructed directly by God and therefore had a full, perfect knowledge of everything. As the traditional Hindu king knows that human life is intended as the opportunity for a soul to evolve its own consciousness and, ultimately, become liberated from material existence, he is conscious that his subjects should be so protected as to attain this highest stage of welfare. It is for this reason that, to this day, many Nepalis accept their king in the traditional way as an incarnation of Lord Vishnu, the protector aspect of Godhead.

Even until the mid-eighteenth century, the kings retained their *Dharma* of protecting their citizens and national prosperity. Unfortunately, the most recent kings' reigns have seen countless antiquities smuggled out of the kingdom, and not a single temple or deity enshrined. The most basic needs of the masses of the people are not met, while the powerful amass fortunes in foreign lands, and law and order cease to protect the vulnerable. But through *Panchayat Raj*, instead of support, the king grew enemies. I would be the first supporter of a king who would save Nepal from ruin—a traditional, benevolent Hindu king. The one person who should gain this realization is the king.

ॐ

In crisis, the mind really runs fast, and sometimes it is difficult to bring it back. I shook my head. There was the interrogation chief in my bedroom, still reading my diary with a keen interest. "I have no privacy," I thought. "I must have written something very personal." From several feet away he pointed out a particular page and asked me, "What is the meaning of this?"

"I do not know what you are referring to and I cannot remember everything I wrote on each specific day," I replied.

He was not satisfied with my answer and I decided not to respond to his further questions.

While this police chief had been raiding my bedroom, the policewoman had been busy herself in my study. She had already selected several cosmetics and hairpins and whispered in my ear, "I want to take these!" I just shook my head, neither yes nor no. She took them anyway. She suggested that I take a nightdress and, before I had time to choose, picked instead a satin Tibetan *bakhu*, which is not a nightdress, but a traditional gownlike Tibetan women's dress, and carried it for me.

The interrogation chief grabbed whatever he wanted from my house and motioned me toward the door and the police van. We had been in my apartment for four hours.

Back at the Police Club, I was taken to the same small room and the vinyl bench. By now, I was too weak to sit up, so I lay down on my side. In front of me, in one of the three entrances to the room, I noticed a microphone peeping from under the door. I craned my head the other way. There were microphones under the other doors also. I closed my eyes and tried to rest, but it was difficult with the bright light above shining into my face.

Lapsing back into a daze of shock and reflection, I found myself wondering at the paradoxes, the conflict and struggle, and the succession of losses that had marked my life: "How hard it is to be myself, forced always to be someone else." It seemed as though I was losing all of the things that I held dear. Momentarily unconscious of my hunger strike, a thought appeared in my mind: "No! I love my life. I still have that. And my spirit."

# 2
.

# "Maybe the Charge
# Will Spring Out"

The next night, feeling very frail and dehydrated, and almost carried by my female guards, I was taken to a big room in the same building. It looked like a reception room. Seated around the table were the IGP, the deputy inspector general, the superintendent of police, and the DSP, and on the table was a crude spread of liquor bottles.

"What kind would you like?" one of them asked me.

I replied, "No. I don't take it."

They persevered, insisting more strongly, but I only replied, "No, definitely not." Here was another trick, I thought. It was not that I had never tasted alcohol. I had tasted half a glass of mild beer maybe once in a blue moon, and I had a close friend who used to make Newari liquor from betel leaves. A few times I had drunk maybe a teaspoon of that at her request. Even that amount had gone to my head. But I had never drunk in public, and, as a custom, it was very impolite to offer alcohol to a woman in Nepali society.

They poured themselves large servings and started drinking. I remained seated. It was late in the night. Occasionally they would give me a glance, but I pretended not to notice. Once in a while one or another of them would repeat, "You really won't accept our request?" I continued to ignore them. Making no progress with me, they talked among themselves. But it was no conversation to listen to. It sounded like prattle, intermixed with real and affected coughing and laughs, and the hiss of their lips as they drew on their cigarettes. Before long the air was thick with smoke and reeking of alcohol. The police chiefs were getting more and more drunk and noisy, shouting loudly to each other, and their eyes were becoming bigger and bigger, bulging as they stared at me from their stupor. I began to feel more frightened. If they did anything to me there was no witness. Perhaps I should call the women guards. Although I was at the point of near collapse physically I was conscious of a surprising mental clarity. I saw danger from all sides. If I stayed inside that room I would be at the mercy of the top four police bosses in the kingdom. I was convinced that they were getting drunk purposely. They could do anything. Already they had tried to make me drink, either to try to loosen my tongue or, given my physical state, to kill me. If I tried to escape I might be shot. The worst thing, I decided, would be to stay in their presence for even a minute longer.

I remembered what my father had told me many times: "Never trust a drunk man. He loses his senses and can do anything." My imagination was running wild. Four drunk men against one weak woman. How will they react? To walk out was to really confront them. My heart had started pumping fast and I was sweating. Somehow, I stood up and walked to the door, and then, just outside their room, I turned around and told them, "Have a good night." From their looks I could tell that I had done something they had not anticipated. They stood up, shouting at me. Ignoring them, I proceeded. The women police guards were waiting outside. One of the police chiefs followed me in anger but when he saw the women guards he stopped, and his bloodshot eyes only leered at us as the women guards took me back to my cell. I sat heavily on my bench and gathered a deep breath, then, after some moments, I found myself shivering uncontrollably and lay down, keeping my eyes wide open.

ༀ

Over the next days I became aware that all of the police—men and women—who came to my room came with some motive. They were trying to get something out of me. Sometimes they would come with their own problem, or sometimes with someone else's. Or they would feign sympathy for me. One day a new policewoman came and began telling a vulgar story. I pretended to respond to make her talk aloud, and she continued talking more vulgarly. I thought that it must all have been recorded.

The following day another policewoman came and started telling me that she wanted her husband, also in the police, to be transferred to the airport customs.

Stepping outside for a moment, she returned with a piece of paper and a pen—items that were forbidden to me. This time she was more specific. She mentioned the name of a close contact of mine working in the government, and insisted that I write him a letter. "Whatever you write I will take to him. Don't tell others I'm doing this," she warned. "If you want to write something about what he should do for you outside, mention that also," she whispered in my ear.

I saw that this woman was also trying to fool me. She persisted until at last I scribbled something. If this was the best strategy the highest level of the police could think of to try to get some incriminating personal gesture out of me, it seemed a cheap effort. My health might have been running down but I found that I was becoming progressively more conscious. I spent hour after hour trying to meditate. They would disturb me. They would be quiet. I would return to my meditation. I reached the point where, despite all their efforts, I could exclude them from my vision and have the experience of being fully alone and transcendent.

One day, a very young policeman entered my room. The policewoman went out and he sat on the bench, as I lay there, as he might with a sister. I was alert for any trick he might play. He edged closer to me and started talking very gently. Then he added, "If the government decides to kill you they will definitely take you to your Koshi Zone. I'm the one who has to drive that van. If you are somehow able to seek political asylum in the British or Indian embassy, then, instead of driving south, I can drive north fast and slip into the embassy. After that it's your responsibility."

I just listened without reacting. He would not give up. I tried to sit up because I felt very uncomfortable with him sitting there. He helped me, pulling me up to a sitting position, and stood in front of me.

I protested to him, "What are you talking about? Why should I be killed? If they want to kill me nonetheless, then let them. Why should any embassy give me asylum?"

He came closer and held my left hand. I thought he was about to say good-bye. I glanced at his face and noticed him looking red and nervous. Then he started to attack me physically. I resisted, pulling my hand from his grip, and stood up. Drawing back a little, he shook his head—apparently in remorse.

I gave his back a sharp pat. "You are my little brother and you are very sweet. Please go now, and send those women in."

Facing the dark room, he rearranged his police uniform, pretending to zip up his trousers, and then without looking at me said ashamedly, "Do not misunderstand."

"No," I replied, "I understand." Then he went. But what I had really understood was that the police were trying every technique they knew to torture and demoralize me.

The women police came back. I told them, "Tell your bosses that I don't need to be disturbed every hour. You are enough for me. Don't let any man come here."

One of them said, "What are we to do? They are much younger than us, but they are officers. When an officer comes, all you can do is salute and go out. That is our police rule."

The other one, indicating the dark room with the open door, said, "Durga *didi*, it seems there is a movie camera fixed in that room." Now I could guess why that young policeman had tried to show his sympathy for me. They were hoping for some action photos to complete my character assassination.

In the evening different women would come for night duty. I think all the police changed shifts at this time. There would be a droning noise like a nest of bees as the incoming and outgoing groups met. Two of my guards left as their shift ended and I remained for a while with only one guard. After a while, she said, "*Didi*, how long do you want to live in this misery? I have a suggestion. I'll help you escape from here."

Before I could say anything in response she had taken my hand and lifted me up. My feet shuffled two or three steps. Then she pointed into the black room.

"Go through here. There's a door on the other side, an exit. Once you're through that you are outside near the wall. Then, if you jump off that wall, you're in the college. Once you're with those professors and students they'll take care of you."

I was not so dumb as to not understand her hidden intention. It was their favorite trick. However, I asked, "How could I do that? Everybody is outside in the evening."

She said, "The best time will be while they are all doing their prayers and national anthem at seven P.M. Only a few guards will be roaming around. I will take care of them."

Too weak to stand any longer, I stepped backward twice and fell down on my bench.

This incident again restored me mentally. My eyes were wide open. I noticed that my breathing was coming in short, fast breaths. The same woman was still standing staring at me.

"What happened?" she asked.

I said, "Nothing. Just relaxing."

In the meantime my two night guards arrived.

Life began at night in the Police Club—rough aggressive shouting, kicking, the thuds and lashes of beatings, the policemen's grunts and cursing as they inflicted their blows, and the awful cries from the victims—"Ayaa, ayaa." My room was positioned so that I could hear captives' treatment from the moment of their arrival. I could even see police vans and other traffic coming and going through the main entrance. There was one louvered window high on one wall of my room. The glass louvers were tilted so that as I lay on my bench I could see a reflection of the events outside. The police vans would halt right below this window, and I could hear and often see the captives. Whoever was caught on whatever charge was pulled or thrown from the van, and grabbed brutally to be taken to some cell.

The noises of torture at night reminded me of a story that my mother used to tell me when I was a little girl. It was about a cemetery of those people who bury their dead, a practice strange to most Nepalis, who prefer cremation. "At night," my mother told me, "some jungle animals go there and dig out the bodies because they are not buried properly. Jackals howl, wolves cry, and dogs bark. Sometimes people from a distance say that they hear human cries amidst all these noises, as if some of those buried were still alive."

I tried to think that all the noises around me were not real, and I wanted to think that even my being there was not true. I looked about me and realized it all was real. The three women guards were sleeping like babies amid the cries and din. I was glad they slept, as I could imagine that I was alone there. My mind returned to a piece of news that a guard had told me earlier that day. He had cried as he told me: "Your friend Sapkota has just been killed. Maybe they'll do that to you."

If the news was true, the man killed in police custody was a schoolteacher who had been leader of the teachers' union. I wondered, how might he have been killed? By being beaten to death? By being shot? Or by hanging? According to law, any political prisoner was supposed to be brought to a court within twenty-four hours of being detained. What law was I imagining in a country where there was no rule of law, only the law of terror? I thought of my Nepali Congress friends Bhim Narayan Shrestha and Yagya Bahadur Thapa. Bhim Narayan had written me a letter just days before his execution in which he had mentioned something about old coins and a handkerchief. I still did not know what he had meant. That was in 1979, when the two were executed at the time of Bhutto's hanging in Pakistan—the incidents that sparked Nepal's 1979 revolution. I wondered in what manner our two men had been killed. I also thought of the Dahal brothers, Thagi, Lilanath, and Khagendra, and of Gokarna Karkee—all Nepali Congress workers who had been shot near Patan's Nakhkhu Jail. The reason the police had given for their killing was that they had tried to escape while being transferred from Central to Nakhkhu Jail. Other prisoners inside Nakhkhu had heard the shots.

This story bothered me. I tried to imagine their last moment of life. As I did so fear crept into my own body. I recalled the escape route the woman guard had shown me five hours earlier and felt sure that I would have become another Thagi. How easy it was for these butchers to take another's life. Who gave them this license to kill?

It was one A.M. and there was another pathetic cry from the north building. It seemed they had started on another prey. One of the policemen had been telling me the other day, "You are looked after very well because we are gentle people here. In Mechi Zone, women are raped by police. Some even become pregnant." What was his motive for telling me that? I recalled a young leftist friend who had been held in Mechi during the late 1970s. While I was chair of the Nepal Human Rights Forum I had tried to see her in prison after I heard of her rape in police custody, but was prevented from seeing her. The policewomen had also been talking among themselves about a drama group that had been massacred by the police in 1978. Women artists in the group had been first raped and then killed. The memory increased my feeling of anxiety.

There are different realities in different places. If you visit a butcher he might talk about how to kill animals. If you visit a saint then you can hear how you can master techniques of unity consciousness and become enlightened. In society we see human beings who may look alike, but their destinies are different, their ways of life are different, and their commitments are different. Some people act by their own free will and make their own choices. Others are told to act this way or that way. In Nepal, it was their established policies that made the police brutal and inhuman. I thought to myself that I could never be in the police. I became frightened even of an injection; how could I insert pins under someone's fingernails or toenails, or into a woman's nipples? It was unthinkable. I recalled how a friend had been tied up and stuffed into a jute bag like a sack of vegetables; then the police had played football with him on a concrete floor.

I asked one of the policewomen whether it was true that the police played football with male political prisoners.

"That is common, and beating with nettles dipped in cold water, and beating with the spiked iron *korra*. All these are very common. These days we have electrical torture also." She laughed and added, "Don't worry, we will not do any of that to you."

She moved closer and whispered in my ear, "Don't tell anybody that I told you this, but listen, if anybody suggests you escape from here, don't do it. That will be the end of your life."

The other two women entered and interrupted her. I pretended to be resting. Who to believe in this place? Who to trust? I was tired of all the whispered messages, the threats, and the pieces of "advice"; they were all the same—designed to break me down.

On the sixth day of my detention a man came in the morning introducing himself as a military doctor.

"I heard you are not eating," he said. "I just want to see how you are doing."

I tried to stand up, but couldn't. I felt a little nervous. I tried again. Then I realized that I was unable to get up.

He asked, "Have you looked at your face?"

"No," I said.

A policewoman brought a little mirror and held it to show me my face. My eyes were hardly focusing, and at first I saw only a blurred image in the mirror. When I made an effort to focus, to my shock I saw three layers of dead skin separately peeling away from my lips, but not completely fallen away, still adhering to the flesh. I touched my lips gently with a fingertip. They were very rough and crusty. My face looked dry and bloodless. The doctor measured my blood pressure and checked my breathing and heart rate with his stethoscope.

He then advised me, "This is not the place to do a hunger strike. If you don't eat, these people will not be too worried. You will be the only one to suffer. Some people can live longer than others without eating or drinking. For you, I would say you have a maximum of another six days left. After that it will be too late."

"At least I want to know my charge. I will continue my hunger strike until I see my letter of arrest," I said.

The doctor replied, "I don't know about that, but as a doctor I can give you only my suggestion. Start with water, and for a couple of days take only liquid, then slowly begin on solid food."

"It is your duty to say so," I replied. "Thank you for your suggestions. I will see how long I can do this." Then he went. Mentally I still had some strength.

In the afternoon the chief of interrogation came with another man, who was not wearing a police uniform. The man was tall and thin, had a long black mustache, and spoke in a shrill, hoarse voice. He introduced himself as a police lawyer. Again I tried to get up with help from the women police, but couldn't.

"Sorry, I cannot sit up."

"That's okay," he said.

The interrogation chief passed a slip of paper to me and said, "This is your arrest letter."

I read it, then asked him, "It is under the Security Act? What is the charge?"

He answered, "We need to take your statement now. Maybe the charge will spring out of that."

The lawyer asked my name, my age, and my father's name. I refused to give my father's name on principle. If I was accused of something, why should my father be dragged into it? Besides, they knew well who my father was. The general custom in Nepal is to write a person's ancestral history on any document, something I had always opposed. I felt that a document is prepared for a specific individual and that it is not necessary to bring all the male ancestors into the picture.

He asked me, "Do you know why you are here?"

"I wish I knew," I replied, "but I do not. I have only just received this slip of paper in front of you, and you have heard the contents."

The interrogation chief asked all three women guards to leave the room.

He continued, "You know why you are here, and we know why. Let's go straight to the main point."

"What is the main point?" I asked.

"The main point is about the crown prince," he said.

I felt my eyes opening wide as a rush of thoughts flooded my mind. I took a deep breath and closed my eyes, pressing hard with the thumb and middle finger of my right hand on each side of the bridge of my nose near my eyes.

My mind went back to an event and some rumors that had occurred five years before, in 1977, the time of B.P.'s return and reconciliation with the king. During those days, *Panchas* with no constituency other than the palace were deeply threatened by B.P.'s return and, in an attempt to convince the king to trust them and take their side, would set up false charges of sedition and conspiracy against democrats. At that time, I had been approached by agents of conspirators who were after the crown prince. It was evening, and three people came to me disguised as beggars in torn and tattered clothes. I was about to go inside to fetch the beggars some *bhikshya* (alms) when one of them said, "We have come to talk with you."

I asked them into my living room.

They said, "We live in India these days. Somebody in Patna gave your name as a contact person in Nepal. So we have come to you."

Curious, I asked, "Why do you want to see me?"

One of them replied, "We're planning to kidnap the crown prince."

The other one added, "We are involved in such kidnappings even in India, so don't think we are inexperienced."

I recalled now how, for a second, I had just stared at their faces at first, quite scared, but then responded, "It's a crazy and wrongheaded idea to harm the little prince," and refused point-blank to be involved.

As they left, they mentioned the area in Kathmandu where they were staying and said, "Don't tell anybody." As they crossed the yard below they were attacked by the big dog belonging to the people who lived on the ground floor. It was a very frightening creature, and after that they never returned.

Immediately after they left, I took a taxi and went to the home of the zonal commissioner, Sunar Prasad Shah, whom I knew well, and told him about the incident. I assumed that after listening to me, he would deal with those agents and increase the security for the crown prince. Over the course of the next several months, the zonal commissioner called me to his house on a number of other occasions to discuss with him every detail of the incident that I could recall.

All that had happened so long before, I had almost forgotten about it. Now, again, a similar incident. I thought, "Why did people have to come to *me* with such proposals? Who might the person be who was sending these people to see me?" I felt myself starting to sweat. What else should I have done when I learned about what was being planned? In this kingdom you were not safe whatever you did. If you spoke up, then you knew too much and you were in trouble. If you kept quiet, then you might appear an accomplice. "Why me?" I almost cried aloud. But the words that came from my mouth were: "What do you want me to say?"

"Say that you knew those people; they were your friends. Say, I got mixed up. I am sorry." he suggested.

I shuddered, and felt my skin prickling with fear. Was I being framed? Were they going to try to make me confess that the kidnap plotters were my friends? I woke up mentally, and said, "Don't try to influence me. I won't say anything that is a lie."

The lawyer rejoined, "Okay, then say what you have to say."

At this moment I heard an unusual sound, the sound of feet dragging along the floor, somebody shuffling irregularly instead of walking. The DIG entered the room, and with him came Shiva Prasad Kangal. *Kangal* means "bankrupt." He had given himself this name when he realized he was the most destitute of all the Nepali Congress activists. More accurately, he was a guerrilla of the party's militant wing. The government had blamed him for several bomb attacks on police posts and other targets around the kingdom during the party's armed struggle phase. A few months earlier, he had told me he was going to settle down. A family in his village had offered him their daughter for marriage provided he had a source of income. So he had started a political magazine, and I had contributed a little cash. He had asked me for a "loan," but in his case I knew that lending him money would be, as the Nepali proverb goes, "lending meat to a dog." Still, I did not mind helping him. Now, with one foot trembling on the floor and the other raised uncomfortably, Kangal could barely stand up. His one arm was dangling limply from the shoulder. He held it steady with his other hand. His face, hands, feet, all the parts of his body that I could see, were bruised and swollen. His eyes too were swollen and red.

Looking at the DIG, I asked, "Did you try to kill him?"

"Not yet," he replied.

Kangal was still whimpering and trembling. The DIG turned his eyes on me and accused me: "You are the brain of the plot, and this one is your co-conspirator." Then he turned to Kangal and shouted, "Eh! Boy, tell in front of your *didi* how much money she gave you."

His eyes looking down at the floor, Kangal stammered, "Eight hundred."

"Did she or did she not say to buy a bomb and throw it at the crown prince?" the DIG continued.

Kangal stared the DIG's face sullenly and replied, "No, she did not give money to me for that purpose."

The DIG reddened and raised his hand menacingly as if to slap Kangal.

I shouted in English, "Don't drag him into this. Whatever allegations you want to bring, bring them against me. Do not torture that innocent boy."

The DIG shouted back at me, "Either you say 'My brain was not functioning, so I spread that rumor,' or say 'I was involved and I regret it now.' "

I do not remember how I controlled myself but I addressed the lawyer: "Eh! You listen now to my story and write down what I say. Don't forget that I'm also a lawyer. If you write down something I didn't say I will not sign it."

The DIG went out of the room, pulling Kangal with him. Other police were waiting outside and must have dragged him away somewhere.

I thought quickly, "This man, the DIG—a Rana—is related to the royalty. By definition, he should be loyal to the King. Either he is very dumb, or he's a traitor."

My mind became newly alert as I sensed the hostility of these men. What they were up to was a trick the government was becoming well practiced in: setting traps and then killing the victims. I tried to imagine who it might be that wanted to get rid of me just at this time when I was settling into my business. But I could not think who this personal enemy might be.

ௐ

The police lawyer prepared his paper, Nepali paper—light brown, thin, and slightly rough-textured, the official paper used for such documents in the kingdom. The interrogation chief brought a little stool for the lawyer to write on and I started my statement, the story of the conspiracy as I knew it, and he began writing. As he transcribed, he worked like the scribes in the courts. Each time he finished writing the last word of my sentence, he would repeat it aloud and say, "Then?"

Here is the rough story of the kidnapping conspiracy that I knew, as I told it to him.

About two months ago, two men in their mid-twenties came to my house in the evening and knocked on the front door. Lama was cooking in the kitchen. I had just finished my evening meditation and yoga and went to open the door. From the top of the staircase inside the apartment, I saw their faces. Kangal was not one of them. They were not very familiar to me, although I remembered having seen one of them once briefly with a group of our Nepalis in exile when I had gone to visit B.P. in Banaras. I stood where I was outside my study door and said, "I'm really busy now. Do you have something important to say?"

The young men said, "We have come with a proposal. Can we come in and discuss it with you?"

"Okay, come in then." I thought that these boys looked similar to a number of students who often came seeking my help in drafting a pamphlet or a statement, or such like.

We climbed the stairs. At the top I did not even ask them to sit down, but stood leaning against the living room door. They stood in the corridor. They were wearing Indian-style shirts over Western trousers and each was carrying a cotton bag slung over one shoulder. One of them took out a round black object from his bag and showed it to me, saying, "Durga *didi*, this is a grenade thirty-six bomb. We want to leave it here tonight. We have a plan you have to help us with."

"If you come to me carrying scary things like that, I doubt very much whether I can help you," I replied. But I wanted to know what they were up to, so I added, "But what is your plan anyway?"

"All you have to do is let us jump down from your balcony to the Indian embassy. And your responsibility is to guarantee political asylum for us if our plan fails."

"I cannot do that. Why do you want political asylum anyway?" I replied.

The other boy explained, "We have a plan to kidnap the crown prince from his school. We've selected the spot where we can carry it out, and thought how we will do it."

"You boys, don't be so ridiculous. And, anyway, what harm has that little boy ever done to you? I don't approve of this at all, so don't even come to my house with such a proposal," I said.

"Durga *didi,* we thought you were a revolutionary and would help us in this plan," they protested.

"I am sorry, I cannot help you in this kind of matter. I do not believe in violence," I replied, beginning to get irritated.

"Okay! We'll go," they said, "but think on this. We might come again."

After they had gone I did not know what to do. Were they government agents trying to provoke or trick me, or exiled members of a political group?

Then Lama said, "Dinner is ready."

"Okay, bring it," I replied.

As he put food on the table Lama asked, "Why didn't you offer tea to those boys?"

"You cannot offer tea any time people come," I evaded, and then asked, "Did you see those boys?"

"Yes, but I do not remember their faces," Lama said.

"Do you remember their general appearance?"

He replied, "Yes, that I do."

I warned him, "If anyone of their appearance, whom you don't know, comes here again and asks for me, don't even tell them what time I'll be home. And if they ask you if they may leave their bags or anything in our house, say no. Okay?"

I told him, "Go and put a padlock on the door from the outside. If anyone else comes they will see the lock and think nobody is at home." Part of the apartment door was made of iron rods so that we could fasten a padlock on the outside by reaching through with our hands from the inside. As soon as the lock was secured, I went to my bedroom. I felt restless, unsure of what to do. Should I tell Shrish tomorrow, or my party president Bhattaraiji, or B.P.? Maybe the boys were just joking. Or maybe they were trying to test me. After some thought, I decided not to attach much importance to the incident.

After a week they returned. This time I had just come back home and Lama had gone out and, as he had not yet returned, I had left the front door open. They came straight up to my living room. One of them was the same chubby-faced boy, while the other was a new face. The one from the previous time asked me, "Did you make up your mind?"

"Don't joke with me. I am not interested in it at all," I replied.

"You must help us," they insisted.

"Absolutely not at all," I replied.

They took out their bomb and asked again, "If the government intelligence suspect us on the street we'll be caught with this. Can we leave it here for tonight?"

I answered, "No. It frightens me even to see it."

"We came with such hope, but you're not helping us. We're really disappointed," the new one said. Then the first one added, "We came to you particularly because your house is in such a good location. If our kidnapping is a success then we are safe. But if we fail we just want to throw this bomb into the school and escape. We want your help at that time to claim political asylum. We've also prepared a pamphlet for the aftermath."

The other boy passed the pamphlet to me. "Now, if you still say you can't help us at all, then you have to do one thing for us at least. Give us eight hundred rupees in Indian currency."

"I don't have that amount of money, and I would not want to give you the money anyway," I replied.

"You can't say that. Until you contribute money we'll keep coming here. We'll be back one day soon. Prepare the money." Saying this, they left.

I read the pamphlet. It was one sheet, and was called "Why the Kidnap of the Crown Prince." Its message appealed to the public to support the kidnapping. I was a pamphlet collector. Pamphlets, whether they were underground, anonymous, or from a political group, were the only source of information you could get in Nepal on contemporary political issues. Several authors, foreign as well as local, had used my collection for source material in writing books and articles.

After I read this one I became really restless. They were planning something very serious. I thought, "Where to go, and whom to tell?" I did not have a telephone to use to call anybody, and at night I would never normally go out unless some friend would promise to bring me back home. Lama returned. He had already prepared dinner. First I went to my bedroom for a brief meditation. Then I ate dinner and told him, "I am very worried. Those boys came again and they are not good."

Lama suggested, "Maybe you shouldn't live in this house for the time being."

"Perhaps you're right," I replied, "but I can't go to anybody else's house tonight. It's too late."

Lama used to sleep in the kitchen. I said good-night and went to my bedroom through my study, locking the door to the stairway while closing the study door. I heard Lama locking the living room door on the other side of the passage. The study room windows were all latched shut, and once inside my bedroom I locked the door to the study. I drew the bedroom curtains, noticing the light in my neighbor's house immediately to the north.

ཉ༅

It was the middle of the night. Suddenly something woke me up—a knocking and rattling sound at the bedroom window right next to my bed. I always locked my windows, but this night I must have forgotten to twist the bolt completely. Somebody was trying to open the window from outside.

I shouted, "Lama! Please come, quick! Somebody is outside the window."

The person outside was tugging at the window. Frantically, I kept pulling at it from the inside, seeing only some shape on the other side of the glass that separated us. Lama had to cross four internal doors to reach my bedroom. Two doors were locked from his side, and two from my side. The seconds dragged. Finally, he arrived outside my room on the south terrace, but I was unable to go to open the door because the intruder was still pulling at the window.

I shouted at Lama, "Break my door and get in!"

Somehow he entered, and instantly the person outside disappeared. It was not a nightmare. It was real and I was frightened to death. Was it a thief? Or somebody come to shoot me? I knew I would not get back to sleep and asked Lama also not to go to sleep. We stayed up the whole night drinking coffee.

The following day, while I was at work, a lady from the British embassy called me to say that my pamphlet collection had been left there. A mutual friend, an Indian lady, was writing a book on South Asian politics using my pamphlets as research material. The British lady asked whether she should bring the collection to the press. I said no, and went to her house in the embassy compound to collect it. The newest pamphlet was still in my purse. While she went to order her servant to make tea, I placed the new pamphlet in the file. I did not want to show it to anybody. After having tea, I took a shortcut back to the press. It was only a three- or four-minute walk from the embassy this way.

The first thing I wanted to do was to go home for a minute to take the pamphlets back, but one of our compositors wanted me in the back room to read a short galley proof. I put the pamphlet file in the top drawer of a cabinet in the front office and locked it, placing the key as usual in the drawer of a desk. As soon as I finished the proofreading, our Toyota client next door called me for some business. I went there and came back after fifteen minutes.

The moment I entered our office, I saw the drawer open. In an instant,

I looked inside the pamphlet file. The new one that I had filed on top was missing. I shouted at the press people inside, "Who came here?"

Shrish had arrived and came out from the back room, asking, "Why? What happened?"

I said to him, "You took something from my file, didn't you?"

"By God, I did not. What was it?" Shrish protested.

One of the boys said that Upendra had come earlier for a while. I told Shrish, "Then he must have taken it."

Shrish asked, "Tell me, what was it? Why are you so nervous?"

I told him the story, then Shrish left by taxi for Upendra's place. After a short while he returned. No, Upendra also swore that he had not even touched the drawer.

I chided our press workers, and asked again, "Did anybody else besides Shrish and Upendra come here?"

One of them said, "Oh, yes! Thapu came and waited for you for a while and then went."

As I heard his name mentioned I was sure that he must have taken the pamphlet. He was also a journalist, but closely associated with the aide of one of the princes. Shrish and I went to find him at his press. He was not there, and I thought that he must have taken the pamphlet to show intelligence people and told them where he had found it. At last, later that day, I met him at his press and told him point-blank, "Will you please return the piece of paper you took from my drawer."

He smiled at me. "What are you saying? I didn't take it. Don't talk so much."

I returned to the press, and then walked through the shortcut, this time to the Indian embassy. I went to see Mr. S. Chandran, the consul, and told him the story. He assured me, "We don't approve of such terrorist acts and will take precautions." The next day the embassy installed a searchlight facing my house from a pole in their compound.

After I returned to the press from seeing Chandran, Shrish, Upendra, and I went to the house of a World Bank adviser, Syd Rose, a British man who was our close friend. His home would be a safe place to talk. We told him the story. All three friends suggested that I stay away from my house for a while. So I decided to stay at Syd's house. I returned later with Lama, and for a couple of days he stayed there with me.

The next day I went to the press as usual. Just as I stepped out to go to Ringmo's to order tea I saw those two boys, the same two who had been to my house the second time. They were approaching our press. I did not know what to do.

Standing there on the street, one of them said, "We have come to see you."

I said, "I told you not to come anymore."

The other one asked, "Have you prepared the money?"

"No, I do not have the money," I answered.

"Until you give us money we will keep coming," the same one insisted.

Just wanting to get rid of them, I said, "Come here tomorrow."

They walked away.

After ordering tea I went back to the press feeling very worried and anxious. Another guest, a man named Setha, had arrived there. Setha was a former university lecturer like myself. Although we had been contemporaries at the university, I knew very little about him as he had taught at a different campus. He too had lost his job, but I learned later it was for different reasons.

While drinking tea, I said to Setha, "I have to go somewhere. Can you drop me?"

He agreed immediately.

In fact, I did not have to go anywhere. My problem was that I really did not have the eight hundred rupees in Indian currency that the two boys had demanded to receive the next day. Therefore, in order to ask him to loan me that amount, I had to tell Setha the story. All I wanted was that after tomorrow they should not bother me. Setha loaned me the eight hundred.

The next morning, from inside our front office, my eyes were scanning the street constantly, and my mind was playing with their promise: after I gave them money today they would not bother me.

I saw them approaching from a little beyond the Toyota dealership and went out and walked toward them. As I gave them the packet of eight hundred rupees I said, "I hope you will keep your word and not bother me anymore."

They said, "Do not worry. We speak the truth. We do what we say."

That moment I felt a great relief.

By this time I had decided to let my party president, K. P. Bhattarai, and our leader and former prime minister, B. P. Koirala, know what was going on. First, I went to Bhattaraiji. He was the only leader of our party who was a real believer in nonviolence. I always felt very close to him for this reason. He listened attentively as I spoke.

"Go and tell the home minister. He will take care of it," Bhattaraiji suggested instantly. He added, "And stay away from them. They are really bad fellows."

I called the minister a couple of times, but he was not available. I gave up.

After this I went to B.P. His comment was, "There is an element within the system which is trying to make my reconciliation with the king fail. Somehow this must be communicated to the king."

I told B.P., "I have told Shrish and Upendra. They might communicate it."

ॐ

Setha started becoming very interested in the affair. I wanted to forget about it and to pretend that nothing had happened. One day he told me, "Durgaji, could you just introduce me to them? I also want to know them."

Shrish, Upendra, and I began to think that he had some vested interest in the plot. Once Setha joked at me, "If somebody gave me three lakhs (three hundred thousand rupees) and asked me to kill you, I would kill you."

I replied, "Am I worth that much only?"

He just laughed out loud. I began to feel uncomfortable as he increased the frequency of his visits to me.

On the fourth day of my stay at Syd's house, Setha came to visit again and sat on the sofa where I usually sat. He did not seem to have much to say. He was carrying a medium-size instrument that looked like a camera. In fact, he mentioned that it was a camera. After he had gone we noticed that he'd left the camera behind where he had been sitting. It was there for several days. Then one day it disappeared. Shrish, Syd, and I used to talk late into the night, but until it vanished we did not suspect anything about that "camera" that might have been recording our conversations.

One day as Shrish and I were working in our front office, the king's chief security officer visited our press and took Shrish away. Shrish came back after a couple of hours and told me, "He's asking about the same thing. He wants you to talk to him and give him detailed information." I refused to meet him. I had already told Shrish everything that I had seen and knew. I did not want to testify in front of a high-ranking military officer. However, I was glad that the rumor had reached up to this level.

But certain people would not leave me alone. Setha, and now a couple of others, seemed very deeply interested in the matter, and began harassing me for more information. It was at this time that I started speculating that somebody very big in the system was behind the conspiracy. The boys sent to my house must have been sent by them. This was how Panchayat politicians had been staging dramas to victimize Nepali Congress supporters. The trend had been for *Panchas* to kill a framed person on a particular sedition charge in an attempt to gain the king's favor and secure their constituency with him forever.

However, in this kidnapping plot it was possible that some faction of the opposition could be coconspirators. If that was true—which I suspected—then the story would run like this: a powerful and high-level faction in Panchayat and a small faction of multiparty advocates had made a working agreement in relation to this conspiracy. The advantage for the Panchayat faction in doing this was that they would gain the king's confidence by declaring, "Look, Your Majesty! You are attempting to be liberal, but your own son—the would-be king—is being targeted and we are the people who found out that the plotter is from one of the liberal groups you are favoring. You need us instead."

The advantage for the opposition faction would be slightly different. This group had not yet been recognized by the king as in the past it had been branded antimonarchical. After the framed plotter—the "suspect"—had been killed, this group would come up with a statement condemning such an antimonarchical action. The Panchayat faction would then convince the king to extend his protection to his enemy, thereby including him in the king's constituency. This would strengthen Panchayat conspiratorial politics further. The plotters would gain the king's enhanced regard. The sole objective of those who joined Panchayat was to get nearer to the king and closer to power.

I do not know how much the police lawyer recorded from my statement. At around eight-thirty P.M. there was an interval. The lawyer and the interrogation chief went out together with the materials that they had been writing. Before leaving, they said, "We have not finished; we'll come back right away."

In a minute another police officer came in and shouted at me in a very rough and abusive tone. By now I was exhausted and sleepy. His abuse had no effect on me and I remember his aggressiveness more than the exact words he used. But from his tone and the protective way he spoke of the conspirators I had referred to during my interrogation, I suspected that he too must have been among them. I could easily figure out that this officer must have been listening to everything from the other room. Otherwise he would not have known what I had said.

The other two came back in, and this one went out. The lawyer asked, "How much more do you have to say?"

I replied, "As much as you want."

"Okay, carry on then."

The chief of interrogation intervened, "But this statement is not serving our purpose—the reason that you were arrested."

"The law is in your hands," I said, "I am simply your captive. You can make any meaning out of anything."

The lawyer said, "No discussion. Go on, go on."

So I continued.

It was the wedding day of the daughter of Syd's landlord, a big affair because the landlord was a well-connected member of the Rana family and had invited everyone who was someone, including the prime minister. I had been invited by the bride, as had Shrish. As the main wedding party was to be held in the house where Syd was living, he had to let them use the ground floor. I went and had a peep from a distance and noticed several ministers and other Panchayat politicians standing around drinking and smoking heavily. I was in no mood even to say hello. So, instead of attending the reception, Shrish and I went upstairs. As usual during these days we busied ourselves by making guesses about who might have been orchestrating all the incidents surrounding the kidnapping conspiracy. It was six P.M. While we were still talking, Syd's telephone rang. Syd answered and gave me the phone. It was Setha wanting to talk to me.

"Durgaji," he said over the phone, "I am in trouble. You have to help me. I'm at the Summit Hotel. Take a taxi and come."

I replied, "I can't possibly do that. How do you expect me, a woman, to come and meet you alone in a hotel at night?" I put the phone down. At this moment I had a very bad sense of foreboding and felt a familiar sort of flickering around my left eye that had always served to warn me of danger in the past.

Shrish, Syd, and I continued chatting. At around nine P.M. another phone call came for me. It was Setha again, with the same request.

"I will definitely not come," I asserted.

"Let me come and fetch you," he offered.

I declined, and then, with another thought coming into my mind, I said, "Okay, I will come. But you be in the lobby."

This time, even against my intuition, I thought that with the help of my friends I would find out what Setha's role was in this affair. I asked Shrish and Syd to help me, and as I expected, they agreed. The three of us became serious and discussed the possibility of some trap being planned for me. Soon we came up with an idea. As a precaution we called Upendra and with his help arranged for two military men in civilian dress to be in the lobby before I reached it. Then the four of us—Upendra, Shrish, Syd, and myself—left for the Summit Hotel.

My three friends waited outside, and I entered the lobby alone. Setha was standing there waiting for me, and asked me to sit in a chair. Offering me a glass of Coca-Cola, he said furtively, "There are intelligence people around here after me. My life is at stake. I will escape from here, but until then you sit here." I saw him give a thousand-rupee note to the counter receptionist, saying, "Do not let anybody go to my room." Then he ran out of the lobby and was gone. My friends tried, but could not stop him.

"Why are you telling this story? How is this related to your conspiracy?" interrupted the interrogation chief.

I replied, "The next event after this incident was you arresting me. Do you not see the connection? My interpretation is simple. Setha must have had a bomb in his room. He wanted to get me arrested red-handed."

"Why should he do that?"

"He used to tell me that he would kill me for three lakhs. Somebody must have offered that money and he was serving somebody else's purpose. He was a stooge."

"Who is that somebody?"

"It must be a big person to plot such a big conspiracy." I mentioned the name of a big shot I suspected.

"We have information that you were the brain of this kidnapping plot."

I could tell that their minds were set against me already. They were under orders, perhaps paid, to produce this outcome. The conspiracy seemed clear now. To vindicate themselves, the police bosses were out to extract a confession from me.

"Are you trying to make up some story?" the lawyer shouted.

I felt as if I had been in a dream and had just woken up. I heard *tang, tang, tang*. Ten times—ten o'clock at night. I looked at them.

My interrogator said, "Sometimes people enjoy creating a torturous situation themselves. Perhaps you are that type."

"Is that a question you want me to answer?" I asked.

"Let us agree on one thing," he said.

"What is it?" I asked.

The chief of interrogation suggested, "Just say, 'Nobody came to my house. Everything is just a rumor. The money I gave to Kangal was indeed to buy a bomb but the intention was not to throw it on the crown prince.'"

"Whatever you want to write, you write it for me," I said.

One of them said, "If you simply say that you were behind the plot then everything will be over."

There was silence for a while. I was sweating. My mouth was completely dry. My whole body was aching from lying on the hard bench and from undernourishment.

One of the two men then said, "In a couple of days a new cabinet is going to form. If the same prime minister returns to power then we have heard that you will either be killed or imprisoned for a long time, maybe for life."

I asked, "Are you saying that the prime minister is the one making me a victim?"

"Let's not get off the track here. Either you know the truth or, as you are alleging, the people you are accusing know what is true."

"We have to make some compromise," the other man interjected. "Say something like you were involved in purchasing bombs."

"If you are not going to leave me without obtaining that confession, then write it," I said, adding, "But what for?"

"Say it was to throw at some prominent person," one of them suggested.

Irritated, but purposefully, I told them, "If you want that, then write that it was to throw at the prime minister himself." I thought privately, "The penalty for this confession will be only ten years in prison for attempted murder; at least that's better than a death sentence—the penalty for such an action against the crown prince."

The lawyer counted the pages aloud, one, two, three—up to eighteen. He asked me to sign each page. I signed. Whatever they wanted, there was their proof of what I had said. They had not read it back to me, so I did not know exactly what they had written down. They left the room a little after eleven at night.

The woman police guards came in and asked, "*Didi!* Why did they take so long?"

"Ask them," I replied.

Although my hunger strike was self-imposed, the reality was that my stomach was chronically empty. I was also being constantly disturbed. People would keep coming at any time, and, whether I wanted to or not, I would have to talk to everybody who came in. There was not much difference between day and night, although nights were busier. All the activities were carried out then—beatings, torture, killings. The next building was more active than mine, particularly on this night. They might have brought in a new prey. The silence of the night was broken by cries of pain. They must have been inserting pins. I became very restless. My hunger strike did not have any meaning for them here. It was three A.M. A male police officer came to my room.

"Did you kill somebody tonight?" I asked.

"You always imagine something big; he is not killed. As a routine treatment he was enclosed in a sack and beaten. But he would not speak a word, so some other police friends put a couple of pins in his fingers. That is all," he replied.

"Who was he?" I asked.

"Not a big shot. It was your cook, Lama," he said.

"No! What is his crime? Just because he is my cook, please don't torture that innocent boy," I shouted, managing through some unseen energy to sit up.

"If you tell this to any other police here I will be in trouble. I will lose my job and be court-martialed," he told me. Then he added, "I am telling you because I feel close to you. I don't know why." The policeman left.

"What could I have done to save poor Lama?" I thought. My eyes watered.

# 3.

# *Netaji*

I was struggling hard not to lose my mind. Physically I had almost gone. Mentally, I think I was still alive. I had heard that people could fast for days and days, and yogis even for months. I was wondering why I was so weak on only the seventh day. I closed my eyes and tried to meditate. Whenever I meditated, memories would return of happier events in my life and better things that I had been involved in. A couple of times I tried to concentrate on the event of my arrest. I wanted the deepest level of my consciousness to tell me what might have prevented me from being arrested. But it was as if my mind would not take up this event—it would not go there—and I decided to give up this exercise.

I found my mind returning to the painful time during 1962 when Nepali Congress people had been subjected to the most inhuman atrocities, which most foreigners might not think possible in our land of gentle Hindus. Tipped off by the new local agents of Panchayat—the *Panchas*—police and army men entered houses to pick up anyone they chose, disregarding any dignity of women or psychology of children. They pierced with bayonets, struck with *khukri* swords, beat mercilessly, and then threw victims from the windows of their own homes. If victims still breathed they were beaten and dragged farther down a hillside until they breathed their last; bullets gave the final wounds.

I recalled the story told by one of our domestic servants, who had served for two or three years in the army during those violent days. He told me how Nepali Congress activists were brought to army barracks and then stripped of their clothes. Then the soldiers used to sit around them asking them to howl like dogs or dance. It was after this that the army men poked them with their bayonets and started inflicting injuries, cutting the body slowly, inch by inch. When the victims began twisting and crawling with pain, they were shot dead. The same servant took me to see an open grave in a forest ravine not far from our house. I saw a large number of headless human bodies, some in decomposed condition and some skeletons. The army men had to forward the decapitated heads to Kathmandu—to the palace, or so it was said. I also remembered his story of how a political person of my district was murdered. A squad of soldiers went to that Nepali Congressman's house. At that time he was in ill health and bedridden, with his wife and children sitting around his bed. The soldiers asked him to get up, but he was unable to rise. Two army men dragged him up and tried to throw him out of the window. He clutched the window railings. The soldiers crushed his fingers with their boots, and when the sick man fell to the ground they kept dragging and beating him down the terrace slopes of his small farm, and finally shot him dead. Unable to tolerate such inhuman happenings, our former domestic servant resigned from the army and returned to our house.

ॐ

It was really difficult to bring my mind back to confinement within my cell. It strayed too far away. I was lying on my back. A guard noticed that I was staring up at the louvered window, where I could see the activities outside reflected. She came closer and watched, then laughed and said, "The police are playing judo and karate. Over there is the training center. We have two Korean instructors who train the police who can then massage the captives. You're lucky you've not been given that kind of treatment so far. I was one of the first batch to get karate training."

"If you hit me even once I might die, I am so weak now," I said.

She laughed. Her other two friends went for tea. My head was itching so badly that I started scratching furiously, but my hands became so tired that I could scratch no longer. She came nearer and said, "Eh! Maybe you have head lice. Can I look for them?"

"It is possible," I replied. "Today is the fifteenth day that I have not washed my hair. I used to wash it only once a week on Tuesdays when I always purify myself and fast for Lord Ganesh. I was arrested two days before my great hair-washing day."

She came closer and started searching for lice. Her practiced finger movements across the scalp, and the ritual clicks as she snapped the backs of her thumbnails together, miming the dispatch of lice, helped to stop the itching and felt comforting. She found no lice. Although it was the tenth day of my hunger strike I was feeling a little more energetic than I had a few days before. I told her, "Now do not disturb me. I want to meditate. If anybody comes tell them that I would not talk for a while."

"How do you meditate?" she asked.

"Close your eyes, allow thoughts to come but detach yourself from them, think your mantra, and let it take over the thoughts as effortlessly as thoughts themselves come," I replied.

"Does it bring peace of mind?" she asked anxiously.

"How otherwise do you think I am managing to survive here? It is through the peace of mind that I create through meditation," I assured her.

A little apologetic, she said, "I know you are about to meditate, but I have something to tell you if you do not mind."

"Oh, not at all. What is it?" As all the police who had talked to me "nicely" had been trying to manipulate me, I was already very wary about this. But I was open to this woman, and ready to give her the benefit of the doubt. I did not know whether she had some hidden agenda. Some had warned me that all police who came to me were briefed to employ some trick. Whatever, this one had been quite nice so far.

She began her story. "My husband is in the military. He is a great drunkard and womanizer. When he married me he had four wives already. But he lied that he was not married. After me, he has married again twice. . . ." She started crying.

There was a moment's silence.

"Where are all his wives?" I asked.

"Two eloped. Two are in the village in his house. And the last two are here in town. He didn't tell me he had married them. One day they got hold of me, and I brought both of them to our *dera* [rented apartment] while he was there. He was surprised at how the three of us came to know each other. I asked for a divorce because I am in a police job and make my own living. I can survive without him. He does not support me at all anyway. The other poor women have no jobs, nothing. But he would not give me a divorce."

"How on earth can he keep that many wives? Even according to Panchayat law he cannot have more than one wife except in certain specific circumstances, and definitely you have the right to obtain a divorce."

"For police and military, what is the law, *didi?*" replied my guard. "I reported it to my boss also, but nobody took any action. Now I am fed up with his behavior. I don't even want to raise this question about how many women he married. All I want is to restore peace in my mind and live on my own."

"Meditation helps to restore peace of mind. If I were out of custody I could help you with the other technical legal problems also," I said, and mentioned the name of a woman lawyer who was dealing with women's cases.

"Okay, you start now," said this policewoman, and sat on the floor quietly as I started my meditation. I do not remember how long I sat there. I must have fallen asleep, because the next thing I knew it was the morning of the next day.

ಌ

The doctor came again. I had absolutely no physical strength left. The policewomen had to help me sit or stand and would hold me for as long as I remained upright.

The doctor looked at me and warned, "Today is your last day. If you do not start taking some water, nobody can save you."

I told him, "I am feeling very strong mentally. I can talk better than I could five or six days ago."

"You are flickering like a candle before it dies," one of the policewomen interjected.

"Even if you want to eat something now," the doctor advised, "you cannot. The only thing you can do is to drink water for a couple of days, then glucose water, after that juice, and then milk. You have to wait at least two weeks before you eat solid food."

"All I am depending on is God. I will see what happens," I said.

"It is my duty to let you know your condition. It is up to you to do what you want to do. In your condition there should be an intravenous administered, but that is not possible here. So my suggestion is that you start with water." With that he left.

One of the guards brought a little water in a bowl and suggested that I clean my face. She also took a small mirror out of her bag and, handing it to me, said, "Look at your face."

I looked and was more shocked than before. I saw a horrible creature— skin peeling off in thick chunks. My lips looked an inch thick, but it was just layer upon layer of peeled skin sticking out. My hands, arms, feet, legs— in fact, my entire body—had become rough and cracked like the hide of a crocodile. A rush of realization came to me. My hunger strike was pointless. I felt akin to a goat seeking kindness from a tiger. All of a sudden a yearning for life returned. I did not want to die, definitely not. For the first time in my life I felt loving and caring toward my body, strongly loving to myself. I told the police, "I do not want to die. Please bring me some water."

One of them went running and brought me a glass of water.

Chanting a short mantra, I told myself, "I am breaking my hunger strike. My Lord Ganesh, give me strength for further struggle." Then I drank the water slowly. I felt slightly light-headed, as if intoxicated. By evening, I felt a little alive.

The next day, a new policewoman, in her fifties, and two young women took over as my guards. The older one told the other two, "If you want to go out for lunch you can go. I will stay here. I am old enough to be with Durga *bahini*. You do not need them, do you?" she asked me, and laughed. They went out of the room.

She said, "They are only constables. I am a *hawaldar*, the rank above them—so they have to obey me. That is how it works in the police. If an assistant subinspector comes and gives me orders, I have to obey him."

She tried to be very nice and friendly. "I have a daughter like you. Although I am a policewoman and have my duties, we can still be close. We can be like mother and daughter. Your poor mother, how might she be feeling?" she added, eyes watering.

I was not melted.

"What a stony heart you have. Why don't you talk to me?" she asked.

"I am just listening to you. You seem very kindhearted. I am sure my mother is sad," I responded.

"How long do you want to stay here?" asked this motherly guard.

"It is not how long I want to. It is how long your *hakkims* want to keep me," I said.

"Oh, *bahini*, if I were you I would not wait until when they say. I would find a way to get out," she advised me.

"Again the same proposal," I thought. "If I keep quiet, she digs me out. If I say something, she takes it steps further. How to react?"

"I need a little rest," I told her.

She came and pretended to help me settle down. I closed my eyes. I had not dropped off fully to sleep. I was in a kind of half-awake state. Then I had a frightening nightmare: somebody was tickling my feet. I looked down and saw them—two very little dwarfs, very ugly, with yellowish faces, looking up at me and laughing. I tried to sit up but could not. I felt suffocated. I tried to kick them away, but they were holding my feet tight. I could not lift my head . . . then I woke up. I was sweating and nervous.

The motherly policewoman was standing there in front of me. "Did you sleep all right?" she asked.

"Yes. Can you give me a glass of water?" I requested.

Nobody else was in the room, so she could not go. She looked around for somebody and said, pointing toward the dark door that was always left open, "Those men are armed guards." Then she called out, "Eh! Inspector *Saheb*, I need help."

A male police officer entered the room.

"Oh! I didn't mean you to come yourself, Inspector *Saheb*," apologized my woman guard.

The man said, "That is okay. What help do you need?"

"Durga *bahini* wants water. I will go and come back quickly," she said, and went out.

Obviously the inspector's entry was unexpected, so he was not briefed. He said to me, "One of your students at Padma Kanya College was my sister."

"That is great. Give her my best," I said.

The woman arrived with the glass of water. Handing over the water to me, she saluted the officer and he went out. After I drank she came closer to me and whispered in my ear, "Durga *bahini*! Do you want to go away from here? Trust me, I can help you."

I looked into her eyes. They were slightly frowning and cool—and suspicious. "Do you think I will be staying here for life? Of course I will go one day," I said.

She thought for a minute and held my hand, and then said, "You must not lie down all the time. You need a little exercise, otherwise your body will become dumb. Come! I will take you around the room slowly."

I was saying, "No, no." But she just pulled me up and held my arms and started walking around the room. After a minute she suddenly pulled me toward the open dark room.

I said, "Don't take me there. Somebody told me there are armed police guards for me. I do not want them pointing their bayonets at my chest."

Saying, "No, no—nobody is there," she tugged me through the open doorway. I found myself in a large hall. On my left was a wall. On my right was a long velvet curtain the whole width of the room. Some light filtered underneath the curtain, and in the light on the other side I saw men's black boots. Obviously the police guards were standing just behind the curtain. We were halfway across the hall. Wherever she was pulling me, I did not want to go there.

I said, "I feel like fainting. Take me back to my room quickly."

She resisted still, and said, "No, I just wanted to show you something, and after that I have a suggestion. We have a proverb, *bahini:* Even if a slave caste gives you a moral teaching, sometimes you should listen. You might think I am just one of the police. But I also have some ideas." Showing her hair, she said, "This hair has not gone gray for nothing."

I resisted. "Okay, I will listen to you. But in my room."

"If you say so," she said, and took me back.

I lay down again. She sat on the floor next to my head fanning me with her sari, and whispered, "Before those two girls come, listen! The place I wanted to show you was where you can easily get away from here. Just go the way I took you. Once you are out of the door on that side, you are out of this Police Club. The wall almost touches the door and it is not that high. You can easily jump. You can do it while I am on duty, so that if anything happens I can distract the other police. Do you understand?"

"I do, but I do not want to," I said.

"Although you are educated, it seems you do not have wisdom," she said.

I did not want to discuss anything with her further. Then I started to feel frightened by her. I told myself, "Keep her busy talking until the other two return." I asked her all about her family, how many children she had, whether they were married or not, whether she had grandchildren, what her husband did, on and on. She started giving me all the details, but I remember nothing of what she said. I was not paying any attention from inside, but outside I tried to show interest, saying repeatedly, "Oh! Yes! How nice!" My throat became so dry that I was almost choking. A little drop of water was left from earlier on. I indicated that I wanted it and she handed the glass to me. I sipped it. At last the other two policewomen arrived, and I felt as though I could breathe again.

She looked at me pointedly and put one finger over her pursed lips as if in a silent "Keep quiet." Then she joked at the other two, "Eh! You two young girls, you took so long. Did you go to find a husband?"

All three laughed loudly.

Another new batch came to relieve them in the evening. Hours later in the night a policeman entered. As usual the women guards left. The man was drunk—I could smell it even from a distance.

He warned me, "I am hearing bad rumors. Do not move anywhere except in this room. They will shoot you."

After saying this he called the three women back and disappeared. One of the three asked me, "Why did *Saheb* only come for a minute?"

"I don't know. I don't even know who he is," I replied.

She said, "He is our new inspector. For us, whoever it is, if they order, we have to obey. That's it."

༄༅

I felt a little more energy now. It seemed even water alone had started restoring my stamina. I did my meditation seated cross-legged on my bench. My day guards had changed again, and as usual whenever there were new police I had to explain to them what I was doing.

One of the women guards told me, "We heard you are going to be taken somewhere."

"Where?" I asked.

The other one replied, "They don't tell us anything like that, but I overheard one *hakkim* ordering others to make ready a van." At her mention of the word *van* the two policewomen caught one another's glance.

Late that night another male police officer came and asked in a very jolly voice, "How are you feeling, *didi*? Is everything okay?"

I just looked at him for a second and ignored his question.

He continued, "After six P.M. we are kings here—us inspectors and subinspectors. All other higher-level officers go home."

I looked at his face again without reaction.

He said, "Okay. Good-night," and turned to go out of the room. After a couple of steps, he turned around and faced me, and said, "There is a very bad rumor in the club. They are talking about killing you. Also they are making a plan for when to take you and how to do it. If they take you by van, then that is the end. The van is all dark and locked shut with little ventilation. I am one of the drivers who drives that kind of van long distance. If they decide to kill you, as a rule you will be taken to your home area, Koshi Zone. But listen and do not tell anybody—if you guarantee us both asylum, I can drive to one of the foreign embassies you know well."

I stared at him.

He went on, "Eh! Durga *didi*, a horrible thing is happening outside. Do you want to listen?"

I said nothing, but in my own mind I asked myself what could be more horrible than what was happening to me. What were they planning next?

He continued, "That poor Amrit Campus student—his skin was cut open and fresh lime juice rubbed in it. That really was too much."

"Maybe police enjoy torturing others. You're also a policeman," I remarked.

"By God, *didi*, I'm not like others. I am also a human being," he said.

I asked, "Why was that student tortured like that then?"

"Are you interested to hear the whole story?" he asked me.

"As long as it's not one of your tricks to make me feel demoralized, then I would be," I replied.

"You don't trust me because I'm one of the police. If you are not killed, then many years afterwards you will realize that, hey, there was one police *bhai* who was trying to be nice to me," said this young officer.

"Okay then, tell me," I said.

He looked around and shouted to the policewomen who were gossiping outside, "Go to the mess and drink tea. I'll stay here for a while."

Then he said to me, "Believe me, and listen to what happened. Four girl students—two from Padma Kanya Campus and two sisters from Amrit Campus—had gone to Pokhara to visit their relatives. The two sisters were found killed and the other two are still missing. The local police carried out their investigation. A forest watchman was the witness of their killing. When he came forward to testify, he was killed also."

I became curious and asked, "Who killed the girls, then?"

"That is the most interesting part of the story," he continued. "There are big shot Panchayat leaders' and businessmen's sons and even the royalty involved in this incident. They were after these girls. They raped them one by one—those five or six men. The two died while being raped. The forest watchman witnessed this incident and knew who the rapists were, so he was also killed. The girls' fathers went to Pokhara to inquire about it, but were told by people, "Do not try to investigate your daughters' murders; big people are involved. We cannot risk providing you any information." The reality is that everybody knows who the murderers are, but because the government ordered a suspect to be produced, the police went to Amrit College and picked up a boy who was close to the girls. He was kept in a van and taken to Pokhara—to the murder spot. Now he's in the process of being tortured to make him confess."

"You are not hinting that I will also be tortured that way, are you?" I asked.

"No, not at all. You always suspect me. I'm telling you what else is going on around our kingdom," said my news-bringer.

"Thank you very much for sharing such news," I said.

"Don't tell anybody," he said, and went away.

After a minute my policewomen entered and told me the same story as well. It was the gossip of the country, it seemed. Poor girls—what a way to die. I found myself wishing they had been first shot and then raped, so that they would have been spared being conscious of the pain and the shame.

One of the policewomen said, "*Didi*, what to do? The police force is not the place to have a job. You have to obey the orders of officers no matter how cruel they might be. If you say no you will be court-martialed. Even if you know the truth, you have to act as if you know nothing and behave like a beast."

ಬಂ

On the sixteenth day, I felt very, very weak again. I had had a horrible dream the previous night. I thought to myself, "This is how you suffer for telling the truth. The police have become like a wounded snake. It seems they are not going to let me live. If I am killed, people will say, 'Eh! She was involved in that kind of conspiracy, so she deserved it.' But if I am not killed, maybe I'll be able to write my true story." I think I fell to sleep with that blink of hope.

The next morning, I found myself wondering why I had been kept in captivity all these days. For what? "The overt reason, the pretense," I thought, "of the government—as I am told by the police, at least—is that I was the mastermind of the conspiracy to kidnap the crown prince." But the covert, the real, issue, I was convinced, was that the young men who had come to me were *their* people, *agents* of the people in power who had staged this plot. If, before my arrest, those who had sent them had been identified, then the real masterminds would have been exposed. From this viewpoint, I realized now that I had made one great mistake, and that was not having met the king's chief security officer when he had asked to see me through Shrish. "Well," I thought, "how could I have foreseen that the real plotters would come after me like this?"

I imagined the public reaction after I was killed. "Who was she?" they might ask. A revolutionary trying to kidnap the crown prince? Why did I need a bomb if I was to kidnap him anyway? Bombs are to be thrown to destroy. "They" would create the story. I was just trying to put the pieces together.

The new guards came. "*Namaste*, Durga *didi*, how are you today?"

"As usual, I am fine," I said.

"We are told there is very heavy security for you today. 'This day in particular you have to be very watchful,' was how we were instructed," the senior guard said.

The second one added, "We heard that the cabinet is going to change today. If the same P.M. returns to power then there will be real problems for you. If a new P.M. comes, then you will be free tomorrow."

The third one said, "Tomorrow the home minister is visiting this place, so the police have started cleaning up and washing all the bloodstains from the cells, and even sweeping the road. All the male captives are going to be taken either to jails or to the cells at Hanuman Dhoka. But we have no idea where you will be taken."

I still had not eaten anything. I had been sipping water only. What to eat anyway? I should have been drinking nourishing juices or milk but obtaining either was impossible. I had no money. Even if I had, I could not send the police out to buy anything. Nobody had asked me if I wanted food. As of that morning my skin had peeled six times.

A fourth policewoman entered and asked, "Durga *didi!* Do you want to take a shower?"

I asked, "Where?"

She said, "I will take you somewhere."

I thought that this might be another trick, so I said, "I am okay."

A male officer came in and all the women went out. He said, "A new cabinet has just formed under the same prime minister. The new home minister is visiting here tomorrow morning. I overheard the IGP talking to the DIG, the SP, and the DSP about your removal from here."

"Where are they going to take me?" I asked. "I do not mind going to jail."

He spoke very seriously. "No, it does not seem like jail. I heard really bad gossip. Since last night the security is very tight here. A van is ready."

"Do not tell me anything, okay?" I said.

"Don't take it otherwise. I'm trying to help you," he said.

"It doesn't help me. Even if I'm going to be killed, I don't want to know. Just shoot me without letting me know," I said.

"I am just warning you about something bad happening. Don't tell the others," he said, and went out.

In a second, the three women returned. One of them said, "*Didi!* today we cannot even go for our lunch or tea. Our *hakkim* has ordered us not to leave *didi* for a minute."

The other said, "We are told not to leave a shawl or anything. *Didi* might kill herself by tying something around her neck."

I listened but showed no reaction. The third woman talked on and on, more of the same sort of rumors, "Some police—male and female—have been bribed by *didi*. . . . She might try anything to escape from here with their help. . . . They are strongly instructed not to come near this room to see you ever again. . . . I heard the IG saying something to someone, I could not see who it was. . . . He said, 'If she escapes I will be kept in her position. . . .'"

I did not know why they were talking like this in front of me. All I needed right then was a warm glass of milk and a soft bed to sleep on. But their disturbance went on until three-thirty P.M. Then they became quieter. The DSP who had come to get me at the press entered my room at four. Being of lower rank, the women left the room.

Trying to look grave, he said, "Life is strange. I don't know whether we will meet again or not." He handed me a new book, saying, "Take this book—you can read it."

I took the book and saw that it was called *The Day of the Jackal*. Just inside the cover page was its purchase receipt. I said, "I don't have this money to give you."

"No, it's a gift," he said, and left the room.

I had not read this book, but was in no condition to read it at this time. The policewomen came back in. I was so weak and tired that I fainted. All I remember was seeing the ceiling starting to revolve, then everything in the room, even the women guards, began to spin. . . .

ೞ

The eighteenth day. At one A.M. I woke up to find a policewoman fanning me. My clothes were soaked with sweat. I wanted to drink some water. One of the policewomen brought water. I drank a little and rinsed my mouth. As I did, I realized that I had not cleaned my teeth or my tongue since the morning of the day when I had been arrested. At three A.M. two other policewomen came and told me, "*Didi*, we have been ordered to get you ready to go."

I shivered, genuinely frightened.

"Go where?" I asked, although I did not really want to know.

"I do not know where, but the van is ready outside," she said.

I talked to myself. They had really decided to take me somewhere without letting me know. So I was on my way to be killed. My mind became numb. All I could see before my eyes were visions of being shot or hanged. I thought that if they should ask me I would say that I preferred to be shot. The mind is so sensitive. Right up to the last breath, it thinks for you which will be the least painful way to go. Another woman guard came, smiling, saying, "Durga *didi*, I am going with you."

"Where?" I asked.

"I don't know where, but it's by plane," she said. "I've never been in an airplane. I'm so happy! Because of you I'm getting a chance to fly. What good luck!" Then she added, "All the inspectors and subinspectors have been told not to go in front of Durga *didi* now. Some of them who care for you might cry, and you yourself might also cry. There is very tight security outside to make sure nobody sees you."

She offered to help me get ready. What to get ready? All I had was the sari I had been wearing for the eighteen days since my arrest and the *bakhu* dress. Anyway, I got ready.

At a quarter to five she said, "Time to go," and held my arm and virtually hauled me out. Some of the police did start crying when they saw me. Their *hakkim* shouted at them, "Everybody get out of sight!" They saluted and disappeared.

I also felt some emotion. Perhaps for myself. Tears came to my eyes. I could not help it. I was human after all. They made me sit in the back of a closed van. The van was dark blue, with a few vertical slits in the sides. It was like a little cell, with no windows. All I heard was police speaking on their walkie-talkies. "Everything ready?" "Ready." "Okay, over." I was being treated like a little animal being sent off to be sacrificed. All of a sudden I felt a surge of energy to fight against this tyranny.

At five-thirty the van was driven away. After a while it stopped. The policewoman said, "Here we are. The airport!" and I could hear the engine of an airplane. I was trying to be conscious and brave. The events, combined with being locked inside the van, made me start sweating.

After some minutes the van was driven right onto the tarmac next to a small twin-engine Otter. The policewoman held my hand and pulled me out of the van, where I saw that there were still more police with walkie-talkies. The woman guard whispered in my ear, "*Didi!* There is a new inspector to go with us. He is not from the Police Club. They have brought him so that you do not know him."

This officer approached and said, "*Namaste.*"

The plane was a flight of Royal Nepal Airlines. Inside I saw an acquaintance, a man who used to work in the same office as Syd. I asked where he was going. He said, "To Sethi Zone." Despite the fact that the police were preventing me from talking, I managed to tell him after we landed in Sethi, "Please tell Syd I am going somewhere by plane but don't know the destination."

After the plane took off again I heard people talking about its final stop—Mahakali, Nepal's most remote western zone. I heard someone say that this was the last plane before the monsoon, because in Sethi and Mahakali the air strips were not all-weather surfaced and the small planes that flew to these destinations could not land after heavy rain.

So! I was being banished to Mahakali. Well, I had never been to Mahakali. I questioned myself, Why there? I came from the easternmost region of the country. Was this to distance me from my acquaintances? I came from the cool hills, and Mahendranagar, the Mahakali zonal capital, was one of Nepal's hottest places. People in the plane were talking about the heat at this time of year, saying that temperatures in Mahendranagar were likely to be well over one hundred degrees, with high monsoonal humidity. Like many of Nepal's new little towns, this one was also named after royalty. I thought about the irony; the meaning of this town's name was "Mahendra's city"—city of the king of Panchayat, the system I hated.

At about two P.M. the plane landed and I started feeling great discomfort. I supposed it was the heat after the noisy, bumpy journey by air. I felt dizzy as I tried to stand up to walk out of the plane. The policewoman helped me to get out. An open police jeep was parked at the foot of the plane's steps, and two others waited a little farther back. The three jeeps, packed with armed male police, drove away with my jeep in the middle.

I had never experienced such heat in my life. My blouse instantly became dripping wet, and wherever my chiffon sari touched my skin it almost burnt. My hair—thick, long, unwashed, and not properly combed for over two weeks—became very uncomfortable. I wished that I could shave it all off. The rays of the sun on my peeling scalp were burning.

After fifteen or twenty minutes, we stopped in front of a place that looked like the police headquarters. Inside, I was presented to a fat, uniformed man who was introduced to me by the inspector as the DSP and police chief of this zone. The inspector handed over a letter to him.

The zonal chief read it and asked me with a rough shout, "Do you know why you have been brought here?"

I said, "If it is to be killed I would have preferred to go to Koshi. If it is to live, I do not mind."

He glared at me as if I was his prey and asked, "Have you not eaten for eighteen days?"

I did not respond.

After a while I was taken to the chief district officer's office, where I fainted. When I regained consciousness, I found that there was a doctor there. He took my blood pressure and said, "You are very, very weak. You need to drink and eat immediately."

I knew that—but wondered how I was going to get anything there, not knowing where I was going to be living.

A man introduced himself as the chief district officer. We knew each other. We had first been acquainted some ten years before when he and one of my cousins had been friends while they both were district education officers. I felt a little relaxed.

He also asked, "Do you know why you are here?"

I replied, "Not really."

He said, "I have been requested to put you in prison here."

"Here means where?" I asked.

He said, "In Mahendranagar Zonal Prison, which is in Kanchanpur District."

I asked, "Are there other women there also?"

"Yes, a few murderers."

He introduced the jailer who was waiting for me in the CDO's office. Perhaps to reassure me, the jailer said, "We will look after you."

The CDO brought a glass of milk from his residence and offered it to me. I drank it and immediately felt dizzy. The doctor noticed this and told me, "As you have not eaten for so long you will feel strange when you start eating solid food."

At four P.M. I was taken to the prison along a very rough, dusty road.

The police who had accompanied me from Kathmandu and the local police handed me over to the jail police at the jailer's office. The inspector from Kathmandu told the jailer, "Please lock her up behind the bars, then we will go."

The jailer replied, "Don't worry, you can go. We'll do our duty."

Then all the Kathmandu and local police said *namaste* and good-bye to me and were gone. The jailer introduced the jail police chief and police guards, and also his subordinate, the *mukhiya* (clerk).

"*Mukhiya*'s house is that one," the jailer said, pointing from his window across a fiery-hot, barren landscape east of the jail office to a small thatched hut. He added, "If the monsoon does not break within a couple of days, this whole district may burst into flames."

Looking at me, the jailer said, "The doctor was suggesting you drink milk. Our *mukhiya*'s cow has just calved, so he can sell his milk to you."

Looking at the *mukhiya,* he said, "From today give her one *mano* of milk each day." A *mano* is our measure of volume, equaling a little over a pint.

*Mukhiya* said, "Okay, I will bring it from tomorrow, before four in the afternoon, in time for the evening meal."

I requested him to bring some in the morning also.

"Very well, I can give you one *mano* in the morning and half in the evening."

I was really reaching my last breath. I asked the jailer where my room was. I wanted to lie down. Standing outside his office, the jailer pointed with his forefinger to the brick prison walls and explained, "This jail is quite big. Behind that wall after a little walk is the Mahakali River; after crossing that you are in India. That section is the male jail. There are over a hundred men, with nobody on political charges at the moment." He pointed to the left. "That is the women's section. Look, can you see behind that iron gate? All the women are waiting for you."

Then he and the police chief walked with me into the jail. The distance from his office to the main gate was only six or seven steps. We passed through the gate and into a narrow yard within the high prison wall. At the end on the right was the big iron-barred entrance gate to the male section. It seemed all the men inside were watching my arrival. They shouted respectfully, "*Netaji*, welcome to Mahakali." *Neta* means "leader," and used with the *-ji* suffix, which denotes respect or reverence, is a title reserved for popular political leaders.

I smiled at them and said, "Thank you."

We walked five or six steps across the narrow yard to another gate, not quite opposite the main gate, where a group of women peered out through the bars. The guard opened this gate and the jailer said to the women, "*Netaji* has come. Behave well."

# 4

## Banished

I entered the women's section. The gate was locked behind me and the guards went away. It was five P.M.

Eleven women were assembled in an even smaller yard than the one I had passed through inside the main gate. There was nothing in the yard except for a solitary, dry water tap. The twelve-foot-high gray prison walls enclosed and dominated the yard totally. An empty brick watchtower overlooked the yard from the top of a single-story building with a flat roof. One of the women introduced herself as Potha and took my arm to lead me the three or four steps across the baked earth yard to a wooden door leading into the little building. My eyes had difficulty adjusting from the intense brightness outside. I dimly perceived a narrow, windowless corridor running from left to right, and could also make out through the pitch darkness another doorway straight in front of me. As my eyes adjusted, I saw that there were some thin and grubby mats woven from rice straw in a row on the concrete floor. On or beside some of the mats were a few meager possessions—one or two items of clothing, a ragged bedsheet, a clay water pot. It was obvious that all of the women imprisoned here had to share this one room, nine or ten feet across and about thirty feet wide. I stepped back into the little passage and followed the woman down it. At the end, the passage turned a corner and stopped. I saw from the row of primitive open fireplaces on the floor that this dark little corner was the cooking area. My guide turned me around and led me the ten yards or so along the passage in the other direction. From the smell it was not difficult to tell what we were approaching. It was in another corner at the opposite end of the passage to the kitchen corner. There was no door. I could hardly see anything. The woman said that there was a toilet hole in the floor there. I dimly perceived it and asked where the tap was.

"There is no tap in here." Pointing at two old tin cans, she said, "A little while back we all contributed and bought these." She added, "This one is for us. There are two Damini [an untouchable group] among us; they use the other can. You have to go early in the morning while the water is coming from the tap outside. We all go then, otherwise there's no water to wash with afterwards."

The stench was making me feel sick. I imagined that there must be excrement all over the floor because it was too dark even to see the hole. "What happens to it all?" I asked her.

"We were also wondering where it all goes, so not long ago we asked. The police said that it falls down a hole and the pigs come and eat it outside the prison wall."

I inquired about my fellow inmates and learned that one was classified as mentally ill and had been imprisoned due to the absence in Nepal of any alternative mental health facility. Two little girls, both three years old, were there too—daughters of two of the women. All of the other inmates were there on criminal charges—mostly murder and attempted murder.

After showing me around all these facilities, Potha, who was the mother of one of the little girls and a sort of leader there, introduced everybody to me. Some bowed down at my feet despite my protests. Some said "*Namaskar*," bowing their heads—the traditional greeting of respect. All were really sweet. Everybody addressed me as "*Netaji*."

I told them, "Don't call me *Netaji*, just call me by my name—Durga."

A little awed or shy due to my presence, they said they could not do that. Some called me "*Saheb*," and others "*Netaji*." They must have seen what a poor state I was in physically, as they all wanted to give me a massage. I declined, but they insisted they should. So I lay down, and the women tenderly massaged my feet, legs, and arms. I felt blissful. Particularly comforting was the relief the massage gave to my leg muscles, which had become cramped from dehydration and tiredness. At last, I thought, I was with the real people of Nepal.

They had already eaten, so there was no food. I was thirsty, but there was no water left in any of the storage pots in the room. The women told me that water flowed from the tap for only an hour or so in the early morning and for a short while in the late afternoon. But that particular afternoon none had come. I looked out and saw that the sun had become a red ball sinking slowly through a haze of premonsoon dust. Then, although the fiery sun disappeared over the horizon, the world it left behind remained like an oven. Intense heat continued to radiate from everywhere—walls, the flat concrete roof of our room, even the floor.

The *mukhiya* returned. He was carrying one new straw mat and a length of handloomed cotton material. "*Netaji*, Jailer *Saheb* has provided this bedding for you," he said to me. I thanked him. Then he moved to lock the door of our building. As a routine, it seemed, the women passed out to him all the pots, pans, spoons—and the one kitchen knife. These utensils were kept outside the door in the little yard. "That stops fighting," the *mukhiya* remarked to me, and as he left, he added, "Is everything okay?"

"Yes, thank you," I replied.

The women moved their empty water jars into the middle of the room for the night. "Bugs crawl around the walls," they explained. "They will not get into the jars here." Then each woman laid out her straw mat in preparation for sleep. The madwoman slept at the end of the room nearest the toilet. An elderly woman lay down with her feet toward the madwoman and her head toward the door. I asked Potha to put my mat next to this old woman's and parallel to the outside passage so that my head came almost up to our door. The others lay down here and there. It was the night of the dark moon, so everything was pitch-black. Mosquitoes whined in my ears and I found it difficult to close my eyes. Potha told me that everybody in jail had malaria several times a year. After a while some of the women started snoring. A woman named Nada spoke out of the darkness to warn me, "Eh! *Saheb*, the madwoman sometimes pulls your ears or pees on you in the night. You have to be careful." Then she too fell asleep. Bima, the madwoman, sang all through the night, something like "Motor came to Baitadi Bazaar." Later I discovered that a gravel road had just been opened from Mahendranagar up into that hill district. The women spoke Nepali, but their language was dominated very much by their local dialects. Consequently, I found it difficult to follow everything they said, although I felt sure that I would get used to it within a few days.

During the night I realized that the male section was on the other side of our wall. I could hear the men talking and coughing or crying. Some shouted the whole night—they must have been the mentally ill. I could not sleep at all. At one point in the night I wanted to pee, and Nada said she would go with me. Holding on to her and feeling my way along the passage, I used the toilet hole. I could not see light anywhere except one dim bulb way beyond the main prison gate, faintly visible as I peered through a crack in our door. I guessed that it must have been where the police guard was standing. I wondered why the *mukhiya* had to lock our door, because the gate of our section was itself locked from the outside. Our gate, the male section gate, and again the main gate were all locked, so I did not see the point of locking our door also. Well, I thought, this is jail. These women must be so used to this environment—they were all sleeping soundly. I lay down again and covered my face with my sari to try to avoid the mosquitoes. But then I became too hot. I uncovered my face again. There was not even a scrap of paper to use to fan them away and cool my head. I sat up and fanned myself with my hand for a while. Sweat trickled out of my hair. I tried to meditate. Even this failed. My eyes were aching from sleeplessness. Then someone rang the jail bell four times— *tang, tang, tang, tang.* "Oh! Soon it will be morning," I thought. The noise of mosquitoes began to diminish slightly and again I tried to meditate. This time it was easier. Not long after, a cock crowed outside the prison— *kukhurikaa.* As if an alarm clock had gone off, everybody woke up, saying to each other, "Ehey! It is dawn." It was five o'clock.

After a while the *mukhiya* came and unlocked our door and returned all the spoons, pans, and pots that the women were not allowed to keep inside at night. I thought, "How nice, the day starts quite early here, and I am with these women—human beings." The *mukhiya* said to me, "*Netaji!* I'll bring you some milk in a while." Then he left.

At seven he came back with my *mano* of milk. I did not have any pots or pans, so Potha offered to boil the milk in her pot. She also said that she would like to cook for me and I accepted. She boiled the milk, but not for long as she did not have enough firewood and had no money to buy more. When it was done, I gave some milk to the two little girls, Krishna and Jayanti.

My first day out of police custody was starting in a prison. Physically, it was not very different, but mentally, the experience was an improvement. I could talk to these women and spend my time more or less as I pleased. At about seven-thirty A.M. yellowish water trickled through the tap. Everywhere around the tap the ground was stained a strong reddish yellow. Having experienced the mosquitoes and now the water, I remembered that this area had been one of the *kalapani* areas where, during Rana rule, people were exiled for serious punishment. *Kalopani*, literally "black water," described a place where the combination of malaria and bad water meant little chance of survival for someone exiled there. So, not much had changed.

After fortifying myself a little with the milk, I felt that I had to wash my hair. It had been smelling bad for a long time, but only now did I feel free to care for myself. Pointing at the tap water, a woman named Madha said, "If you wash with this water your hair becomes very sticky because the water is so thick."

"Where do you wash?" I asked.

"Here—at this tap. It's the only place," she replied. Then she added, "Maybe if you request, Jailer *Saheb* might send police and get you some other water to wash your hair."

"No, if you wash here then I have to wash here too," I said.

As I did not have any soap, one of the women brought some mustard cake, explaining, "We all wash with this. The ration money isn't enough to buy soap."

"Well, I will try this too," I said.

She helped me with preparing it. First she soaked the cake in water for half an hour. But then, by the time she started working it into a paste in her hand, ready for application, the water stopped coming from the tap. So I decided to wash the next day.

A little hesitant, another woman, named Chiad, asked me, "Is it your fourth day?"

"Of what?" I answered.

"Of *nachune*—when you are not touched," replied the woman.

This is the way Nepalis refer to a woman's period, the first four days of bleeding each month when a woman becomes untouchable. During this time, even in her own house a woman sleeps a little apart, often on the floor on the far side of the room from the door. And others cannot eat food touched by her. She stays away from everything for four days and on the fourth day washes thoroughly to be purified. Untouchability is directly related to concepts of purity in Hindu society. In the case of menstruation, a woman is considered impure only during the first four days of heavy bleeding after which, if she is in good health, the bleeding should cease in any case.

I said, "Why are you asking?"

"We wash our hair only on the fourth day of our periods, just once a month," she explained.

I told her, "No, it's a little less than a full month since I last washed my hair, but it has become all entangled and knotted and smelly. Maybe coming it would be easier if I could wash it."

"Oh!" said the woman.

The jailer arrived and shouted from outside, "Hey! *Netaji*. What is your news—everything okay? I wanted to suggest one thing to you—don't drink the tap water without first boiling it."

I replied, "Okay, Jailer *Saheb*, thank you for your suggestion."

He called for Potha and shouted at her, "Will you feed *Netaji* your food for now, I will do the account later."

"Okay," she said, and he went away.

At nine A.M. our food was ready, and it was time for everybody to eat. Potha called me to the kitchen and served me first. The food consisted of rice and two very hot green chilies, and salt. The children ate the same food. I could not question anything. However, I told her that I could not eat chilies. Therefore I started eating the rice with the salt. Every time I tried to chew, my teeth would crunch on a stone, and the rice smelled very bad—like a dead animal. The smell was so bad that I almost vomited, but I tried to pretend that I was eating. Then I told them, "I just had that milk, and it seems that I do not have any appetite."

Potha looked at me and said, "What to do, *Saheb*. I don't have any vegetables to cook. Maybe tomorrow we'll send a policeman to buy a vegetable, and I'll cook it."

"Don't worry," I said. "Whatever you eat I will eat. I'll get used to it."

But I just could not eat that rice. I took my tin plate outside to see in the daylight what kind of rice it was that smelled so bad. I had never known rice like this. It was dark, almost black in color. Then I noticed numerous long, white, whiskered grubs mixed in with the black stuff. It was my first food since breaking the hunger strike, and at this point I did vomit. My body was demanding something pure, gentle, and good, like fruit juice, but even the water was not drinkable. All I could do was to wait for the *mukhiya* to bring some milk at five P.M.

Even in the morning the sun was hot, so we had to stay inside the room. While the others were washing their dishes, the woman named Chiad came back inside. She noticed that I had not eaten much, and observed the rice.

"Potha is a nomadic, tribal woman," she confided. "She does not care if she eats rice with worms in it. She never cleans her rice anyway. As I am the only Brahmin in here it is very difficult to maintain proper cleanliness with the kitchen and the food. All I do is try to keep my own little area clean. I don't say anything to the others." Then she added, "If you wish, I can cook for you."

Chiad's concern about cleanliness reflected the high standards of purity Brahmins, as the highest Hindu caste, are supposed to maintain in order to carry out their traditional duties. *Brahmin* literally translates as "those who posses knowledge," which is why higher-status Brahmins traditionally became gurus, priests, physicians, and advisers. Cooking became the lowest domestic position poorer Brahmins would perform. Certainly, in Nepali society all Brahmin and most non-Brahmin families able to hire domestic staff would tend to hire a Brahmin man or woman cook. Commonly, a Brahmin student boy, who would have received his sacred thread (a purification ritual usually performed for boys after they reach eight years of age), may be offered free accommodation by a family in return for his cooking. Such families prefer Brahmin cooks provided they maintain their daily observances of meticulous washing, wearing of clean white cloth while cooking, and meditation, chanting of mantras, and worship—observances that impart the quality of *sattva,* purity of body and mind, which is naturally of value in food selection and preparation. Generally, these cooks are pure vegetarians, although a few might occasionally consume the meat of a goat offered for sacrifice.

For a moment Chiad's offer to be my cook seemed appealing. Then another thought came into my mind. "I have found a job for myself here—to clean the rice and instruct Potha how to cook in a better way."

Everybody returned to the room. Potha came up close to me and, kneeling down, holding my feet, said in a very apologetic manner, "*Saheb,* teach me to cook city food. I will cook."

"I'm also from a village, so don't worry—we'll cook together," I replied. "All we need is to clean the rice. That I will do. Then we need some vegetable to go with the rice."

"How about some buffalo meat—it is cheaper than a vegetable. The police say it is killed near here," said Potha.

I told her that I was completely vegetarian. No meat at all. Potha tut-tutted, staring at my face in disbelief.

Then the women all began telling me their personal stories. Each one had a tale that was at once poignant and tragic.

Our atmosphere was shattered by a sharp cry from the jailer: "Eh! Women—where are you? It is ration time." It was twelve o'clock. Everybody ran outside. The jailer and the *mukhiya* were standing outside our gate; there were two other police officers with them. I was standing behind the other women. The jailer called, "Where is *Netaji?*"

I went forward and said, "Here I am."

"These women get fifty *paisa* and one *mano* of black rice a day, but because you are a political prisoner, you will receive one rupee fifty and one *mano* of white rice a day. Now the problem is how you will cook—you do not have a pot."

"Potha will cook for me, and I will teach her daughter how to read and write," I said.

"Not Potha; she doesn't know how to cook for you. Take that Chiad—she is a Brahmin like you," he said.

"No, no, I am quite happy with Potha. She has given me food already," I said.

A Brahmin, conscious of the concepts of food purity of our caste, he shook his head disapprovingly and said, "Okay, if you say so. You can change later if necessary."

Today, for the first time in twenty days, I had cash in my pocket—one and a half rupees, the equivalent of five American cents. I thought of all the necessary items I might have liked to buy, such as cooking oil, matches, firewood or charcoal, soap, salt, or spices. If possible I would have liked to drink tea in the morning and eat fresh vegetables. Oh! It was all going to be way beyond my limit. I decided to live day by day. I remembered that from that one and a half rupees I had to give seventy-five *paisa* to the *mukhiya* for milk.

"*Mukhiya Saheb!* I will pay you every week, okay?"

"Okay," he replied.

Then I decided to use the one and a half rupees to buy a vegetable for that day. Potha warned me, "These police cheat. Don't give them all the money." So she sent only fifty *paisa* to buy a vegetable and with that the police bought a good-size white radish.

I told Potha that I would clean the rice, and did so. My white rice was enough for myself, Potha, and Krishna, as we all ate very little. Potha decided to sell her rice through the police outside so that we could have some money to buy oil, salt, a vegetable, and eventually lentils. I felt a little awkward eating white rice while everybody else was eating the smelly black rice, so I told Potha to sell the white rice and cook the black rice for me also. She brightened up.

"That's great!" she exclaimed. "White rice is expensive. We can make enough money to buy lentils and other things if we sell it."

I said, "Do it. But I still want to clean the cooking rice."

She wanted to make sure, and asked, "You really mind those little worms in the rice?"

I laughed, "I do, Potha. You don't mind if I throw them out before you cook, do you?"

"No, I don't mind," she replied simply.

So the permanent agreement was that we sold the white rice, I cleaned the black rice, and Potha did the cooking while I taught Krishna. Jayanti also wanted to learn how to read and write, so I would have two students to begin with.

I still had the yellowish black, pasty mustard cake for washing my hair. It had been soaking from the previous day, and because of the heat, had started to smell quite sour. In the morning there had been so many activities going on that I did not get a chance to use it. First, the *mukhiya* had brought my milk, which I had to strain through a corner of my sari and boil; then I had to clean the rice; and then the little girls wanted me to teach them the alphabet and how to count—they were so excited at the opportunity to learn. So I had decided to wash later in the afternoon when the water came at three P.M.

Everybody else filled up their clay pots—a time-consuming process because the water flow was very slow. Then came my turn to wash. As I had no extra clothing to wear except my *bakhu*, I decided to wear just my petticoat, which I tied around my chest. Then I applied the mustard cake to my entangled hair, and, after rubbing it thoroughly as the women had instructed, I began to rinse my hair under the tap. The thick-looking yellow water mixed with the mustard cake and proceeded to turn my hair into a great, thick lump. I could neither get rid of the sticky mustard paste from my hair nor could I leave it the way it was. All of the women came to the rescue and tried to help me. At last one of them said, "You have such long and thick hair that this mustard cake was not appropriate." This certainly sounded like a correct statement. Until I had met these women, the main function of mustard cake that I had known was its property as a thickening and hardening agent. Throughout Nepal it is used as a kind of glue or sealant applied to all kinds of baskets woven from bamboo. Smoothed into the cracks, it seals them and hardens to form a durable plastered surface. The other use of mustard cake that I remembered was from home. My father used to mix it into milled corn and cook it for our water buffalo. He said it made them generate more milk. As I was thinking about this, the water stopped coming from the tap. My heart stopped momentarily. Now I could think of only one way to get rid of this great lump, and that was to cut my hair very short. Potha sent a message to the jailer to ask if he would lend me his scissors for the task.

He came out shouting, "You women know that you cannot have any cutting instruments inside, even for a minute. Why do you need scissors?"

When Potha explained what had happened, the jailer wanted to see for himself. I wrapped my sari around myself and stood inside the gate.

"Oh, you *are* in a mess," he said. "Let me see if I can do something." He went back to his office.

After half an hour the jailer returned and said, "Never use mustard cake again while there is scarcity of water. For this one occasion only I have made arrangements to help. There is a private house nearby where they have a tube well and they have agreed to let you wash your hair there. Two policemen and two of these women will go with you. I will be watching from the office. Go straight there, don't talk to anybody, and come straight back. Don't tell the CDO or anybody else who visits here, or I will lose my job."

I promised everything. Accompanied by two policemen and two of my fellow inmates, I went fully dressed to the nearby house to wash myself. Their tube well was out in the open. I kneeled under the tap. The women worked the hand pump, and out gushed the water. The two policemen watched as I washed. Much of the cake in my hair washed out, but a good amount remained caught in all the knots and tangles. The women offered reassurance on this, saying, "It will fall out after your hair dries." I trusted what they said. When I had finished washing, I walked back to jail dripping water across the baking hot ground. As I had no towel, I changed into my *bakhu* and the women began helping me untangle my hair.

I had a constant craving for fruit juice. I gave a little money to the jailer to buy a small can. The man who was sent by the jailer came back with a big open bottle containing some sickly-looking, deep-pink liquid. I told the jailer that it was not the kind of juice I wanted. "If you can't get it, never mind," I said.

They insisted that the liquid was juice, and that it was the only thing available in town. So I said, "Okay," and took the bottle inside.

The other women were excited to see it and remarked, "Eh! This is the sweet water sold by Indian hawkers that you can buy in town."

"Do you know how they make it?" I asked.

The women explained: "They mix sugar with water and add colors. You can buy any color you like!"

I gave the bottle to them, and they drank it down happily. For them it was a little luxury.

I still had the problem of drinking water. I discussed this with the jailer. Because clay pots were cheap, he suggested buying one for boiling the water and another for storing it. I gave him one rupee and from that money he purchased both. I made a fire from three or four little sticks of wood and balanced the clay pot above the flames on three stones. The water boiled. On its surface a skin formed—as if it were boiled milk, except that the skin was a yellowish brown color. I decided to strain the water through my sari— the only piece of thin material I had. I put the water in the other clay jar and let it cool. Even then, another skin formed on the surface, so I skimmed this off. There was my drinking water. At least it was better than drinking straight from the tap as everyone else did. The women were always ill—either with diarrhea or stomach pain of some kind or fever.

The first ten days were quite interesting and encouraging for me. I almost forgot how I had spent those eighteen days with the police in Kathmandu. After a week, everybody said they wanted to join the little class I was running for Krishna and Jayanti, so even the old woman, Sama, at the age of sixty-nine, became a student. Everything was verbal to begin with because there was no paper or pen. All I could do was to get them to memorize the Devanagari alphabet and numbers. After we had been going for a few days, I talked to the jailer about this.

"I will give you a pen and one piece of paper every day," he responded, "but you have to give them back to me in the evening so that I will see the proof that you are teaching them and not writing letters outside."

I agreed.

In the evening there was nothing to do anyway. It was very dark in the room. So whatever I had taught them during the day I would get them to practice verbally at night. After two weeks a prisoner from the male jail and a policeman wanted tutoring because they were planning to sit for the School Leaving Certificate examinations from jail. The jailer gave permission for this for an hour a day as well, and I would sit on the ground inside the gate while they sat outside the gate. I taught them any subject they wanted.

During these days I had visitors on two separate occasions—Nepali Congress colleagues from Mahendranagar and student leaders. I knew one of them immediately—Tarini Chataut—and he introduced the others to me. One good thing about working for the Nepali Congress was that even if you might not have met the people in the party, you knew their names, and when you did meet you naturally felt close. They were like family to me. They asked if I needed anything. There were no end of things I needed, but I did not want to appear demanding, so I replied, "No, there is nothing. If you could come to visit me once in a while that would be the greatest thing." I thought that having been exiled to such a remote region was turning out to be not so bad after all.

They also asked me what my charge was. I said, "No charge. I am being held under the Public Security Act." That was true according to the arrest letter I had been given.

After these two visits, however, not even a mouse came to see me. Actually I had not expected anyone to visit me in the first place. I recognized that the whole purpose of the government was to send me this far away so that nobody could find out where I was. Even if other Nepali Congress colleagues came, I was sure that permission to visit me would be denied. If I was to be treated like any other prisoner, then why had I not been taken to the women's prison in Kathmandu itself? It surprised me that I had even received those two visits, and I was not surprised when nobody came anymore.

One day the jailer brought some food, soap, juice, and a little money. After the hair-washing experience I was especially thrilled to get the soap. Handing these gifts over to me personally, he said, "If asked, do not tell anybody that I brought this for you because the instruction now is that nobody should visit you, and that I should not give you anything anybody brings here. A lot of people have come to see you bringing food, but I could not allow them to give it to you, otherwise I would lose my job."

"Who sent these things? I would like to think of them," I asked.

"Somebody from the Fuel Corporation, I think his name was something like Koirala," replied the jailer. (I still do not know who this was.)

He came closer to the gate and whispered from outside, "The prime minister's brother was here in town. People are guessing that his visit was related to your presence here and that he was the one who instructed the local administration that you should not be seen by anyone."

The next day a policeman gave me a couple of newspaper cuttings secretly and told me, "If anybody knows about this, I will be hanged."

"Don't worry," I replied.

The cuttings were from the local papers—although one was from across the river in Hindi—and were about me. I gathered two important pieces of news from these cuttings. The first was that I had been sent to Mahakali "to keep everything secret in Kathmandu" and that the prime minister's brother had indeed visited Mahakali and stopped all visits to me. However, when asked by a local journalist (or Nepali Congressman, I forget which), he had stated that he was there on a "private visit." The second thing I learned was that because the government had stopped my visitors, the local students had organized a one-day *bandha*, or strike, to protest against the government's action. I felt greatly cheered by knowing that there were friends outside thinking about me.

Now there was no hope of any friends visiting me, and nothing to do except teaching the women. That too was very limited because of the lack of writing paper. I remembered the book—*The Day of the Jackal*—that I had been given by the interrogation chief who arrested me. I picked it up and read it in one sitting. When I closed it I took a long breath and thought,

"So! They are trying to make me the jackal who is killed at the end." I read the book again and underlined every line that stated the ideals of democracy and how difficult it is to live as a democrat. Then I resolved that one day I would reveal the facts of what had happened during this autocratic rule. I prayed to Ganesh, "If I do not die, let me not forget to write a book. People around the world should know about this kind of staged conspiracy, victimization, and torture."

After reading the book for the first time, at around midnight one night, I was dying to go to pee. I got up and looked toward the toilet in the black darkness. I really become frightened by darkness, and was about to wake up Madha to go with me. All of a sudden I heard what sounded like men marching on parade on our roof. Very startled, I sat down again on my bed, and as I did so, I felt as though somebody was jumping off the roof, crying. A deep sense of fear gripped me. It seemed as if someone was trying to enter our room. "Madha, Madha!" I shouted.

She woke and asked, "What happened?"

Then I thought to myself, "Maybe because I read that book I have had a nightmare." So I said, "Oh, nothing serious. But I felt as if somebody was trying to come in here."

She came to my bed, held me, and said, "Eh! We haven't told you yet. This room of ours is haunted. Some time ago, it was used for male political prisoners, and the police told us that some of them were killed in here. That's why, once in a while, they still haunt the place. Even the police no longer go up to the watchtower above. One policeman died up there after the prisoners were killed. No one knows why. He vomited blood a bit before he died. Everyone suspects that he was frightened to death by one of those spirits. We were very frightened in the beginning. Now we are used to it."

"If everybody else is asleep and one person is awake and the ghosts come, it must be very frightening, mustn't it?" I asked.

"If that happens you have to wake the others up and start talking. Then it stops," she replied.

While we were talking, everybody, including the madwoman and the two little girls, woke up. We continued talking until two A.M. By then everyone wanted to go to pee, so we all held one another, each hanging on to the back of the one in front, and marched in a line through the blackness to the toilet. Naturally, everybody was scared to be the first, but elderly Sama volunteered to go in front. After that night I never drank anything after three P.M. out of fear of going to the toilet at night. The other women did the same.

I experienced the haunting five times during the four months I spent in this jail. Once the sound was like one person shouting and another sobbing in pain. The women thought that the political prisoners must have been killed by bullets, which was why we sometimes heard the sound of shots. The haunting was a strange phenomenon. The sounds would wake you from deep sleep, and for as long as you lay there in a kind of half sleep you would continue to hear the sounds vividly—frighteningly real. But the minute you started talking and became totally awake all traces of the haunting would vanish, as if your consciousness had switched to another state and had left that spirit world behind.

Some nights were so very hot in our room that, despite the danger of snakes and scorpions, we all decided to sleep outside near the tap. I requested the jailer to allow us to do this, and he ordered the *mukhiya* not to lock our door for a while. The women were not worried about creeping creatures on the earth, but I was, so the police lent me a coconut-string bed from their barracks so that I could sleep up off the ground. In the morning I would give it back to them. In the middle of one of these nights outside, I heard the haunting again. Outside the sounds were even more frightening than inside because we were lying right under the eaves of the roof. I felt as if somebody was throwing stones over me. I shouted and then in a second everyone else began shouting. But the stones turned out to be hailstones! What relief we felt as we ran inside and laughed in the darkness. Fierce, powerful lightning and thunder ripped the dead night sky. The monsoon had broken. The next day the police told us that some people in the town outside had been hit and killed by lightning during the night.

Now that the rain had come, the prison became humid as well as hot. I developed a rash all over my body and intensely itching hives on my face and arms. Coming from the cool climate of the hills, this place was like a furnace for me. "Well," I thought, "this is also an experience in my life; if it was not for the government of Nepal I would never have had this chance. Even if I had come here, it might have been only in the winter."

I think I lost almost 50 percent of my hair during that monsoon. All the other women also complained that their hair had almost completely gone. They all had very short hair of uneven length. "In the beginning we felt sad. Now we think, why care for our hair while our whole life is in this hell," Madha commented.

For weeks it rained and thundered heavily. My fellow inmates kept talking about floods, worrying lest some of their people back home might have been swept away. They cried. Nada and Mebu were particularly anxious because their parents' houses were on the edges of little streams in the hills, which during the rainy season often experienced flash floods. Both had lost their goats and cows in floods in the past. The other women tried to comfort them, saying, "Look at how we're living here, and who cares? Our minds on our relatives and their minds on the stone." It was a Nepali proverb.

Despite the women's unhappiness as they thought of home, I quite liked the rain. Gradually it cooled the air. Also I have a fascination for heavy rain, thunder, lightning, and, most of all, the great black clouds. You can feel the new air mass enveloping your world, the movement of everything, and you become more expanded, more imaginative. It was true that from here there would be no communication with the outside world during the monsoon. No airplane, no bus; if somebody wanted to come to Mahendranagar they would have to travel by train through India and then cross the border at the Mahakali River. No one was going to visit me anyway, I thought. Was I thinking selfishly? Not really; this rain might be good for the farmers as well.

The women wanted to sing their local songs and asked me to play drums with an aluminum plate. The theme line of their song was, "I am on this side, you are on that side; with something in between so we can never meet."

Over three months had passed. I had had no news from outside and no contact with anybody. My life was this one room, the cooking corner, toilet, rain, mud, heat, police, jailer, the *mukhiya,* and these women inmates with whom I had nothing in common except that we were women and we were all in jail. However, they were now becoming my close friends. We started communicating better. I learned their languages quickly and taught them to read and write simple Nepali. I taught Krishna and Jayanti a few English words, and how to count up to one hundred in Nepali and up to twenty in English. It reminded me that at around their age I had learned from my father how to count up to one hundred.

I thought that luckily my mother had never been imprisoned. At least I had not spent my childhood with her in jail. Yet my childhood and early teens had not been free from challenge and tension. A thread of memories broke loose within my mind as it unraveled the past.

# 5.

# Early Life
# and Politicization

For better or worse I am what I am because of my family.

We had a patriarchal system at home, where all decisions were made by my father and were followed by everybody else. Well—not entirely. My mother, Yoga Maya Pokhrel, used to make decisions about the kind of food to cook, who should clean the house, and who would husk the rice or grind the wheat. She would supervise the maids and servants—both permanent and seasonal. She herself was never idle. She would create work. Even if she sat resting for a while her hands would be doing something. My father was fond of saying, "There is only one sin in this world and that is to sit lazily twiddling your thumbs without doing anything, wasting time. Time will not wait for you." His logic was that each lost minute in the approach toward death is one that could be used to create something valuable to fulfil *dharma*—one's duty or divine purpose in life. Therefore, Mother always had some work to do.

My father and mother had a typical traditional Hindu family relationship. Their marriage was arranged by their parents when my father was nine and my mother was seven years of age. Every morning, she would bow down at my father's feet in case, during the night, her feet might have touched his—a sin for a devout Hindu wife to carry. She would not eat anything until she drank a little drop of the water left from washing my father's feet, because according to the Hindu religion a husband is the representation of Lord Vishnu and the wife's protector. This was her gesture of surrendering to her lord. My mother always wore red vermillion in her hair that parted on the crown of her head, a red *tika* on her forehead, a wristful of red bangles that jingled cheerfully as she moved about, and red clothes—the sign of a married woman with a living husband. Every evening she would prepare the five-stranded kapok cotton wicks and ghee (clarified butter) for our copper-bowled oil lamps and would place them first in the worship room, kitchen, and front doorway. She would then step into the courtyard outside and place one on the *tulsi math*—a raised bed found in every Hindu family yard for the sacred *tulsi*, or basil bush, in which it is believed the protecting Hindu deity Vishnu also resides. After these observances, my mother would once again bow down at my father's feet for blessing.

Although she never ate with my father, she would always eat from the same plate after he ate. Father had two sets of dinner plates, one of fine brass and the other of silver, each with matching side plates, bowls, and goblets for water. After eating, he used to leave a little morsel of food—one mouthful—which my mother believed would bring her good luck. These observances were effortless, and routinely performed. In making decisions, whatever Father said she would echo, and she was very persistent in implementing his decisions. That was her role, her *dharma*—her righteous religious duty in the cosmic, societal, and family order of things.

In public, and generally at home as well, my father was very soft-spoken. But in certain situations, he could roar like thunder. But Mother was always serene. In all of my life with them I did not see her sad or unhappy. She was always the same—mild in manner, soft in speech, gentle in humor. Father always wore fine ironed clothes while Mother always wore very, very simple clothes. This was the one thing that used to make my father cross with her. But it just came from her natural humility.

Apart from seeing to the careers of his sons and grandsons, Father's life as a physician and community leader was devoted to the health and governance of the people in Dhankuta and the surrounding hill districts. He had studied Ayurveda, the classical Vedic science of health, at Banaras Hindu University in India. The term *Ayurveda* means "the science of life" and is a branch of ancient Vedic knowledge that deals with health as the integration of spirit, mind, and body in both preventing and curing illness as well as enabling a person to achieve the full purpose of human life.

Father lived quite a slow, yet busy, life. Early in the morning, long before dawn, to influence the day with positivity, he would start chanting verses from the Vedas. First of all, he would chant a salutation to his spiritual guru, followed by other mantras invoking the presence of various deities and honoring the mother goddess, the earth. My father would carry this initial consciousness throughout the day, and if, at some moment, he might burp or release gas, he would pinch his ear as punishment and chant an appropriate verse seeking pardon for polluting the environment. While he was engaged in his predawn chanting, I would prepare the ingredients for the worship ritual before the priest arrived at around four A.M. Since the time of my great-grandfather, our family had engaged a priest for daily religious rituals.

At around dawn, Father would make a fire in the kitchen, where, in the center of the room, we had a brick-and-mud oven built into the floor. For fuel we used local firewood. My father would first prepare food for the calves of the cows and buffaloes that lived on our farm. Then the servants and maids would gradually arrive and take over. After that my father had the habit of smoking a *hukka* pipe before he began his morning ablutions. He had a big *hukka*, its lower bowl made of heavy engraved brass and a long upper section of fine crafted wood and cane with an engraved silver mouthpiece. Every day he would put fresh water in the bowl, then light the charcoal fire at the top and pack in the tobacco. He used to sun-dry fresh tobacco leaves from our own garden, then crush and mix them with molasses to make his smoking mixture. His theory was that while smoking was bad for health, if you smoked the *hukka* in this way the dangerous elements were filtered out as the smoke bubbled through the water. He might have been right. He certainly did not ever have any disease related to smoking. Quite often I would help him prepare his *hukka* and loved its quiet hubble-bubble sound.

Even while smoking, Father was always busy reading something. He used to subscribe to many research magazines from India in both Hindi and Sanskrit, and would buy most Hindu texts dealing with spiritual and health matters. When it was his *hukka* time whoever in the village was free used to gather around to listen to him, and he would read aloud and give interpretations for them in Nepali. If nobody was there he would read quietly to himself.

After *hukka* and toilet, Father would shower in cold water before performing his personal *puja* [worship ritual] and meditation in the worship room. Father would complete his own ritual with *pranayama*, yogic breathing exercises. By then it would be nine o'clock and time for his morning meal. When he returned home from work in the evening he liked to do something involving physical labor, such as tilling the garden, where he raised a rich variety of vegetables, fruits, flowers, and Ayurvedic herbs. We always ate home-grown food.

Father's own father, my grandfather Pandit Veda Nidhi Pokhrel, was renowned throughout the hills of eastern Nepal as a *rishi*, or sage. He was a scholar of the Vedas, and, in his later years, adopted the simple garb of a renunciate—namely a *dhoti*, or loincloth—and marked his forehead with broad horizontal splashes of sandalwood paste, the sign of a Shiva devotee. For a period of years he had dwelled in a cave, meditating and gathering wild forest products for food, clothing, and shelter. During this time of solitude, it was said, he became enlightened.

As part of his devotion to the spiritual path, my grandfather visited India's holy places on a number of occasions. He was a true yogi who had attained the yogic state of knowledge of past, present, and future. Thus he had knowledge ahead of time of the moment at which his "death" would occur. While my father was still studying in Banaras my grandfather told my grandmother and other family members that he wished to return to Rishikesh, known to pilgrims as the Valley of the Saints, to give up his life and to be reborn. "No one should cry," he said. "Don't think that I am dying. I am simply going to change this old body for a new one." One of my uncles accompanied him to Rishikesh, where the Ganges roars on its path from the Himalayan snows of its source high above Badrinath. After giving his son a final blessing, Grandfather performed a last *puja* ritual. Then, on the bank of the Holy Ganges, sitting cross-legged in the lotus position and doing *pranayama* breathing, he "left his body." In Sanskrit we call a person with such developed consciousness a *bramhagyani*, "one with eternal knowledge." For my father, his father was nothing less than an incarnation of the Divine.

After completing his doctorate in Ayurveda, my father visited Kathmandu to inform the Rana prime minister, Chandra Shamsher, that he was now qualified for work in the health service. The prime minister ordered him back to India for further practice. This time he was sent to Calcutta to work under a very renowned physician. After a year, Father received the title Vaidya Bhushan, "Jewel of Physician," and returned to Kathmandu. The prime minister then commanded my father and some colleagues to formulate a tonic to be named, in characteristic Rana humility, Chandrodaya—after himself. My father duly prepared the tonic, which was sent to Japan and Germany for analysis and clinical tests. After the results came back highly favorably, Chandra Shamsher gave my father a cash award and posted him back to his hometown of Dhankuta—which was also the Ranas' eastern capital—establishing at the same time a hospital where my father could work. For the hospital, the prime minister selected the name Tribhuvanchandra Ayurvedic Hospital, after himself and the then-still-imprisoned Shah king. Father was appointed chief medical officer for the entire eastern region of Nepal, and remained working there in Dhankuta for thirty-seven years until he retired in 1966. Just before the 1950 revolution, the second-to-last Rana governor, Shrish's grandfather, dismissed my father for a year on suspicion that he was a Nepali Congress supporter. After the revolution, B.P., while visiting Dhankuta, reinstated him. Despite the dismissal, Father and Shrish's grandfather remained close friends.

Besides running the hospital, Father would make an annual visit to every village in our region to give cholera and other vaccinations. Many patients would come to the house for treatment even during weekends and holidays, and for emergency treatment at any hour. Father used to perform basic veterinary treatment as well. He taught me some of the basic techniques of medicine, including Ayurvedic preparations. Whenever he was not at home I ran the home clinic. My mother also performed certain medical treatments, such as helping with childbirth and lancing infected wounds.

In community affairs my father was the *mukhiya,* or mayor, for some twenty villages in the Dhankuta District, widely scattered over three or four "foothills" of four thousand to seven thousand feet. He was responsible to the Rana governor during Rana rule until 1950, and thereafter to the district magistrate until 1960. As the recognized headman in our local community he would often hold *lok adalat,* "people's court," meetings on the stone-paved patio outside the entrance porch to our house. Everyone concerned, as well as other interested villagers, would assemble there. The aim in our Hindu concept of justice is to establish a situation where wrongdoers feel remorse rather than bitterness at their punishment, and come to a deep realization of their misdeeds. As soon as a defendant freely admitted guilt, others among the assembled would be asked for their views on the appropriate punishment. After this, my father would consult the culprit. Was he or she satisfied with the punishment? This would be the first test of realization. I must have witnessed dozens of cases at our house, although at that time I was too young to understand the moral forces in action in these gatherings.

Another duty of his was to supervise the management of public forests. If villagers wanted to cut grass, fodder leaves, or firewood they were supposed to consult him and he would tell them how much they could cut, and from which part of the forest. This system of local forest husbandry conserved supplies for everybody.

The dominantly Brahmin village of Kachiday was my birthplace. It comprised mostly the extended Pokhrel family, whose ancestors migrated to the east from Pokhara in the west six generations ago according to the Pokhrel family genealogy. Five thousand feet up on the west slope of a ridge, Kachi-day was situated below a mature pine forest. The Newari Bazaar town of Dhankuta, one hundred and fifty miles as the crow flies due east of Kath-mandu, remains the capital of Nepal's eastern region even today.

Above the Dhankuta ridge was a backdrop of the world's most majestic mountains—the Makalu, Chamlang, and Sagarmatha Himalayas to the northwest, and Kanchenjunga to the northeast. Sagarmatha is known to the rest of the world as Mount Everest.

My father built our family house after his father separated the family land. Besides the Rana governor's palace, ours was one of the few large houses in the area. In those days, no one was allowed to have a building larger than the Rana's house. It must have been a big undertaking at that time, when every roofing sheet, length of timber, and sack of lime had to be carried from the roadhead in Dharan on a porter's back. The huge flag-stones for the courtyard were carried up from a river four thousand feet below.

Upstairs were six bedrooms, the family worship room, a south-facing ve-randa, a balcony stretching the full width of the house on the east side, and three other small balconies. The third-floor attic was a large room where we stored food grains year-round. On the ground floor was a spacious kitchen, various storerooms, and Father's work area. In accordance with architectural principles laid down in the Vedic texts, the front door faced the east and the covered entrance porch, with its built-in, wide wooden benches on which Tibetan carpets were laid, served as the reception place for visitors.

The whitewashed mud-brick and timber house nestled in about two acres of natural garden, dark green with orange, mandarin, lime, lemon, grapefruit, litchi, fodder, herbal, and ornamental trees. Near the house were banks of flowers and medicinal herbs. Surrounding the garden, hillside ter-races of maize, mustard, and other crops produced a patchwork of textures and colors.

No horns or engine noise from motor vehicles disturbed the natural har-mony of the farms and villages around Dhankuta. Since we had no elec-tricity, we used paraffin lamps, and cleaning and lighting all six of them was my duty each evening. Once in a while I would also sweep the floor or fetch water from the well. In these remote hills, there was no dependable piped water and certainly nothing like a telephone. Until I was a teenager I never saw a motor vehicle. The nearest traffic was in Dharan—a long day's trek away through a deeply cut river valley, up over an eight-thousand-foot ridge, and then down again to the lap of the foothills bordering the *tarai* plains.

১৯

I was born by the fireplace on the clean, cow-dung-plastered mud floor of our kitchen. "It was after the evening dishes had been washed up," said my nanny, which means between eight and nine at night. Childbirth in our society is an exclusively women's affair, and my father was upstairs. As Hindu society places high value on sons, my father strongly desired his last child to be a son because he had four daughters already and only two sons. Throughout the nine months of my mother's pregnancy, the astrologers assured him that the baby would be a son. Then, just before the birth, the astrologer closest to my father confided that although the signs still favored a son, some stars were not now so favorably positioned and he might have a daughter. The astrologer added, however, that if it were a daughter her qualities would be those of a son—strong and powerful.

After my birth, someone must have had the courage to convey to him the news he did not want to hear. When he heard he showed no interest in my arrival at all, and did not even come down or inquire about my mother. Instead he went to his bed, and then early the next morning disappeared. He did not reappear even for the customary name-giving and purification ceremony on the eleventh day—a most significant ritual in any Hindu family. In my father's absence my close aunt, along with our family priest, performed the formalities at which my secret astrological birth name was selected. I do not know when my father eventually returned, or where he had gone.

Until I went to primary school I had no given name; neither was I told my astrologically determined birth name. Some in the family called me just *Kanchhi*—"youngest female." My mother called me *Chhori*—"daughter." My father only used a rather derogatory diminutive form of address in Nepali that I do not want to repeat here. Of course, other people around the village took their cue from my father and used this name as well. So I grew up with that. Interpreted kindly, it meant "smallest one."

On my first day of attendance at school I had to give my name to the teacher. I had no name to give. So when I returned home I asked my father what name I should tell my teacher.

It was then that he said, "Your name is Durga."

How deliberate his decision was to choose that particular name I do not know. Durga is the Goddess of Power in Hinduism. Riding astride a fierce tiger, with her eighteen arms she battled all of the demons in creation for nine days and nights until she emerged victorious on the tenth day. Every year Hindus celebrate this day during the Dasain Festival (*Dashera* in India) as Victory Day, the triumph of good over evil and ignorance.

In later years, whenever he would harangue me for disobeying his wishes, Father used to say that perhaps it was because he had chosen this powerful name that I had been influenced by its strength and had become so ungovernable. Once in a while, Mother did tell me that even though I was not an obedient daughter, when Father wanted to feel better about me, he would console himself with his astrologer's prediction that I would indeed be as good as a son. Yet, when it came to certain issues there was no getting around the problem that I was a daughter. And so I grew up with this cloud over me, and my father's constant "ifs"—"If you had been a son. . . ."

Despite this, my earliest memories are of him holding me in his lap, until I was about six years old, and telling me all sorts of stories based on the Vedas and the great epics, the Mahabharata and the Ramayana. After I was six I used to sit beside him. Every evening after dinner he would read these texts for the whole family. We would all gather by the kitchen fireplace as the maids and servants washed the dishes and cleaned the hearth of impurities by rubbing and then rolling over it a sticky, fresh pat of cow dung to which any food remains adhered. Then they would apply a watery coat of red clay that hardened quickly to form a new, clean surface. Their duties finished, they too would sit cross-legged on the floor to hear Father's lecture.

Some of the Sanskrit verses he recited I would memorize. When Father first heard me chanting these he was considerably impressed and proud, and after that he would take me to literary and other local meetings where he would recite his poetry. He would teach me Sanskrit verses from the Bhagavad Gita to recite by heart at the meetings. By the age of nine I was writing simple lyrical poems, and whenever I accompanied him to the meetings I would recite my own poems, for which I received several awards.

From the age of six or seven I used to tell everybody that I would be a doctor when I grew up. When, on one occasion, I told this to my father, he replied, "We will see. I always wanted your eldest brother to be a famous doctor and the second one to be an engineer. The first one is doing what I dreamed, but the second one was never interested in his studies." After I earned the best scores in the first grade of my village primary school, he took me to the girls' school in the bazaar and admitted me in grade five, skipping grades two to four.

My father and I remained very close until I reached the age of twelve. Then, when I began my thirteenth year, there was suddenly a big gap between us. As was the tradition when a daughter reached maturity, he began to speak to me only through my mother and started to look for eligible boys for my marriage. I felt depressed and frustrated and asked my mother to tell him that I would not like to get married. Rather, I wanted to study as my eldest brother had. I soon heard my father roaring at my mother, "No, definitely not! He is a man. She is a woman. She must realize that." Then he lowered his voice and said, "I wish Krishna was a daughter and Durga was a son." Krishna was my second eldest brother.

ಬಲ

It was during this same early period of distancing from my father that I suffered another psychological blow that would affect my relationship with my family deeply.

"She looked exactly like you do," remarked one of our maidservants one day as I approached our village returning from school.

"Who did?" I asked.

"Your mother."

Perhaps I appeared puzzled. It was a little difficult for me to imagine how Mother might have looked when she was younger.

The maid continued, "She was so kind to us all as well. I know she left plenty of wealth for you. Lots of jewelry."

"I don't like piercing my ears or nose, so perhaps I don't want any jewelry," I replied.

All of a sudden a strange, creeping feeling of suspicion spread over me.

"Wait a minute," I uttered. "Why are you saying 'my mother, she *was*'? What is wrong with her now?"

The maid came closer and whispered in my ear, "Your mother was different. She died after you were born. But don't tell anybody that I told you."

I felt jolted through my whole being. Fury exploded within my mind. Already I had enough to fight about with my father. Now what was this secret that had been kept from me? I did not know how I would control myself. I charged home, my eyes not even seeing those whom I passed on the footpath. I looked at no one as I entered our yard. I felt as though they— all members of my family—were sugar-coated quinine. I spoke to no one. I ran upstairs and sat on my mother's bed and cried. Then I determined to confront somebody. I went to the room of my aunt, my father's sister—a child-widow who had been ordered by her in-laws to die as a *sati* (by immolating herself on her dead husband's funeral pyre), but luckily she had escaped and now lived with us. I asked her straight, "Do you know about my own mother?"

There was a moment's stillness as tears filled her eyes; then she replied slowly, "She was very good."

"Do you have her photo?" I asked.

"Nobody has one. A photo of her was taken once, but I think that it was destroyed."

I was silent. I felt suddenly as though everybody in the house was an alien to me.

This feeling lasted for many days until I replaced it with a demand, my right to know who my real mother was. Slowly, from other relatives I came to know that the mother who had given me birth, Prem Kumari Pokhrel, was my living mother's own younger sister. My living mother had suffered from some recurrent illness. An astrologer suggested that until my father married a second wife, she would not recover. In turn, my living mother worried that if my father married an unrelated woman, that new wife might mistreat her stepchildren. With this anxiety, she had requested that her father arrange her younger sister's marriage to my father. Thus it was that my father, at the age of thirty-four, married my birth mother when she was twelve years old—younger than his first daughter.

My reaction to these revelations was to revolt against everything and everybody in the house. Many times I behaved fiercely like my namesake goddess. I wrote several poems and short stories and a novel in search of my mother. One of my poems received a national award. While I was reciting this poem at a competition I noticed my father break down and cry. However, my relationship with my father had undergone a fundamental transformation.

When I entered ninth grade I was selected by the "senior sisters" to be president of our school union. Perhaps they selected me because I was already perceived as being courageous and vocal. I held that position for two years, through the ninth and tenth grades. In the tenth grade our senior sisters who had just graduated from school came to me and said that there was to be a meeting of student leaders in one of their houses in the bazaar. Naturally, as student president, I was to attend the meeting. In the room were six older boys from Dharan and Biratnagar colleges.

It turned out that this was no ordinary meeting of student leaders. In fact, it was to be my first political meeting. The six older boys spoke of many political things that I had never before known. They told us that beyond the imprisonment of democratic leaders, thousands of other party political workers had been arrested and murdered. It was deeply shocking. Inspired, I became intensely determined to fight against the inhuman political system that was governing the country.

The student leaders explained how all student unions across the kingdom had to work for the release of the country's elected political leaders. An underground pamphleting campaign had to be mounted. They promised that they would supply the pamphlets to us by sending them through some unidentified person. They ended by saying that Panchayat was mutilating our society and we all had to work together against it. We promised to follow their instructions. At the end of the meeting, they gave me some stamps, pads, stamp pad ink, and a membership book in which to write down the names of new members, and instructed me to do this recruiting work very secretly and to not keep any of the materials at home.

I took their instructions about secrecy very seriously. Could I trust anyone in my family with a secret? I began by experimenting with a couple of my girl cousins who were attending school with me at this germinating stage in my political activism. Often, my political activities caused me to skip classes or return from school late. I tested how much I could trust my cousins by telling them some little piece of information that was inconsequential. "Promise not to tell anyone?" I would request. By the time I reached home, the little "secret" would have arrived already and Father would interrogate me. As a result, from that time in my early teens I began to live a double life. My cousins were always on time arriving at classes and returning from school, and would create gossip about what might be the cause of my lack of punctuality or attendance. The trouble they sometimes caused made me wonder if they wished, on some level, that they too were involved with my activities even though their main objective was to earn reputations as obedient daughters.

Often, Father would reprimand me based on my cousins' reports, but my grades saved me. "Is studying hard important, or passing the exams?" I would retort. More and more, I led a secretive, autonomous inner life, not telling my father or friends what I was really doing. I made one exception, and that was a much older relative who agreed to keep everything for me in his trunk in his house. However, even he did not know exactly what I was doing. All I told him was that the documents were very secret and that he should not reveal anything about them to anybody. His father and my grandfather were brothers. But his father married a Newar girl from the bazaar, which meant that his caste was downgraded from Brahmin to Kshatriya. His wife had died young and he was living with his four sons and one daughter. I used to call him "Babu." He was very reserved, inward, and private. Whenever I needed supplies I would go to meet him secretly and he would give them to me. Since my own brother Krishna was in Panchayat, I felt that he was the main person to hide my activities from. In retrospect, I can see that, during these early years, my later lifestyle was being fashioned. As time went on, I would be better able to operate free from the timeless pulls of family status, loyalties, aspirations, and expectations.

ॐ

The same year that I joined the underground political movement, King Mahendra visited Dhankuta. As the president of the school student union I was included in the town Panchayat's King Mahendra Welcome Committee and was given the honor of meeting him and Queen Ratna in their camp. Although I was excited, I was unprepared for the walk up to their tent. Every two or three steps, some military official or palace courtier would draw near, stop me, and instruct, "You must understand: do not smile, do not point your hands while talking, stand at a distance, and while talking press your hands together as if you are saying *namaste* and bow your head."

By the time I was halfway to the tent I wished that I had not come at all. But having come that far, I sensed that it would have been fatal to retreat. Finally, I must have reached the place where they were holding court. Here, the officials no longer spoke loudly but rather attempted to issue their instructions with sign language. I walked on. A military man stopped me and commanded, "Only up to here," pointing to a spot on the ground immediately in front of me.

I responded innocently, "No! I have come to see the king and the queen."

Then he pointed ahead and said, "There."

And there they were, seated in front of a charcoal stove outside their tent, warming their hands. It was winter. I had imagined that they would be very big or fearsome in some way. When I saw them sitting together in front of a fire, just like my mother and father, my heart stopped racing and I repeated with only a little nervousness the phrase I had been instructed to say along the path to the royal tent: *"Darshan gare sarkar."* This was the royal form of "I greet Your Majesties." In the tension of the moment, however, I forgot to tell my name and position, to bow my head, or to keep my hands pressed together. A man just outside the tent, hiding from them, was trying to catch my attention and signal with movements of his head, body, and hands how I was supposed to be bending forward with my hands pressed together in respectful greeting.

The king noticed that I was being distracted by someone and asked me, "What is your name?"

Feeling as if I had just awakened, I immediately told him my name and put my hands together and bent my head down. After I had said everything I was supposed to, he asked again, "Why did you come to see us?"

I replied, "Because I am the student president."

"How did you become president?" he inquired further.

"The senior sisters appointed me," I answered.

He continued, "Where is your house?"

I promptly pointed with my right hand and said, "Right there, a little bit farther down from this forest."

The man outside gave me a very stern look. Pointing was clearly not what one did in front of Their Majesties. I became nervous again, and forgot for a second time about my hands and bowed head. Noticing how awkward I was feeling, the king said, "Not necessary to do, you don't have to do," which put me at my ease and made me feel much better.

Then he asked, "Are you going to perform anything else here?"

"Oh yes, I am going to recite some poetry tomorrow night."

The king and the queen both asked several more questions, and I found them to be warm and friendly. Then, a military officer came close to me, saluted them, and informed me that my audience was over. I pressed my palms together and politely bade them farewell. Then I turned and left. I had been told to retire from their presence backward so as not to show them my back. I forgot. On my return, the man outside chided me for pointing and said that I had not behaved properly.

"The king asked me where my house was, and it was right there," I responded. "What was wrong with pointing with my hand?"

When I noticed how cross he was with me I became more defiant. "Hide your king and queen then, so nobody comes to see them," I challenged, and kept on walking. I heard him murmuring something. He likely thought me an unruly girl.

The following evening, I recited my poetry in a public contest and received an award from the king. After that I was invited to several district-level functions. Royal recognition had brought me to the attention of the local officials.

಄

About four months after my meeting with the king and queen, our school was preparing to celebrate Queen Ratna's birthday. In honor of the auspicious day, a formal ceremony was being planned on the town's parade ground. I was selected as student representative to give a lecture that would exalt Her Majesty's noble deeds and wish her a long life on behalf of all the students. All of the district officials and dignitaries were there.

Less than a month before, I had heard from two new underground leaders from Dharan that it was the king who had imprisoned our party leaders and caused the killing of so many innocent people, and that our fight was against him and his system. They specifically noted that celebrating the birthdays of the king and queen was unnecessary.

As I prepared my lecture, I thought, "Here I have a chance to give voice to my new political understanding." So, to begin with, I recited a short piece of poetry wishing her a happy birthday. Then I began my speech, saying, "It is just a formality to wish her long life. It would not make much difference to the state of affairs in the nation whether she really lives long or—"

I had not completed my sentence when the inspector of police shouted out from behind, "A little too much," and the announcer grabbed the microphone from my hand.

My voice is quite loud and I shouted, "Why did you select me if you don't want to hear what I have to say?" and left the gathering.

The next day, the inspector and the chief district officer must have complained about me to my father, for he called me quietly close to him and said, "You know, you should not have made that remark."

"I had not even finished when the inspector disturbed me. I might have concluded very nicely," I responded, reflexively maintaining the veneer of normality that I attempted to preserve at home.

"From now on be very careful what you say," my father admonished me.

A surge of outrage and injustice welled up within me, and I declared, "From now on I am not going to take part in any other Panchayati events." With that I rushed out of his sight, and away to be with my own thoughts and feelings. Things had suddenly changed. I had declared my political interest and views and there was no going back from that. I went to my room, where I could watch the swaying pine trees and listen to the soothing whisper of the wind in their branches. Monkeys were crashing about and screeching in the trees at the edge of the forest. In reply, our watchdog offered an occasional bark.

"Durga"—my father was standing in my room speaking to me—"I hope you are not a communist; you know that if communism comes they will nationalize all of our property."

I just listened to him. I knew that I was not a communist, and I interpreted Father's comment as a green light to continue my activities. In retrospect, my father's remark reflected a deep concern for traditional Nepalis because, in addition to the loss of an asset, loss of family property meant the fracturing of traditional inheritance systems, the erosion of land-management responsibilities, and loss of social standing. Land, rather than money or possessions, was the basis of wealth in this agricultural society.

ॐ

The authorities now guessed that I was on the wrong side and became watchful. Early on the morning of the day following the queen's birthday celebration, some illegal pamphleting was done around the bazaar. The authorities suspected me. Two policemen came to our house and took my brother Krishna away. After a while, he returned with them. He asked me to make tea. I prepared it and he took it outside. Whenever unfamiliar visitors came to the house, women were not supposed to go out on any pretext. As no servant was at home, Krishna took the tea out himself. After a few moments, when the police were drinking their tea, he came back inside and asked me if I knew about the previous night's pamphleting. I said no. In truth, I had nothing to do with that particular effort. At that moment, Father came down from his rituals upstairs, and Krishna explained the trouble to him. He looked at my face and I looked back at his. Then he turned to Krishna and instructed him, "Tell the gentlemen outside 'my sister is not involved in any activities of that kind.' They should never come to this house again for that kind of inquiry." Krishna went out, and I went upstairs.

ཉྫ

During my last days in high school an incident occurred that characterized dramatically the widening gulf that was developing between my father and myself. By an established tradition in Dhankuta, the teachers would take students from both the boys' and girls' high schools for a picnic just before graduation. It might have been designed to prepare them for college, since Dhankuta had only one college and it was co-educational. I told my mother about the planned event, and after talking to Father, she came back and said, "Don't even mention the word *picnic* to him again. He has become so irate and now he will not allow you to go."

The day of the picnic came, and I sat in my room at home imagining what the others might be doing. Just as I was thinking, "By now they must have reached the meeting place," I heard the noise of girls not far from our house. As I looked out from the balcony, there were all of my friends and teachers approaching merrily along the footpath leading from the forest. How I wished that they had not come. I knew that I would need my father's support for issues of far greater significance than this picnic, and I had already emotionally detached myself from this event. I hid in my room, directly above the front porch where Father was sitting and watching their approach. I hoped beyond hope that my father would not vent his fury on them. The gate was opened and our front yard suddenly filled with excited girls. Then one of the girls entered with a teacher and told my father about the picnic and asked him where I was.

I heard him reply, "No, Durga is not feeling well, she cannot go."

I did not hear what they said, but my third sister, Devi, was visiting us at the time and she came out and talked with my father. Somehow, Devi convinced him that I should be allowed to accompany my friends on this, the last event of my school days. Reluctantly, he agreed, but then made the teachers promise to bring us back by five P.M. What he did not know was that boys were also going to the same picnic. In Nepali society, a picnic attended by boys and girls was seen as something of an unseemly occasion.

Later that day, Father went to the bazaar and in passing mentioned the picnic to his friends. Then the awful truth came out. He rushed home and roared, "Devi! You are helping to ruin your younger sister! If we permit her to go on a picnic like this we will never be able to arrange her marriage with a high-level family. We must send someone to go and haul her back home."

Devi urged him to wait another hour since it was four o'clock already. "He waited restlessly until five," she told me later. Then he ordered three of my male cousins to go out and search for me and to drag me back home. Up at the picnic site I had already reminded my teachers and friends that when my father said "five" he meant "five and no later!" Although it was only four-thirty, it was now early winter and darkness was falling quickly. The teachers from the boys' school were fiddling with the Petromax pressure lamp, trying unsuccessfully to light it because of a strong wind. Finally, half an hour later, at exactly five o'clock, it burst into life, shooting out huge flames and then gradually settling down to a healthy roar. With the trail brightly lit we began our descent home. It took an hour. At six P.M. we reached my house. From a little distance I saw my father waiting in the yard and noticed that he was very restless. I told two of my friends and a teacher who had accompanied me home that they should not venture any nearer, so they only accompanied me to the gate. Slowly, I walked down the steps onto the patio expecting Father to bellow at me. He did not even look at me, but turned and stared in the other direction. I passed him, entered the house, and went straight to my room.

Later, at dinner, in front of all the members of the family, his lecture started: "This is the first and last time that you go to any picnic. Only vulgar people go to picnics. From now on, you will not go out of this house. You just stay at home and study and I will take you to attend your final exams. That is it, as far as education for you is concerned. And after your exams, you will get married to whomever I decide upon." I kept quiet like an offender in his people's court, charged before my own community with an offense of which I felt utterly innocent.

After this episode, I never participated in any frivolity or social activity that might aggravate the tension with Father. For the sake of keeping a superficial peace at home, I made a deliberate choice to surrender my youth for a covert political life. "Very well," I thought, "that is the end of my social life. But it doesn't really matter. It's all in preparation for the struggle that lies ahead." The picnic was child's play. I had been meeting young men in underground activities for two years. If, instead of a picnic, the event had been a political meeting, I would have attended without even telling Father. Oddly enough, contact between boys and girls through political involvement was more socially acceptable. After the picnic, I knew that it was no longer possible to be direct and open with my father in any aspect of my life.

The picnic episode was likely the point at which he lost all control over me. Because there was no openness between us, I could never discuss the divergence that was growing in our relationship. His practice of talking to me through my mother had destroyed the rich bonds between us. If he had continued to communicate with me directly, our relationship might have developed differently and my confrontational behavior could have become less pronounced. But the gulf separating us was to grow wider still.

After my high school exams were over, I learned through my mother that my father was seriously looking for a boy with whom to arrange my marriage. I felt desperate at the thought of my life's being sidetracked in this way. I was conscious that I had my own life—my own goals and political commitment. Moreover, this commitment had its own time frame, a timing that marriage would truncate because no conventional Brahmin husband in Nepal would allow his wife the freedom to pursue a political destiny with its accompanying dangers. As I considered the "threat" of marriage, I began to question what was the point of living. So, I said to my mother, "If Father is serious about this I will commit suicide rather than be married."

I went straight to Father's clinic and swallowed ten doses of a potent Ayurvedic medicine. It turned out to be a stool softener. The outcome, though dramatic, was not death. To my relief, neither my mother nor my father told anyone else about this.

After this incident, Father mellowed very slightly with regard to my ambition for further study. However, my wish was to attend a college where I could study science. As Dhankuta had only a liberal arts college offering majors in economics, politics, history, and literature, this would have meant leaving for the capital, Kathmandu, to study at a science college. Father was horrified. "If you were my son," he roared, "I would send you away just as I sent your brother off to study. But you are a woman. Where can I send you? And with whom? I do not want to send you to Kath-mandu—I had a very bad experience while I was a student there myself. And India is too far away—I cannot send you alone. So just forget about it."

I could see that he was not going to budge on this. It struck me that a hunger strike might dramatize my case to my father and bring about con-cessions in my favor. So the hunger strike began. It also did not work. I sustained my fast for two days and then my mother came at night with a delicious meal and fed me, saying, "You must eat enough to fight with your father. If you are weak, you cannot fight." I was defeated, and a couple of months later I was literally dragged off to the local college to begin my un-dergraduate studies. My mother tried to console me and pointed out, "If you do not study what is available here, your father is going to marry you off." When put this way, it was clear that I had no choice. Being forced into liberal arts against my will only had the effect of intensifying my sense of political purpose. I resolved to be committed forever to the struggle in Nepal.

Soon after my undergraduate program began, I decided to tour all the hill districts of eastern Nepal and create a network of like-minded students. There was no way of obtaining my father's permission to step out of the house on such a venture, so I waited until the winter, when Father, ac-companied by most other family members, made his annual two-month visit to our farm down on the warmer *tarai* plains. My mother stayed be-hind. This time, Father wanted to take me to the farm with him, but I gave the excuse "I would prefer to stay with Mother," and he did not insist. As soon as he left, I began making my own plans. Mother opposed my tour, but I knew that she would not tell Father. If she did she would have been in trouble herself for allowing me to go. I urged her not to worry about me and warned her against mentioning my tour to any of our neighbors. Then off I went, leaving home for a month and a half. Thinking back now, there was clearly a great advantage in not having telephones in those days in rural Nepal, for the only way my father could communicate with us at home was by sending a letter if he happened to find someone traveling back to Dhankuta.

I was just sixteen, and I took as a porter a boy thirteen years of age who, perhaps from early malnutrition, looked no more than an eight-year-old. Most of the time I had to shoulder the luggage myself, but at least I had someone to talk to each long day on the stony trails and dusty footpaths. We climbed the spine of a massive ridge until, after walking through a forest of rhododendrons draped with mosses and orchids, we crossed over a bleak, ten-thousand-foot-high pass with close views of the Kanchenjunga massif. For days we climbed and descended the great ridges of these Himalayan foothills, sometimes walking for hours without passing another traveler. Once in a long while there would be a small tea stall on the trail where we could take some refreshment. At night we usually stayed as guests in the home of a local student or a Nepali Congress activist.

My tour was very successful in meeting other students and senior Nepali Congress workers, and creating a network among them in those very remote areas. But in one place I faced a threat from communists. During the day, I had held an open meeting with all senior students at the local high school. The reason I had kept the meeting open to all was that this community was considered progressive—and anti-Panchayat. That night I was staying in a small lodge run by a woman, and at about ten o'clock she woke me up to tell me that within half an hour some communists were coming to harass me. "They might even kill you," she warned. Luckily, another democrat student, who must have been a year or so younger, had that day volunteered to accompany me to the next place, and he and my porter were sharing a room so we all would be ready for an early-morning departure. I knocked on their door and shared the threatening news with them. Worried, we had no time to think and left quickly before the communists arrived to attack us.

It was pitch-dark with no moon as the three of us started without using our flashlight along a narrow, treacherous path down a steep hillside. From the dense jungle on either side we could hear the cries of jackals, and I began wondering which was the lesser danger—a confrontation with communists at that lodge or the jackals or a leopard or a bear in the blackness of the forest on this unfamiliar trail. I had never been afraid of communists before, but the landlady's words—"They might even kill you"—kept ringing in my ears, assuring me that the threat I had left behind was more frightening. We stumbled on and on downward, fording a river at some time after midnight, and then clambered up a four- or five-thousand-foot ascent until, high on a ridge at about four in the morning, we heard the grunts of pigs and a cock crowing and knew that we were approaching a habitation. Rather than arriving so early, we decided to sit and wait for the day to dawn. For the first time since we had left the lodge we discussed our fear as we had journeyed through the night, and we realized that instead of escaping we could have sought refuge from the communists at a sympathizer's house in the same village. Then, as if to dissolve our doubts as we shivered in the predawn darkness, nature provided us with a most spectacular sight. The shadowy outline of Kanchenjunga suddenly turned red, then pink, orange, pale yellow, and finally—though the world all about us remained dark— pure white. It was as though someone was beaming a gigantic floodlight only on the snowy mountain. The source of this wonder, the sun, was, until this time, being felt nowhere on the earth where we were, nor anywhere else that we could see. It was the most majestic scene I had ever witnessed.

An elderly lady had come out of a house and was carrying fodder toward a cowshed. She saw us and asked who we were and where we were going. As we talked, we came to know that for the next sixteen miles there were no tea stalls or other houses. I offered her money, and, a little hesitant at first, she made us tea and then rice and vegetables, and we were on our way. The remaining week of my tour went well. My student companion returned to his home, and I made my way back to Dhankuta with my little porter, arriving home with aching legs and swollen feet two weeks before Father's return from the *tarai*. Mother never revealed anything about my trip to anyone.

There was one district center I had not managed to visit, though I had written to the students there promising to come. It was as if God provided me with the opportunity to go there, for one day some friends of my father's came and took him on a trip to a faraway village for two weeks. This time I asked one of my younger cousins if she would like to accompany me. She was excited at the chance because one of our relatives was married and lived near my destination. The day after Father's departure, we left too. We set out on foot at four o'clock in the morning and, after six thousand feet of ascents and six thousand feet of descents, we arrived thirty miles away at six in the evening. Except for the leeches that attached themselves to our legs each time we sat for a rest, we had no problem on this journey.

It was most important to return home before my father did, so we stayed away for a week and returned on the ninth day, a Tuesday. A couple of hundred feet above our house in Kachiday was a very large rock that provided a fine vantage point for viewing our village and the valley far beyond. As we arrived home, we sat on this rock and I called out "Ama" to my mother in the yard below. She looked up, but, to my consternation, did not reply. Instead, a moment later one of my aunts appeared and shouted, "You wait there, you naughty girls. Durga, your father is back and is very angry. He is complaining that you have returned on the ninth day and, even worse, on a Tuesday. Don't you dare come down!" I saw Father come out of the house and then one of our servants climbing toward us who told us that I should not enter the house until after it was really dark. According to my father, doing that would avert the bad influence of having returned on the ninth day and a Tuesday. We followed this instruction, and waited where we were until night fell. To my surprise, Father did not scold me at all for having gone away with no guardian and without his knowledge. His wrath was concentrated entirely on my failure to be aware of the proper timing for traveling that is laid down in astrology. For several days I really felt rather guilty this time.

Father began talking about my marriage very seriously. He would discuss his daughter's marriage with any Brahmin who had a son, as if he had ten daughter's marriages still to arrange. Over time, I developed a hatred for marriage and involved myself more openly in extracurricular activities and politics. I felt as though I was being pushed into rebellion. I was only in my mid-teens, yet whether at home or from the government I faced opposition.

I did quite well in the national Intermediate Arts Examinations, and Father decided to postpone my marriage for another two years so that I could continue working on my B.A. in Dhankuta. During my B.A. studies I became even more politically involved but also did well scholastically.

After my B.A. results were issued he said to me, "Now you are a graduate, you must understand your father's anxiety and help to make his burden light."

"I want to do my master's now," I replied.

He roared, "No, definitely no! You know where you have to go for your master's—Kathmandu! Do you think I can send you to Kathmandu? No, you must agree to do what I decide for you now."

If I had said anything more he would have just become further enraged, so again I kept quiet. But I knew that he would not say no to his eldest son, who was still in England, or to his first grandson—my eldest sister's son— who was older than I and was studying geology in Russia. I wrote letters to them both, requesting them to write to Father in support of sending me to Kathmandu for my M.A.

Around this time, Father brought a couple of goldsmiths to the house to prepare the necessary jewelry for my marriage. They stayed for two weeks and produced several items. However, I paid no attention at all to what they were doing and showed no interest in the wedding set they made. Within a month, letters from my brother and nephew arrived to convince Father that it would be a good idea to send me to Kathmandu for my master's program. After reading their letters he was annoyed with them as well. But I had a few older relatives, both male and female, who had also just completed their bachelor's degrees the previous year, and he talked to their fathers. It turned out that, as my father was the eldest and most senior family member, the others were waiting to see how he handled my case and told him that if he would send me to study for my master's degree then they would send their children too. Pressured by his eldest son and grandson, and then by these relatives' expectations of him as the model of wise decision making, Father most reluctantly decided that I could go to Kathmandu for my master's.

So, I went off to Kathmandu. Every week, Father wrote me two letters. One would be of a general nature about how to take care of my health and so forth, which I could share with others. The second one would be confidential, concerning my marriage in two years' time to whomever Father would choose. But now distance and experience in dealing with the matter were on my side.

# 6

# Profession, Politics, and Family

I was a first-year master's student of modern political history. It was time for the annual election of student union officials, the only ballot that in Nepal's suppressive political environment served as a kind of opinion poll and indicator of general political trends. This was especially true because we had only one university in the whole kingdom where intellectuals could exercise some limited freedom. We democrats won a landslide victory, with not a single communist elected to the committee of thirteen. The progovernment students received only two votes out of a total of about two thousand. I was elected and given the portfolio of cultural secretary.

Although I was very active in extracurricular activities and had to spend three months in hiding at one point in order to avoid a political purge, I was nevertheless a good student and managed to complete my master's degree on time. I decided to go back and teach in Dhankuta Degree College, which my family had been instrumental in establishing in 1957 soon after the fall of the Ranas. For me, teaching there would be like going home. I knew as well that because of my political record a job in a private college was all I could hope to get.

The college's managing committee was anxious to employ Nepali and, if possible, local professors and said yes immediately when I contacted them. So I went back to my hometown, staying with my parents in Dha-ran on the way. My father was very happy with me now because he thought I was going to be a professor. Nonetheless, the evening before I left for Dhankuta he reminded me, "Now you are more responsible and mature. But do not forget that you have to get married. I do not think you are mature enough to decide on a husband. Anyway, our society is not like Western society. Here parents have their duty to arrange their children's marriages. The only thing you have to do is to say yes to the boy we pre-pare. Whenever I am ready I will send you a message and you must come." I said nothing.

I left for Dhankuta on foot at four in the morning and arrived at six that evening. The next day I started teaching.

Not long after I had started teaching I arranged a meeting of demo-cratic students, including recent graduates of the college. My objective was to organize a democratic student union. The students nominated me as their president and we formed a strong executive committee of students who were genuinely committed to democracy. Our purpose was to create a forum not just for students but for democrats of Dhankuta generally. It was risky, of course, and because of the Organization Control Act—the Panchayat system's legislation that the local panchayat and police would use to ban any form of social or political organization they did not want— there was no way our union could be registered.

It was very important to me to become established in Dhankuta. My ex-perience of society at that time was that if you were engaged in some kind of income-earning activity then you could more easily win people's confi-dence and influence them. I knew many political colleagues across the king-dom who were out of a job and finding it very difficult to be integrated into society—or, in other words, to *win* society. If you were in the opposition the local government was always on the lookout to hit you in a weak spot and spread misinformation among ignorant people.

Within six months I was quite well established in the college and decided to go to Banaras to meet our leader, B.P., whom I had never met before. This was in 1972. Banaras was the headquarters of the Nepali Con-gress in exile and also one of the holiest places of pilgrimage for Hindus, so, for a Nepali Congress worker, visiting Banaras was like killing two birds with one stone. Even my father could not say no to this trip. Instead, he remarked, "I hope your wisdom will grow through the blessings of Lord Bishownath [another name for Shiva]." I had two other representatives from Dhankuta with me—Yogendra Hari Shrestha and Shyam Raja Shah. Durga Subedi, a close colleague from B.P.'s hometown, Biratnagar, was the leader of the trip. He had been to Banaras several times before, and shortly after our visit achieved notoriety by successfully hijacking a Nepal National Bank charter plane between Biratnagar and Kathmandu and diverting it and its cargo of thirty-one million Indian rupees to Bihar, India, to enable the exiled Nepali Congress to launch the armed struggle.

When we arrived in Banaras, B.P. asked us to stay with him at his house, where we stayed for two weeks and had some long discussions about Nepali Congress policy in general and about increasing the influence of the party in Dhankuta. I recall B.P.'s telling us, "The king is not the target of the Nepali Congress; it is his Panchayat system. I have full confidence that we will restore democracy to Nepal." Hearing B.P.'s determined words produced within me an even deeper feeling of commitment to the cause of democracy. From my inner heart I surrendered myself to whatever struggle lay ahead.

We became enamored with B.P. Tall and fine in appearance, with a sparkling face—what a charismatic personality he was. More than that, he emanated such natural friendliness and was so attuned with his cadres that he made one feel comfortable immediately. It did not surprise me that King Mahendra was awed by him, although I must say that King Mahendra, too, had a strong personality. I began to think that a psychological tussle between these two giants might have been one of the reasons for the 1960 coup. The prime minister had been everywhere in 1959, with everyone mouthing the initials "B.P." He was popular, impressive, and had a radical new governing policy for the kingdom—populist socialism. The king might not have been able to suppress a doubt that the prime minister would topple him.

B.P. awarded me with "active" (as distinct from "ordinary") membership in the party, a status that would formalize the activities I initiated on behalf of the party in Dhankuta. Knowing that it was very difficult to reach and involve people in remote districts, he suggested that we run the party also in the name of the student organization. Then he gave us all the necessary stationery for issuing ordinary memberships in the Nepali Congress. I did not forget to get some *Prasad* from the temple and water from the Holy Ganges for my family. From both points of view I felt that our trip had been highly successful, and we returned to Dhankuta with new inspiration.

Back in Dhankuta the local authorities were suspicious about our trip, and we noticed that we had become targets for surveillance. Nonetheless, as B.P. had suggested, we began talking to people about the Nepali Congress's goal of restoring democracy and, while maintaining secrecy, signing up as ordinary members of the Nepali Congress all those who supported the party's aims.

Overtly we organized many social activities like literary readings, music competitions, and sports events. But covertly we started organizing politically. This meant drawing a membership from people who were genuinely committed to restoring democracy and sending the membership lists and donations to our leader in Banaras. One of the important points about having a roll of paid-up members was that it helped our exiled leader identify state agents who tried to talk their way into the Banaras headquarters. We worked through an underground network of contacts throughout the district. I myself toured all the villages. In each area we would start by making contact with people who we knew had spoken out against Panchayat, and from there get leads about others who supported the Nepali Congress.

As a teacher I liked to create an open, friendly atmosphere in class so that ideas could be freely explored—an approach that stood in contrast to the prevailing political climate. Neither did I consider that my job was confined to the classroom. Highlights of my teaching experience were two tours of Nepal of more than a month each that I organized for a mixed group of students—a bold step in view of the traditions that kept girls especially under parental watch at all times. Students joined the tours from all classes in the college, and we raised money as we went along by performing cultural shows. It was an opportunity for the students to see the country at firsthand and to learn about the political forces shaping their destiny. However, all that the authorities noticed was that I met Nepali Congress people around the kingdom, and toward the end of our second tour, I was imprisoned for four months.

The second tour had coincided with the government's enforcement in July 1973 of its New Education System Plan (NESP) at the university and colleges. The goal of NESP was not educational but political: "To produce citizens loyal to the Panchayat system and the Crown." All private colleges were nationalized, and politically sensitive colleges were either renamed after some member of the royal family or were downgraded. The teaching profession was made transferable to any college within the kingdom. It was not necessary to consult the teachers concerned. All colleges were changed into campuses and were brought under Tribhuvan University. As T.U. was now the only umbrella institution, the king, who was T.U.'s chancellor, became chancellor of the whole higher education system and appointed the vice chancellor, rector, registrar, and deans for the various departments. Thus, our private Dhankuta Degree College was changed into the Dhankuta campus of T.U. and was demoted to undergraduate level, becoming like an American community college.

I was thinking of starting a signature campaign to restore Dhankuta's status as degree college. The loss of bachelor's degrees would severely disadvantage girls in the region, as cultural constraints would prevent them from traveling away from the region to pursue their studies. It was a great blow for women's education. However, anybody who protested against the new education system would be arrested under the Public Security Act.

On the day that the NESP was enforced a telegram arrived for me. I was to be transferred immediately from Dhankuta to the Padma Kanya campus in Kathmandu. It was a shock, and was clearly in retribution for the student tours and my other extracurricular activities.

The farewell from my students and colleagues was an emotional one. All the student representatives who delivered speeches cried as they spoke. The farewell songs were melancholy and the poetry was sad. When my turn came to speak I too could not suppress the tears. The whole hall was crying and everybody was serious. It was as if we were saying good-bye also to freedom of education.

I said farewell to Dhankuta, wondering if it might be forever. It was one of the saddest moments of my life. The previous eighteen months in Dhankuta had been fulfilling professionally, politically, and from a family viewpoint, because, in my parents' absence, I had acted as guardian for my schoolgoing nephews and nieces. This dislocation must have been happening to college teachers all over the kingdom, as the government was using the NESP to separate politically active teachers from their support bases. But, as I pondered the meaning of my transfer to the capital, I felt that there must be a deeper explanation for it that I would understand later. This time, Father did not oppose my move to Kathmandu because my eldest brother was now well established there as an eye doctor, and, by custom, I would be living with him. The university authorities allowed me one week to make the move.

ཀ

Although Padma Kanya was a girls' college it was a much larger campus than Dhankuta College. I had been assigned to teach two new courses on Chinese and Japanese history to an undergraduate class of two sections each with about two hundred students. I taught Nepal and Europe to graduates.

As a history teacher, I started taking my students on all-day excursions to nearby historical sites. Naturally the students were very delighted, as this had never been done before. However, after I had taken two groups out, the assistant campus chief called me to his office to warn me about getting too close to the students, saying that the campus chief had ordered that I stop such extra activities. I should just "teach the students from a distance." I felt sickened at finding these fawning Panchayat supporters appointed as campus chiefs.

As a result, after two semesters I was transferred to the National Development Service (NDS) of Tribhuvan University's central campus in Kathmandu.

NDS was a new two-semester program required of master's students between their two years of classwork. It had been initiated because of pressure from certain international advisers and was designed to bridge the gap that was perceived to be growing between Nepal's urban and rural populations. The students had to go to a rural village, teach in a junior or high school, live with a rural family, and help with health, agriculture, and construction work. They received a supervisory visit every month and a 150 rupee stipend. At the end of their stay, students were required to write a village profile and a development plan.

There could have been no job I wanted more. I was the only woman supervisor, and it seemed as if the position had been designed for me. Padma Kanya's campus chief indeed did me a favor unknowingly when he recommended my transfer. While teaching at P.K. I had already helped NDS in my spare time with the site-selection process for girl students, and had found that the director at that time was quite a nice man. I went to work there happily, and soon was out in different parts of the country supervising both male and female students.

During the two years of my Kathmandu career, September 1973 to September 1975, I lived alternately with my brother and with my eldest nephew. In that first year, while I was staying with my brother, my parents came to Kathmandu several times to arrange my marriage. In the twelve months of our calendar, which begins in mid-April, only six months are suitable for wedding ceremonies according to Hindu tradition and the science of Jyotish (astrology). Whenever father visited during these auspicious months I would become restless and wish that time would fly quickly by. Because of this problem we were unable to establish any natural relationship. Whatever I tried to do to please him, he would only respond, "Your doing this will not make me happy since you have caused me so much pain by not getting married. Even the sight of you just adds more anxiety for me." What could I do and how should I have felt? I was determined not to marry, but my father kept on insisting that I should. Yet at the same time my heart was full of love and care for my dear parents.

Eventually I moved to my nephew's house just to escape from Father's sight. One day my parents came to see me there. My father had another complaint: Now that I had left my brother's house what might society think? Quite frankly, I was fed up with our conservative society and especially with my Brahmin caste. There was no freedom for doing anything you wanted. Women who did cross the boundary were heavily criticized.

If they did not heed the criticism they were ousted by their social group, which meant being isolated. If you survived all the gossip for a long time and proved that what you were doing was worthy, then people might shut their mouths and evaluate your deeds and achievements. But if you stayed as you had started then you became as rubbish.

The question was this: How long could a woman sustain a struggle when everyone told her the traditional Hindu wisdom that she was *abala*, "without strength," and from birth needed the protection of a male throughout the various phases of her life—as a daughter, wife, widow, and old woman?

My father was not interested in how I was managing in my new job in Kathmandu. After a three- or four-hour lecture on the impropriety of my remaining single and living away from my brother, they wanted to return to my brother's house. Once again I too moved back to my brother's, and they decided to go back to Dharan until there was another astrologically suitable month for marriage. At the start of our lunar year my parents returned to Kathmandu. This time Father was determined to use force if necessary to fulfill his duty. I was equally determined that he could not force me to marry as long as life remained in my body. He marshaled all of my relatives to try to convince me. One after another, different family members broached the topic, and each time I would explain that the issue was not one of convincing me about the values of marriage. It was that I simply did not want it. Father, from his side, was equally determined to make it happen. When eventually all his efforts to convince me via others had failed, he sent word that he wanted to talk to me directly. My parents and I sat together in my room in my brother's home.

As usual he began: "You must allow me to fulfil my duty. Tell us whoever you want if you have any in your mind, but it must be a Brahmin. Even now you are too old for a Brahmin girl to be married. After twenty-four women are old in our society. I married your mother when she was seven and all of your sisters were married young. It does not matter for men. But if you hesitate now then you will never be married."

I drew on all my strength and spoke out, "I do not mind that. I can live my life without ever marrying."

He became fierce and roared, "That is exactly what I do not want to hear. You must obey what I say. You have become so undisciplined. The one mistake I ever made in my life was to send you for an English education. I had some doubt then that that beef-eating education would harm you. All I can do now is regret it. But that will not help much. There is only one way to solve our family problem, all you have to say is yes, then we will start talking to the eligible boys. Whoever we think is the right type for you we will decide. I can consider one thing—if you want to have a look at him before marriage we can arrange that. This is my decision. You cannot say no." Then he went upstairs.

My mother stayed with me. Through tears I told her, "Only my dead body could get married, not me."

Two months passed by in this state of tension. I still had to go to work at NDS every day and found relief in the work with my colleagues and students. Somehow I was able to keep my mind and body together. As he had vowed, Father started searching out a husband for me. He began the task through our relatives. He would come with some name that one of them had suggested. I would say, "No."

"Okay, then, the next one," he would say.

Through negotiations with other families he made some prestigious matches, but after I continued to say no, one day he exploded, "Okay, if you do not want to get married, then just kill me! I am old anyway."

"It is better if I die," I replied.

The last of the three possible months during which marriage could be performed passed by. Now there would be no marriage dates for another four months, so he decided to go back to Dharan. Before leaving he told me, "I am tired with you now. I came to Kathmandu twice solely for this purpose. In the future you wait and see; if you do not marry you will feel lonely. All your relatives are married and have children. You will regret it. In Europe and America women marry as late as thirty or thirty-five. But we are in Nepal, and here we do not have that system. To bring that system here would be immoral. What pleasure is it to get married when you are that old anyway? You might not be able to bear children. I am not going to come ever again to ask you for this. You must come to your own realization about it and then inform me."

Once again they returned to Dharan.

Subsequently Father wrote several letters to my brother reproaching him for not being able to convince me. In a letter to me he wrote that one of his own brothers had suggested to him that they should just tie me to a pillar and finish the marriage ritual, and then I would be forced to go to the man's house. Father expressed regret that he had not been able to do that. My brother then started nagging that because of me his relationship with our father was going sour, though both of us knew that there was more to it than that. At times I felt like giving up everything and going away and being a yogi.

At work, it was time for the NDS students' evaluations. However, at the time that the first batch of students was completing its field service the NDS director changed. In evaluating student performance, the new director was passing some students who had abandoned their village postings and had returned home. I protested, warning him that if students who did not get a fair deal created any problems, I would not be on his side.

He replied, "I know students' psychology. No matter what you do, you can't satisfy them."

The next day, after he posted the results, those students who had been unjustly evaluated gathered outside the office shouting that they were picketing us. For the rest of that day we were locked inside. Simultaneously, the next year's batch of students arrived and demanded a higher stipend, transistor radios so that they could listen to the news while they were out in the villages, and one or two other things.

The next day they held a meeting to discuss among themselves their demands and how to advocate them. I was there. Some T.U. officials, who were actually Panchayat agents, must have informed the government about this meeting because, not long into the meeting, *Mandales*—hired thugs the government used to infiltrate other student organizations on the university campuses, break up meetings on or off campus, and harass members of the political opposition—arrived to interrupt it. On this occasion, they not only heckled but set about beating democrat students severely. Some students lost their teeth. Later the police also entered, physically attacking one of the campus chiefs.

The negotiation process between the government and the students started the following day. The students' demands were basically related to the NDS and were quite genuine. If students boycotted NDS for a year there would be no students in the university the year after. Also, higher education was receiving substantial foreign aid, along with foreign advisers, and the government was worried that it could no longer finance higher education if this assistance was reduced. The whole situation had been artificially created by some of the university authorities and the government. Finally most demands were met, but because of the university's handling of the episode that led to the riot, revenge was taken on twenty-two well-known professors who had been blacklisted as critics of the government.

We were all expelled from the university. Among our number was one of the most senior professors at T.U., a man who had been a founding member of the university. I faced six different political charges, including involvement in party politics and assisting students to write political pamphlets. The only other woman who was expelled was a communist. Our expulsion followed the Panchayat regime's characteristic pattern of getting rid of opposition.

There was nothing I could hide from my family about this dismissal. Because it was a political expulsion, the government media had announced it even before I received the charge sheet.

After the dismissal a number of my friends who had also been expelled began coming to my place for consultation on what to do next. It was an easy convening point because my brother's house was right in the center of town. To tell the truth, the day I received the expulsion letter I felt relieved. At least this one problem was finished, over with. There would be no more office duties and political infighting with those half-baked people. But the reality was that I would have no income, and my brother had been warning me constantly against involvement in political activities.

On my birthday, September 5, my brother came to my room early in the morning before going to the office. He spoke tersely and without emotion: "All I can say is either you choose politics or family. I don't have much else to say." Then he left and my sister-in-law went with him without saying anything.

It was an unexpected ultimatum, and I felt very depressed. When the maid came to call me for food shortly after, I told her I was not feeling well and did not want to eat. After a while she also left the house and I was there by myself. In my mental state at that moment I felt that I had a choice between committing suicide or breaking with my family no matter what society would say. I looked in the mirror. I loved my being so much, why should I commit suicide? What wrong had I done? Then I remembered what an astrologer had predicted one year before, and this restored my strength. He had told me, "Nineteen seventy-five will be the beginning of your journey toward severe struggle. . . . No matter how much struggle you have, keep restoring your strength." At that moment I made the decision to leave my family.

But where would I go? How would I explain why I needed a place for myself—an unmarried woman, and alone, with no job? I could imagine the gossip that would build up. I did not have much time to waste. Then I remembered an acquaintance of mine who lived alone. Although we were not very close, I thought I would ask her if she would accommodate me for a while until I became brave enough to live on my own.

So I went to her office and simply expressed a desire to visit her.

With corresponding simplicity she replied, "Okay, come."

That was the only response I needed. Immediately I went back to my room at my brother's house, took my two suitcases and books outside, put them in a taxi, and went to her place. She was living in a charming one-bedroom house on a hill. It was so peaceful and silent there that it stood in marked contrast to noisy New Road, where I had been living. After all the tension and pressures this place was exactly what I needed.

"As long as you do not get bored with me, I would like to live with you," I told her.

She said, "Okay, we can live together as long as we do not get fed up with the arrangement."

I did not realize at the time that she had been married and divorced, which is as bad as things could get for a Brahmin woman. As a result, she had been blacklisted in our social circle. But the good thing about her was that she did not mind what others said about her and did not need to maintain some ideal image. I was alone at her house every day for the whole day, which gave me all the time I needed to think creatively about my life. I had been expelled from everywhere. However, my brain was still functioning.

It took some time living there for me to heal myself and restore my energy to face society.

# 7

# Struggle for Survival

One day while living with my not-so-close friend, I realized that I should be living on my own. But where to go? And in whose house should I live? It seemed I was not strong enough yet to live on my own. Was I still a little concerned about what society would say? I think I did feel self-conscious, and I wanted to find out how to live on my own and yet avoid the inevitable gossip. To avoid such gossip I rented the first floor of a two-family house in the middle of a very conservative Brahmin clan community. Not a single person there was out of the mainstream—that is, in opposition politics. Also, one of my cousins was married and living around the corner. My idea was not to tell any of my political friends where I was living. Now I could hide my head for a while.

As I had enough money to pay six months' rent, I paid in advance. I was hopeful of finding a means of survival within that time, so I moved to the house. I bought the bare necessary utensils for the house. There were three bedrooms. I locked two of them because I would never need them. All I used was one room. I practiced living on a minimum. I ate once a day, only in the evening. If I ate during the day, then I would not eat in the evening. Prior to this I never had liked bread, but I was now virtually living on it because that was the cheapest food I could buy.

I discovered that five minutes' walk from me a journalist from Dhankuta was living with his family. He knew my family well, but was of a hill tribe ethnic group that was not conservative like Brahmins. I felt quite comfortable visiting them once in a while because I had to show them no formalities. Although some people warned me later that he was working for Nepal intelligence, that did not bother me as I was already blacklisted by the government anyway.

A month and a half after I left my family it was the time of our biggest Hindu festival, Durga Puja, and three weeks later Bhai Puja. I decided to renounce such occasions. During Durga Puja I was supposed to go to my parents and seek their blessings. What blessings would I have sought, and what could they have given? It was the same with Bhai Puja. How could I worship my brothers? I could not live in pretension, especially with my own people. I either wanted the totality or I wanted nothing at all. Therefore, as I could not fulfill the duties of daughter or sister, I felt no obligation to fulfill other formalities that were empty for me. The path ahead was long and not familiar, but it was clear that I had to travel it by myself.

One night toward the end of my fifth month on my own I could not fall asleep until midnight. However, I had turned off the light and my eyes were closed. As I was about to doze off, I heard several sharp impacts on my bedroom window. Was it my imagination? No, it was real. I was very frightened. I shouted in alarm, hoping that the people upstairs would call out "What happened?" or "Don't worry." But there was no response. However, their dog barked and the stones stopped hitting the window. The next day when they saw me they did not even ask me what had happened during the night. As I reflected on this I realized that I had been silly to expect any response from them. The man upstairs was the nephew of the 1975 prime minister and, by virtue of this, he had inveigled the king to make him education minister. Within a few months of our expulsion from the university, the king ousted both uncle and nephew from their jobs on corruption charges.

I thought that I would go to my journalist neighbor's to tell him what had happened at night. Only his wife and the children were there, so I stayed and had tea with her. It was Saturday, the only weekend day in Nepal. Everybody affiliated with the system was going around the valley the whole morning visiting ministers and the king's secretaries to gain their favors. He must have gone for that buttering ritual, I thought.

After he returned I told them what had happened during the night. His reaction was, "It is quite a safe neighborhood. Nothing has happened the six years we have been living here." Then he thought for a minute and added, "I wonder whether your upstairs neighbor himself sent someone to do that, or did it himself?"

Their house was right on the road. I heard a loud palatal click sound. It reminded me immediately of one of my relatives because he and I used to call each other from a distance with this tongue sound. I stood up and looked out through the window, and it was indeed my relative!

"What are you looking for?" I asked.

"I came to see you but did not know which house you were living in, then I heard your voice and called you," my relative said.

I asked him to come inside. This was the first relative I had met since I had left my family. He looked unhappy, and as I saw no sign of his opening up, I questioned him about his worried appearance.

He replied that he had been going toward the house of my cousin who lived in the same neighborhood. As she saw him approaching her place she had said, "If you have come to ask which house Durga is living in, don't even come near me—just go away."

Pained by this encounter, he confided in me, "I went to say hello to her and I heard you were somewhere here too, so I just wanted to ask if she knew."

I gave him a little chocolate and joked, "It seems you are still a baby! Don't worry, take some comfort with this." He understood.

After having tea I took him to see where I was living. Although I had joked about what he told me, I felt quite deeply hurt at hearing my cousin's comment. One of the main reasons I had selected that community was because of her symbolic protection. I had imagined that people would remark that at least I was staying near my married cousin. From this day I realized that I was still living a superficial and pretentious life. I thought, "I have become a hypocrite, proving to people that I could live on my own and at the same time seeking social protection." At that point, I wished that I was a nobody, that I did not come from a high-caste, prestige-conscious family. If I was nobody then it would not matter what I did. I would be left alone. I did not yet appreciate that my culture and my class could work for me, no matter how much I hated it for its restrictions. I was later to realize that I would have been dead if I had not been who I was.

Evening was approaching. It was time for my cousin to leave. I walked with him as far as my journalist friend's place, and he continued on. Inside the house I requested the journalist to find a place for me. He said he knew a vacant apartment a little farther down the hill. "I'll take it even without looking at it," I affirmed.

He warned me, "It is not a Brahmin neighborhood, and it's right on the road."

"It doesn't matter. I think I've crossed that stage already," I said.

He promised to go and negotiate for me with the landlord while I waited in his house. Before long he returned with the news that the landlord agreed.

The environment was pushing me more and more away from the little remnant of belief I still had in "society," a society that called itself "higher caste" but was really feudal and opportunistic. The more I heard and experienced the social gossip that was intended to humiliate and weaken, the more I strengthened mentally. The basis for this strength was realization. In this process, several times during these months I literally felt that there had been a thin veil like a cataract over my eyes that I had wiped off with my hand, and that now I had begun to see better and better. I had this experience simultaneously in social and political terms. In both realms I developed detached attachment. I knew that no one could have been more attached than I was to the two things I valued most—family and freedom. But no one understood my attachment to either. So I detached myself from their fruits. It was not that my commitment to the democratic struggle lessened an iota. Nor my love for my family. I would never hesitate in the genuine service of either. If anyone needed my help it was there. But I detached myself from worrying about what anyone thought, or about what might become of me. Socially and politically, I knew what I was. I often ponder even now whether this psychological reorientation happened only to me, or whether it is that I feel so because I can express myself. The more I experienced injustice, and social and political attack, the more I felt resilience rising from my alienation. I wondered how many more people in Nepal and around the world might have faced similar dislocation under tyrant regimes.

ळ

Next morning I hired a pushcart with two coolies to shift my stuff. The distance was not that great, so it was quite an inexpensive move. At around ten A.M. I moved into the new place. It was on the ground floor, one very small bedroom, a very, very small kitchen, and a little corridor that served as a living room. There was no bathroom, but there was an Asian toilet—the squatting type. If the floor space of the whole place was taken together it would have made one full-size bedroom. The landlord entered and asked me who else was with me. Ignoring his question, I asked where I would wash myself. He explained that I had to get a bucket of water from the kitchen tap and, opening the toilet door, place the bucket in the toilet entrance. If I wanted to wash my hair I should squat in the living room with my head toward the toilet. If I wanted to wash my body, then I should stand or squat in the toilet and face the living room. There was no dispute about that.

He asked me again who else would come. I replied nobody else. Then he went away. There was no ventilation except through a small window in the toilet. I closed the door to the outside world. The place looked like a dark tunnel. I thought that in my poverty this place was the best bet for me. It was half the price of the previous house. Besides which, I had really only been camping in one of its rooms. To have some light while I arranged my possessions I opened the door.

After I had finished, I felt that something was not quite right. It was all the framed photographs of members of my family that I had displayed around the room as usual. But now they appeared to be laughing at me with scorn. Until this moment, I had not been aware of how disturbing their presence was for me. Perhaps in my subconscious mind one of my "mes" had been seeking their symbolic protection. "Well, not anymore," spoke an inner voice. I took every photograph out of its frame and tore it into pieces. Now every frame was empty, a gaping hole. For a moment the thought came to smash the frames as well and throw them outside. Then I thought, "Wait a minute! Why not frame photos of someone who cares about you?" I went through all the photographs of myself, which I kept in a large envelope, and selected those that comforted me. I put them into the empty frames. They looked back at me with feeling, warm and full of life. I took a deep breath and spoke out loud to myself, "There! I have someone dear in my life who will always be with me. Myself." It felt so good to have discovered how my own photographs could offer comfort. It was not my ego that desired to be surrounded by images of myself. It was desolation.

I closed the door again. Evening came, and then night. I felt lonely and nowhere. However, I had the comfort of "myself." Overcome with tiredness, I went to bed.

∞

I had one regular appointment to keep each month. At the Kathmandu District Court, a suit had been brought against me by the national Panchayat member representing the Nepal Women's Organization—one of the six class organizations within the Panchayat system. Amid all the pressures I had been facing at home and at work—before my expulsion from both— this case had come as yet another slap in the face. The case was dragging on and my distaste was growing for the whole episode and the system that it seemed to represent, and there seemed to be no way for me to retaliate. Suddenly, one day I had an idea. There was going to be a national fair in Kathmandu—an event that would be patronized by the highest in the land and attract huge publicity. I applied for a stall even though I was not sure what I would do in it. Business was a Vaisya caste occupation, not suitable for Brahmins, but I was determined to do something that would create some sensation. "What could be the worst business for a Brahmin and a teacher? Yes! A shoe shop," I thought. Traditionally such business was the province of the Sarki, a "lowest" untouchable caste of shoemakers. Darjeeling shoes were famous in Nepal, therefore I went there to buy some.

After a couple of days, I was back in Kathmandu with my shoes ready in the stall for the inauguration of the national fair. Some of my friends came and pinned a sign over the stall saying A BRAHMIN PROFESSOR'S SHOE SHOP. It was a sign of the tremendous sympathy I had from the people. The stall became an afternoon meeting place for our friends. But whenever customers came I busied myself cleaning the shoes. Most of the regime's so-called big shots visited my store.

While I was not busy in the stall I started writing short stories and poetry. I even sent an entry for a national song competition to the Ministry of Education after I saw an advertisement calling for entries. Believe it or not, one of my songs was selected and I received a cash award. But until I left Nepal in 1983 I never heard my name mentioned even though the song was recorded and I heard it broadcast several times on Radio Nepal's children's program.

I must say that politically it was a successful venture to sell shoes, though financially not so good. Of course, my father was extremely cross with me for doing such menial business. Finally, a few days before the end of the fair, when it became too political, I was asked by the fairground manager to close down my shop. I did not want to be too confrontational so I obeyed.

ॐ

I had spent the little money I had on shoes, and I was living a hand-to-mouth existence with no savings and no job. As winter came, the nights became colder in Kathmandu. As it would cost money to buy a quilt or a blanket, I decided instead to transfer my kitchen into my bedroom. My kitchen was just my little baked-mud electric cooker, locally made. You could carry it in one hand. Its single ring could heat one pot or pan at a time. To some extent it would keep the room a little warmer. Many times it had fused, causing the thin coiled filament to burn through. I had mended it myself by stretching out the coil a little longer and joining the disconnected pieces. With this cooker now glowing a dim red in my bedroom I would work on newspaper articles or write a short story for my own satisfaction.

Every day I would go out on the streets of Kathmandu in search of work, often walking ten miles a day. In the evenings I would return home tired and hungry. There was no refrigerator, and all the food I had was uncooked rice, a few vegetables laid out on an empty sack on the floor, and, of course, bread, the one food I never liked. If I did not eat I would faint, so I would prepare and eat this one meal of the day quickly and then decide whether to write until late or go to sleep early.

There was no hope of a job for me in the government, so I tried to find work in the private sector. However, each time I approached people in business, I found that, while they expressed sympathy for what had happened to me, they were unwilling to employ me out of fear that they in turn might be blacklisted. One day, out of frustration, I went to a travel agency to see if I could guide its tourists. After all, I was a history lecturer. The travel agent replied that until I had tourist guide training I could not be a guide.

I was walking in the street like a lost person when I met a communist friend of mine. I did not tell him the whole story but mentioned the training. To my surprise, he said, "Oh! I am going to do that also. I am going to apply tomorrow. That's the last day."

"I met the right person," I thought. He explained to me what was necessary for applying. Talking to him for half an hour made me feel lighter and happy.

The next morning I walked to the tourist guide training center and was there to submit my application at ten A.M. On the way home I met another friend. He asked me where I was coming from, saying that I looked more cheerful than before. Had I found a job?

"After two months a job is guaranteed," I told him, laughing.

"How do you know so much in advance?" he asked, surprised.

"I am going to guide all the foreigners in our kingdom," I joked.

"Oh, no! I hope you are not going to do that training to be a tourist guide," my friend exclaimed.

"Why not?" I asked him.

"Do not get involved in that cheap profession. I won't even say hello to you if I meet you after you become a tourist guide," he warned, and made a bad remark about it.

"Do you think I'm afraid of that?" I replied, and said good-bye to him. No matter what, I was determined to do it. I had no role model and did not believe in them. I never aspired to be nice like that woman, or gentle like another woman.

Within a week I was notified about my acceptance for the tourist guide training. I smiled to myself and thought, "Now I am in line to guide tourists around my country."

One day while I was in the middle of an anthropology class one of the center's *peons* interrupted the class and said, pointing at me, "You have a phone call."

"It can't be for me," I replied. "I don't even know the phone number of this place, and I never asked anybody to call me here. Please tell the caller that it might be a wrong number."

"No, it is for you," he insisted, absolutely sure.

The instructor suggested, "Go and see, and then come back."

"No, I'm not interested in talking to anybody," I said.

My communist friend, who was sitting next to me, said, "It might be that your father died of a heart attack, or your brother died in a car accident. Why don't you go and at least you will know what happened."

Still hesitant, I went to the room where the telephone was. My communist friend had been right. It was an important call from the secretary of Her Majesty the Queen of Nepal. She had granted me an audience in a couple of days. This was in response to a request I had made. I wanted to tell her about my expulsion from the university, and about the way people like myself were being treated under the Panchayat system. Her secretary was calling to brief me how to enter the royal palace.

I told two of my Nepali Congress leaders about this. They said that it was my chance: "You must go and tell her whatever you feel like telling her. You won't be expelled from the party on the grounds that you met the queen." So I went to see her with an open mind.

I gave my greetings to her. I am sure that this time I did them more correctly than the time I met her mother-in-law, Queen Ratna, many years before in Dhankuta. She was alone in the room. I had never been so close to her, and I noted that she looked graceful and pretty. Pointing to a sofa, she invited me in a friendly voice to sit down. I sat, and then remembered that I had been told not to sit down. Nevertheless, I remained seated.

I told her my story in detail, explaining what had happened at the university and how much I and others had to suffer as blacklisted people.

She asked, "What do you think you would like to do?"

I expressed my desire to devote myself to preserving and researching various cultural and historic places in the kingdom, mentioning those needing immediate attention. She encouraged me to do so. Thanking her, I left the palace after an hour. I told a few of my friends that the queen had been very receptive.

I continued my training. In the meantime I consulted some of my former professors who were experts in reading inscriptions and dating statues. They were very interested, especially knowing that this work was among the queen's interests. Everybody gave his or her word to cooperate. So I went to the site I had selected. I took a photographer to shoot detailed photographs of all the statues, idols, and temples, and mapped the site. Finally I prepared an album of all the photographs and illustrations.

I approached the queen's secretary to arrange to see her again. When I met her I handed over the materials I had prepared. To cover the initial costs I had mortgaged my jewelry with a goldsmith. I had not hesitated to do so, knowing that the queen herself was behind my project.

By now I had completed the other training and had obtained my license as a tourist guide. But that was not what I was interested in. I invested all my energies in this conservation research. One day the prime minister informed me that he had been holding a substantial sum of money for my project but that "it was the last day of our financial year and if that money was not transferred into some account it would lapse." According to His Majesty's government regulations the funds could not be made over in an individual's name without a cabinet decision, and there was no time for that. So the money ended up being transferred into the Tribhuvan University account.

The vice chancellor at that time was a communist. I went to him several times. He kept saying, "Yes, but I have to fulfill some formalities. Don't worry, sooner or later you will get the money." I waited and waited, but he never handed over the funds. When two months had passed since my last audience with the queen I wrote her a letter explaining the difficulty I was facing because my funds were being blocked. By this time the prime minister, along with his finance minister, had been dismissed by the king for a scandal involving the overinvoicing of carpet exports.

At last, I learned that a meeting had been called in the Ministry of Education with the following agenda: "To hear what Durga Pokhrel wants to do." It was a typical meeting of the Nepali bureaucracy, with officials present from every department that had anything to do with education, history, conservation, research, archives, museums, and so on. The bureaucrats now wanted to "collaborate," but when I firmly refused to allow my research to become entangled with the bureaucracy, they promised to write a letter of explanation to the queen. I do not know what they did. I never got that money.

Finally the inevitable happened. I had photographed an extremely rare three-and-a-half-foot-tall "standing Buddha" of black marble. It was a true antiquity, dating back to the sixth century. My heart longed for its preservation. When I went back to the site a day or so after my discovery it was missing. The local people commented, "We knew some big smuggler would take that."

Disillusioned, I gave up the project.

"Well," I thought, "at least I have a license to be a guide." I went to a travel agency and met the director. He interviewed me. At the end he said, "We definitely need someone like you, and I am very impressed with you. But there is only one problem with this agency. You see, [here he mentioned the name of one of the royalty] owns this travel agency, and I am a little reluctant to hire a controversial person. I am sorry."

I also thought I had better stay away from a royal personage's travel agency. So I went to another one. Its director said the same thing. I wondered how many travel agencies belonged to the royal family.

On the road I met another guide who had received his training with me and had started working immediately. I asked him, "Which travel agency does not have any royal family's shadow?"

"It seems you have been going to the wrong ones," he replied. Then he gave me the names of four others.

I did the rounds. Three of them informed me that they had to deal with the government every day, so they were sorry. At the fourth one, I met a pleasant middle-aged lady. She said she could not hire me but that I could do freelancing. That was what I wanted, freelancing! A couple of times I did guide tourists. After that I found it inconvenient because I did not have a telephone, and had to walk half an hour to reach there every day just to ask whether or not she had tourists to guide.

Then, outside her office one day, I noticed a bunch of small teenage illiterate street boys speaking in foreign languages with some tourists and pleading with them to be allowed to take them here and there. I questioned myself, "Am I competing with them?" Here were Nepal's real "freelance tourist guides." They were the ones who needed this kind of job. I knew they did not have the government's training, but they had market experience. During the 1960s these kinds of Nepali kids had spent months and months with Western hippies, sleeping on the pavements of Freak Street and learning their languages. What else to do when you were homeless and uneducated? Hippies were gone, but the trend of such boys emerging on the streets was growing. These boys could never be hired by the agencies as they were, but if they found some kind tourist they could do the job— maybe in a more interesting way than a formal guide. Altogether I took groups four times. Then I decided that was not my *dharma*.

ରଙ୍

The rumor of my meetings with the queen had spread all over Kathmandu and as far as the country's eastern zone. My father wrote me a letter based on what he had heard through the gossip channel. He wrote, "I heard you were offered the position of zonal commissioner or assistant minister on condition that you write a statement saying that you no longer remain with the Nepali Congress and want to work for Panchayat. You never listen to anybody. Your B.P. is not even allowed to enter our borders. All the Nepali Congress will be killed, and so will you. Why don't you surrender to the queen and get some great position? Everybody does the same here. All one needs is their blessing. If you do not follow what I say then the time will never come for you."

I had nothing to say in reply, and did not write back.

Some of my colleagues also became sarcastic about my meetings with her. One of them told me, "Durga, even if one really drinks only milk in a bar, people will not believe it." There was no point defending myself. I thought, "Let people believe whatever they like to think."

The queen's birthday was approaching. To my enormous surprise, I was invited to be in the birthday celebration committee. Very dubious about this honor, I nonetheless went to attend meeting after meeting. Along with two other women I was given the responsibility of producing a birthday souvenir magazine, which I proposed should be called *Aishworya* after the first name of the queen.

As expected, the articles submitted to the committee were mostly ones in praise of the queen, and I discovered that I was also expected to edit articles written by relatives of these progovernment women on the committee. One of the women asked me if I could write an article about the queen in her name for *Gorkhapatra*, the government Nepali daily. Without hesitation I agreed to write for her. Soon I was contacted by three other women and two men for the same purpose. Both men and one woman were government ministers. I found it very easy to write about the queen because there was nothing complicated about her. My articles were straightforward, with some flattering language to polish them. Suddenly the realization came that I could earn a livelihood from writing.

As I wrote articles for various people on the occasion of the queen's birthday, I did not have any idea how much to charge. After they were over the hangover of the birthday I went to see one of the ladies for whom I had written. She was very pleased with the article, and told me that she had received a very good response from the palace itself. Without my even asking for money she gave me a thousand rupees. I thought she was too generous. The other one gave only five hundred. The remaining two gave little. I did not complain, as I had never done this before and did not know what to expect. I thought that perhaps the last two did not get good feedback. One of the men was an assistant minister. He gave three hundred. The other man was a cabinet minister. He called me to his residence and asked me whether I could write two more articles—one for the coming Constitution Day, and the second for an Indian magazine. I agreed, and he gave me two thousand rupees.

I began to feel much more confident that I could live on my own with ease. All I had to do was wait for the birthdays of the royalty and go around to these people offering this service. Within a short period of time I was able to write any kind of article featuring Panchayat, the king, the queen, Democracy Day, Constitution Day, or the queen mother. All government and Panchayat-backed newspapers used to abound with such articles on these occasions. Several times I even wrote speeches. Some of my political colleagues started questioning why my visits with such *Panchayati* people were so frequent. I used to smile and ask them, "Why do you want to know everything that I do?"

It was not that I was happy about what I was doing. I had tried other things, but failed. I was sure that this ghostwriting opportunity had come to me simply because the gossip about my audiences with the queen had spread everywhere. So these people might have mistaken that as a sign that I was no longer in the opposition, or something like that. I never tried to merge my means of livelihood with my political conviction, but lived with the paradox. I certainly did not discuss my strange situation with anyone. It was a question of "What else to do?" I had a right to survive. I was not stealing or harming others. I did not believe that the articles or speeches meant anything. Perhaps they bought people a margin more false credibility in the palace, if this was how loyalty was evaluated. But nobody outside the system, or probably even inside it, paid any attention to what they said anyway. Everyone knew it was eyewash. I thought, "I am just being paid for my labor." This might sound unethical, but what were my choices?

I was feeling a little relieved about my financial situation. But I was not satisfied with the place where I was living. It was so depressing. Also the owners—both the husband and the wife—were becoming too "concerned" about why I was living alone, why no family came to see me even during religious festivals and holidays. I came to feel that it could be dangerous for me to live in this environment because this kind of person could create trouble. This was at almost the peak of my ghostwriting, and my present location was perfect for me from this point of view—one of the ministers for whom I wrote lived right next door to me. What I needed was a nicer place to live in the same area. There was a big house nearby. It was as if the owners sensed my problem. They offered me two rooms, a bath, and a kitchen. A close friend wanted to live with me, so I went to tell her and we moved immediately into this new house together.

*Aishworya* was partially successful, but I was not satisfied with what I was doing. One day I meditated for a long time. At the end something very clear came to my mind, and that was that I should start publishing my own work. Visiting the Information Department, I discovered that there was no way I could register any publication in my own name because of my police record. However, there was a law whereby, even without registering, anybody could publish a souvenir book or magazine on special occasions like Their Majesties' birthdays or our New Year. For the moment this would solve my problem.

I decided to publish a souvenir book on the king's birthday, and put together articles on one of his interests—the theme of development—in both English and Nepali.

On their birthdays the following year I did the same thing. This time, I wanted my *Aishworya* to be serious and to focus on women's issues. Except for one piece, which I had to write for a progovernment friend, none of the articles were queen praisers. I was not trying to flatter Their Majesties. I genuinely believed in the monarchical system for Nepal. Whether then or now, my ideas have been the same. What I never liked was the absolute power of a monarch.

After I presented my own magazine *Aishworya* to the queen I met nothing but confusion, with even Nepali Congress people making allegations that the queen had helped me to get it published. I did not care. I had proved to myself that I could publish on my own. And I had found out a secret: On such occasions, even if you published advertisements for businesses and government agencies without their prior consent, they would not hesitate to pay you for them. Normally, advertisements depended on some minister's phoning the concerned organization, which would then grant you one as a favor to that minister. After this success story I just laughed to myself. Simply because I had met the queen a couple of times and had published a magazine named *Aishworya*, it seemed that all doors were opened for me in this little theater of dancing attendance.

By publishing such magazines I developed tremendous confidence. At the same time I recovered from the poverty in which I had been living for almost a year. From 1976 through 1977 I did quite well in printing and publishing, and even hired a houseboy for cooking and cleaning. I was constantly meditating and practicing yoga, and I cultivated the habit of thinking positively about any eventuality.

For the first time my brother Krishna came from Dhankuta to visit me, and he stayed for two weeks. Perhaps it was his way of saying that he had not discarded me. I appreciated his coming. He had not fulfilled the scholarly or professional dreams of our father, so his influence in our family decisions was not great. But he would report back to our father on how he found me. I never wanted to be seen to be defeated by circumstances and thanked God that when he came I was no longer going through those lonely bad times. I was surviving. I wanted to make a positive difference in the lives of people around me who were suffering because of the oppressive system.

ॐ

Early in 1978 I received an invitation to attend an international conference on human rights in Hong Kong. It would be the first time in my life that I would be traveling to a foreign country with a passport, since there was no passport requirement between Nepal and India.

Getting a Nepali passport was not a right in itself, as the government had a very strict policy toward issuing passports. The government's policy was simply to prevent the opposition from going abroad lest we be vocal against the system. When I applied, the Foreign Ministry told me that the Home Ministry had ruled that it could issue me a passport only if I could produce a recommendation from a gazetted first-class (high-ranking) officer in the government administration. Obviously, it assumed that no senior government official would risk his neck. However, I had a distant cousin who did not use Pokhrel as his last name, and he was in a very influential position. I went to him and asked for his recommendation.

Laughing, he said, "I will do it for you, but I hope you will not do something naughty so I have to lose my job."

I joked, "Don't worry. Even if you lose it now, when we come into power I will reappoint you with double promotion!"

On his recommendation the passport was granted.

It was a weeklong conference. I was elected to the executive committee of the forum and also presented a country paper on human rights violations that I had prepared with the great help of B.P. and Bhattaraiji. On my last day in Hong Kong, a reporter from the *South China Morning Post* interviewed me. She asked a number of political questions and at the end of the interview asked, "What do you want to do with your political system?" "We want to overthrow it," was my response. There was no time subsequently to go through what she wrote, and I never did see her article.

When I arrived back in Kathmandu on the morning of the next day, I was met at the airport by police, who seized my passport and then released me. I tried to figure out why they were doing this, but could not work out whether it was related to the interview, my paper, or merely my participation at the conference. I concluded that it must have been the interview. How quickly they had seen a copy of the paper. Within two or three days I was arrested under the Passport Act, under which the government could bring an action against someone traveling without a passport, on someone else's passport, or on an expired passport. None of these contraventions applied to me.

I was held in police custody at Hanuman Dhoka in Kathmandu's Durbar Square. Inside the shuttered front windows on the first and second floors were the cells—small, cramped cubicles barely wide enough for one person to sit down, yet each sometimes holding several captives. I was alone in my cell because I was not allowed to mix with others there.

It must have been the worst cell in the whole world. No sun, no light. There was just a crack between the wooden shutters of my window, but if I squinted hard all I could see among the temples outside was the terrifying black figure of Kal Bhairab, a representation of Death. If I turned the other way I faced an iron-barred gate onto a narrow corridor and then a row of cells opposite. Those cells had little barred windows. The only air to breathe came through those windows, but if anything came it was the foul smell from a refuse heap in a courtyard in the middle of the building where the police threw their leftover food. Once a week, a Pode (a member of the untouchable garbage-cleaning caste who pick up excrement from the streets using two buffalo ribs) was brought to clear the mess. Sometimes prisoners undergoing interrogation to force a confession were made to eat from the refuse heap.

At the left end of the alley between the cells on the first floor was a very dark corner without light or water where captives were supposed to relieve themselves. A policewoman came once a day to ask me if I wanted to go there. She would guard me if I went, but as soon as I came near the stinking piles of excrement I would start to vomit. It was then that I began to practice mind-body control. I could control my bowel movement for four days. And I would even wait to urinate until I felt as though urine would burst through all the senses of my body. The compulsion to release it came when I felt urine might make its way out through my ears. Food was very irregular. A few times a friend of mine sent a plate, and a few times the police would provide something. I preferred not to eat every day in any case, and even then I kept to dry foods. If, as Hindus say, prison is synonymous with hell, it was certainly so in this dark dungeon.

To begin with, I was not allowed to have visitors, nor could I consult with lawyers. After a month I was taken to the District Court, where I saw several lawyer friends who were going to plead on my behalf. Only when I was in court did I see the cutting from the *South China Morning Post*. If the government had brought a suit against me for what I said in the interview it would have been difficult to escape from the serious political charge. But because the authorities were trying to frame me on a violation of the Passport Act, my lawyers very skillfully prevented the court from paying attention to the contents of the newspaper. They forced the government prosecutor to focus only on the Passport Act. At last, after ten months, the case was decided in my favor and I was released.

တ

One of the agenda items at the Hong Kong conference had been the establishment of national forums to work on human rights issues. When I was freed from custody, I called a meeting of about a hundred people to pursue this. The participants chose me as chair of the forum. There were seven other committee members. The first thing the new forum did was to prepare a list of all Nepalis who had been imprisoned, exiled, or killed after 1960 for their political beliefs. To prepare a comprehensive report for restricted circulation, we interviewed leaders of all political ideologies in Nepal.

On United Nations Human Rights Day, we organized a symposium on human rights in Nepal. As Nepal was a signatory to the United Nations Human Rights Charter, the government could not prevent us from holding this event. The conclusion we reached did not surprise us but was no less grave and shocking. Since 1960 to date the human rights situation had been worsening in every respect—political imprisonment, people missing from police custody, political killings, and torture. The symposium also pointed out the degree of professional insecurity that prevailed so long as anybody could be expelled from any job at any time. This showed how far the government's human rights violations extended beyond explicit political opposition to victimize anyone on any pretext. We decided to keep up a level of pressure through periodic petitions and delegations in order to let the government know that the people were conscious of its activities.

We started our action program by seeking out some independent lawyers to take up cases of underaged children who were being kept behind bars. With great difficulty we prepared a list of cases. None of these juveniles were being held on major charges. Another of our intervention areas related to intercaste marriage. Across-caste love affairs might always have existed in our society to some small degree, but they were never condoned in customary law. The advent of intercaste "love marriages" was therefore a phenomenon most conservative Nepali parents were utterly unprepared for, and was emerging as a severe social problem. Prevailing law allowed a girl of sixteen and a boy of eighteen to freely choose a life partner. We of the forum entered the furor at this point by facilitating and sometimes actually arranging intercaste marriages of such couples. I remember first recognizing at this time that human rights issues extended beyond political killings, imprisonment, and harassment to the social realm of domestic tragedies.

ಇಿ

It was now late 1978. Although political parties were still banned, our activities were no longer underground because of B.P.'s return from exile. The Nepali Congress even had an office in town, if not a signboard and its flag. Because of political pressure, the government enacted a law permitting monthly or less frequent literary magazines that were not news oriented. I applied to register *Manas*, a Nepali-language monthly, and *Horizon*, an English-language quarterly. Both were registered. However, the law made it clear that before releasing any issue in the marketplace, four copies were to be sent first to the zonal commissioner. If his people found even a word that they thought was objectionable, they would seize all copies and ban that issue—or even the publication itself. Thus, I was still in a very risky business.

Around this time, my female friend decided to move and the house became too big and expensive for me alone. The landlord had also become rather cool since my arrest. One day a friend came to visit and told me that she knew of a house in Lazimpat the top floor of which was available for rent. I liked this place better than anywhere I had lived in Kathmandu and moved immediately.

My days of humiliation were over. I went everywhere without hesitation. Even when people asked me about my living alone away from the family, I could command the logic to satisfy them. I had proved that I was good at marketing any publication. Therefore, my desire now was to start a press of my own to publish *Manas* and *Horizon* and branch out into other publishing and printing work. I talked to some of my Nepali Congress colleagues—including Bhattaraiji—who all said it was a good idea, but nobody came up with the idea of going into partnership with me. I needed a partner.

One day I had gone to the Gorkhapatra Corporation, the government-controlled media house that put out the *Gorkhapatra* (Nepali) and *The Rising Nepal* (English-language) dailies. I was visiting in order to solicit people to write articles for my magazines. There, in one of the offices, was Shrish Rana, whom I had first met briefly during my student days. Now he was working for *The Rising Nepal*. Shrish offered me tea and promised to write an article for me.

He joked with me, "Let's run a newspaper together!"

"With a former *Mandale* and a Panchayat hard-liner's nephew—not likely!" I laughed back.

Shrish's and Upendra's paper was coming along quite well. And now they were looking for a press to buy, as was I. There was a press for sale in town that I was thinking of buying and running commercially. All of a sudden I heard that Upendra had bought it.

One day Shrish came up with a serious proposal of managing all our three publications together and running what was now Upendra's press. I accepted his proposal with an open heart. It was not a very big operation, but we ran the press and the papers quite successfully despite the political controversy we created.

တ္သ

"Well," I thought now, from the humid heat and stench of Mahendranagar Women's Prison, "one of the reasons the government had targeted me must have been my success at running the newspapers." Unless you surrendered to them, they would paralyze you and, if possible, finish you. In this paralyzed state in jail all I could hope for was that they would not take my life.

# 8

# Central Women's Prison

ne early morning at four A.M. the jailer came to the gate and shouted, "Oh! *Netaji*, you have to get up soon. People are coming to get you at five o'clock. You have an hour to get ready."

I stood up and responded, "Okay, Jailer *Saheb*, but who is coming and do you know where they are going to take me?"

He said, "The CDO told me last night that if the sky clears a little, a helicopter is going to come from Kathmandu. But he did not tell me where they are going to take you."

The sky was heavy with dark clouds and it was raining a little. Once in a while I saw a flash of lightning and heard thunder. "Perhaps the helicopter will not be able to come," I found myself hoping. "Disturbance again," I thought. "I was just settling here peacefully."

All my fellow inmates started crying aloud, "Maybe you are going to be released. We will be orphans here again. Don't abandon us."

I thought, "These poor women—they do not know how anxious I am myself, not knowing what is to come next." I said, "Don't worry, I will write to you. I cannot promise that I will come to see you again because it is so far. But after your release, if any of you want to visit the Pashupatinath temple in Kathmandu, come! You can be my guest."

Sweetly my inmates prepared the traditional vermillion *tika* paste Hindus use to mark someone's forehead as they bless them or pray for their protection before a journey. Then they informed the male prisoners that I was about to leave. At five A.M. sharp, the jailer and the *mukhiya* were at the gate. I asked the jailer if I could offer tea to my fellow inmates before I left, which meant that one of the police would have to run to town to buy it. He agreed. I gave him money for about forty cups of tea.

The jailer said, "We have to wait for the CDO and DSP to come to take you anyway. The sky is still cloudy. It might be delayed."

I asked him again, "Where do you think I am going to be taken?"

"I heard Kathmandu," he said.

Tea had just arrived when two jeeps also arrived to take me. We could not drink tea together. The women put the *tika* blessing on my forehead and, bowing down at my feet, cried emotionally. The male prisoner and policeman I had been teaching also put *tika* on me. Everybody cried, and I cried too. I felt quite attached to these inmates. All of the men inside the male section were waving good-bye from beyond their gate.

Just before I left I said loudly, "Everybody cheer up! Wait and see, we will bring about democracy in Nepal one day." They all clapped. And I left the jail.

I thanked the *mukhiya* for his cow's milk, and the jailer for being nice to me. He was going with me in the jeep as well.

I was taken to a military barracks. A number of government office chiefs were assembled there, including the zonal commissioner. It was the first time I had met him and most of the others. Outside in the garden there was a fire burning and a big white mark on the ground. Somebody asked what they were for. One of the military replied, "So that the helicopter can see where to land." I thought to myself, "Oh! It is true what the jailer was saying about a helicopter coming to get me."

It was still cloudy and raining slightly. At eight-thirty A.M. we heard a sound from somewhere up in the clouds. Everybody who was inside rushed out and started peering up into the sky. After a while a military helicopter broke out of the clouds and made a perfect landing on the prepared spot in the barracks garden. I saw the same inspector and policewoman climb out who had brought me from Kathmandu by plane.

They greeted me with "*Namaste.*"

I asked, "Where are you going to take me now?"

The inspector gave me the kind of laconic reply that I had by now almost forgotten. "We are just the followers of orders from above. Whatever our *hakkims* say, we do. This time they have asked us to take you back to Kathmandu," he told me.

There were also two military men—a captain and a major who intro-

duced themselves as the pilots. Just before I entered the helicopter I gave
the government officers who had assembled a brief lecture about the kind
of democracy I and others were fighting for. For the first time in my life I
felt I was really a *netaji* and that it was my duty to express something on
this occasion to this assembled group. "Even if I am to be killed," I thought,
"at least these government people will know my political beliefs." As a formality I thanked them for their help. I do not know who it was, but one
of them replied, "We could not look after you well because we had so many
other things to do." Then I climbed aboard.

The helicopter took off at nine A.M. It flew low along the steamy valleys and narrow gorges between the steep hillsides, all lush and green with
monsoon crops and vegetation. Whether helicopters always flew this way,
or whether it was because of the weather, I was not sure. I was very scared,
but not by the flying. At every bump or turn in the air my heart would
pound quickly, and fear would return: "Will I be killed and pushed out into
the jungle?"

After an hour of flight, I noticed widespread flooding of the land below.
Then for miles and miles as we passed over the *tarai* plains and lower hills
there was nothing but stumps of trees. The ground looked like the scabby
naked skin of a mangy dog. "Oh! Of course," I thought to myself. "This is
the legacy of the Referendum—deforestation." "*Nepal ko dhan hariyo ban,*"
people used to say—"The wealth of Nepal her green forests." In one decade,
from 1970 to 1980, it went. It was political gambling. To buy out possible
defectors from the system, and to entice multiparty people to their side,
the government had unashamedly offered plots of forest land as one of its
last desperate bribes. Finally, in the Referendum, trees had been the currency traded for votes supporting the system.

Tens of thousands of acres of forest were treated in this way, like loot to
be plundered. Nepal's hardwood timber was very valuable, but instead of
being managed and harvested in the service of Nepal's development, it was
all cut and exported privately to sawmills in India. The plots of the "loyalists" were left rough-cut and naked, the purpose served. Then another
*Pancha* would steal the land and make his farm. This was what had ignited
the other issue—landlessness. The simple villagers from overpopulated
hills who had tried to acquire empty land—neutral people, not Panchayat
loyalists—were massacred.

I asked the policewoman, "Am I going to be released?"

She replied, "I don't know anything. All I was told was, 'You go to get
your *didi* back because you went to take her there. This time you'll be going

in a helicopter.' I was so delighted. Because of you, I got a chance to fly in an airplane, ride in a train, and now in this helicopter."

"Where did you go by train?" I asked her.

She said, "After we left you at the jail, there was no flight back to Kathmandu because that plane we came in had turned around within a few minutes and gone back. There was no other way, so the Inspector *Saheb* took me back to Kathmandu via India by train, then bus. It was so much fun, although it took four days."

The helicopter journey took four and a half hours. At last I saw dear old Kathmandu down there in the wide valley floor that now looked lush and green with its patchwork of paddies. The pilots landed in the military section of Tribhuvan International Airport. Before they disappeared I thanked them for bringing me back safely.

I was taken from the airport in a closed police van. It drove here and there, up and down, street after street. I did not understand what it was doing or where I was being taken. At last it stopped. I was back at the Police Club. They left me in the van for an hour. There was nobody to talk to except the guards, of whom I was already tired. I had eaten no food the whole day, and had had nothing to drink. My mouth was so dry that I tried to generate moisture by imagining all sorts of spicy food. This did not help. The other anxiety was whether they were going to keep me in the same cell as before. Even as I began thinking of that, I started to sweat with fear.

A thought appeared in my mind: no other woman political figure in the country had been humiliated, tortured, or treated in this manner. I caught myself beginning to feel defeat. Then another me protested. No! It was not defeat: I was in the process of sacrificing my life so that democracy would eventually be restored.

A new policewoman appeared and said to the other one in the van, "Eh! You go now. I am told that I have to go with Durga *didi*."

"Where are we going?" I asked her.

"Inspector *Saheb* is coming. He'll tell you," she replied.

Another policewoman came, and some more men. Altogether there were seven guards. One of the men joked, "*Didi!* The prime minister gets seven bodyguards, and you also have seven. What's the difference?"

"Nothing, except that I would never like to be prime minister in this Panchayat system," I replied.

"If you do not wear a *Panchayati* hat then you'll have to live your life in jail," he said further.

I was in no mood to extend the conversation, and said nothing.

The driver arrived and started the van.

"Where are you taking me now?" I asked, not to any particular person.

"To Central Jail," came the response from the inspector.

ॐ

No one can imagine my inner joy at that moment. Even though I knew from past experience that life in Central Jail would not be as peaceful as with my inmates in Mahakali, at least I was going to be with other women and not alone in the Police Club. Probably I would know most of them. They would still be there from three years before when I had been with them for some of the months of my detention under the Passport Act. "Also," I thought, "this is Kathmandu—the capital. I might have visitors." How wonderful it would be to see friends after so long. I became poetic just with this thought and wondered how I would have felt if they had said I was to be freed.

The van stopped in the muddy cul-de-sac in front of the Central Jail office. The jailer and the prison inspector were waiting for me. They were the same people I had known before. I felt relief. My seven guards handed me over to them and the jailer offered me a cup of lemon tea. How good it was to drink tea after four months. I had forgotten how hungry and thirsty I was. After tea the jailer looked at me, then looked at his watch and, with an eye movement toward the door, said, "Time to go."

I stood up. "I hope you will look after me well here."

"If you behave well," the jailer replied, "then as much as the law allows, I will."

He also stood up and escorted me out as far as the jeep. "Take Durgaji, our guest," he ordered the police. "She's not new. Tell the women inside that they should behave properly with her."

ॐ

"Oh! It is Durga *didi* come back again," shouted all the women at the prison gate when I stepped out of the police jeep moments later.

The police escort handed me over to the police guards inside the prison and to the *Chaukidarni*. This was the title the jail's authorities gave to the chief of the internal jail administration, which was run by the inmates themselves. Literally, *chaukidar* in Nepali means "watchman." The title had been adapted for the jail's purpose using the female *-ni* suffix. The jailer and inspector selected a woman they considered a tough murderer, who could control other women physically, and who would not hesitate to carry out any cruelty. She would always be a woman on a murder charge, someone who had endured at least fifteen years in jail, someone who had shown an ability to keep a distance from others and who had demonstrated an aptitude for the role during her time as a *kamdar* (worker), the lowest rank in the criminal administration. Above the *kamdars* were *naikes* (foremen) and the *Mul* (main) *naike*, who reported directly to the *Chaukidarni*. One *naike* and two *kamdars* were appointed by the *Chaukidarni* in each criminal cell. There were thirteen cells in the two main criminal buildings, so there were thirteen *naikes* and twenty-six *kamdars* in the *Chaukidarni's* team.

The sole responsibility of the criminal team was to carry out the *Chaukidarni's* orders for the management of daily prison existence. The jail's office was concerned only that she kept other prisoners under control—by whatever means. She was answerable to no one for the means that she selected. To distinguish other prisoners from the criminal hierarchy, the rest of us were known by the English word *public*.

The *Chaukidarni* and her workers had some enticing benefits. Their official privilege was to receive the same polished white rice as political prisoners received, and one rupee fifty *paisa* per day. Everybody else received smelly parboiled rice and only fifty *paisa* (half a rupee), as in Mahakali. The workers also took unauthorized but condoned profits from feeding the mentally ill, known inside the prison as *pagal* (lunatics). At ration distribution time the *Chaukidarni* and her gang would collect *pagal* rations according to the number of *pagal* each had responsibility to feed. Assignments were up to the *Chaukidarni's* whim. But *Mulnaike* would get at least two to feed, each *naike* would get one or more, *kamdars* could be allotted one on a daily basis, depending on the *Chaukidarni's* generosity, and the *Chaukidarni* would take the rest, which would be as many as ten.

Without exception, all *pagal* complained that they did not receive enough to eat. Perhaps their provider would dish them up a mean portion of smelly rice swimming in salty water, sometimes with some flakes of vegetable. If the provider took rations for ten *pagal* that would mean ten pounds of rice and five rupees. She might use only five pounds of rice and one rupee a day. The rest was saved. In this way the *Chaukidarni* became the richest prisoner.

ဢ

I stooped to enter through the little door within the main gate.

The *Chaukidarni* addressed me: "The jailer told us that someone very important was coming and that we should clean up everywhere and prepare a room for her with only three other inmates plus her two personal police guards."

She went on, "We thought it might be somebody elderly whom we did not know. If we had known it was you we would have told him, 'Ah! She's one of our friends. We'll take care of her, don't worry.' Anyway, we're very, very happy to get you back here."

It was evening. They had already eaten, but had prepared food for me. I ate in the *Chaukidarni*'s room. For the first time in four months I had a meal of rice, lentil soup, and a vegetable dish. I thought that they must have gone to some expense to prepare both lentils *and* a vegetable. It tasted so good.

After finishing eating on the floor, I sat on her bed of two wide planks supported at each end by a mud wall one foot high. It was comfortable— she had accumulated plenty of jail bedding during her fifteen years inside. Starting upward from the planks, she had two rice straw mats, three kapok-stuffed cotton mattresses (each one three inches thick), two kapok-filled quilts (one small and one large thick one), and a kapok pillow. And she was using one rice straw mat on the floor. It was luxury.

Above her bed hung her handbag, and in a little cavity in the wall where a few bricks had been deliberately omitted during building to make a tiny recessed shelf (normally used in Nepali households as a shrine), the *Chaukidarni* kept her cheap Indian face cream, makeup powder, bangles, and traditional marriage necklace.

On a little table next to her pillow was the prison's only radio, provided by the office and controlled externally. All other stations had been blocked except for the government-run Radio Nepal. Like private radios outside, it was run at high volume, and the programs could be heard across the jail compound. Later, I found, however, that I had to strain my ears to catch any news, because if ever I approached the *Chaukidarni*'s room when the news was being broadcast, her radio would be mysteriously switched off. Political prisoners were prohibited from hearing news, but I never knew how the switching-off was achieved.

ဆ

At five-thirty, the *pagal* were pushed into their cells like goats into sheds and were locked up. Half a dozen of them were left outside, immobile and shackled, some by their wrists and ankles, some just by their ankles or by one wrist or one ankle, to iron posts or to huge iron cart wheels lying on the ground. They were naked or wearing nothing but a torn piece of filthy cloth hung by a string or cloth remnant from their waists. Their hair, cropped short, was uncombed and tangled and gray with filth. Their bodies bore the cruel scars of countless tortures.

I heard the policemen calling from outside, "How many inside?"

A female night guard inside gave a reply, and the gate was locked from the outside. Policewomen rattled the gate from the inside, and policemen rattled it from the outside. "Everything okay?" "Everything okay," they asked and answered each other.

A gong sounded—*tang tang tang tang tang tang.*" It was six o'clock. The sound came from the military barracks next to Bhadragol Jail, over a hundred yards away. I had seen the gong several years before when I was visiting a friend imprisoned in Bhadragol. Every hour the duty guard struck it as many times as the hour with a hammerlike iron rod. On the half hours he would beat it just once, a short *tang.*

Now we were on our own, all accused of something except for three regular policewomen and two extras assigned for me. From outside someone switched on the lights.

The *Chaukidarni* ordered a *naike* to shout for everyone to assemble for *bhajan* (prayer). All the women, including the police guards, hurried to congregate for the chanting on the ground in front of the *Chaukidarni's* room. I also joined in the chanting. After *bhajan* they arranged a little singing and dancing to welcome me. In a strange way I felt at home.

It was just after six-thirty P.M. when I finally went to my assigned room. Coincidentally, it was the same upstairs room where I had been kept previously. All three roommates—Mara, Kripa, and Susa—I had known as well, although they had not been my roommates at that time. Mara, a high school girl, was accused of murdering six members of her family at the age of thirteen and was serving life imprisonment. Three years before when I was imprisoned there I had taught Mara and arranged through the jailer for her to sit for the High School Leaving Certificate examinations from jail. Mara had passed and now told me proudly that she was teaching the adult literacy class inside the prison and that Susa and Kripa were two of her students. Kripa was accused at the age of fourteen of being involved in killing five people in her family because she had been the only survivor in the incident. She, too, had been sentenced to life. Susa was charged in connection with the death of her husband and two children. The police had forced her confession by gouging her back deeply with their bayonets and rubbing chilli powder into her eyes. Her badly disfigured face had a frightening appearance, and she had a permanent limp. Now they were delighted we were sharing a room. Susa was a *kamdar* and Kripa was our room *naike*.

I went over to one of the windows of our room and lowered my head to peer down at the yard below. Directly opposite and about twenty yards away

was the *Chaukidarni*'s block, a single-story structure that included the policewomen's room and another room for five of the so-called *pagal*, who
were in fact not mentally ill at all. The *Chaukidarni*'s room was at the end
nearest to the main gate. From my window I could not quite see the entrance area, as it was obscured by the northern end of the *Chaukidarni*'s
building. But to the left I could see the other two-story building like mine.

Straight ahead, below my window, was a shabby low building for the
other *pagal*. It was built of mud packed hard into a framework of rough timbers and sticks, and was roofed with corrugated iron sheets. Viewed from
the side or the back, the building looked and functioned like a rabbit hutch
or chicken shed set two feet off the ground. Underneath was a collecting
area for droppings that fell through toilet holes in the mud floor of the cells
above. The litter had never been cleaned out since the shed was built, and
had accumulated into a mountain of excrement that flooded into the jail
yard whenever it rained. I became conscious of its nauseating stench.

The four buildings—the *Chaukidarni*'s to the east, the *pagal* shed to the
south, my building on the west, and the other criminal block on the northern side—enclosed the jail yard. About halfway across the yard toward the
*Chaukidarni*'s block was a forbidden spot beyond which we "public" could
not go. Forbidden by Hindu custom as well as by the jail administration,
this was the place where the dead were laid—the *chita*. It was a platform
of raised ground about a foot high, the size of a coffin. Next to it was a
bricked-in, raised bed—the *tulsi math*. A leaf of the sacred *tulsi* bush is traditionally placed in a dying person's mouth. It is believed that Lord Vishnu,
the Protector, resides in it and that by doing this the person will attain salvation.

Behind the *pagal* shed was a dirty wasteland, bigger than the public yard,
which you had to cross to reach the toilet holes under the south prison wall.
A small area of this wasteland that was close to neither the toilet footpath
nor the smelly back of the *pagal* shed nor the toilet holes had previously
been used as a garden.

I asked Mara if they were still using this wasteland for communal gardening. "Ah! Every now and then," Mara replied. "*Chaukidarni* has so
many problems managing it. The area is too small to allow individual plots
of more than a square foot, so they are never able to distribute them fairly.
Gardening initiatives always end up in such a great fight that the organizers give up and prohibit gardening again for a while."

Kripa added, "Not to mention the *pagal* who go and eat anything they
see growing there! Also there's never enough water."

"But there's always manure if you don't mind using human stuff," laughed
Susa. "You can just collect it from under the *pagal* shed."

"Kasa the Sarkini [shoemaker caste] used to do her toilet right on her garden," Kripa continued. "By the time she'd done her stuff and washed her bottom, it was very fertile and watered! *Chaukidarni* was mad at her when she smelled the garden, but Kasa said she always covered the stuff over."

I laughed with my companions. It was good that we were only four. The *Mulnaike*'s room, in the building nearer the gate, was also less crowded. She had two *kamdars*, one *naike,* and one public with her. I knew that the women from the untouchable castes, about nine or ten of them, were all kept in one room. The rest of the prisoners were divided equally over the remaining twelve criminal cells, averaging seven or eight per cell—although during student unrest numbers in the rooms could rise temporarily to as many as fifteen. Our room was not big enough for four women, even without the police guards. But I supposed that I did not have any cause for complaint. In Mahakali we were eleven in a room not much larger than this.

"How many are we in the jail now?" I asked Mara.

"About eighty public, including forty *pagal,* and now yourself. And then there are forty of us," replied Mara, referring to *naikes* and *kamdars*.

I imagined all the cells as I had known them before. All criminal cells had about the same floor area, twelve feet by six feet, but the downstairs rooms were the worst because their ceilings were only four and a half feet above the floor. Also, as the floor was bare ground, these rooms were constantly damp, and mushrooms, and even grass, popped up there and on the lower walls that were always green and gray with algae. The women occupying these rooms suffered chronic rheumatic pain from the chill.

The upstairs cells were about a foot higher, although you had to stoop to enter through wooden, shutterlike doorways, and you had to remain stooped after you were inside. Two small barred windows gave a little light in each room and a view down to the goings-on in the yard.

In whichever room you lived there was only one workable sleeping arrangement. Everybody would lie on the floor side by side with heads to one wall like sardines in a can, so close that they could hardly help touching each other.

At their feet, at the bottom of the opposite wall, were their "kitchens." Each woman had a wood-burning *chulo,* three points built up from the mud floor close enough to each other to hold one cooking pot. Beside her *chulo* was her pile of firewood, a few utensils, any purchased foodstuffs she might have, and a round clay pot for storing water. A few women who had been inside more than ten years might have saved enough to buy a small tin box for their personal possessions.

To create more space, every morning each woman would roll any bedding she had into a small bundle. Only once a year, with the *Chaukidarni's* permission, could the women lay their bedding outside in the yard somewhere in the sun to dry out and reduce the bedbugs.

The first four to six years were the hardest for the women. Newcomers usually slept on the bare floor because the jail issued bedding only once every other year at the major religious festival of Dasain. If she came just after the distribution she might have no bedding for two years unless someone happened to have an old straw mattress to give her. You could tell how long a woman had been inside by the thickness and width of her bedding. Every second year each woman was entitled to one rice straw mat and two kilograms of kapok and sufficient cotton fabric for a quilt and a mattress two-and-a-half-feet wide and an inch thick. The cotton fabric came from the weaving factory in the men's prison, and the woman had to purchase her own needle and thread. After two years, the woman would receive another issue and would add more kapok to her first mattress or quilt. After four years, she could re-cover the original bedding and fill a second mattress. The straw mats rotted in the damp conditions and rarely lasted more than two years. A sari and blouse were issued each year. If a woman came with any spare clothing she was safe. If not, she was in trouble if she missed that year's issue, because, if she had no money, there was no way she could afford to buy clothing from outside.

I thought to myself that much must have happened to these women since I had last been with them. Poor souls, I knew the stories of how they had been made "criminals."

Just then I heard footsteps on the stairs up to our room. My three roommates put fingers over their lips and whispered to each other. It was a *naike* and two women police officers—my night bodyguards.

One of the policewomen took me aside and warned me in private, "Do not be too close with these women. All three have the most dangerous murder charges. One is a killer of six, another a killer of five, and the other a killer of three. That is why they were selected to be your roommates."

"Do you think I am afraid of them?" I replied.

The policewoman warned again, "Just be careful."

I wondered whether the police were trying to intimidate me or to stigmatize me by placing me with their three "worst murderers." But I was too tired right then to care. The previous night I had not had a good sleep in Mahakali. Also I had been awakened very early.

I lay down on the bed that Mara had prepared for me—a straw mat and a two-inch-thick kapok mattress she had to spare from her prison issue. I must have gone to sleep instantly. In the middle of the night I was awakened by a nightmare. I was shaking with fear. Where was I? In Mahakali? In the helicopter? I could not tell where I was. Above my face was a blinding bright light. Was I in the Police Club? I glanced around quickly. I saw the others. All had covered their faces from the light with a bedsheet or some other material. I listened to the sounds of the night. Outside all was still save for the barking of street dogs.

I felt like going to the toilet. It was a great effort to go there alone as it was a long walk, perhaps forty yards, to the toilets across the wasteland. At night it seemed like walking through a tunnel of darkness. So I woke Mara. As soon as we stood up Mara shouted to the night guards on duty, "Eh! Durga *didi* and I are coming out."

"Why?" was the answer.

"Just to pee," replied Mara.

"Do as much as you want," came the reply.

By this time we were at the door. So we went outside. Mara said, "Let us not go to the toilet. It is very scary at night. At night everybody pees anywhere out here except just in front of the houses."

I was used to this practice already.

Returning to the room, she explained, "If anybody goes out after six-thirty P.M. without their permission she is punished, and it could be very serious."

"Oh, no problem," I said. "I would be happy if they came and took me to the toilet." After haunted Mahakali I would even ask a police guard to take me through the blackness.

We were quiet as soon as we entered our room.

I could not go back to sleep and tried to meditate for a while, lying in bed, but every hour the women on duty came to wake everybody, shining a bright flashlight in our eyes. I remembered in the past how it had taken me a week to adjust to the activity of the nights here. As the military barracks' gong "tanged" each hour, the patrol would make its rounds checking each room and counting the inmates. The policewomen joined the patrol every second hour. Every hour every woman would be awakened.

"Sleeping, *dijyu* [respected sister]?" a bittersweet voice would ask and at once torment you as the torch shone into your face.

You had to open your eyes to prove you weren't dead. If you were fast asleep you would be shaken into wakefulness. Once you groaned "Yes" they would leave you for another hour. If you were lucky you might sleep soundly for two hours, from four to six A.M. At six you might be deep in sleep, but if you did not get up immediately the duty *kamdars* and police officers would soon rouse you.

At one A.M. I heard a policewoman saying to me, "Earlier on when we

came to check, we tried to wake you up but you were so fast asleep you
didn't wake up. We left you alone thinking you must have been very tired
coming all the way from Mahakali."

"Thank you for being so kind," I responded.

As I lay there for the rest of the night my mind became very, very active. Again I began analyzing the situation in which I had been made a
victim. Three trains of thought were running simultaneously in my mind,
as they always did. I used to call them "my three mes." The first was saying, "If you want to live in your country, live the way other people live and
keep your mouth shut. Even if you know or hear anything risky, keep it
within yourself. Don't even tell the toilet. Even walls have ears. Go and
butter up the palace secretaries and become a minister or take whatever
blessing they give you."

A second "me" was saying, "No! That's running away from reality. *Maya*,
delusion. You should not hesitate to tell the truth even when your life is
in danger. If everyone hides the truth, who will break the ice? Truth-
telling is bitter when everything is based on lies and pretension. But truth
is truth, reality, and it will unveil itself one day. All you need is patience.
In this path you have to face much opposition. But eventually victory is
sure."

A third "me" was mediating: "This is a discussion with no end. Those
are extreme poles, two different paths. If you want to fulfill immediate am-
bitions, then take the first path. Otherwise wait until the time comes to
act like the second. Now is the time to be moderate." So! I smiled to myself. The third train of thought was my moderate one. While lonely in
prison, how satisfying it was to be able to carry on a three-way conversation with myself. As the months passed, I created a habit of occasionally
detaching myself from others around me in order to be by myself with these
voices of reflection.

ನಃ

Next morning the *Chaukidarni* brought me a glass of tea. What a privilege.
I could not believe it, and asked her, "Why did you trouble to bring this
all the way up here? If you had shouted 'Tea' from your room I would have
come jumping for it."

She winked, and said, "I thought, 'Why trouble *Netaji*?'"

"Where's your tea then?" I asked.

She said, "Wait a minute," and stood up. Actually, she had to bend her
head because the ceiling was so low. Looking out of the little window she
shouted loudly and with authority, "Eh! *Naike!* Bring my tea quickly."

A *naike* brought her tea in a minute and offered it to her graciously, her left hand touching her right forearm as she said, "Here it is, *didi*."

"You go now," ordered the *Chaukidarni* roughly.

We both sipped the beverage—the normal jail version of steaming weak sugar and black pepper water, without milk or tea leaves. I could tell she wanted to talk to me. She asked me how Mahakali was. I explained the conditions there, and added, "This is heaven compared to that. Those poor women—I feel so sorry. . . ." As I said this, the thought crossed my mind that there was much torture here as well. But at least the women here had some exposure to the world outside, whether it was the presence of city policewomen or the visits inside the jail of cottage industry personnel. To me this place felt like "light" compared to the "dark" of Mahakali.

"Why don't they ask for a transfer to Kathmandu?" she asked.

I explained, "To bring them to Kathmandu would mean flying them in an airplane or bringing them by train via India. Neither is possible in their cases. The government won't spend the money to bring them by air, and taking them through India is out of the question." I added, "Anyway, they were nice. The main problem was language in the beginning."

The *Chaukidarni* laughed, and said, "I'll tell you a story about how they speak. One of my cousins married a girl from the west who used to say all sorts of funny words. We used to laugh like anything. One night we were sleeping together when, suddenly, in the middle of the night she called out, 'Sun, sun.' I asked 'Where?' She replied, 'On my bottom'! I thought she was dreaming. But she got up and sat on the bed, still saying it. Do you know what she was trying to say? That she felt hot on her back!"

I joined her in laughing.

The *Chaukidarni* said that she would collect my ration and feed me. I agreed.

ॐ

After a week, Mara became my cook. It was more convenient for us to eat together, and we ate slightly above the prison average. As she had no case to fight in the courts, she was not trying to skimp by saving from her ration. We both received the same white rice and could afford a *dal* (serving of lentils or other pulse) and one vegetable every meal—and sometimes also a chutney of tomato or cucumber with salt and lime.

For three months, we drank morning tea together whenever we could afford it. For a little luxury Mara and I had bought some sugar and tea dust. It was not possible to have tea every day, as preparing it meant buying sugar, more firewood, and occasionally milk also. Later, I stopped drinking tea frequently and finally altogether, as I became conscious of how others were feeling. To them my drinking tea was a great extravagance. "How lucky!" they would remark. "Maybe she gets money from outside." No other women had tea dust, and they could not even afford the firewood for boiling water. Only during illness, stomach or back pain, would they make the "jail tea" as a luxury.

Gradually, I adjusted myself to daily life among my inmates. I learned from observation that it was futile to rebel against the jail system. Also I came to know about the life of each and every inmate and, thereby, grew to understand the culture of this forlorn community and consciously became a member.

ॐ

At six A.M. every morning your head would ache from lack of rest. But you had to get up quickly anyway. If you did not, you missed fetching your day's water, which you had to have for cooking the morning meal. But before that, the first task of the day was to trek across the wasteland to the toilet holes. For eighty people there were seven holes in a line a yard apart and a foot or so from the prison wall. Within the row there was no privacy at all, but the seven women squatting together and chatting there, knees almost touching, were partially screened from others in the queue by a two-foot-high wall. From the queue all that was visible was a row of heads. The toilet holes were very narrow to prevent escape. It was not a joke. One of our party leaders, Ganesh Man, had actually got out through one of these holes in one of his famous escapes from the male prison next door.

Water is used rather than toilet paper in Nepal, but even water was lacking at these toilets. The *Chaukidarni*, her workers, and the three policewomen allowed only themselves near the tap first thing in the morning, and would take fresh water with them across to the toilet in a personal can or jar, then return to the tap and wash hands, face, and feet. Their used water drained from the standpipe down a ditch into an open catchment behind the second criminal building, and this dirty water was all that other women would use for washing their bottoms after going to the toilet. A few women who found this water too dirty took a little clean water from their scarce supply in their earthenware pot. I was one of them. The Nepali social custom is that once you take a vessel to the toilet (which, except in modern urban homes, is always outside in the yard) you cannot bring that unclean object back inside the house. In jail this custom prevailed at least. Women in some cells had grouped together and raised twenty *paisa* to buy empty bottles or cans that were shared for this purpose and kept on the ground outside.

Except to quickly pass urine, I used to go to the toilet only once in two or three days. It was so filthy and smelled so bad that you did not want to go near the area if you could help it. I raised this issue with the jailer. Could he not arrange some water to clean the toilets even once a month? He was receptive. As we had one Pode caste woman with us in jail, he gave the *Chaukidarni* authority to appoint her to clean the toilets once a week. For that she was made a *kamdar*, although instead of taking the white rice ration that went with that status she took a double ration of the regular bad rice because of the little baby she had to feed. She was happy. She was even provided with the customary equipment of her trade—two buffalo ribs— for pushing the waste down the holes. It was at this time that she scraped out the ditch to make the catchment for the dirty washing water.

After toilet, women would congregate at the tap. Most had to wait in line for their morning splash. Only the administrative gang could actually gather there, plus the Brahmin widows who had insisted on this right for their religious rituals. The group at the tap would start their morning chorus, the hawking sound that greets the ear near any habitation in Nepal after dawn. "*Adladladladl, kghghaa, thukk!*" each would go several times, to clean out lungs, throat, and nose with a practiced sequence of gargling, retching coughs, noisy spitting, nasal water inhalation, and nose blowing into fingers. The noises of all those with colds and coughs would be especially expressive. "What a cold I have," a woman would announce, surveying the expelled phlegm in her hand, then flicking it away randomly.

Once the members of the administration were thus cleansed internally, they could then wash face and hands and become pure to dispense water to others. Everyone else had to go through the same procedure except that they could not do it around the tap space. Some had a little tea glass and would offer this for the *kamdars* to fill. Those without such vessels would cup their hands, and whatever they could hold sufficed for gargling, nose cleaning, and splashing face and hands. To accompany their "bath," like all good Hindus they would chant some version of the holy rivers mantra: "*Hara Kasi, Hara Gange, Godavari Saraswati. . . .*" (Chanting the names of holy waters is believed to invoke the healing and purifying power of such waters, just as chanting the name of a deity, or of Lord Krishna, invokes the deity's or the Lord's presence.) In Hindu society you cannot eat or drink anything until you have splashed your face. Then you are pure to fetch water.

Water was scarce. As in Mahakali, it only came through the mains for one or two hours each morning between six and eight o'clock and sometimes again for about the same time in the evening. Sometimes it did not come at all. There was a very dirty, hundred-gallon emergency tank that the fire engine would come and fill when the prison had run out of water. Although, when it came, the water flow was feeble, it did flow continually. Nevertheless, access of the public to it was rationed. The *kamdars* would decide who needed how much water and when.

All those who had earthenware pots would place them in a line with all of the others. Actually there were two lines, one for the untouchables. Provided the *kamdar* filled it full, whatever your pot could hold—one or two gallons—would be your "share," which you would keep in your room and use for drinking, cooking, washing, and washing up. Inmates had to buy their own pots. If they did not have a pot then life was very difficult. They would use their little cooking pan. Many newcomers were in this position for at least six months until they could save enough money from their ration to buy a clay pot.

Each morning while water flowed from the tap, two or three women would wash their hair, body, and clothing at the standpipe, wearing a petticoat or *lungi* from chest to knees, as is the custom in the villages of Nepal. As in Mahakali, one's monthly wash occurred on the fourth day of menstruation. Sometimes as many as five women's fourth days might coincide. The criminal administration kept track of every woman's period. If anyone lied and tried to wash mid-month the punishment was a session of torture. Old women who no longer menstruated could also wash once a month. All except the *pagal* enjoyed this monthly privilege. The *pagal* could wash only twice a year, not at the tap but separately behind their shed, using a few cans of water from the dirty emergency tank.

A few women made pads from torn cloth to absorb their menstrual flow, but as in the villages, most of the blood soaked for the four days into the sari or petticoat. After the Pode woman made the catchment, washing these clothes out at the tap was not allowed because it would pollute the catchment water. Just a panful of water had to do. No soap. Wood ash was the laundry detergent. Women said saliva worked like soap to remove the bloodstains, so they would gargle and spit on the soiled areas and rub to get the blood out. But the clothes could not be washed properly this way. Still, they would be laid on the ground to dry, mixing with dust and dirt. Tetanus occurred not infrequently, especially from reusing the pads.

After three years, inmates might have accumulated one change of clothing from the jail issues so that they would not have to wear the same blouse a whole month before being able to wash it. No one had a nightdress; all wore the same sari night and day. Again, some of the longer residents might use an old torn sari or petticoat for nightwear. For reasons of religious purity, Brahmin women cannot wear the same clothing for cooking as they wear while going to the toilet or while sleeping. So at these times they would wrap anything around themselves in order to keep their sari pure. Sometimes, if one of the old widows was forced to sleep in her sari and then continue wearing it in the morning, she would put a little fresh water in her hand, walk over to another Brahmin woman wearing a gold nose ring, touch the water on the gold, and then sprinkle her sari to purify it. Because she could not wash her sari properly she would chant a prayer asking, "God make my clothes pure."

*Man changa ta kathautima Ganga* ("If the mind flies as free as a kite, then wherever water can be found, that is the Holy Ganges"). Because the tap was the only source of "pure water"—water direct from a source and untouched by anyone—the space around the standpipe was especially meaningful for the few more elderly Brahmin women. Everywhere else was filth, excrement, deranged cries of the *pagal*, and other disturbances to consciousness. Inside a room first thing in the morning another woman would be having her period, or of lower caste, or still unwashed on her fourth day, or cooking rice already—all of which defiled the room for ritual purposes. So after prolonged requesting they won the concession from the *Chaukidarni* to use the tap space as their sacred area.

"*La, la, la!* Their God will not come to see them if they worship in other places. This spot is very holy like Pashupatinath," the *Chaukidarni* had said sarcastically as she broke the precedent of not generally permitting public near the tap. So while the rest of prison life carried on its anarchy, the old Brahmins would melt into this sanctum and, facing just the wall of brick, as if seeing beyond it in the direction of Pashupatinath, would please the deities and perform their meditation.

After my six-thirty A.M. wash, I would go and meditate. Then only would I drink morning tea and, after a while, eat the morning meal with Mara. Before we stopped our morning tea routine, I would sometimes drink tea before rinsing my face. Usually this was when I was having my period and would not feel like trekking down to the tap early in the morning. The elderly Brahmins would notice my absence instantly.

"Is *Maiyaa* not well today, or what? What happened, dearie?"

They had not seen me washing to be pure. I would feel very awkward not keeping up my *dharma* properly, and used to reply, "I have a little tummy pain."

Because I was Brahmin they expected me to perform my duty every day. For the first time in my life I realized with fullness what it meant when others expected much of you. As I became more conscious of this, I began to feel guilty if I had been negligent.

ဘ၁

There were two meals a day, and only one issue of rations. Besides the rice, the women would eat whatever they could buy from their allowance. It would be either *dal* or a vegetable, never both. No spices. Just salted water. A drop of mustard oil would be used for flavor. Lower-caste women might save food from the morning to eat in the evening. But Brahmin and Chhetri women would not eat leftovers and had to choose between having a full stomach of rice in the evening or in the morning. Usually they chose evening because rations were distributed at midday so they could send for a little vegetable before three P.M. There was no way to buy fresh supplies before seven the next morning, so the morning meal was always the leanest.

Few could afford matches. Those without would wait until they saw smoke coming from someone else's room and then borrow a burning fragment with which to light their own fire. Throughout the day, these women would be collecting any little leaves or pieces of paper the wind blew in from outside. And they would cut their firewood into small fragments that kindled more easily. In most cells there would be eight women pursing their lips in synchrony and blowing their damp fires into life. The jail procured the cheapest, poorest-quality firewood for the women to buy, and it gave off a pungent smoke. Twice a day, eight fires were smoking inside each small cell, and it was no surprise that all the women had chronic chest and eye conditions. Women living on the ground floor had the greatest difficulty in completing their cooking. The actual cooking might not take more than twenty minutes. But their firewood was always damp, as was their *chulo* fireplace.

Between nine and ten-thirty in the morning, life relaxed a little. The *Chaukidarni* and most of her gang would go to play around with the outside male police at the gate, so the public were less closely watched for a while. All women, and even the children under five, would light up a *bidi* or paper cigarette. Both were small cone-shaped cigarettes. The main difference was that "papers" were wrapped with thin paper rather than leaf. But the strongly aromatic mixture of raw tobacco and molasses inside was the same, and they were both the home-manufactured products of a cottage industry and were sold on the streets. Smoking was the one source of contentment that no one denied herself, and I was no exception. One *bidi* would be smoked three or four times so as to last the whole day, and would be tucked above an ear while not in use. Sometimes three or four poorer women would share a single *bidi*, smoking it right down to the last tiny remnant. When the butt was discarded, one of the five *pagal* girls who were allowed out would run to where the fragment had dropped and would wrap it inside a leaf or bit of paper and suck noisily to draw out one final puff.

After a smoke, the women started telling their dreams, most sitting in pairs, one in front of the other inspecting the other's head for black lice and nits. Whenever one was found it would be killed on the scalp with a quick, slicing pinch of the thumbnails. Others would search their blouses for white lice.

If she had had a bad dream the woman would start crying deeply: "Oh no, love for me has died at home" or "My mother must have died or is very ill. What I see in my dreams always comes true."

After bad dreams the belief is that if you tell a lower-caste person early in the morning you avoid its bad result as the bad *karma* of the dream is carried by someone whose own *karma* has already made her "low." Conversely, if you have a good dream you either keep it to yourself or tell someone of higher caste. Because of this, women would queue up to tell me their good dreams, while the unfortunate untouchable women would become offended by always being told bad dreams.

When a woman had a good dream she might interpret, "Ahah, today some news will come for me" or "My husband [or "my poor mother"] still remembers me, it seems." Hiccups were interpreted in a similar way, with the woman consoling herself, saying, "At least I am remembered." But if the throat tickled it meant someone was being critical of you. "Whoever it is, why are you talking of me? Oh! May you also be in trouble and know how difficult it is here," the afflicted woman would curse.

Before a woman received news from her natal home, it was believed, a crow would perch above her cell and caw to warn her. "Oh! The crow cawed this morning," the woman would let others know. "Maybe my mother or father is dead. Or my little boy? What could have happened?" Within days the police would inform her of the message.

"My sole is itching and throbbing. Someone will come," another woman would say. And a visitor would come.

They had no other communication with the outside world. Nothing except dreams, cawing of crows, itching soles, or eyelids flickering with intuition. Older people at home had taught me all these phenomena, but it was in jail that I first came to believe in their validity.

೧೧

At ten-thirty the *gurumaas*, female teachers, would arrive. The women's prison had two little cottage industry units—hosiery and knitting—and the teachers were assigned to the prison by His Majesty's government's Cottage Industry Department after many demands by female political prisoners. The *gurumaas* were supposed to arrive at ten, which was the HMG office hour, but as they first had to sign the register at their own office, by the time they reached the jail it was sometimes as late as eleven.

They were supposed to stay until five, but, because inmates had to eat by four, the *Chaukidarni* would start disturbing their class from three "tangs" onward, scolding any trainees, "You can't just sit there knitting. You must go and cook." Also, if the teachers had stayed until five they would have witnessed the feeding and ill treatment of the *pagal*. So they had to leave by three-thirty. Subtracting the half hour or more when they left to buy their midday snack, they ended working a three-hour day, which was not unusual in government.

The cottage industry activity was a production and training program, but as with everything in jail, and in the rest of the kingdom, participation was rationed arbitrarily and production was mismanaged. Trainees were selected through a nepotistic political process in which *gurumaas* had no say at all. All they were instructed to do was to teach whomever was sent. The trainees earned a wage of fifteen rupees a month for producing sweaters and gloves and the like, and for sewing and tailoring. There were two knitting machines on which two or three women worked each day. They could knit and hand-finish two sweaters in that time worth at least twenty rupees in total. In theory, revenue above the exploitative wage returned to the department. But much of their production was "commissioned" privately by the police and others. Entire wedding outfits would be sewn for free.

The *gurumaas'* presence was a limited, positive force. On the positive side, a few women learned and earned something, although many prison women were very skilled already in carpet weaving and other occupations. But the problem was that the *gurumaas* also posed a threat to the criminal administration. "Whenever we set our feet inside here our hearts start racing," they once whispered to me. "Who will be hanging? Who will be bruised and beaten?" Even though most of what was done was hidden, still what they saw was awful.

As a result, the teachers were restricted to their two classrooms in the building nearest the gate and were prohibited from going anywhere else or talking to anyone. They were the eyes of the outside world, and therefore a threat, and so they were literally shut inside, the doors closed. Once after I invited the teachers for tea, I was warned very violently against this. The jailer also told me not to mix with visitors from outside. On another occasion, a teacher got into trouble with the jailer. A chained prisoner had been crying for water and the teacher had tried to give her some. It was reported, and the jailer had instructed her not to pay attention to anything she saw inside.

Ever-present *naikes* and *kamdars* acted as informants of the *Chaukidarni*. If any woman commented on the system she would be reported, and that evening after *bhajan* she would receive her "repair"—after others had left the yard and gone inside. That was when the *Chaukidarni* always ordered her crew to stay behind to be instructed on whom she had decided needed torture that night.

"Bring that one here outside, she must get treatment," she would order.

Soon painful cries would tear the stillness, sometimes for hours. More lashes. More cries. Until she was locked away with the *pagal*.

ૹ

"Everybody go inside. *Inside!* Men are about to come bringing rations! After they arrive no joking or laughing, or there'll be treatment."

Thus the *Chaukidarni* would clear the yard of women before the distribution of daily rations at midday. Except for those in the cottage industry, all had to stop their dream telling and smoking and get back in their cells. Only the *Chaukidarni* and her crew stayed in the yard. A few of us would nip behind my building to be invisible for a few minutes and continue talking. I used to join them or go to my room to keep clear of the open vulgarity between the men and the women. Without interruption the entertainment was always vulgar. Even about knitting a sweater someone would say, "How much have you completed?"

"As long as a penis," would come the reply from whoever was knitting.

"No, just a *puti*," another would joke, mentioning the female organ.

"Bring it out, bring it out! Let us see how much you've done," a policeman would suggest.

"Okay, give me some rupees and I'll lift my sari."

It was their greatest time to entertain themselves. There was nothing else for them, and so I never gave them a disapproving look. But they would be as embarrassed as I was if they realized I had overheard. The male police and the *Chaukidarni* in particular would turn red.

To distribute the rations, six men would enter. Two male police officers, the Central Prison or Bhadragol *Chaukidar*, at least two male *naikes*, and a jail office clerk. Ration distribution was the sole opportunity for relations between male and female inmates. Therefore, so as to maximize time for talking and joking, it would be drawn out into a very slow, two-hour exercise. The only females there would be the *Chaukidarni*, the *Mulnaike*, and one or two *kamdars* and *naikes* selected for that day. The rest of the crew had to hang around in the wings just in case the *Chaukidarni* shouted out, "*Kamdar!*"

"Yes, ma'am, yes!" one would say, running.

"That *pagal*, take her out of the way and tie her up," the *Chaukidarni* would command suddenly, and then resume her roll call by instructing the *Mulnaike*, who would tell the *kamdar* to shout out the name of a room *naike*.

Whichever room's *naike* had been summoned would report back. Then the *kamdars* and public of that room would be called one by one. "Eh! Kali! Eh! Kanchhi's turn. . . ."

One male *naike* would dispense the white rice, and the other the gray parboiled rice. As soon as the men had measured the miserable rice and fifty *paisa* into a woman's plate she would place it on the ground and *namaste* first the *naike* and then all the other men—the customary Nepali way of showing gratitude. All the time the men and women would be talking filth, and the policemen would be enjoying viewing each woman, their eyes on the lookout for any lunatic women who were not fully clothed.

The women would then take their rations to their rooms and come out again. The *Chaukidarni* would usually be too absorbed in the gossip to notice what was going on. Gradually a small crowd of amused women would build up to look at the men and listen to the unrepeatable conversation.

"All you women, why have you come back? As if you never saw a man's face before! Clear out!" the *Chaukidarni* would eventually react. And the women would disperse.

From their ration the women were supposed to buy *dal*, vegetables, oil, firewood, soap, matches, cooking utensils, their clay pot, and anything else that a woman might need. And what they could save paid for their lawyer. All this was possible only through starvation. Outside prison, fifty *paisa* would not even buy a cup of tea. Perhaps half a little glass of tea. When the police did the women's shopping they would charge them double, so their fifty *paisa* was devalued to perhaps twenty-five. The police could not afford to be honest. Sometimes a criminal would ask, "Are things so expensive?" But this was like baiting a tiger. The policewoman would jump on such a woman, grabbing her braided hair tightly behind the head, and shout aggressively, "You fucking father's daughter. Do you think I ate your money?"

All the petrified prisoner could do was seek an apology. If she was one of the public, she would be a victim of torture that evening.

The morning meal had to be eaten by eight, and the evening meal by four. Although no one had a watch or a clock, we could tell the time from the "tangs" from the barracks. As soon as we heard three "tangs" in the afternoon we would rush to our rooms to cook. After eating, you quickly cleaned your *chulo* with mud and cow dung supplied by the police every now and then.

At one "tang" after four "tangs" everybody had to leave their cells to wash up the utensils. Everybody had the same utensils, which they had purchased from blacksmiths in the male jail. A small rice pan, a frying pan three to four inches in diameter, an aluminum plate, and a rice ladle—that was it. There was no soap powder or liquid. Prison routines were those of village Nepal. The women would scour their pans with ash and mud, then rinse them with a trickle of water. If the rice had burned, the pan would be scoured with some precious charcoal from the fire. The room *naike*'s duty at this time was to report anyone to the *Chaukidarni* who failed to do her chores on time. The penalty was "massage." If somebody felt too ill to eat she would have to say so in advance.

From four-thirty to five P.M. was a sort of time-out. Inmates could entertain themselves, even talk aloud and joke. Some walked up and down in pairs. It was a strange moment in each day. You lived in fear, terrorized for twenty-three and a half hours. Then for half an hour it was turned off. You couldn't really relax or forget. You were too deep to swim to the surface, only to have to plunge again. This was the emotion in the lyrics women sang. Someone always brought out a small drum, and together they would harmonize in their nostalgia, one woman's voice talking to God, the others behind her in chorus and dance.

> *Our childhood we spent playing,*
> *To government we sacrificed our youth;*
> *What will we do*
> *If we are free when we are old?*

> *I'm at my last breath*
> *To hear your voice,*
> *And you my voice.*
> *There are high high walls*
> *If you hear, come and save me.*

> *All the lucky women were taken by the train;*
> *We unfortunate were brought back on the truck.*

> *Let us forget what happened to us, everything,*
> *A new road let us make,*
> *Where we can walk freely, making new dust.*

The lucky ones from their villages had married men working in India. How happy to go by train, they thought. But these women had not married and had stayed behind, unlucky. There were many, many songs, including some recalling Rana times and some Nepali Congress songs singing of democratic hope.

As in the past I sang with them or played the drum. Lunatics sitting in chains on the steps would watch and jiggle any part that was free. Deep within the foul cells their faces lit with joy and longing.

"Would you like to dance and sing?" I asked them one day.

"Oh, yes, if we could."

I asked the *Chaukidarni* to allow them.

"Oh, yeah! Maybe you want to turn this whole place into a *Pagal Rajya* [a kingdom of the insane]," was her reply.

Some weeks later she relented and allowed some women whom she considered to be less insane to participate in the music once a month. A *naike* would give orders as to who could or could not come out. Doors were opened wide for the others so that they could watch. As we made music in the yard, the women who remained in those stinking holes achieved their own wild experience of freedom and union. And the "lunatics" who came out danced the most brilliantly of all.

At five sharp it all stopped.

"Everybody to rooms!" one of the *naikes* would shout.

Room *naikes* and *kamdars* would make sure everybody was in their correct room, and would order them to stay inside until the *Chaukidarni* gave the order to come out. Then all the crew would report in front of the *Chaukidarni*'s room. *Kamdars* would start counting the lunatics. All *naikes* would shift around the corner to the main gate to take a peep at the male police officers outside. This was the time when the police guard changed and the women might catch a view of the men leaving their barrack room across the gully zipping up their trousers as they dressed for the night shift.

At five twenty-five policewomen would arrive at the gate in preparation for the night shift. The day guard would hand over duty to them. As the new guards took up their positions sitting just inside the gate the "tang" for five-thirty would sound, and the *Chaukidarni* would shout, "Eh! All *naike* and *kamdar*, didn't you hear the time? Get going and lock the *pagal* and see if anybody else needs to be chained tonight."

They would rush about as if they might receive some award, and count all the lunatics again. And, perhaps to please the *Chaukidarni*, they would always find one or two who needed to be chained.

"This one was a little stubborn, not agreeing with what was said," one might report.

The *Chaukidarni* would bustle into her room with authority and return with some handcuffs or chains. Handing the instruments to the *kamdar*, she would announce, "I'm going to the gate to see what those police girls are doing. If anything else comes up you call me."

This would be the moment when the five girls from the *pagal* cell in the *Chaukidarni's* block would make a last-minute request to go and pee. *"Tah! lagan ko belaa hagan*. What were you doing till now?" the *naike* in charge would mock, using a Nepali proverb. Literally, it meant "the moment of marriage, and you want to crap." Sometimes they might be permitted to go. Other times their request would be refused, so they would have to go for thirteen and a half hours without peeing. The other lunatics lived and slept in a toilet.

*Bhajan* time at six P.M. was my most treasured time. Everyone closed their eyes. Hands would be together in front of mouths in *namaste* to God, in readiness for fifteen minutes of mental peace and perhaps transcendence. And the chanting of the *bhajan* prayer, in less-than-perfect Sanskrit, would begin. Spontaneously a different woman would lead the chanting each night. Usually she would be higher caste. The tribal women could barely follow the words and would murmur *"Na na na na."* But, however obscure its meaning might have been to them, all women learned the prayer in some fashion within a week of arrival.

The program included shorter *bhajans* of Radha, Krishna, and Ram, including the *"Hare Krishna Hare Ram"* *bhajan*. But the main *bhajan* was a prayer to Narayan, another name for Vishnu the Protector. Its message was the oneness of Hindu deity, how God had been reborn again and again as Ram, Krishna, Buddha, and other different incarnations to protect the good and to punish evildoers. For the prison women, it was a reassurance. God protected where no human offered protection, and invoking the ideal virtues of these deities would burn up the *karma* of past actions and purify the inmate from the stigma of prison hell.

All the women wanted to be at the prayers. Some, perhaps, because torture would reward those who were absent. Each day, for those few precious moments, the rulers and the ruled within the prison became one, bonded together in a shared synergy. Few eyes remained dry. All felt the same wounds. Women became one in awe of *dharma*, the expression of sacred ritual that enables one to perform one's righteous duty and to escape the punishment of past *karma*. Through this *bhajan*, the two meanings of *dharma* came together: *dharma* as personal duty and *dharma* as sacred action. Minds transcended the daily struggle and were momentarily transformed.

After finishing the prayer some woman would lead the praises, others

shouting the chorus: *"Panchayat ki Jaya, Sri Pach Maharaj Dhiraj ki Jaya"*—
"Victory to Panchayat, Victory to His Fivefold Majesty." And the *bhajan*
program would be over.

*"Namaskar Durga didi. Namaskar Chaukidarni didi. Namaskar Mulnaike
didi. Namaskar hei mitini. Sabailaai namaskar. . . ."* For five minutes this gentle hubbub went on as every one of eighty women saluted each other by
rank and by name, each calling out in a voice a little above the other, turning around where they sat if necessary to greet those behind them. The little *pagal* girls would call out from their locked cell, "Hey! Our greetings also,
Durga *didi, Chaukidarni didi*, and all."

After the ritual one evening during this first week I gave public expression to my views: "You know why I am here? Because I opposed the Panchayat system. If, even here in jail, you all shout victory to Panchayat then
I do not want to come to this *bhajan* again."

Several women asked excitedly, "What to say in its place then?"

I suggested *"Pashupatinath ki Jaya"*—"Victory to Lord Shiva."

The *Chaukidarni* immediately approved this radical change, and from the
next day there was no more *"Panchayat ki Jaya."* Women flooded over to
me, nodding. "Because of that Panchayat we became victims here in jail.
We never wanted to call its victory, but we could not say anything for fear
of trouble. Thank you." The police must not have understood the significance of this change, or else they did not oppose it or report it, because no
negative response came back to us from the jailer or the inspector.

As soon as the *bhajan* was finished, the *Chaukidarni* would order, "All public, go to your own rooms! And no going to others' rooms and chatting."

Everybody would rush to the toilet holes for their last chance. I would
go as well to avoid having to get permission later from the night duty *kamdars*. Then each woman returned to her cell, worn down by another day,
maybe hungry, maybe beaten, feeling dirty, perhaps sick. More than anything in the world she might long for a peaceful sleep. Not in her own
home, next to a loved one, or with her child. That would have been dreaming. A cave would do, or bare ground. Anywhere, alone and undisturbed.
For here in jail there was no refuge, no escape, no curling under your quilt
or covering your eyes from the shadeless bulb that shone all night long. No
relief from torment. Only the mad had no light bulb. Perhaps they had
peace in there. For us, night terror had begun, too terrifying even for the
police to handle alone. While they slept, criminals did the guarding. It was
frightening to walk about the jail at night. The *Chaukidarni* would announce the duties. One *naike* and two *kamdars* would be on duty throughout the dark hours.

Out of the stillness one would hear an eerie call: *"Khabardar, khabardar."* Every minute between the hours of seven P.M. and four A.M. the criminal guards would call out this eerie chant.

*"Khabardar, khabardar,"* the mild feminine voices would call. Literally it meant, "Beware, beware." But it was more than some warning that they were on duty, awake themselves. It felt more like an appeal to some spirit force to lighten the fear, some strong hand to ward off danger. And as if to answer each appeal, from across two walls in Central Men's Prison, a distant male voice would echo, *"Khabardar, khabardar,"* and then again a more faint *"Khabardar, khabardar"* would follow from Bhadragol Prison, over a hundred yards away. The male voices were harsher, but at times their pitch would vary as if to code a meaning. "Beware, beware. Careful, careful," went the gentle duet, like a love song cloaked in torment. A bleak romance.

# 9.

# Where the King Could Be Cursed

It was eleven in the morning, December. The muddy yard outside was still frosted as occasional sunshine broke through Kathmandu's morning fog. Most of us were huddled inside in the traces of warmth from our extinguished cooking fires. A few last wisps of damp wood smoke drifted from the cell windows across the compound. Suddenly everybody sensed that it was less cold outside, and our little public yard filled. All were aching for fresh air, some warming sun, and to stretch their limbs.

"Eh! *Bahulai, bahulai,*" a woman guard yelled from the gate, using the derogatory Nepali for "lunatic."

"Heh, *Mulnaike, kamdars,* all of you be ready. It seems a 'lunatic' has been brought in!" the *Chaukidarni* responded with importance, shouting at the top of her voice and striding roughly the few yards from her room to the gate. Her summoned crew ran shouting to the gate like tigers to a goat.

"Well now, you have brought one early today," the *Chaukidarni* commented.

"Tah, you fucker, take in your old mother!" the guard ordered savagely, shoving a bewildered woman into the pack.

The *Chaukidarni* was unmoved by the rudeness addressed to her, and simply shifted it to her crew. "What are you farting around here for? Move quickly and take this lunatic to her place!"

Pushing, poking, piercing, tugging her hair, pinching her cheeks, slapping her face, the pack hustled the "lunatic" into the compound. I caught sight of her. She was a nicely dressed village woman in her early twenties, but her face was drawn and had a lost and wounded look. She seemed in deep shock.

"Hey, hey! Today our snack has come!" the pack was chanting. "Oh, but so thin, it won't be enough." They mocked her slight build.

"But her breasts are looking big, aren't they!" Her sari blouse had wet patches from her leaking milk.

"There's a little son or daughter, isn't there?"

They fired questions too fast for any reply.

"Sit there! That is your place." The *Chaukidarni* shot an order in lowest Nepali, pointing at a spot of ground in front of the lunatics' cells.

The *Mulnaike* stood vacantly expecting the next directive. She was a quieter, slight-statured, handsome Chhetrini woman, adorned with ornaments, bright red bangles, heavy gold traditionally embossed earrings, and a nose ring. Her upright form spoke of a good family. Raped by her father-in-law, she was serving a life imprisonment term, like many other women, for abortion.

"Why are you staring at this lunatic like a mute looking at a banana?" the *Chaukidarni* shouted at her with deliberate vulgar emphasis. "Choose some suitable *naikes* and *kamdars* for her treatment." The *Chaukidarni* looked down at the new arrival and continued. "This one looks quite thin. Maybe two and four will do."

There were some prison-made tin plates lying on the ground near the torture spot where some *kamdar* had washed them after feeding the lunatics. The *Mulnaike* picked up one and banged it dramatically, as if to call order in some great hall, and ordered all *naikes* and *kamdars* to be present. They were all right around her already but, to show their presence, jostled and reshuffled themselves without actually moving anywhere.

"Now, you *naikes* and *kamdars*," the *Mulnaike* tried to order with authority, pointing at two *naikes* and four *kamdars* in turn and calling their names. "It's your duty; do your work."

Looking at other criminal inmates, she issued another command: "All public go to your own rooms. All others be somewhere in case we need you here." The public dispersed. The *Mulnaike* came up to me and spoke more softly. "*Bahini* [little sister], this kind of thing should not be seen by you; it's dirty work. You should go to your own room."

Being one of the public, I too returned to my cell. But from my window I could see everything.

The little yard became almost empty. But as the crowd melted away, in front of the lunatic shed the half dozen shackled and almost naked lunatics remained. One had a deep gash across her forehead that a *kamdar* had inflicted with an iron rice ladle during her most recent weekly treatment day. Under the rags worn by a thick-faced fifty-year-old woman an awful bloody and dirty mass of flesh the size of a giant mango hung crudely—an inverted uterus or cystocele condition.

The *Chaukidarni* was now sitting back on her doorstep nearby, drawing heavily on a cigarette. "Hey, those *pagal*, what are they still doing watching around here?" The *Mulnaike* jumped to the order, grabbing a long stick. Holding parts of each others' bodies, tumbling over one another, the half-naked women were herded back into their cells. *Kamdars* locked their cells from the outside.

The new woman appeared already worn with exhaustion but looked around. Then, with almost normal curiosity, she smiled weakly and asked simply, "Why are these women naked here?"

The *Mulnaike* laughed. "Wait, wait. Now your turn will come and you'll know why they are naked."

From the tiny window in my cell, I watched the six on duty ready themselves, tying up their braided hair and smartening their bright traditional quilted muslin blouses. Those wearing *lungis* hurriedly tightened them. Others with saris pulled them up above their knees, tucking the folds into their waist strings. Some came equipped. The *Mulnaike* ordered "Start!" Our three women police guards, dressed in smart khaki saris and coats, and blue berets, paced up and down, passing between the naked shackled *pagal*, preparing to watch all that occurred.

The newcomer was still sitting where she had been ordered. Madu, a *kamdar*, marched around her. "Get up!" she ordered rudely, physically pulling at her. "Eeh, it seems this is like a little bird, so light."

Others started pulling at her sari. The new woman resisted, pulling it back and trying to keep it properly in place. The *Chaukidarni* had already begun her usual practice of calling out orders from her doorstep. Now she addressed the woman using vulgar words: "What's this, feeling shy? You wait. We'll pull all the hair from between your thighs and you'll know how shy you can be!"

The group overcame her hopeless attempts at defense and unwound her sari, then tore off her petticoat. There was nothing left underneath. Her blouse had press studs, so it came off in one pull. No bra. She became nude very quickly. She tried vainly to hide her breasts and pubic area but others pulled at her arms. I could see her trying to cry though the tears and even deep sobs would not break out.

Two *kamdars* started pouring cold water over her from head to toe with a food bowl, decanting from a large clay pot that had been brought over. The others joined in with handfuls of fiercely potent nettles tied with rags, and commenced the beating. The woman was kicked, beaten, and slapped in every part of her naked body. As the treatment got under way, the group started laughing as if at a fair and shouting rhythmically, "This is what you've come here to eat! Uh! Eh! Uh! Uh!"

"Aha, that's right. Do like that. Yes. Pull harder like that," the *Chaukidarni* kept calling out. Once in a while she leapt up at a *kamdar* who she thought was not performing properly. "Put the nettle water in the proper place. I'll do it to you if you can't do it to her, and then you'll know how to do it!"

Before lashing with the nettles, they dipped them into the freezing water. This made them sting like lime squeezed in a fresh cut. Very soon a frightening rash blistered up red all over the new woman's body.

From one of the criminal cells near me somebody murmured, "Poor woman, who might she be?" The *Chaukidarni* overheard and recognized the quiet voice. She marched over and pulled the woman out into the yard by her hair, throwing her down in front of the bruised, naked newcomer. "That's your old mother! Go on, bow down, bow down at her feet then!"

The quiet voice pleaded for forgiveness, "Excuse me, *didi*, from now on I will never say anything like that again."

The others were still beating and pouring cold water over the "lunatic." Her cry could still not break out properly. She just sobbed with stifled sounds.

I had moved back outside and could hold back no longer. I had not witnessed this ritual before in daylight. Other sessions had always been in the evenings, after lockup, and I had only heard the screams and cries.

"At least spare her life," I called out.

The *Mulnaike* came over to me. "Sister," she said, "do not be around here. These are all filthy women. You should stay far from this. It does not suit you to take the side of any of them."

I could not say anything, and returned again to my room. I had learned already it was dangerous to confront the *Chaukidarni*, particularly in front of others. She had the license to kill within the prison. Even the jailer had warned me not to intervene.

For several hours the new woman lay naked, dirty, and bloodstained on the ground, her awful nettle blisters and bruises turning from harsh red to blue. Every now and then a *kamdar* would go close, uttering some nasty remark to the near-lifeless body: "You must do what we say after coming here.

Whatever the jail rules are, you must follow them." Finally, after everyone else had eaten the evening meal, the *kamdars* dragged her, still naked and unconscious, to the wide step in front of the lunatic cells. There they raised her up and handcuffed her wrists to the projecting beam under the eaves of the corrugated iron roof that was reserved for this torture. Her ankles were chained, one to an iron wheel, the other to a heavy bell-shaped weight. Bent forward, spread-eagled like a collapsed X, the woman was left hanging from her wrists all that night.

The next morning at six-thirty as I went to rinse my face at the tap, I stared silently at her dreadful-looking body. The *Chaukidarni* was sipping tea noisily through her lips, but caught my mood and ordered some *kamdars* to unchain her. She fell unconscious onto the dirt. "It seems this woman has hysteria," the *Chaukidarni* said to a nearby policewoman, using the English word she had heard in prison and trying to wake her up by teasing one of the unconscious woman's soles with one of the previous day's nettles.

"Eeh, up, up, up!" she tried to command.

The woman did not stir. "After the sun's higher her brain will also warm up and she'll get up," she concluded.

By eight o'clock I had finished eating, and resumed knitting a sweater in front of the *Chaukidarni*'s doorstep.

Two hours passed. At ten o'clock the woman stirred and opened her eyes. I stopped knitting and went over to help her sit up. A *kamdar* noticed and brought back her clothes. She stared at them, expressionless, for some minutes and looked at herself. Her body was red and swollen. A little blood still seeped from one corner of her mouth, or perhaps from her cracked lips. Weakly, with repeated little hand movements, she slowly spread some folds of her sari over her front. As she did so water started welling in her eyes until it overflowed nonstop down her face.

I went in to the *Chaukidarni*. "Can I give her a glass of tea?" I asked. The *Chaukidarni* replied with angry sarcasm, "Why only tea? Give her a full meal then!"

While walking across to my room I heard the *Chaukidarni* tormenting the woman: "Listen, you fucking woman, this is not the place to cry."

I took a glass of tea.

After sipping tea the woman slowly examined her battered body and wrapped herself loosely in her sari. The *Chaukidarni* came over to her. "Look, this is a prison, you have to live here." She pointed at a grimy little doorway just behind them and continued, "Your room is that one there. There are seventeen other *pagal* just like you in there. After going in you shouldn't quarrel with them. You must stay nicely together."

Gradually the woman raised herself onto her knees and crawled painfully through the doorway into the darkness. She lay down on the damp, stinking ground and curled up for warmth and so that her feet kept distance from the hole in the center of the cramped floor area, soiled with excrement. Around her, her mostly naked roommates scratched at their skin with long black fingernails. She slept all through that day.

Her name was Juki, she told me later. She was the mother of two children—a two-year-old son and a daughter of six months. She used to milk the four cows she and her husband had on their small farm just north of Kathmandu. He used to go around selling the milk on his bicycle. Like most of the prisoners this woman was innocent of any crime. She was in jail because her husband had bribed his police friends to send her away as a lunatic because he wanted to marry another woman.

Juki's brutal initiation was a kind of rite of passage. It was meted out on most newcomers and served as a physical and symbolic preparation for the jail's organizational culture. This was a culture where anarchy, subjugation, arbitrary justice, and inhumanity prevailed, one where pain and torment had to be borne without feeling. Only some of the underage girls who had been illegally imprisoned and the elderly women escaped the worst forms of jail initiation. Most of my companions were like Juki and had committed no crimes. Surely, there could be no more tragic violation of human rights in the world than the suffering of these women, tortured as they were from the very beginning of their victimization at the hands of the police outside to the point of their incarceration in this prison. But throwing them into jail on alleged criminal charges or as lunatics was not the end of their torture.

To be in prison in Nepal was not merely a question of serving out a sentence. By being inside long enough to understand the system of criminal rule I came to realize that with the sentence began a life of torture—mental and physical. Again, this was not just the torture that a person feels by being in prison, shut away from her normal world. It was worse than that. On a daily basis she would receive torture at the hands of the criminal inmates. Many times I struggled to reach some explanation for the regime of torture in this dumping ground for the unwanted. The Brahmin widows used to say that their torturers were in the hell of prison, so they were behaving like Yama Raj, the God of Death. I concluded too that the prisoners drawn into the criminal administration were those who had lost consciousness. The effect on many of these women was to produce not realization of any criminal misdeed, but rather minds full of revenge—minds that could fall from higher consciousness into a game of survival of the fittest. In this, they came to reflect the servants of the Panchayat state who had victimized them and sent these women to prison according to their own vengeful intentions.

The prison hell experience did not pull everyone down. A very few did not participate in the game. They were the greatest sufferers physically, but spiritually were the most purified by this hell, and their consciousness became highly sharpened. In many women the hell experience also produced a burning political consciousness in opposition to Panchayat rule. Previously these women had posed no threat. But having been made victims, locked up, and tortured, they ended up cursing their rulers. Throughout the duration of their sentences, constantly, every day and every night, innocent women cried against the lawmakers of the kingdom. I viewed their suffering as a kind of *tapasya*, or austerity, whose influence would destroy evildoers, and liked to think that the power of their curses would inevitably bring bad luck on our rulers and lead to their ultimate downfall. In this way I used to think that on a collective level these women too were our martyrs, living death every day, some actually dying, to kill the autocratic system.

Jail was institutionalized torture. Petty injustice and torture formed the rules and regulations under which women lived on an everyday level. Their object was to maintain a regime of unconsciousness, compliance, mindlessness, and inhumanity. In this state, no display of conscious personality, no normal human feeling, and no interpersonal relationship could develop in either direction—affectionate or aggressive. There could be neither closeness nor enmity. No one could laugh loudly, or the reaction would come immediately: "What happened then? Why so happy? You'll be next for treatment. . . ." Neither could anyone be seen crying, or she would be assailed with "Who died then? Who told you? Come on now, has your husband died? Your father died? Your mother? Why, why?"

It is difficult to imagine how human beings, especially two women, could live near to each other in neither closeness nor distance. If two women talked together two or three days continuously, that was closeness. In the same way, if they did not say anything to each other for two or three days then that was enmity. Someone, anyone, could notice and report, and treatment would follow. Gala did not talk to one of her roommates for three days and was fed sewage from the toilet. Madu and Desa were roommates who had become close friends. For this they were both beaten with nettles and transferred to different rooms to be separated. Ruse talked to her friend aloud, so a male *naike* was brought to give her a sleeping injection. She did not wake up for forty-eight hours.

No warmth was allowed. In winter, even if one woman had no mattress or quilt and accidentally in her sleep became partially covered by the quilt of the woman lying next to her, the night guards would wake both women and separate them straightaway, warning them not to sleep close together. Because of congestion on the floor it was hard for the women's bodies not to touch. And in Nepali society it is very normal for women to share a bed together, as if sisters.

One day Chasa asked Kasa if she had seen her missing potato. Spies immediately reported her question to the *Chaukidarni*, who ordered a *kamdar* to present Kasa before her. The *Chaukidarni* was not interested in hearing what Kasa had to say. She had stolen a potato so *kamdars* were ordered to "repair" her. In a minute they stripped her naked, blackened her face with charcoal and oil, and locked her in a lunatic cell for twenty-four hours. Kasa had a ten-month-old baby that was still breast-fed. It cried the whole day and night, separated from its mother, left with another woman.

So it went on. Jaade was chained to an iron wheel and left outside on the ground one December night because she cried while remembering her six-year-old daughter back home. Kaga did not obey the *Chaukidarni*. Therefore all her pubic hair was scorched off by pouring hot ash over her genital area. Sau was handcuffed and her feet padlocked to the big iron bells and wheels on the ground and left there spread-eagled all night. Sau's misdeed was to tell a doctor that they were thin because they did not get enough to eat. That was the only doctor's visit during that whole year, and, because of its outcome for Sau, I regretted later that it had been arranged by the jailer at my request.

Initially, I found it very difficult to tolerate this inhumanity. I began thinking that if I saw these events every day and night I would go mad, and if I became mad I knew where I would be kept. From my room I could see the whole yard, everything that went on. I wondered if the government had put me there intentionally. One of my visitors told me that the zonal commissioner had already spread a rumor around Kathmandu that I had gone crazy in prison. He was even telling people, "She might have been crazy before her arrest, but she is worse now and needs to go through treatment." I thanked my Lord Ganesh that my daily meditation was keeping me from madness even amid all the horror.

After about two months, I made up my mind that torture was the routine of daily life in the prison. It was not that I no longer felt abhorrence, because nobody deserved such cruelty. Yet after witnessing the horror repeatedly, my own realization grew that I was living in the same water and had better not confront the crocodile. In this netherworld, one had few choices: Keep clear of the system and survive. Slide into lunacy. Or rebel and die. So I tried to live the way they did by following all the jail rules. Other political prisoners came for a week or two every now and then, during periods of student unrest, and used to disregard the criminal administration. For example, they would not ask the night guards' permission to go and pee after six P.M. I always did. I tried constantly to unite the women. They bore the same wounds. All were victims in some respect.

The most common mild form of punishment was to be locked up with the lunatics for twenty-four to forty-eight hours. It could happen for any reason, just through the whim of a police guard, the *Chaukidarni* herself, the *Mulnaike*, a *naike*, or even a *kamdar* with the *Chaukidarni's* approval. Once some leftist college students were with us for a week and started complaining about the conditions. The *Chaukidarni* ordered them to be locked up. I begged her not to do it, convincing her that they were just young city girls who did not know much. She was not happy with my interfering, but withdrew her directive. "It is *Netaji's* order that you cannot lock up these queens," as she put it.

Because the girls were there on political charges I was instructed not to talk to them. However, I took a chance to communicate with one, advising her that they should live quietly or face trouble. They soon went away anyway. Afterward the *Chaukidarni* held a meeting with her crew, declaring that in future when other girls were brought they would be subject to the same rules as others or be punished as others. "It seems our *Netaji* is not going to be released soon. Therefore from now on whoever political comes, *netaji na setaji*, let us not think any longer that she is here. Things must be done according to our jail law. That is my decision," announced the *Chaukidarni*, referring derogatorily to me.

More severe torture was practiced with regularity, keeping us all in quiet terror of the crocodile. One of the crudest practices was to force a rough stick into a woman's vagina. I feel like fainting even to remember seeing this done. This, as well as heavy beating, may have been why so many of the women suffered from inverted uterus, cystocele, and rectocele conditions, as the wall of their vaginas must have been torn by this treatment. And as if this was not enough, these very protrusions would be beaten sometimes, causing the women acute agony and bleeding.

Another sensitive area attacked was the nipples, through insertion of needles. And needle insertion under the fingernails was also practiced, as learned from police custody. Women were hung upside down by their ankles from the torture beams. And vicious beating was just ordinary, five on one.

One day I saw a police guard holding a woman's head from behind by the scruff of her neck and thrusting her mouth into a pile of excrement. The Pode caste woman had been ordered to bring the excrement to the yard for this purpose from the toilet.

After witnessing what happened to innocent Juki, I determined to see the jailer. I wrote three request letters, sending them through the women police guards inside and the outside male police. One day in early January I received the news that he would see me. Two women guards and the *Chaukidarni* came to my room to call me.

I went over to the main gate and stepped out through the little doorway with the two women guards. The *Chaukidarni* remained inside. A Russian-made military jeep was parked there. The customary two policewomen and five armed policemen were waiting for me in the back. I was bundled inside the cramped canvas canopy with them, facing backward and unable to see anything. After halting minutes later, the police unhooked the jeep's tailgate for me. I stepped out. I was surrounded by grim, high-walled buildings. On my right was the entrance gate to the Men's Central Prison. Ahead was the low gate of Bhadragol Jail, where the regime dumped for severest punishment those it most wanted to get rid of. *Bhadragol's* literal meaning was "chaos." Experienced opposition friends said it was a fitting name for one of the worst jails in the kingdom.

To the left was the gate of the military barracks. Seeing the armed military stationed next door I felt anew how easily the military could be used if the regime wanted to reinforce the police to quell any prison rebellion. They could butcher everybody if they wanted to. I shuddered as I do when passing a butcher's shop. I too was a prisoner.

The police escorted me as I climbed the narrow flight of steps up to the jailer's first-floor office entrance. It was a small old building tacked onto the men's prison wall. From there the jailer could view his microcosmic kingdom.

"*Namaskar, namaskar,*" his staff greeted me respectfully, standing up as I entered. "*Jailer-saheb* is inside there." I walked across a threadbare jute carpet that was almost indistinguishable from the mud floor of the clerks' office. At the far end there was a very grubby green curtain in the doorway into the second, even smaller room, which was the jailer's. I entered. He was dressed in Western clothes—shortsleeved shirt and trousers—but, to keep national dress alive, he was wearing a Nepali *topi* (hat). He looked pleasant enough, a typical gazetted third-class officer, a bureaucrat with a noticeable paunch.

The jailer invited me toward a rough-hewn wooden chair with ringed tea glass stains on its flat arms. Smiling a little awkwardly, he offered me a glass of lime tea. I took it and placed it on one of the rings on my chair arm as he said to me, "You look quite okay really."

"What did you expect, that I might have died or be about to die?" I replied, unable to keep myself from expressing everything that was on my mind. Then I backed off a little. "I do not know how long you can talk to me. I have come about a case from inside. Throwing these women in prison was enough. Why so much torture also? I cannot go on seeing all these kinds of behavior. Anyone could go crazy in there."

The jailer was polite. "Oh, don't worry about time. Tell me then. What is the problem?"

I thought for a second. Had he not understood? What was *not* a problem? But before I could begin he did, perhaps sensing the horrors that I could not express. He knew the problems well. "With you being here, I have become so relieved," he offered.

But I was in no mood for wasting time. "Don't joke," I said. "There are so many serious matters. I am sure you can do something."

"I will try. What are they?"

I described Juki's treatment to him, and related her story and then, with almost mad hope, challenged him: "Why not do something to get her released? What could the procedure be?"

His initial reply brought me back to earth, as I might have expected. "It is very easy to bring a lunatic here. But anyone brought here in a lunatic case is very difficult to take out. There has to be a guardian. They can only be taken away if some family member comes and takes responsibility for anything that happens afterwards. Besides, all these women here make some kind of excuse."

I tried again. "She said her husband bribed the local police. Why not get other police to go and interrogate him and get him to admit that he bribed. He lives right close by here. That would prove she's not a lunatic."

"Pokhrelji, you know that could never happen, no matter how much you are depressed by her story. To do that I would have to request up to the CDO. The district would have to request the zonal administration because only they could ask the DSP to place an order on the local police or send detectives to investigate. I have no authority to make all this happen. I don't think it possibly could happen because nothing like that ever did before. There is no regulation for such a procedure, and the channels are so complicated."

I tried once more. "I had a dream it will happen, so please try because she is the wrong person to come to prison." In fact, it was true. I had had this dream.

"To make you happy I will try," he agreed.

After the jailer agreed to try for Juki's release I spoke on. For a quarter of an hour I briefed him on everything I could think of that was abnormal about the prison. I became quite emotional, and found myself forcing back tears as I appealed to him. "Torture is too much on everyone, and the condition of the *pagal* is inhuman. Their rooms are like a sewer. Those chained or hung the whole night scream and cry. I cannot bear listening to it any longer."

"Oh, but all that is just normal," he said routinely. "But anyway, about the lunatics' rooms—I will see whether I can send some disinfectant spray."

With his *topi* cap tilted low and rather inanely over his forehead, he glanced from side to side, then uttered the practiced laugh of the system. "What to do, Pokhrelji. The Home Ministry does not sanction a budget for doing anything. Jail is last priority. With no funds I can't change anything, and I can't do more than what I am told by the ministry. If anything happens, say a prisoner escapes, I have to be substituted. All I can do is 'laash ki shaash.' "

The jailer had invoked an awful concept from Nepali law that had been lifted out of context to become the one base rule of prison administration. Literally, the expression translates as "dead or still breathing." What it meant in the prison context was that whether anyone died or survived was no one's concern. It derived from Nepali law regarding those facing the death penalty. If such a person was very ill and could not walk, execution was stayed until he could just walk, still having a little life. In running the jail, the jailer was responsible only to keep the inmates inside. If a prisoner died, then it was just a question of handing over the *laash* (dead body), if there was anyone to claim it. If not, a lowest caste Pode was called. If the victim did not die within the term of imprisonment, the jailer's responsibility was only to produce the *shaash*—still-breathing body, even if at the point of death. The jailer was not liable if prisoners suffered sickness or injury, if they lost a leg, or a hand, or an ear, or their teeth, or even if they were killed. Relatives could file no claims on the government. The jailer's sole instruction was to prevent escape.

The friendly jailer looked at his watch. "Oh, it seems it's time for you to go."

"Can I walk back? I would like to get a little exercise at least," I requested.

"No, the order is not like that. I do not have that discretion."

"But I will not try to escape. I will go sincerely back to my jail with the seven police," I tried once more.

"No, just think it is for your security," he advised. "*Namaskar* Pokhrelji."

I left feeling weak and heavyhearted. Maybe he would do something for Juki, but my only other accomplishment had been to secure perhaps one can of disinfectant. Had he ever smelled the inside of a lunatic cell, I wondered. What had I expected? I knew what he had said was true. Prison was the pits of the wretched Panchayat system, the last priority. I was glad I had not mentioned anything about the purpose of my visit to the other women. At least I had not raised any hopes.

I made the return by jeep as ordered. The jeep halted, turned awkwardly, and backed up toward my prison gate. "We've arrived," the police guard said. I stepped down again. This time the jeep had stopped a yard or two farther from the gate than usual. Windowless barrack rooms for the police guards faced each other on either side of the street. My guards were all stamping to attention, each one saluting and coughing abbreviated "Sa'b" sounds, as they did whenever they saw a higher officer. I glanced left and saw the police inspector standing in front of a tiny low doorway in an otherwise unbroken stretch of wall. I could see past him through a dim wood-beamed entranceway into a derelict little courtyard. He was the highest ranking police officer in charge of security in our jail.

He grinned impishly, and this time I recognized his clownish red face. He was a satirical comedian, famous on Nepal radio and on stage. He had a butterfly mustache that made you feel like laughing just seeing it. Seeing him in uniform, I wondered whether he really controlled his subordinates or just made them laugh.

"The house where I live is this one," he said to me, gesturing with a wink to a couple of little windows in the wall above him. From up there he could oversee the whole women's prison compound.

"If there's any emergency then maybe I can shout from the inside. Maybe you'll hear," I joked, half seriously.

"Oh sure!" said the jolly man.

As I was talking to their *hakkim*, the other policemen did not insist that I reenter my jail. He waved them away tediously, reminding me of his comic acts. What a double personality, I was thinking. How did he reconcile his odious duty with his off-duty life of humor?

Like the jailer, he too seemed to be able to read my mind. Silly eyes twinkling, he chuckled. "What to do, Pokhrelji. Have to look after your tummy. Many mouths to feed. I'm the only one earning. My wife hasn't been to school like you, eh! How are you living? I hope you are doing okay. If there's anything I should do, tell me maybe."

We said good-bye to each other: *"Namaste."* Then he ordered the jeep to leave and turned back into his little doorway. I walked a few steps and reentered the jail through its little gate.

The jailer did make the unheard-of request for Juki. Unbelievably, a report came back after two weeks. The husband admitted that he had bribed
the police to remove Juki to prison as a lunatic. "What Juki said to you was
correct," the jailer reported laconically. Though I was still imprisoned in
uncertainty myself, I felt a little inner peace.

Juki received a message that her husband had been brought to take her
back, but no longer feeling safe to go to his house, she refused to be taken
by him. "He might play another trick," she said she feared. Through the
prison police she asked the jailer to call her mother. Somehow the jailer
managed this too, and she was handed over. Juki made history and left the
lunatic cells of Central Women's Prison. I do not know what happened to
her husband. There was no one to bring any case against him, and the local
police would have remained his friends. The *Chaukidarni* might have been
worried about losing the profits from handling lunatic rations. "If *Netaji* goes
on staying here, maybe all these lunatics might go away" was her sarcastic
epilogue to Juki.

But a few days after I saw the jailer, he did also send two male *naikes* with
the promised can of disinfectant spray. Once.

જીજી

Faces peered out of the *pagal* cells. One dirty naked woman beckoned me
from within. Holding my nose, I approached the woman's doorway.

"Hey, Durga *didi*, don't go inside there! You might faint with the smell,"
cried Mara, pulling me away.

"It's okay, Mara, don't worry about me." I thanked her and looked into
the dim interior. The woman pointed to her foot. It looked about to come
off, the flesh of the leg and ankle separated by a ghastly ulcer that had probably been caused by prolonged gripping in rusty shackles.

I asked her how it happened.

"In this graveyard what does not happen?" she growled.

The only remotely health-related practice was when the *kamdars* forcefully cut the lunatic women's hair about once every two months. It was
cropped so short it might have been shaved. Women who had been
married outside would cry terribly when this was done, screaming, "My husband is alive; I will not be cut," because shaving the head symbolized wid-
owhood. Even the lunatic women were traditional and conscious enough
to know and feel this.

The woman's mud-floored cell measured about twelve by fourteen feet.
North facing and with no windows, it had no source of warmth except the
lunatics' bodies. For ventilation there was just the little Nepali doorway I
was blocking, with its pair of twelve-inch-wide wooden half doors that

closed in the middle like shutters and were locked from the outside with a little chain and padlock at the top. Because of the padlocks these lunatic cells were the only places in the jail that could be locked, and so they were used also for locking up any criminals who were in the process of being tortured.

Inside, the cell was no better than a pigsty. In Nepal pigs are traditionally given no bedding and are cleaned out rarely—unlike goats, which are housed in much cleaner conditions. Cows, being sacred, are always kept clean and are given bedding of rice straw and husk. In this woman's cell there was nothing on the floor except two or three worn and grimy straw mats. Chaba, who shared this cell, had a thin rag covering her mat. The other sixteen or seventeen lunatics lay on the bare floor, avoiding, if they were conscious of them, the two holes in the floor. Those who were of sufficiently coherent state of mind defecated through those holes onto the mountain of excrement below. The less mindful did their business anywhere in the cell. Sometimes the holes would get blocked and one of the *pagal* would be told to push through the blockage with a stick and scatter some ash—the only sanitizing substance available. After ash was sprinkled, the women used to pick up some from the floor and rub it in their sores. They used to think anything dry might cure their wounds, often applying dust even though it only aggravated them.

I had been standing in the doorway for only a few seconds. Already I noticed some fleas on my foot. The cell was jumping and crawling with parasites. Even bedbugs were so many that they were crawling out of the entrance. A few of the women had scabies as bad as any street dog, and soft white grubs wriggled in open sores resulting from scratching, beating, and shackling. I supposed they were fly larvae.

They were caged like animals, I could not help thinking, living amid their own and others' excrement. Because of profiteering by the administration, the lunatics had to fight over whatever prison-issue sari material reached them. Most of them received at best only one sari length in which to live day and night for the whole year in that filth, without ever being able to wash it. The cloth became rotten within a few months, so they had nothing left to wear.

In the beginning of my first term of imprisonment I used to feel most uncomfortable seeing so many nude women around me. In Nepal, a Hindu country, you never see nudity even among your own sex. Only during the great Hindu festival of Shivaratri, the Night of Shiva, celebrated at the end of February at the Pashupatinath temple by tens of thousands of Hindus from all over the subcontinent, you might see a few naked yogis performing austerities. Even then, one naked yogini woman was once taken by the police to prison. Otherwise, except in the private bathroom of an urban home, a woman cannot even take a bath unless she is covered from her breasts down to below her knees with a *lungi* wrap of material.

Nepal is not like America, where I went once (only!) to a swimming pool and found the changing and shower rooms full of nude women. Imagine my embarrassment when one of my Harvard professors walked over stark naked to talk to me. I was seated in my bathing costume, with a towel wrapped around me like a *lungi* on top. I could not even bring myself to look at her face, let alone see what was straight in front of me at eye level. Would one ever see one's guru like that at home? A male Nepali friend told me that American men walked around in the same way in their changing rooms. In America that was from individual choice and cultural freedom. But in this Nepali jail the nudity symbolized the negation of our cultural norms by a bestial regime.

ಞ

I remembered Shagi. She had been one of the longest jail residents on a lunacy charge. In the beginning I had not realized she was a lunatic. She was a fair, handsome woman who walked in an erect, graceful way. She wore her ragged prison sari with a kind of town sophistication even though it was now her only covering. She remained careful in some forgotten way, and concerned about her appearance, making instinctive gestures of adjusting her sari and her now-filthy, matted hair, moves reminiscent of some high-society past. But I never saw her in criminal groups, so one day I asked the *Chaukidarni* what Shagi's case was.

"She was brought as a *pagal*," replied the *Chaukidarni*.

"But she doesn't look like one," I said, showing my curiosity.

"Aah! Back then she had the most extraordinary crazy story of love," the *Chaukidarni* said, half dismissing her while yet hinting at some juicy, scandalous tale. "If you're so interested in that kind of thing there are at least four other love-lunatics in here whose romances failed."

Shagi, who had overheard, was looking at my face and smiling.

"Eh! C'm'ere then! Our *Netaji* wants to talk to you. Your lover or husband's name . . . tell her, she might know him," commanded the *Chaukidarni*, giving Shagi her chance.

"What is his name?" I asked Shagi.

Arranging her sari politely around her head, Shagi smiled coyly and revealed his name.

"Hey, I do know him!" I confirmed.

"Really! How do you know?" she asked, obviously excited.

"He was home minister a while ago." How could I not have known him?

"Oh! If he could just take me back I would go to heaven," Shagi beamed.

Shagi had been this Panchayat politician's lover. They were of the same caste, and even Shagi's family did not object once they knew. Their affair continued for eight to nine years, and was well known throughout Kathmandu high society. In Hindu custom once a person takes another in his or her mind and thinks of marriage, this means they are mentally married. If the man dies the woman will consider herself a widow. Even to think of another man would be a sin. Shagi was this kind of woman.

But the politician married someone else.

"Ours was not just a short affair," explained Shagi. "For years he said he would marry me. Finally he did not. Yet we had both accepted each other with *man* [mind], *bachhan* [words], and *karma* [action]. How could I possibly not be his? It was a social disgrace for me. Other men would never marry me because all knew of our affair. His other marriage was a great shock to my family. I smelled of him, and still can think of no other. And who did he marry? Someone not as pure as I am. She was a widow of a different caste."

Shagi explained how even after his marriage she continued to visit him for a while. His wife did not know this in the beginning. Then one day she went as a visitor to the minister's quarters.

"I cried before him. But he had to leave for his office so he could not see me. His wife came into the room. 'She is also a woman,' I thought. I was practically her husband's wife, too. I still call him my *sriman*. I imagined she might be very kind and say 'Come stay with us also,' because at that time it was still common for men to have more than one wife. Most of those ministers and politicians had two wives, or at least a wife and a concubine. So I told her about our affair. I said to her, 'You are the queen now, I do not mind. But I am so much in love with him. If only you would allow me to live in that servant's quarter I will be happy just to see him from my room, going out and coming in by car. I will never even talk to him.' "

I could comprehend Shagi's mental state. Her wish to be his second wife was nothing irrational, and in her mind she was his spiritual, not physical, wife.

His physical wife did not say anything in reply, and Shagi left. But after a couple of days she went again. She described her action: "How could I stop my mind? It kept telling me that if I kept on worshipping, even a stone would one day get melted. But on this visit, before I was even admitted anywhere near the visiting room, some police came in front of all the people who were waiting and took me away. They did not explain anything. I was brought straight into this prison, pushed physically."

Shagi cried, "My only desire in life now is to go out from here and see him smile, and then die so that in our rebirth we meet again. Oh, Durga *maiyaa*, say something about him for me to hear!"

"Why to say anything about such a rotten man who could put you in prison as a lunatic?" I protested.

"No, I must do *tapasya* [austerity]. In every *Purana* and *Mahabharata* love story, women always got whatever they sacrificed for. If I do *tapasya* in this life then I will be with him in my next life. Parvati did *tapasya* for Shiva and won him.

"I feel so miserable in here, all the time thinking of him. But one day he might just wake up and feel the vibration and hear my cry in the wilderness. Then if he sees me in this condition he will not tolerate it, and will take me from here. Now he may have forgotten. He might not even know I'm still here. It was so long ago. But one day he must realize that I'm still here."

Full moon and dark moon would make some of the prison lunatics wilder or more subdued. Therefore every full moon and dark moon all lunatics would receive a powerful sleeping injection. The jailer and inspector used to arrange for a criminal from the male prison to come over and administer the injections. Afterward the lunatics would be unconscious for at least twelve hours.

One evening this was done. Quite late the next morning Shagi had still not woken up. I asked the *Chaukidarni* why Shagi had still not been seen.

She said, "Oh, she is still sleeping. Maybe the man last night gave her an overdose. It will take a little more time for her to wake up than the others, that's all."

I asked the *Chaukidarni* to order her *kamdars* to bring Shagi outside.

Two went inside and pulled her out and carried her by the feet and armpits, her head lolling backward beneath her crumpled shoulders. Shagi was laid out on the bare ground. I put a drop of water into her sagging mouth. It would not enter. She was dead.

The *kamdars* picked up her body and dumped it on the *chita*, where it remained, lonely and small, all the rest of that day and the next night, draped with her sari. The next day the jailer sent two Podes to collect her body. Besides street and toilet cleaning, another role of this caste in Nepal is to deal with vagrant dead bodies.

Susa told me, "Now that you are here, she was taken the next day after she died. Otherwise the dead sometimes remain here until they start smelling. Nobody can say anything about it."

ཅཚ

My gaze returned, as it so often did, to the naked figure of "lunatic" Saacha, hung, as Juki had been, from an eaves beam between the stone pillars of the *pagal* shed. When I had left to see the jailer she had a fragment of ragged cloth tied above her sagging breasts. It had just covered her as far down as her private area. Now it had been stripped off and nothing was secret. She looked bone and skin only. A reddish pink lump of flesh was hanging down a hand's length between her spread-eagled thighs.

"Does it hurt, Saacha?" I asked her.

"It hurts so much. What to do? If there were a little oil, it would be easier."

She meant to push it back in. But I could not dare to give her any. Anyway, it was almost always like that. At the beginning I used to think of raising one or two hundred rupees a month through friends outside and trying to solve the prisoners' health problems. But the administration warned me strongly against helping, interfering, or giving the other women anything. I was told, "While you are here, do not think we are against what you are doing. But it's the order that you should not be close with any of these women."

Once in a while I used to make the *Chaukidarni* laugh. "I hope *Chaukidarni* will not chain me there, will you?" I would say.

"If necessary I will chain you also, *Netaji*," she would reply, winking at me.

Saacha's left leg was gripped tightly by a heavy rusty iron chain and padlocked to the six-inch rim of a solid iron cart wheel lying at an angle on its hub on the three-foot-wide step outside the lunatic cells. It was so heavy that it could be moved only if several women righted it and rolled it as a wheel.

Today her right ankle was chained also and locked to one of the solid-iron bell weights. It, too, needed two or three strong people to lift it. Both her ankles were sore and bleeding a little. Her wrists, handcuffed to the roof beam, looked painful also—swollen, bruised, and dark from multiple scars.

Underneath her was a stained, damp, stinking area of floor where the excretions from her bladder and bowels fell day after day. Sometimes when she defecated there, the *Chaukidarni* would scream at her, "Why do you do that there?"

"Where to do it then?" Saacha would challenge simply.

The *Chaukidarni* would be enraged. "You are talking with me! Who do you think you are talking to?" Then she would turn and shout at some *kam-dars*, "Take that shit and force it in her mouth." A *kamdar* would lift some with a stick and do so.

Now I sighed deeply. "Oh, *Chaukidarni*, I can't look at that thing hanging out of her like that. Let us do something for her, then only I can talk to you. Mara, please go and get me a glass of water before I faint."

The *Chaukidarni* gave the order. "Eh! *Kamdar*, that Saacha's right hand, unchain it, will you."

Immediately two ran over and unchained it, and gave Saacha a rag. With painful slowness Saacha pushed the protrusion back inside her with her one freed hand, and a *kamdar* helped her wrap the rag around her body.

"Do I look pretty now?" Saacha asked me.

"You always look pretty, Saacha," I replied.

The *Chaukidarni* intervened: "Hey, how much are you going to say to a madwoman? The lunatics will go on talking like farts after soybeans if you don't stop."

Just then someone's visitors arrived at the gate and the *Chaukidarni* and the women police officers jumped up to be there. Always the *Chaukidarni* detailed one *naike* and one *kamdar* to be on duty at the gate. If there was any movement outside they would shout for her: "Eeeh! *Chaukidarni*, a person to meet so-and-so has come!"

The *Chaukidarni* would rush straight to the gate herself to verify who was there and issue clipped commands: "Aha, eh, okay—wait, wait!" she would call, as if she were some big *hakkim*. Then she would shout into the little jail yard, "Eeh! Mara [or whoever], your visitor! Where are you? Are you dead or what? C'm'ere. Run! *Munti*." The language would be most abusive.

Knowing that they should be far from the gate whenever a visitor came, the other women dispersed. But I remained where I was near Saacha.

"Saacha, you really are pretty," I told her, meaning it.

Her face had all the classic features of Brahminic beauty—strong curved eyebrows, fine Aryan nose and face structure, deep dark eyes, high forehead, and perfect teeth, though she could never clean them.

"*Didi*, if only I could wear an untorn sari and blouse and could put red *tika* on my forehead, and comb my hair, then I do look pretty," she assured me.

She touched her closely cropped hair. "I also used to have thick long hair like yours. Now, here . . . all of us . . . they cut our hair by force. How do women look without hair? Like a scary ghost, that's all."

Before I could respond, she went on talking in her hoarse voice that had broken from so much ranting and cursing. She spoke ever so low now, not because of fear of being heard but because her cystocele was back inside and would slip out if she raised her voice or coughed.

"My husband's maternal uncle is Nepal's ambassador to Germany," Saacha revealed. "I was married in a nice family and have a little girl. My husband had gone to a foreign country. After he came back I was happy and so excited. I have no idea what I did that I should not have done and that made my mother-in-law think I was mad and send me here. Always my daughter's memory returns to me. How big our house was! What tasty food we used to eat! The nice clothes! Durga *didi*, I'm also a daughter of a big house. I used not to talk like this when I first came here. But these women torture me—so why keep quiet? Which incarnation's sin brought me here, I wonder. Even if I was mad how could I get cured staying here in this condition?"

I followed her cracked lips as they moved. Her skin was ash colored, dry, and flaking, weathered as rough as buffalo hide. Fingernails and toenails that had not broken off were over an inch long, ingrained with black grime. From her body it was hardly possible to tell her skin color, but her face was brown.

"Why are your feet and hands shackled like this? Are you very naughty?" I teased her gently.

"They used to tie me only by two legs and the left hand. But I started cursing them with my right hand because I was in so much pain, unable to sit or sleep day or night. Now they chain my right hand also. But my mouth is still free.

"If I have to die, I will die not caring what I say. I might as well say what I feel like saying, after all this torture. If only my husband or my mother would know I am kept like this. Perhaps they would come and get me out. But nobody takes them any message."

Saacha started crying. "What happened to my little girl? I used to care for her so much. She used to sleep with me. Now I have to be in this grave-yard. Where is that God? I'm always looking for Him. Why does He not hear my cry?"

I began to feel nervous as she started to curse. I knew the risk of her speaking out like this. As soon as she became more boisterous the *Chaukidarni* would call the police: "Her disease has gone up and she's giving us a lot of trouble. Report it to the jailer, will you." Out of fear the women police would always do whatever the *Chaukidarni* said. The report would reach the jailer, and he, without seeing anything for himself, would select some *naike* or *kamdar* from the men's prison to come and inject her to make her senseless. The first time I saw them injecting Saacha like that it appalled and scared me. Then I discovered they did it once or twice every week to somebody. The prisoners sent around from the male jail had no training at all, but if anything went wrong nothing would be done to them.

Mass injection days were dehumanizing to watch. *Kamdars* would force the *pagal* women one by one, screaming, to the step in front of the *Chauki-darni's* room. They looked like animals being driven to be slaughtered. If a woman resisted, *kamdars* would flatten her on the ground, standing on her legs with hands on her body while a male criminal rammed the dirty needle into a bony thigh. If she became unconscious on the spot four *kam-dars* would lift her limp frame by the wrists and ankles, one *kamdar* per limb to avoid touching her filthy body too much. Then they would literally throw her like a sack from the doorway into her stinking cell. Most of them knew that would happen, so they ran back to their cells immediately after the injection before they dropped. All were truly terrified, and cried from the pain of the one big needle that was used for everyone. But within seconds whatever it was in the syringe sent them senseless for many hours wherever they fell.

Before Shagi was killed, Saacha used to be left outside unconscious wherever she had fallen after the injection, her feet still shackled. These days she was taken inside a cell like the others. Maybe my concern over Shagi's death had had some impact, and now I was not supposed to see in case Saacha died outside one night.

Poor Saacha, the only time she could lie down was after her sleeping in-jection. Sometimes she would lie sleeping through a night, a day, another night, and into the next day. Otherwise she never slept. The aftereffect of the injection was intense thirst. Saacha would be hanging again from her beam by this time and would cry out, "I'm so thirsty. I need water."

One of the crew would reply insensitively, "Your mother will bring you water. Is that why you're crying?"

"Please give a little, and I will give you a blessing. A blessing given by a Brahmin works, you know!"

"Hah! You think your blessings are any good to us!"

Then Saacha would start her cursing. "Curse you, all of you—*Chauki-darni, Mulnaike*. Die! The lot of you. Kill me if you want. I'm a Brahmin. If I curse you, you'll all go to hell."

Often Saacha would get carried away. "May the whole government go to hell! May the king die! May the queen die! The zonal commissioner, the chief district officer—may they all die! The police! They are all the king's messengers. Let them all die! They were the ones who brought me here. Poor me! Me, *abala*—a woman without strength. I have done nothing wrong."

I would reach up and pour a little water in her mouth. Her cursing would cease, and she would bless me. "Durga *didi*, may progress always be there for you. You helped a person in trouble like me. God will see!"

In the year that I was there Saacha was released from her beam twice in order to wash her body. Standing above her slightly, a *kamdar* poured cold water on her body from a little tin can. Saacha would slowly let her hands feel the swollen sores and bruises.

An abrupt order would be fired: "Do it quick. Do it quick! Or you'll see what will happen if you delay."

Saacha would not reply but would murmur under her breath, "How it hurts. Oh! What a place to have come." Then she would start rubbing her skin. But as soon as the layers of grime started to soften there would not be enough water to rinse away the loosened dirt. There would only be two or three canfuls, and the *kamdar* would not let dirty Saacha touch the water. The water was not there according to Saacha's need, just however much the *kamdar* felt like pouring. I used to think how unimaginable it might be, how it must have itched, and how Saacha might have felt the itching. I wondered how it was that she was still alive after all this treatment. Then slowly I lived with it as normal. There was nothing I could do.

For me Saacha became a heroic figure. Her story and her daily torture symbolized at once the suppression of consciousness in our society and the strength of resistance, the resistance of *abala*—the second word for "woman" in Sanskrit—"without strength." As I gazed at her hanging form I thought of my other friends in the democratic political movement. Eleven men known to me had been killed since 1979 in police custody and in jails. Saacha was still alive and resisting.

# 10

.

# Dead or Alive

gain the guards started whispering in my ears. I hated this kind of "sympathy." It reminded me of the Police Club. After six in the evening when they came on duty I could not even talk to the three inmates in my room. If I did, they intervened: "We have to follow orders. We were told you should not talk much to others here." In my present vulnerable situation I did not want to discuss anything with them. They could report or distort anything, and the authorities could make any meaning from their reports. I kept quiet.

After a couple of weeks, one of my night guards told me, "Tomorrow morning there is going to be very tight security outside the jail and up to the jailer's office. Has anyone told you that you might get transferred or anything?"

"No, I do not know anything," I replied.

The *Chaukidarni* came up to my room and told me in front of my guards, "I heard bad news about you." She continued, her eyes watering, "Not long ago while there was tight security at the men's jail, early the next morning two of the political prisoners were taken away and they never returned."

I asked, "What happened to them?"

"They were shot dead. Did you not know?" replied the *Chaukidarni*, and added, "I have been told to prepare you at six in the morning."

"No problem. I'll get ready at six in the morning. Don't worry," I said.

She left, very unhappy. One of the policewomen said, "We are told that we cannot sleep tonight."

I wanted to be away from everybody and to be by myself. So I lay down, covering my face with my quilt. The other three inmates were already in bed. I could not tell whether they were asleep. The "clock" rang eight. At night it sounded as though it was somewhere next door. Immediately after the eight "tangs" two women police guards, one *naike*, and two *kamdars* came around for checking. As usual they woke everyone up. I too removed my quilt to show my face. After they left I closed my eyes and tried to meditate. It was difficult in my mental state. I had thought that by coming back to Kathmandu everything would be solved. I could live in peace here with these criminal and lunatic inmates. I was worried: "What will happen tomorrow? Will I be transferred again? Where? Are they going to take me to my hometown? It is just one-way traffic. I have to do what I am told to do."

I heard a cock crowing somewhere outside: *Kukhuri-kaa*. The two policewomen had been murmuring the whole night. I was awake, but I stayed sunk in deep thought with my eyes shut. It must be four o'clock. Yes, it was—the iron hammer went *tang, tang* . . . four times in all. The guards came to check our room again. This time the *Chaukidarni* also came. She said, "Maybe you should get up."

The other three also got up. The *Chaukidarni* proposed, "Let's all go to the toilet; there are enough holes for seven of us."

Mara said, "How about water to take to the toilet? It hasn't come in at the tap yet and we do not have enough."

The *Chaukidarni* said, "Oh! I have some and you have some. That will be enough." And she went and brought some water.

There were only four tin containers to take to the toilet. The *Chaukidarni* solved the problem by assigning the biggest one to my three inmates for their combined use, one for the two policewomen to share, one for herself, and one for me. By this time it was four-thirty A.M. We all went to the toilet. After we returned from our group toilet trip the *Chaukidarni* shouted to one of the sleeping *naikes*, "Eh! Bring some water."

From her sleep she replied, "Yes, *Chaukidarni didi*! What did you say?"

The *Chaukidarni* went a little closer and shouted, "Your father's pee! I said, bring some water!"

She brought some water instantly.

Instead of soap, each of us held some earth in our left hand ready to purify the fingers used for washing after toilet. The *naike* poured water into my hand first, then into the *Chaukidarni*'s, and then into the policewomen's.

The *Chaukidarni* decreed, "Today let these three also become queens." So the *naike* poured water on the hands of my three roommates also. After this we went back to our rooms.

Snatching the vase from the *naike*'s hand, the *Chaukidarni* said to me, "Okay, you wash your face also now. The tap water won't come in time for you to get ready." As she poured water on my hands, I washed my face and rinsed my mouth. Then she said, "After putting on your sari, come to my room. I'll prepare tea."

I put on my sari. As I slipped on the matching blouse I got a shock. I found that I could put three fingers up the sleeve and still move them around. The blouse hung emptily over my front. How thin I had become. Mara looked at me anxiously, conscious of how ill-fitting the blouse looked. I combed my hair.

Kripa asked, "*Didi,* how about a red *tika?*"

"I always used to wear it, but since my arrest I haven't had any," I said.

She offered her miniature bottle of *bindi*—and with its small applicator put a dot of the red liquid on my forehead. I was quite sad not knowing where I was going to be taken. I could not say anything to my roommates. Crying, they begged, "Please come back soon."

"I'll try," I said, and left the room with the two policewomen.

The *Chaukidarni,* offering the tea, apologized. "No milk in jail."

I said, "I know it. Don't worry."

It was six o'clock. I heard the conch blowing and bells ringing from a radio outside the jail. Radio Nepal was waking up the kingdom. I always loved this prayer—Shiva's *bhajan.*

We waited and waited in the *Chaukidarni*'s room for over two hours.

Finally, at eight-thirty A.M., somebody shouted from the gate, "*Chaukidarni,* it's time." She, my two bodyguards, and the two night duty guards led me to the gate. Outside, forming a line from the gate to the back of a police jeep, were five armed policemen and two policewomen. The first policeman stamped to attention and presented arms, greeting me with a customary "*Jaya Nepal, didi,*" and then said, "Enter the back of the jeep." As I passed the rest of the police in line, each one saluted me formally and repeated "*Jaya Nepal*"—"Victory to Nepal."

The two women helped me climb over the jeep's high tailgate, not easy in a sari, then they climbed in and sat on either side of me. Three policemen with guns sat opposite, and the remaining two closed the canvas canopy and went and sat in front.

I had not given up asking where they might be taking me. As if they would tell the truth, I asked, "Where are we going?"

One of them—he might have been the senior one in rank—replied, "Sometimes even we do not know what we are doing. We just follow orders."

I did not see a friendly face anywhere. These were all new. I decided not to talk. I chanted my mantra to myself, one that all Hindus chant for good luck before undertaking some task or going away. I could see nothing outside as we drove along, so I had no idea where they were taking me. After an hour of fast driving the jeep eventually halted. When the driver stepped out I ventured to peep outside. Even just glimpsing the entrance I could tell that it was the attorney general's office at the Supreme Court. I felt a little relieved. But why on earth, I wondered, had the police driven around for an hour when the distance from the jail to the attorney general's office was only a ten-minute walk?

The driver came back and said, "This isn't the place. It's in the next building." Now I guessed that they were taking me to the Supreme Court. I thought to myself, "If these police had only asked me I would have told them where to go."

The driver started the jeep again and drove to the next building. Then, with the two policewomen—one on each side—almost holding me, two male police officers on their left and right with guns, one armed policeman in front and two behind—they paraded me up the stairs and into a second-floor chamber. It was nine forty-five A.M. Office time in Nepal begins only at ten A.M., and people usually arrive late. Yet a large gathering of people was already seated on about eight rows of long benches. At the front were chairs for the lawyers on the right side, and in the center was a raised platform and desk for the judges.

We all sat down in the same formation as we had walked in. I was hemmed in on every side by more police and guns. One of the policemen behind me told the crowd, "This is not a public hearing. You all go out." Some went out and some stayed. In the meantime five private defense lawyers came in from a side door on the right and sat in their assigned chairs. I turned and smiled at them, but a policeman warned me sternly not to look at or speak to anybody. As soon as the two judges entered through their door, everybody stood up and a number of people from outside entered at the back of the courtroom despite police objections.

I had absolutely no idea what charges would be brought against me or why I had been brought to the court. I thought to myself that if they brought a charge based on what the police wanted me to confess, the law provided me with a chance to make a fresh statement in court.

Then it started. One of the lawyers pleading on my behalf addressed the bench. "*Sriman* [Your Honor], it seems to me that Durga Pokhrel was in the habit of wearing a sari every day, but then one day she decided to wear jeans. The authorities saw her and thought, 'Oh! Today she looks smart. Maybe she is trying to do something to disturb the peace and security of the country. We'd better finish her off!' And she was arrested on such a baseless assumption. She must be released immediately."

The others took turns in pleading my defense. As there was no charge from the prosecution, the defense was focused on the illegality of my arrest. The gist of their reasoning was that Durga Pokhrel had been arrested because of malice on the part of the government. "From the minute of her arrest until this present moment the government has followed no legal procedure. Durga Pokhrel's detention was illegal, and every minute that she is kept behind bars will be illegal. She must be released as soon as possible."

I started to become excited. "The happiest moment in life will be when I get back my freedom," I thought. But then, like a shadow, a sudden strong feeling of foreboding gripped me, and the familiar flickering signal spread across my eye. A bad sign. Perhaps some wrong would occur after my release.

The judges listened impassively to my lawyers' arguments. It was impossible to guess at their thinking—but the case seemed clear, the facts simple. After a lengthy series of presentations, one of the judges announced tersely "Adjourned until next time," rose, and walked out of the chamber. His colleague followed. There was a gasp from the crowd.

We all stood up as they departed. The courtroom started to hum, and my lawyer friends looked at me with sympathy in their eyes. Everybody else was watching me, too. The police glared back at the crowd.

I took a quick chance. "What's going to happen next?" I asked the lawyers.

One of them replied, "We thought you'd be released today. Now this adjournment sends a completely different signal—we really can't tell what will happen. The judge's 'until next time' could mean next week or next year. They're buying time. All we can do now is hope for the best."

Then the police started dispersing the crowd and ushered me from the chamber through a side door. A crowd had assembled near the police jeep. The armed police stayed tightly around me, telling the crowd, "You cannot talk to Durga *didi*," and ordering me, "Don't speak to anyone."

What was there to say to the people anyway? I thought that the bad feelings and sense of foreboding I had had turned out to be accurate. But there was some small mercy in the fact that no charge had been brought. If they had charged me with the conspiracy to kidnap the crown prince, that would have been the end of my life.

I was taken back to jail—directly this time—in five minutes.

ဢ

Back inside, the other inmates were happy. I had not "disappeared." Trying to lighten the situation, I told them, "It was only to go to the Supreme Court."

"What was the charge?" Kaga asked.

"There was no charge today," I replied.

She could not believe it. "How can you be taken to court without a charge?" she protested.

The *Chaukidarni* replied, "I'll tell you what her charge is—she is the stepdaughter of the government!"

Everybody laughed.

For me it was as though for a long time I had been practicing to fly and finally, just as I was about to take off, a poacher came and cut my wings. Or as though I had been walking for days and days, with my feet and arms so swollen that it was difficult to move any one of them. After eating that evening, I even did not go to join the evening gossip and *bhajan*, but sat quietly in my room. This was the only time I could be alone.

I asked myself, "Why do you feel so sad? Because you could not be released today, be with your friends outside, be having fun? Is your life only for that? No!" My realist self spoke up. "This is the road I have chosen—to work against this Panchayat system, which has caused so many innocent people to be victimized. If I do not sacrifice, how will this inhuman system be swept away? The political opposition's duty is to root out the tyrant system from our country and bring a new system—a system where people can say no or yes freely, where they can say good or bad, where they can discuss their problems frankly, and where they can freely organize themselves. To live will be a right, not a mercy. And to have a full stomach every day will also be a right."

"I must not feel like a coward," I thought. "Many of our people have already been killed, made homeless, imprisoned. . . . I am not the only one. Whenever 'you' have to face trouble, 'you' think 'you' are the only one. That may be common human psychology—but it is not true. At this time I am the only woman victimized at this level. But, how many men must there be next door in the Central Male Jail and in Bhadragol and in Nakhu and out in the districts?"

I remembered stories of many freedom fighters around the world. How hard their paths had been. In the end they were victorious because the free-dom and democracy they fought for was the cry of the people—the voice of truth. *"Satyam eva jayate,"* as the Sanskrit expression puts it: "Truth is always victorious." Just thinking this made me feel better. I felt part of the ongoing drama of history. While authoritarian rulers introduced their rule using force, killing those who resisted, democracies were restored by the collective power of the minds of the people, with their hands empty. The tyrants used arms against these people, too. In the processes of losing and restoring democracy there are always casualties.

ཉ

The next day, still weak from my experience in the Supreme Court, I was sitting on the step outside the *Chaukidarni*'s room when, without warning, I fainted. It was the first time that I had fainted in jail in public. There had been other times when I would feel myself about to faint, but somehow I would manage to reach my bedding and lie down on the floor until I felt I could stand up again. Now my weakness became a public "concern."

The *Chaukidarni* and the police must have reported the incident to the jailer, because the following morning I was taken to a health assistant at the jailer's office. First the health assistant weighed me. I discovered that, despite having gained some weight since leaving Mahakali, I now weighed only ninety-six pounds—twenty-four pounds less than usual. Then the health assistant looked at my eyes and, deciding that I was anemic, said that he wanted to draw my blood.

I refused. I had never had blood drawn in my life. The very thought of having needles inserted into my body frightened and appalled me. I heard the *Chaukidarni* and the police guards murmuring to one another that they should hold me so tight that I could not move. Then, before I had time to realize what they meant, I was forcefully held and felt the pain of a needle in my arm. As I felt my body draining of energy, I fainted again.

After I recovered, someone gave me a small glass of milk, then I was taken back to prison. Some inmates looked and remarked, "Eh! How weak you are. We thought you were at your end." The policewomen supported me as I made my way across the yard to lie down. That was the last time I ever saw the health assistant, and no one paid further attention to my "anemia."

One Sunday at around eleven A.M. I was talking as I often did with one of the alleged *pagal* girls when the *Chaukidarni* came running over and stopped me with the reprimand "What are you doing chatting away with this *bahulai* [madwoman]? Someone wants to see you at the gate."

I asked, "Someone from the jail office or the police?" These were the only people I was allowed to see and I was not eager to see any more of either of them.

She said, "Come with me and you will see who it is."

I followed her. I could not believe it. It was my friend and business partner Shrish Rana. I had been thinking that I would never be allowed to see any of my friends again.

I was not mentally prepared to see a close friend like him. I almost broke down with emotion. He was wearing dark glasses, and his shaking voice indicated that perhaps he was trying to hide the emotions that he, too, was feeling. All I could say, in broken sentences, was, "Please push for my release, no matter where you have to take the case." I was trying to indicate that he should take it to the royalty, but because the police were writing down everything it was difficult to be explicit. All I remembered him saying was, "From now on we have to seek permission to see you every Sunday."

After a short while the police accompanying him said, "Let's go, ten minutes is up." I felt as though I had a hundred and one things to tell him but that someone had forced a gag over my mouth so that I could not speak.

When I was back inside, everybody came pressing around me like leeches, asking who had come and what he had said.

The *Chaukidarni* winked with a big grin as she exploded, "God! He was a handsome one—who on earth was that?"

Someone else marveled, "His eyes were godly like in our paintings."

"And his mouth was 'ready-made' as if some craftsman formed it," another inmate added.

A Rana *pagal* had also peeped through the gate, and now pronounced with respect, "Eheh! He looked like a Ranaji for sure."

But all I needed at that moment was to be with myself in peace. With all these inmates around me I was not even free to think about how I felt at seeing a friend after five months. It was so suffocating there. No matter how deep the wound was within you, you had to project normality. Imprisoning someone was not the end in itself. It was just the beginning of the end of your freedom. If only there was at least a separate cell provided for political prisoners, then I would have had some time to myself. I had almost forgotten how those hours, days, and now months had gone by. They already felt like a story that had never happened to me. Shrish's visit had jolted me back to the first day of my arrest. How sugar-coated that police chief had sounded when he had come to our press with such an evil motive. If only I had suspected him at the time, I might have escaped and disappeared. But there was no reason to suspect him. Everything else had gone so well that day that I had not foreseen any danger.

Perhaps because Shrish had been with me when he came, they had been unable to make me "disappear"? Then, just as this thought came, for a second, another thought crossed my mind. It was a thought that had disturbed me a couple of times during those eighteen days of police custody. What if Shrish deserted me, ducking out from being my witness? It was an unthinkable thought. Yet, when everything seems against you and so hostile, in your imagination even your friend becomes the "hard-liner" who does not save you. But now that I was beginning to get glimpses of those who were behind the plot, Shrish's role was becoming very clear in my vision. I thought, "Beyond politics and business, the human relationship is always there, tender and supportive." His visit confirmed this to me, although, besides resuming our friendship, I could not speculate at all about what he might now be doing to help free me. Nevertheless, just by thinking this little positive thought I became happy.

In a few days the police resumed their whispering. One said, "We've heard bad news about you." The other guard added, "Maybe they're about to transfer you somewhere else."

I told them, "Don't tell me anything—even if I am to be taken to be killed, okay?"

The first one murmured on, "Don't you think that those men from the male jail would have tried to escape had the police tipped them off that they were going to be killed as they were transferred to another prison?"

"It is just the person's luck," added the second one again. "Even if you try to escape, if you make it you are safe, but if not the police will shoot you anyway."

The other one winked at her friend and said to me, "If there is anything like that, we'll inform you. Don't worry."

I did not want to respond, but could not help it—they were looking straight at my face. Therefore I had to say, "Oh, I'm not worried about anything."

"Early tomorrow you're going to be taken out again," the *Chaukidarni* told me.

This time I was sure that I was going to be taken to the Supreme Court, because of the way that the judge had postponed my case the previous month.

The next morning at five they asked me to get ready by six-thirty. But this time without saying anything I delayed. I ate my morning meal at eight as usual and only then got ready.

At nine-thirty the same police team as before arrived at the gate to collect me. This time they took me straight to the same Supreme Court chamber, where I sat in the same position as before. As on the first occasion, I was not permitted to talk or to look at anybody's face. But before the judges entered, from overhearing some of my friends chatting on the balcony outside, I learned that my fourth elder sister, Subhadra, had managed to file a *habeas corpus* writ against the government. A lawyer friend had contacted Subhadra in Kathmandu while she had been visiting other relatives there, and had encouraged her to file the writ. Otherwise she lived two hundred miles away in Dharan. It seemed that B.P. had prompted her action in order to find out whether I was alive or not.

I thought, "So this is why I was brought back from Mahakali—because of *habeas corpus*." This was a writ that could be filed only by a relative to produce a missing person before a court to release them from unlawful restraint. Somehow Subhadra had been prepared to take the risk.

The judges entered, and immediately I heard the space behind me fill up with the crowd that had been waiting outside. Very alert, I listened closely as the lawyers pleaded again on my behalf. What I gathered from today's pleading was that it was very fortunate that Shrish had been present as a witness when the police chief took me away from our press without a warrant or arrest letter. Because of this, my sympathizers had become worried. I had been considered a missing prisoner.

I learned, too, that there had been three pleadings before I had even been produced in court the last time. After the first hearing, when the writ was filed, the Supreme Court sent a letter to the Home Ministry asking for my immediate release and arguing that imprisoning me without making public the charge was an infringement of natural law. In response, the ministry had denied that I was even arrested. That response of the government must have been very badly motivated, I thought. They must still have been thinking that I could be persuaded to escape so that they could finish me off on the grounds of "attempting to escape." But because Shrish had witnessed my arrest, the court did not drop my case and became firmer with the ministry in its next pleading. The second Home Ministry response stated that while I was in detention in Kathmandu, I had tried to "provoke" the police and, as a result, the police had been forced to take me to Mahakali. In its third pleading, while I was still missing, the Supreme Court had issued an ultimatum that gave the government a period of time in which it had to produce me in its chamber—alive or dead.

I was surprised that the government had not brought the great charge that the police had wanted me to confess to, and I was one hundred percent sure that I would now be released.

Durga Pokhrel's childhood home in Kachiday, Dhankuta District, Koshi Zone, in eastern Nepal.

Durga at age seven, seated second from left, with her family.

The young teacher, at center in sari, with her National Development Service students at Tribhuvan University in Kathmandu in 1975.

Addressing a meeting at Kathmandu's Rotary Club on Human Rights Day in 1977.

Imprisoned frequently for her pro-democracy activities, Durga drew strength from many sources to sustain her in the darkness of Nepalese prisons. She inherited her spirituality from her grandfather, Rishikalpa Pandit Veda Nidhi Pokhrel (right), and her father, Kaviraj Narapati Pokhrel, pictured above in his Dharan dispensary in 1982.

Kathmandu's Central Women's Prison in the 1990s. This is the prison's main gate, with the visitors' reception area in the foreground.

The prison yard with the author's cell window at the far left on the second floor. The wall on the left was constructed after her release to segregate the mentally ill housed behind it from those imprisoned on criminal charges.

The building where prisoners deemed insane—*pagal*—are still kept. Durga frequently saw prisoners hung by their wrists from the roof beams between the columns and tortured.

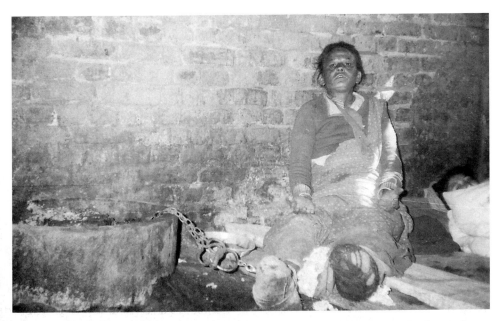

Inside a typical *pagal* cell, a woman suffering from what appears to be gangrene of the feet lies in chains.

In exile in Minnesota with her hostess, Beverly Thompson. Durga had shaved her head in mourning for her father, an act of bereavement traditionally undertaken in Nepal by sons. (*E. Thompson*)

In 1985, Anthony, whom the author had met in Nepal just days before her escape, came to Cambridge, Massachusetts, where Durga was studying at Harvard. They soon traveled to classes together on a single bicycle.

When Durga and Anthony were able to return briefly to Nepal in 1986, he became a Brahmin in preparation for their Hindu wedding. In the center is Durga's cousin's wife, Ranjana Pokhrel. (*G. Bodeker*)

Durga's former partners in the Star Press: Shrish holding her son Samyog (the king's palace is in the background), and she and Upendra Rana entertaining fellow students on "Nepal Night" at Harvard.

Today in the United States: Durga and Anthony with Tapasya, Shristi, and Samyog.

Suddenly I heard one of the judges announce, "Postponed until next time," and they disappeared. I could not believe it. Something was very wrong. Now I was really shaken. And angry. Everybody in the courtroom looked at me in sympathy and started talking at once so that I could not distinguish what was being said. The police were trying to disperse them, but no one was paying any attention. The noise was like a fairground. Despite the bodyguards' protests I called out to one of my lawyer friends, "What's going on?"

He replied loudly, "Be courageous! We'll try our best. There's something in the government's mind that we don't understand."

The police took me down from the building to the jeep, dispersing the crowd as we went. Amid the jostling, one of my friends managed to tell me, "When you weren't released last time we knew that this would happen. Usually in *habeas corpus* cases the Supreme Court has to release the prisoner the day she is produced to the court. What it means is that the judiciary is not independent in our country."

A little nervous, the police actually pushed me into the jeep and quickly started it and moved. Shut in the back with my guards, I was in a state where I could think of nothing. The jeep lurched out of the driveway onto the road back to the prison. Consciously I cleared my mind and as my almost watery eyes dried and widened, I felt myself toughening, fresh and strong for whatever lay ahead. I returned to my prison home. I really felt that it was my home now, the home of the victimized, and that all the inmates were my family members. "Nothing is meaningful outside," I thought. "It is all absurdity."

As I entered, the *Chaukidarni* asked, "What is it? You look so happy now!"

Before I could reply Kripa chirped, "Maybe Durga *bahini* is going to be released today."

Mara lamented, "No, no, *didi*! I haven't prepared enough for my exam." (I had been helping her study for her B.A.).

By this time everybody was around me. I announced loudly, "Don't worry. Maybe I am going to live with you people forever."

The *Chaukidarni* laughed. "I knew that."

"How did you know?" I questioned her.

She pointed with a quick eye movement toward our police inspector's quarters outside and revealed, "I also have my intelligence sources. When you were not released the first time I guessed that was not a good sign."

I was in good humor, and challenged her and the authorities. "I want to say this in front of everybody, *Chaukidarni*. From now on, don't you or the police impose too many rules on me. I want to live happily here."

The *Chaukidarni* laughed merrily but still towed the line, insisting, "You have to follow the jail rules."

"I will, but not too much—okay?" I said, and added, "You people don't have police guards in your rooms, so why should I?"

"For that you'll have to talk to the jailer and the inspector," she commanded.

The next day I sent a message through the police to the jailer asking to see him. I felt positive that because I had not been released he would see me instantly at my request. I dressed in my sari, ready to go out.

"You're being released today, or what?" the other women all said, staring at me. I felt peculiar dressed up like this, as if in my "best" to go out somewhere special. Yet it was to see my jailer.

I was still chatting in the yard when the policewomen came over to tell me, "The time has come for you to go. People from the jailer's office have come 'round to get you."

As usual, I made the short journey by jeep, and climbed the flight of steps up to his office.

"*Namaskar*, Jailer *Saheb*," I greeted him. "I have a few things to request."

He returned my greeting and, still staring at some paper on his table, asked, "What are they?"

I thought that he was not paying any attention, so kept quiet for a minute and looked around feeling lost and distant.

Putting the paper aside, he looked at me and asked again, "What are they?"

I was about to open my mouth when he pressed the bell. A man came in; he must have been the *peon*.

The jailer ordered him, "Hey! Make a nice cup of tea for Durgaji."

The *peon* saluted and went out again.

I opened the conversation. "It seems now that I'm not going to be released soon. The first thing I request of you is to discontinue sending those women guards to my room. I want to live more freely."

"They are for your security," the jailer replied. "You never know what those criminals could do. If anything goes wrong in the case of a political prisoner, I would be responsible."

I said that I was not afraid. "What is there to go wrong? I'm quite happy with my roommates."

The jailer pressed his bell again, this time to order one of his staff to call the police inspector. Looking at me again he explained, "I cannot decide by myself on this, so let the inspector come."

Within a couple of minutes both the *peon* with the tea and the inspector arrived at the same time. The jailer and the inspector discussed my request for a minute, and in an agreeable tone the inspector warned me, "All three women with you are here on serious charges of killing many people. If you feel comfortable with them I will arrange that the police don't stay with you at night."

"I am positive that I don't need them. The women do not scare me," I assured him.

"In a couple of days I will stop them from coming," he promised.

The jailer asked what other requests I had.

I told him, "Because of the smoke that the cooking fires produce when my roommates all cook inside the room at the same time, my eyes are being affected. There's a small passage outside our room—if we could cook there it would be more healthy."

The jailer agreed that my food could be cooked outside, but not that of the others. Then after I explained that Mara cooked for me, he conceded that hers, too, could be cooked outside with mine. With only the two other inmates cooking inside the room the smoke problem would be reduced to some extent.

My third request was about my visitors. I wanted visitors to be allowed, and on a regular basis. His reply was that he was arranging for me to meet no more than five visitors at a time for a maximum of ten minutes on Sundays and Thursdays. Police would be present together with someone from the jail office to write down everything my visitors and I talked about. If a government holiday fell on one of my visitors' days then I would not be allowed visitors on that day.

My last request was that the jail administration should not impose too many rules on me. That, the jailer said, was something I had to sort out with the inmate administration inside. Even if the jailer said no to everything, I had no choice. I thanked him.

I was taken back. As soon as I entered the *Chaukidarni* asked me, "Okay, what did you say, and what did he say?"

Everybody waited curiously for my reply.

I joked, "I said to the jailer that I wanted to be *Chaukidarni*, and he said okay."

The *Chaukidarni* looked at me again, "If you become *Chaukidarni* how do you think you're going to run this jail? You don't even like to see a mouse beaten." Then she added commandingly, "Here the rule is *laash ki shaash*—Panchayat's code of conduct," repeating the base rule of prison that I had heard from the jailer.

"One thing I could never do would be to push a rough stick into Saacha's private part, if that's what you mean. I can't even look at such things that you all do," I told the *Chaukidarni*, "but you know well how I control my-self in this place—through meditation. If I could teach everybody that way of settling their minds, then I could easily keep order here and jail would be a peaceful place."

She did not want to listen to the last remark, but reverted to my first. Coarsely she joked, "Instead of a rough stick, you can demand a smooth, long eggplant. That will go easily."

Thinking it better not to take the conversation further, I said good-bye and went to my room. My two police guards came for three more nights, and were then withdrawn.

Sunday came—the first Sunday after my meeting with the jailer, and I waited expectantly in case some friends might visit me. I was very excited. I was also worried that whoever came might think that I was very depressed after not having been released by the Supreme Court. How to tell them that I was feeling perfectly normal now, and could face life in jail as long as necessary? I felt like having a cup of tea. I told Mara, and within twenty minutes she prepared it. We drank together. It was eight-thirty A.M., so we ate our meal as well. We laughed with each other that we had not had to use extra firewood today because she had made tea at the same time as the rice.

My excitement was growing. I put on my sari. Since my last court ap-pearance Mara had used a small piece of white material of hers to make a sleeveless sari blouse for me. Normally I did not like wearing sleeveless blouses, but the choice I had now was either my old ill-fitting one or this sleeveless one. I did not mind either one, but Mara was a little fashion con-scious and suggested the sleeveless one looked better because it fit well. To please her I wore the one she had made, covering my bare arms with the length of my sari that draped from my shoulder.

I had one pair of sandals for all purposes. Nothing else really—no cream, no lotions. Even outside all I used to use was a little face cream once in a while. A red *tika* dot on my forehead was my only "makeup." But here I could not afford to buy it. It would cost three rupees even for a little bot-tle that kept for a year. But spending three rupees meant two days' ration money. I could not dare to do that.

I came down and waited in front of the *Chaukidarni*'s room, which meant in front of the *pagal* cells as well. They were all curious, seeing me wearing a nice sari. I explained that it was the day for my visitors, but they were not sure whether I was telling them the truth as everybody else could receive visitors at any time between six A.M. and six P.M. any day. Rarely if ever did a visitor come for any of them.

At eleven A.M. a policeman shouted from the gate, "It's time now for Durgaji."

The *Chaukidarni* and two policewomen took me to the gate. Of course, the *Chaukidarni* stayed just inside. She was also a prisoner. I stooped and lifted my sari slightly to get through the little half door within the main gate, then I saw Shrish again, this time accompanied by Manjoor World, chair of a private social service organization. Outside in the little covered porch where the police guard was posted, there were two small benches about six feet apart facing each other across the entranceway. Shrish and Manjoor were asked to sit on one bench. Beside them two men sat down ready to write down whatever we said. I sat on the bench opposite with the two policewomen standing immediately behind my back. This was my first official visitors' day.

Shrish opened, "When you weren't released on your first appearance in the Supreme Court we suspected something wrong was going on. Now there's to be another day when you'll appear. Let's see if we can do anything then."

I said, "Even if not, don't worry. I'm prepared for nine months away." Usually arrest under the Security Act lasted for nine months, although I knew that the act also provided for detention to be extended every nine months once, twice, or three times. It was a tricky situation.

We could not talk about anything else openly because every word we spoke was being recorded. In this awkward way we looked at each other, our mouths performing some sort of conversation that I could not remember much of even immediately afterward. How quickly ten minutes vanished. I had to say good-bye, and they disappeared back into the city. I felt teased. There was so much to tell them and to talk about, but I could not say much.

A week after my second appearance I was taken to the court again. Quite frankly, now I did not even want to go; it was too humiliating. Nonetheless, I was dragged like a sacrificial goat to the contemptible chamber again. Everything was the same. But this time the absurdity of the whole drama was transparent. Just a look at the judges' faces belied the pretension that they were listening to the lawyers. I could tell that everything was already predetermined.

Finally one of the judges stood up and announced, "Dismissed."

"Dismissed" did not mean that my case had been dismissed and that I was free to go. The judge was simply referring to the plea my lawyers had made against the illegality of my detention. Thus, "dismissed" meant that the government had succeeded in proving that my detention was not illegal so that I could continue to be held under the Security Act.

I felt like punching the judge's nose and holding his neck and asking him, "You damned crook, what did you dismiss? Did you get a big bribe from the government? Confess it! Confess that you are not independent, but that you act exactly as you are told to from above."

But in reality the only thing that I could do was to follow the seven armed police to their jeep and go back to prison. I felt like a defeated foot soldier taken by the enemy. A pawn taken near the end of a big game. Now the drama of *habeas corpus* was ended. There was, after all, no real *habeas corpus* in our land. But then, I thought, at least I had been produced to the court and was alive. I could just as easily have been killed in police custody like others. Now, for me, there was no more anxiety about going to court, or anticipation of other charges. Nonetheless my mind remained busy, curious why the government could not bring the charge to which the police had tried to make me confess.

On the second visiting day, my father, my sister Subhadra with one of her sons, and two of my friends came. I saw that my father's health had deteriorated. Water filled his and Subhadra's eyes. He was eighty-two years old. Until just six months before he had looked radiant. All his life he lived with total mindfulness within his Ayurvedic regimen, which made him fit, slim, and almost youthful with scarcely a wrinkle. Even his hair was still shiny black with only a dozen or so gray hairs. The only reason Father ever used to feel a little old, he would tell me, was because at the age of seventy-six he had replaced all his teeth with a set of dentures. Father hated the word *old*. Whenever my mother called him "old" he used to give his definition of *old* as "whoever looks really old, with head bent, back hunched, failing eyesight, weak hearing, and mucus and saliva dripping from the nose and mouth, crouching down facing into a dark corner. It is your mind which makes you think you are old; it is not your age."

Now, seeing his health deteriorated, I felt deeply saddened.

"How is your health?" I asked.

For the first time ever he used his taboo word, *old*. "My old body is not much use for anything. I wish I could be inside and you could be released so that you can be active."

I did not expect this from him because he had always been against my being in opposition politics.

But now, sitting on the bench, he exhorted me, "Whatever the government wants you to say, say it. Write, sign, and come out."

"If I say what they want me to say, I'll never come out," I said seriously.

He sighed, then revealed, "I went to the prime minister because I thought it was my duty to go to him first as he is from our district. He said to me, '*Guruji*, if it was under my control I would free her now, but this is a palace matter—I cannot interfere. One thing I can assure you is that, instead of twenty years, if I can I will try to help so that she's imprisoned for only ten years. Other than that there's nothing I can do."

I told my father, "Maybe he was not the right person to go to."

One of the policemen quickly interrupted, "That kind of talk is not allowed here."

My father rebuked him, "Why is it not allowed? This is my youngest daughter." Then Father continued, "I have sent a petition to the king also. I don't want to die leaving you in jail."

The police said several times that the time was over. I had to go in. Before I went my father admonished me, "Do not lose patience, and do not lose your consciousness. Meditate as much as you can."

"That I am doing," I said, and went back inside. I was not allowed to wave from inside the gate.

As soon as I stepped inside, my eyes as always met the naked form of Saacha, hanging as if crucified from the beam. As I stood opposite her, she asked, "Durga *didi*! I heard your father came to see you. Did he bring you lots of money? If he did will you buy a *bidi* for me?"

I replied, "Whether he brought me money or not I'll buy you a *bidi*." Then I thought to myself, "It would have been good if Father *had* brought me some money."

I was still there talking to my fellow inmates when a police guard came and said, "Jailer *Saheb* wants to see you."

I thought, "Maybe he is going to allow me to see more visitors in his office. I went with the usual number of armed guards in the jeep. My mood was mixed—a little happy, a little lost, a little sad, but not contemplative.

The jailer asked, "How was the meeting?"

"What to say, maybe it was okay," I replied, unsure of what was in his mind.

He became serious, "Our boys were complaining that you and your father were talking about something undesirable. I'm warning you, that could delay your release."

I turned a little angry. "Okay, don't allow my visitors to come then. When someone like my father comes he likes to tell me a few of the things that are going on outside. If that's not proper, then why don't you brief my visitors exactly what they should say and should not say before they meet me?"

Handing over two hundred rupees to me, he said, "Your father and

Shrish wanted to leave you some money. I said not to leave more than this because if you have too much money inside your life could be at stake. Don't tell anybody that you even have this amount."

The jeep took me back. I started questioning myself how to use this money. Should I buy lots of sugar and tea? But to last how long? Or should I buy another sari to wear, or a nightdress, or good vegetables and fruit, or what? I decided not to use it in buying various foodstuffs as that would offend others. So I asked Mara what were the most urgent things we needed. She said, "Tea dust, firewood, cooking oil, soap." Soap seemed a good idea, as we used the same detergent for washing ourselves that we used for washing clothes. Mara calculated that all the immediate necessities would cost thirty rupees. I would still be left with one hundred and seventy rupees. I did not know what to do. What a paradox, in a situation of scarcity you did not know what to do with that little extra money when it came to you. Before my arrest I would spend two hundred rupees just to have pancakes and coffee with a friend at the Annapurna Hotel. Now this money seemed such a big commodity. I decided to improve my knitting, and sent fifty rupees to buy needles and wool. It was really a good investment. I learned to knit from the other inmates, and even learned how to make rugs.

I still faced one dilemma—whether to start smoking filter cigarettes. Before this arrest I had never smoked in my life. Yet, in Mahakali even a three-year-old girl used to smoke the locally made *bidi*. I was out of place. The way Potha used to offer them to me, I could not refuse. She would bend down with the *bidi* in her right hand, left hand holding her right, and beg me, "*Saheb*, just a puff—it is mild." I could not avoid it. Within a month I became a chain smoker. I did not have any preference. Whatever was available, *bidi* or paper, used to satisfy me. "Yak" Nepali filters used to cost about ten rupees a packet, while *bidi* cost only thirty *paisa*. I decided not to spend so much money on smoking filters. Also, I did not know how long I would be inside. If, as the prime minister had told my father, he was going to make it ten years, then there was no way I could afford expensive cigarettes anyway.

One day during a visit, Manjoor noticed that the thumb and first and second fingers of my right hand were all burned black. He asked me how that had happened. I had to admit that it was from smoking *bidis* down to their last puff before my fingers burned.

He offered, "I will supply you 'Yak' cigarettes."

I thanked him, but refused. "No, don't do it. You don't know how many I need these days."

"I will buy one pack a week," he insisted.

I did not want him to bring them, but he did, and I kept quiet about them. In one packet there would be twenty. Dividing by seven meant not even three a day. It was nothing like enough, and anyway I still did not want to live differently from the other women. Nonetheless, Manjoor started sending them as he promised. Only when I was in my room with just my three roommates did I ever take out one of my filters and pass it around so that we each took a few puffs. In the yard I smoked *bidis*, which I shared even with the lunatics.

Shrish thought I might be released after my ninth month was completed. Privately, I too was sure that I would be. During these whole nine months I had very few visitors. Even my supposedly very close female friends did not come. From my huge extended family also no one came besides my father, Subhadra, my second eldest brother, and three of my nephews, who came once. Whenever my friends or family came I received a treat like some bananas, oranges, or biscuits. That was a real luxury and I would share whatever it was with the other inmates. I did not feel like eating anything by myself. On two occasions, foreign friends sent me a surprise through the jail office. A plate of good Western vegetarian food, sent by Syd, arrived on one of these occasions—it was on my birthday, which I had forgotten all about. Only two days later did I realize that the food had come on that day. Even then, I imagined that it had just been a coincidence.

Once in a while I would wonder why my other friends did not come. But after my father's visit I could guess that if the rumor going around was about a "palace matter," then who would risk coming to see someone involved in such a matter?

One day Manjoor came to tell me that my landlady wanted to rent my apartment to the Indian embassy military man living in the floor below. I had already arranged to pay the landlady rent in advance and wondered why she wanted to move me out. What would happen to all my belongings? I asked Manjoor to talk to her nicely. "If it looks as though I will be here for a long time, then I will arrange to be moved from there," I said. "Otherwise I will need a place to live after I am out."

Manjoor came again on the next visiting day and reported, "She heard through the zonal commissioner's office that you are involved in some trouble with the palace, so she doesn't want to rent her house to you anymore. Together with the Indian man she has dumped all of your stuff in one little room, and he has already moved up there."

What could I do? The government had the power to manipulate as it pleased. I never imagined that my landlady would turn against me in this way. She had always been quite agreeable. Anyway, I had a little valuable property that I would need sometime if I was ever released. I decided to write a petition through the jailer to the zonal commissioner. In it I mentioned the amount of cash that I had kept in my trunk, and the items of gold jewelry and silver—precious family heirlooms given to me by my father and mother. I also had one hundred heavy silver British Indian coins. Other things I was less worried about. I wrote out three copies of my petition and sent one to the jailer, one through him to the zonal commissioner, and kept one for my own records. Whether the jailer forwarded my petition or not, I had no clue. Even if he did, what would the zonal commissioner do—the same man who had told my landlady of my involvement in a "palace matter"—no doubt assuming that I would not be released?

I think I became irrational sometimes hoping that government people would do something to help me. Why should they? If they could do anything good for me, or for anyone else like me, then they would not be trying to liquidate me. I was in no better a situation than the women around me, imprisoned on alleged criminal charges. They had been targeted by the local *Panchas*. I had been targeted by the highest level *Panchas*. One could expect anything in this arbitrary environment of victimization.

# 11
.

# Petition
# to the Wrong Door

verybody was guessing that I would be released after completing nine months because this was the maximum that someone
could be detained at one stretch under the Public Security Act.
When only fifteen days were left I started counting down the hours. One
day before completing my nine months I was absolutely ready to be released
the next day. My heart was beating quickly with anticipation. Just one more
night. I started feeling that in some ways I would miss this environment.
Normally one could never live in such oppression and misery. But the realization came to me that if my sentence here were not for life, then I could
turn this experience into something worthwhile by writing about it. Then
it would have been worth sacrificing nine months to be here. I had already
spent over a year in various jails and police custodies before this. Those
experiences also entered this fresh realization, but having realized it, I did
not desire a day more of the torture and frustration.

We were eating our morning meal as usual. Two heavy tears dropped
from Mara's eyes. Kripa and Susa got their chance and started crying aloud.
I was sad for them, too. I told them that I would always be with them in
my spirit. Somehow we finished eating. I offered them my remaining filter
cigarettes. I was not going to smoke outside.

At around eleven we were about to go out into the yard when the
*Chaukidarni* came running over, saying, "People have come to see you."

I replied, "Today isn't my visiting day, so who could come?"

Anyway, I followed her. Outside the gate two men from the jail office and two unfamiliar men were waiting for me. The policewomen asked me to remain standing inside the gate. One of the unfamiliar men pushed a piece of paper through the gate and gave me an order, "You have to sign here."

I asked, "What is it?"

"Oh, it's just a formality," replied the man.

"I won't sign anything without first reading it," I said.

"Okay, read it then," he said.

I read it. It was an extension order for my imprisonment for another nine months.

I refused to sign it and told the men, "I will only complete my first nine months tomorrow. I know that under this act detention cannot be extended unless I am first released even if only for five minutes."

The men absolved themselves. "We don't know about that. We're not the lawmakers. We just have to follow the orders from above."

"Go and tell whoever it was that sent you that I did not agree to sign because it is illegal to extend a prisoner's detention order inside jail," I told them, and turned back into the prison yard. My fellow inmates all started asking me if I was going to be released today. I announced that my stay with them had been extended for another nine months.

After an hour the same men returned, this time entering the jail along with some male and female police officers. Again they pressured me to sign the order. I declined. Finally they posted the arrest letter outside my door. This would have been a legal notification outside prison if I had declined to sign, or if I had been underground or had otherwise escaped arrest. But for a person already detained in prison, it had no legality. I thought, "What is legal about any of this in my case anyway? From the very beginning up to now all the government's actions have been lawless. I should not expect any legal action from them."

I could say that I was very unhappy, but really I was not. Immediately, I converted all my past days' excitement about release into fantasy. This really helped. You can fantasize about anything you want. You just let your mind run far away in quest of something that is not available and then pretend you got it. Being that which you quest, even for a moment, helps you feel free from the pull of that desire. You can feel it, caress it, observe it, and analyze that state of "you," and then allow your mind to let go of it. I brought my mind back. As I came back I felt as though my mind had traveled straight up to the sky vertically, perhaps because within the prison walls there was no horizon. Maybe because of this, instead of returning slowly my mind came back so fast that it fell down as it landed. I was left with the same shaken feeling as you have sometimes after waking from a frightening dream.

After being served with the extension of a further nine months, I began to accept that I faced real uncertainty. I reconciled myself to an imprisonment of anywhere between eighteen months and the ten years that the prime minister had told my father. What other option but acceptance remained anyway?

As usual Shrish came on visiting day. He seemed worried. I did not blame him. It must have been very difficult for him to manage the press on his own. I had heard, too, that Upendra was not quite well, and so was unable to help Shrish properly. On top of that, Upendra had his other full-time job. Shrish had come with a proposal for me about the press. A close friend of his was expressing interest in running it. I also knew him. On a personal level he was not a bad sort, but politically he was the former president of the government-backed student union and was still closely associated with the prime minister.

I told Shrish, "I definitely can't be in partnership with him. On principle it would be impossible. But I'm not in a position to suggest anything, being locked up here, so you decide whatever suits you."

Shrish mentioned that the friend had said that he could run the paper, not the press. We left it up to the friend to decide where he would fit in.

The other matter that Shrish discussed with me was that he would try to seek an audience with "Number three." I agreed. We had to talk through a sort of code language. "Number three" became our way of indicating the king's youngest brother, who was Shrish's class friend.

With the *Chaukidarni's* permission, I started offering tea to my visitors, which meant my visitors along with all the other hangers-on—policemen, women guards, and the jailer's staff. At least twelve cups of tea were involved each time. I had that money now, so I could afford it. The advantage of doing this was that the time it took for tea to be made, handed around, and consumed bought me a few more minutes' time with my visitors. Also, while everybody was busy sipping their tea my visitors and I could talk a little more freely. Mara used to make the tea. In deference to the other women's feelings, by now I had given up the habit of drinking tea inside prison altogether, and drank only when I had visitors.

After Shrish left and I went back inside I had much to think about and many ideas to play with. Playing with ideas was the best part of being alone and, as a political prisoner, the only one in my category. I thought deeply about Shrish's first proposition. My intuition told me, "No, definitely not. It's difficult enough being a partner even with Shrish and Upendra. Even now I am attacked politically. If this friend of theirs joins our press, there will be no way I can defend myself. It's absolutely impossible." Also, I was not sure about this new man's intentions. Why did he want to come and be a partner with a Nepali Congress-run business, and especially at a time when I was locked up? The only explanation my mind could find was that because of his political persuasion he was being sent to sabotage the reputation of my paper and my press business. I reached the conclusion that there was some maneuvering going on in the government's chess game. The next time Shrish came I decided to tell him my opinion in no uncertain terms. It would have to be a matter of "either him or me."

I turned my mind to Shrish's second idea, of meeting "Number Three." If the king had not heard what had really been going on, now he would come to know and maybe he would realize that I had been trying only to save his son's life. I was not a culprit. Perhaps if the king understood this he would grant me mercy. As this thought came to me, I felt ready to do anything, even to stand on my head. I smiled to myself while thinking this, because in fact standing on my head was the simplest thing for me—I was well experienced in yoga at that time. As I reflected, I began to feel a little flash of light somewhere at a deeper level. A few days later, I meditated much longer than ever, very deeply, and on the third night after that, I had a very positive dream that the king would do something good for me.

The next day Shrish came and through the usual hints and obfuscations somehow made me understand that he had secured a chance to meet the youngest prince, and that the royal response was that I should write a petition to the king. I signaled to Shrish that I agreed. But about the press question I told Shrish that if I had been out my answer would be a straight no. But in my present position I could only consent to Shrish's managing the press in whatever way he could in order to keep it going. As usual, I waved good-bye and stepped back inside the gate.

As I thought more about writing the petition to the king I became quite excited. While there is life there is hope, I reminded myself. After all, the king was the Supreme Law Giver. The Supreme Court had been powerless to vindicate me. But my last hope would still be the king even if I were in a case with a specific charge. Also, I did not harbor any personal animosity toward him. Politically, as a democrat, I wanted the king for Nepal. Traditionally and spiritually as a Hindu also, I respected the ideal of a benevolent king. I was critical only of those kings whose actions strayed from their *dharma*, or the moral duty of protecting their subjects.

"What are you thinking about, *didi?* You still haven't changed your sari," Mara said, interrupting me.

"I don't believe it," I exclaimed. "I've been in this room all by myself for half an hour!"

"*Didi,* today's the fourth day of both Kripa's and Susa's periods, so they had a wash in the morning and also took all their belongings outside to air in the sun. If they don't stay out there with their things a *pagal* might crap or pee on them, or bring something from the toilet and wipe it on their mattress," explained Mara, accounting for my roommates' absence.

I changed the subject back to my plans, telling Mara briefly that I had to write a petition to the king and that I needed some plain paper. She gave me two pieces, and I went to the schoolroom. First I meditated. I received a really positive feeling about what I was going to do. Then I wrote it.

In the petition I did not explain the whole story that I had to relate during police interrogation. The main point I made to the king was, "If I am imprisoned for the reason that the government is alleging, then I deserve more punishment—imprisonment is not enough. If I am not guilty then my arrest is very illegal. I did not receive justice from the Supreme Court. Therefore I am petitioning Your Majesty for justice."

Next day, early in the morning I sent it to the jailer, attaching a little note to him explaining how important and urgent this petition was, adding that I would be grateful if he could forward it directly to the king. Anyway, just by sending this petition I felt a little relieved. I was conscious that the government had already succeeded in putting me into such a trap that there was no way I could satisfy everyone that I was not a culprit. But what mattered was that I should convince the king that I was not.

When it came to others, I never tried to convince anyone about what I thought or did. I was vocal and critical about government policies. That by itself was more than enough for the people in power to want to make me the scapegoat of any conspiracy. Now I thought, "Thank God I'm still alive! I can expose those people involved in this, and maybe eventually they'll be punished." Then another inner voice admonished, "No, what are you thinking? Who could punish them? They're in power. All of them are in power to shield themselves, to remain pure, to pretend they're good. There's nowhere you can complain about them. The leader to whom you would complain could be one of them." A third mediating voice counseled me further: "Whom to trust? The palace? Who is the palace? That's the most intrigue-ridden place of all. If it was the king or the queen alone, then there might be some hope. They might listen to you. Otherwise, Durgaji, you will inevitably bear the stigma that the conspirators gave you."

When your fate has been toyed with by someone, you feel utterly help-less. You know what the truth is and how innocent you are, but people have forged the circumstances to project you as something completely different. The most unfair aspect of your situation is that there is no channel through which your voice can be heard by anyone. I had been itching in this irri-tation for nine months. But now at least I had started the process of com-munication. I went to bed that night feeling more relaxed.

The next morning I had just finished my food when a crow landed on the roof above our room and cawed raucously. Mara stopped what she was doing for a second, looking up and listening, then said, "*Didi*, you must be going to get some message today."

"Oh, how could that be?" I replied incredulously. "I only sent the peti-tion yesterday. It takes time to reach the palace and to be acted upon. I don't think there can be any response yet."

The crow did not give up until the *Chaukidarni* came across the public yard shouting, "Eh! *Kaag*, what news have you got for our *Netaji*? It's not good cawing. He is cawing nervously." Then she came up to our room to say, "This is not good news he's bringing."

I queried her, "Why do you think it's for me? It could be for anybody."

"No, he's perched just above your bed and his beak is pointing down to-wards your pillow," she emphasized.

"Nothing could be worse than what has happened already," I assured her.

I lit a filter cigarette and offered it to her. As a person, the *Chaukidarni* was fun, with a really lively sense of humor—though mostly very vulgar. But she was illiterate, so I excused her.

At around nine-thirty A.M. a policewoman shouted up from the yard below, "Hey! That *Chaukidarni*, where's she lying dead?"

The *Chaukidarni* went out, shouting back rudely, "Whose mother-in-law or father-in-law came then?"

After a couple of minutes the *Chaukidarni* sent her *Mulnaike* to our room to tell me, "It's your visitor, Durga *bahini*."

I did not believe her. "Don't be silly, how could I have a visitor today? It's not Sunday."

"True! It is your visitor." The *Mulnaike* described him: "He's tall and has a mustache."

I could not figure out who it could be. Then the thought crossed my mind, "Could it be that lean lawyer who wrote my statement during the police interrogation? He was tall and had a mustache."

I had not combed my hair and was not wearing my sari. I told the *Mul-naike*, "Please go and tell him that it will take me a few minutes to come."

"You don't need to dress up," the *Mulnaike* advised me. "There are no police with him, and nobody from the jail office to take notes, so you'll have to talk to him from inside the gate."

Now I was sure that my visitor was that police lawyer.

I walked across the yard toward the gate. A tall figure was standing in the shadows under the porch. I approached nearer until I caught his stare. It was not the lawyer. It was Setha, the one who had called me to meet him that night in the Summit Hotel. I halted instantly to turn back to my room. But before I could take a step away he grabbed my attention.

"You gave the petition to the wrong door," were his words.

I hesitated. I did not want to see this man ever again, but he came with so tempting a message that I could not stop myself from reacting.

"What do you mean?" I questioned him.

He said, "The petition should go first to the prime minister."

"Who is greater?" I asked. "Your prime minister or the king?" I did not wait for his comment and walked away back toward our cell block. I thought to myself, "Now it is obvious who the people were in the plot. They are exposing themselves."

But it seemed that I now had a serious problem. The petition I had sent only the previous day might not have gone to the palace at all. How did this man know that I wrote the petition? Did the jailer call his big boss, the home minister? Did he then tell the prime minister, who sent this man here to harass me once again, twisting a knife in the wound? What had happened? What a mystery. There was no way I could find out. I could only signal something about the problem to Shrish on the next visiting day. Maybe he could decipher things somehow.

After this incident several other unwanted visitors came to the gate. The intrusions became wearisome. Finally I had to write a letter to the jailer saying that I wanted to meet with only certain people. I wrote down the names of those I would see.

Shrish came on the next visiting day and asked whether I had written the petition. I explained what had happened, and he suggested, "Write it again today. I'll wait at the jailer's office and get the registration number to give to 'Number one.' "

I agreed. Immediately after he left I went into action. In the second petition I mentioned the first one as well. As I went through these motions I felt as if I were entering data into a black box and could only wait and see what the output would be.

After sending version two to the jailer through the police I went back to my room to relax—if there was anything like relaxation. Only Mara was there.

She remarked, "It will be so lonely if you go out."

I assured her, "Perhaps I can be more effective outside than being locked up in here."

She also had to go to see someone down in the yard, so I had a few moments of solitude. I began to doubt that there was any way of getting even a hint of whether my petition would reach the palace. And even if it went, whether the king had received it. Even if he did, what would be his reaction? All these anxieties started building up in my mind. The only thing I could do was to activate my whole mind and body toward positivity and meditate longer.

On Thursday there was a little commotion near the gate. A rumor spread like wildfire, and within a minute an excited bunch of women came running over to where I was sitting in the sun with Mara.

Breathlessly they reported, "Someone just like the king is here! Big, royal-looking, with dark glasses. Is it the king come to meet you, Durga *didi?*"

The *Chaukidarni* summoned me to see my visitor. It was Upendra, the queen's uncle and my colleague from the press. He was accompanying Shrish today. A religious man, he had brought me the full text of the longer invocation to Lord Ganesh. This is what I had been so desirous to have. To his devotees Ganesh embodies the qualities of humility, cheerful obedience, and self-discipline, and when worshipped he opens doors and brings success. The long prayer assures you that even as you chant the verses—allowing your consciousness to dwell on his image and in the supernatural influence that the sound of his names produces—all fear will vanish, and whatever you desire with good mind and trust will be fulfilled.

Shrish kept repeating "Number one" and simultaneously nodding his head positively, which I took to mean that my petition might have reached the palace. We were being extracautious. If the clerks wrote down even one careless word our whole plan could be disturbed. Shrish put a finger to his lips to remind me, and I kept quiet about this most vital topic for the rest of the time while we had tea together. Then I went back inside, waving good-bye.

When visitors came I used to feel like a little blink of life had shown itself on a dark canvas of death. Many times I had no visitor, either because nobody came or because it was a government holiday. Those days were especially sad ones for me. I would begin thinking that if I was going to remain there for the time the prime minister had indicated to my father, then I would become as forgotten as the other inmates around me.

I decided to perform an extended devotion to Ganesh. It is a ritual that a Ganesh devotee follows at any time when in special need of good fortune to influence the course of destiny. We believe, too, that it helps to make one's consciousness more open and responsive to wherever nature is leading. It involves some fasting and chanting of the longer Ganesh mantra one hundred and eight times, usually over four days starting on Saturday morning and ending on Tuesday morning—the day marking Ganesh's birth. On the third night, the night before the Tuesday morning, I had a powerful vision of Lord Ganesh himself showing me kindness. Seeing this, I thought that my experience of refined consciousness had reached its climax. I stayed awake with this vision for the rest of the night as one always should after a revelation of this kind.

The dawn paled the sky of Tuesday—the day I always fast for Ganesh. On this particular morning I began the final devotion of the four-day ritual and fasted all day. As I slept that night, I experienced what *bhakti yoga* Hindus would call the supreme manifestation of their devotion. I was visited by the Living Ganesh in a dream. When I awoke I found myself still tingling from his presence. The dream happened at between two and three o'clock in the morning. The duty *naike* and *kamdars* and the police guards came and disturbed me on their rounds at three A.M. But I did not mind. The dream was complete, and I had no regret that they woke me up. For the second half of the night I did not want to go back to sleep anyway. I did not want the best dream of my life to be diverted by another, perhaps bad, dream. It was easy to stay awake for another three hours. The light shining away above my head was good enough to look at. The night guards' noises would continue for another hour. The rest of that day I really managed to feel alive.

On my next visiting day I told Shrish that I might be released soon. He was not very sure because he did not have any feedback. But I was absolutely positive that the palace must have received the right information about the plot. In my mind I saw only the king as the palace because I did not trust the palace courtiers—some of them knew about this scandal and were suppressing it. If the king was reviewing the information then maybe the conspirators would be punished and, while I did not expect any reward, at least the king would return my freedom to me. I decided to live in this positive hope.

Only Shrish knew about my petition to the king. My other occasional visitors must have given up on me by now. After the nine-month extension of my sentence most of them stopped coming. I did not blame them. It was troublesome to get to see me. One might get to the jailer's office only to find that somebody else had already seen me, using up the one ten-minute visit I was allowed that day. Even if someone happened to be the first visitor of the day, he or she had to wait until the jailer's men were ready, and then wait for the police. In the meantime another friend might telephone the jailer to fix a time to see me that day. The first visitor would then be asked to wait until the caller turned up. If by that time more than five people had come, one or more would be denied access. Nobody could spare the whole day waiting around to see me just for ten minutes, and even then not to be free to talk. I realized, of course, that all this was precisely what the government was planning for me—that I should languish in prison until I was another forgotten case. But even as I thought this, my hopes were not killed.

ဘ

One evening, just before the gates were locked, I heard a great commotion out in the yard. I had heard nothing like it since the day in my childhood when there was a mad dog in Dhankuta and twenty or thirty adults and children had all been shouting at once to try to frighten the dog from biting somebody.

Mara came running. "*Didi, didi,* some catastrophe is about to happen!"

"What?" I asked, alarmed.

"Two *kuhirinis* have been brought. They don't speak Nepali and *Chaukidarni* has given the order for their treatment like new arrivals," Mara explained, still breathless.

*Kuhiro* means "mist" in Nepali, and is our colloquial term for white people because of their light-colored eyes. I hurried out and saw indeed two white women seated on the step outside the *Chaukidarni*'s room.

"Does anyone here speak English?" one of them was calling out excitedly in an American accent, unwitting of what was being planned.

One of the *naikes* was replying in Nepali, "Whatever you are saying, we don't understand. But we have to carry out our job." With this she went forward and started trying to pull at the dress of one of them, saying in Nepali, "You have to take this off, off!"

Others started heckling and jeering. But the white women did not understand a thing and were laughing.

"Laugh now, laugh, that's okay. What will result from your laugh you will see!" *Chaukidarni* spurred on her workers: "Get on with it. Open their clothes, panties and all; then they'll understand!"

The *Chaukidarni* moved right up to them and shouted into their ears, "Under what case are you brought?" People tend to think in Nepal that if you shout loudly enough, foreigners will understand your language. But in response the white women were just laughing.

I decided the moment had come to intervene. I asked the *Chaukidarni*, "Can I talk to them?"

She relaxed her usual rules. "I am told that you can't talk to anyone, but we have to know their cases, so you may ask them." Then she turned to her crew and remarked, laughing, "I'm sure the police must have found these *kuhirini* sleeping with men on the open street."

From her perspective the guess was not unreasonable. During the 1960s and early 1970s Nepal was a paradise for hippies. The lasting impression this era left among the common people of Nepal was that any white person was a hippie and of loose character. These women inmates had seen many female hippies brought in by the police for antisocial activities in public places. Even among other Nepalis, because of the hippie period, white people are generally taken to be Americans, and all Americans are thought to be hippies or, if not, then CIA agents. However, I knew otherwise and said to these two white women, "Hello, can I help you?"

"Oh, you speak English!" one said, obviously relieved.

I explained to them briefly the way the prison was run inside and who the *Chaukidarni* and other crew were. Then I told them that as a matter of routine the *Chaukidarni* wanted to know their charge.

"Where is your arrest slip?" I requested.

"We don't have one," replied one, and then revealed, "But we are here for gold smuggling."

It was lucky that they did not have an arrest slip—I was spared the problem of explaining their charge. Had the *Chaukidarni*'s workers known at that moment that it was gold smuggling goodness knows what would have happened. They could have been murdered that night. Already speculation was growing over their gold hairpins, but I defused this by saying, "Oh, they're not real gold, just a golden color—they're very common in America," even though at that time I had never set foot outside Asia. It was good that they did not have more gold jewelry—they could have been in danger. I suggested to them not to reveal their charge.

I told the *Chaukidarni*, "They were coming from Hong Kong and were arrested at the airport. They do not know the cause. Maybe they did not have permission to enter Nepal or something like that, they cannot tell."

But instinctively she guessed. "Maybe gold smuggling."

In a way it was not surprising that she guessed right. This was the peak of gold smuggling during Panchayat rule. Many top Panchayat politicians, bureaucrats, businessmen, and even military and police officers were involved in moving gold illegally from Hong Kong and Bangkok via Nepal to India, where the import of twenty-four-karat gold was prohibited along with other foreign goods.

Anyway, for the safety of these two foreign women I had to lie. The night of arrival was the most dangerous for any newcomer in jail. Even if someone were killed, if the murderer was from the administration she would receive no additional punishment to the term she was already serving. Staying overnight and the whole of the next day, the newcomers would circulate among other inmates inside and become noticed by the outside police, making their position stronger. Because of my intervention these two were not mistreated, but the *Chaukidarni*'s crew were not very happy about this.

I was curious to know how on earth the girls had become involved in gold smuggling in the first place. They were both very pretty—fair-skinned, but with dark hair, eyes, and eyelashes. They wore no makeup, so the natural light shone from their faces. All the inmates remarked that they were the prettiest white women they had seen, and that if they dressed in saris they could look Nepali—a compliment. Talking with them for a while, I learned that they had been coming into Nepal as ordinary visitors. In Hong Kong's airport a man introducing himself as a businessman asked them to take gold to Nepal for him, offering to cover their airfare and a luxury hotel in Nepal and to give them extra money for gifts for friends and family back home. So one girl carried six kilograms of gold and the other girl two. At Tribhuvan International Airport in Kathmandu they were caught by customs officials. In such smuggling cases, if the officials and duty police were not bribed in advance by the concerned "businessman," the carrier would be handed over to other police. Then by law they had to be taken to prison, from where they could fight their cases.

The two Americans were provided with food by the *Chaukidarni* that first night, for which she would reimburse herself from their next day's ration. Later, we had a little celebration for our new inmates—a few songs and dances in which they were invited to join, and just some chatting and laughing. Then they were asked to sleep in the women guards' room next to the *Chaukidarni*'s. The next morning, with the *Chaukidarni*'s permission, I was able to invite them for tea in my room. However, I did not have an opportunity to tell them much about myself except that I was a political prisoner.

৩৩

All the messages that I was getting from outside were that I should not hope for an early release. Even my landlady sent a final message through Manjoor, and one of the policewomen, saying that if nobody would remove my belongings then she would bring in someone from the zonal commissioner's office and throw my things on the road. I had nothing to say. What could I say if the government people were still pursuing me so badly that they would do anything to harass and hurt me? It seemed they wanted to dispose of anything to do with me, whether it was throwing my belongings out or myself in. I decided that the problem with my landlady was just another small test to make me stronger. I detached myself from my belongings. After my release I could always stay with some friends who were not afraid of me. If I went to my father he would not close his door. Detaching myself from those material belongings and opening this positive channel of thought made me feel good.

# 12

·

# Farewell Without Good-bye

Chait, half March and half April, is the last month of the year according to our Bikram Sambat calendar and the beginning of the very hot premonsoon season we call summer. A very long time ago, the main Hindu festival of Durga Puja used to be celebrated in this month. One of the things about Dasain is that people tend to eat too much, and once after Dasain it so happened that most of the people fell sick. When this happened the ruler thought that holding Dasain in summer was ill advised and decreed that henceforth the main Dasain festival should be celebrated in October. Nonetheless, people still celebrate Chaite Dasain as a mini-festival in the buildup to the monsoon.

Some of my fellow inmates proposed celebrating Chaite Dasain inside jail. I was a little reluctant. Being a strict vegetarian and not believing in animal sacrifice, I had never enjoyed the way Dasain was celebrated. One of the main events of Dasain is the sacrifice of animals—goats, chickens, buffalo bulls, or anything except cows, according to caste.

Instead of celebrating Chaite Dasain, I proposed that we celebrate the Nepali New Year's Day, which would be the first of Baisakh, in mid-April. They agreed. It was to be an unprecedented event inside the jail. I helped with the organizing. All the women contributed whatever they could offer, whether a few rupees or a few *paisa*. We made a menu of a potato *tarkari* (a mild curry), cucumber *achar* (chutney), and *khir*—rice pudding spiced with cardamom, cinnamon, sultanas, cashews, and sugar, a traditional Nepali dish. For most it would be the first time they had tasted anything different in years.

On the last day of Chait, our New Year's Eve, the jailer sent policemen to take me to his office. As usual I went by jeep with the seven police guards. As I entered his room he said, "The zonal commissioner wants to see you."

"What next?" came from my lips, unintentionally.

"Maybe he wants to discuss something," suggested the jailer.

"Why? I don't see any point. I'm not really in the mood to go and see any government people whom I can possibly avoid," I told him.

Looking into my eyes, he insisted, "This is his order. You have to go to his office."

"I suppose I don't have any choice," I said, and followed the seven policemen back to the jeep, wondering, "Am I on the road to slaughter again?" The zonal commissioner was the one person I least wanted to meet again. But here I was on my way to see him—a key player in the whole saga. Whether or not he was involved directly, he was responsible for the situation. Yet although charged with keeping his zone's "peace and order," he had not made any effort to investigate the plot. Instead he had imprisoned me. If he was not a coconspirator himself, why had he not come to see me during my police custody and tried to uncover the truth? I was sure that without his green light that kind of conspiracy could not have been staged. Either he was one of them, or he was very weak and stupid at providing security.

They took me on the five-minute drive to his office. The jeep stopped. I felt as if I had woken up. Outside his door was his guard. I moved forward, telling him that I had been asked to come.

"P.A. *Saheb* is in there with him. Let him come first," the guard instructed me.

In a few minutes the zonal commissioner's personal assistant emerged and asked me to follow him into a large meeting room. "Wait here. *Anchaladhishjyu* will come soon," the P.A. told me.

The room looked like a big conference room. I sat in a chair that was alone in a corner. The P.A. left me there and closed the door and went out. I could not guess what the drama might be now. I had lost all faith, if I had ever had any, in Panchayat government officials. In my experience, they were always devious and double-dealing.

After a while the *Anchaladhish* entered the room. To show common courtesy I stood up, placing my hands flat together, and said, "*Namaskar.*"

He also did the same to me and very politely requested me to sit down. I looked at his eyes. They were extremely big, cool, and cruel. I had known him in the past. But I did not remember noticing then the evil look I saw now. Maybe I had developed a feeling of hatred for these people whose action had always been to crush the popular movement and cover up the reality from the king, helping him into his "Emperor's New Clothes." But one day the king had to realize how he had been made naked. I hoped that it would not be too late for him.

As I stared at him he said in a labored, artificial tone of voice, "Durgaji! I have a very good piece of news to tell you. That is why I wanted to meet you myself and congratulate you."

I did not show any enthusiasm. For a year I had been listening to this kind of language. I hated it. Whether it was a police constable, a police chief, or a zonal commissioner—they all spoke in the same insidious manner. I looked at the floor. If I let my tongue loose I might say something very nasty, so I controlled myself. Then I asked, "What for, to celebrate my anniversary?"

"Whatever happened, it happened, Durgaji. It's gone. You have to forget." He went on, "*Maharajdhiraj*, His Majesty himself, has ordered your release tomorrow, on New Year's Day. Therefore I thought I must let you know personally. That is why I asked the jailer to send you here."

I was looking at the man, but my eyes were unfocused, my gaze far beyond him. I did not feel overwhelmed with happiness. Rather I felt the futility of all my suffering, and how unnecessarily I had been made a victim. A year of my life had gone, and for what? I could have been killed, but for him it was just a normal event to be announcing my release. I found the song of my inmates playing in my mind. *"Our childhood we spent playing. To government we sacrificed our youth. . . ."* In my case, I had spent altogether just over two years imprisoned. And I had sacrificed my childhood and youth; there had been no play.

I averted my eyes and looked at his feet as I told him, "If I am released, it could only be by the king's order because the government wanted me imprisoned for at least ten years for a crime I did not commit. If I am given the chance to have an audience with him I'll tell him the truth so that the real conspirators get punished." I indicated to him my knowledge of who they were.

Becoming rather serious, he said, "Yes, yes. You must tell everything. As a matter of fact, His Majesty wishes to see you. In any case, what kind of friends do you have in my relatives Shrish and Upendra—they should have come and told me the truth. If they had, you would not have had to be in jail."

His expression belied nervousness. I had developed a theory of my own by this time of "fifty percent truth." No matter how open people might appear to be, they tell you only fifty percent of the truth. In some cases this might not be intentional behavior, and in some cases it might not be necessary to reveal the full facts. But in most cases people lie. Maybe *lie* is too strong a word for concealing truth. I am not saying it is necessary always to tell one hundred percent of what you know. You can communicate something quite convincingly with only half the data. But there's always the rest of the story—the other half. So now, as I listened to this man, I knew that perhaps twenty-five percent of what he said was truth—that is, my release by the king. The other seventy-five percent I was not interested in.

After a while he took me into the waiting room where my guards were. They all saluted him and then took me back by jeep.

In the jailer's office, I told him why I had been called by the *Anchaladhish*.

Not believing me, the jailer declared, "It never happened before that a political prisoner could know beforehand about his release. You must be joking."

Just then the phone rang. It was the *Anchaladhish* on the line. Replacing the receiver, the jailer looked a little serious as he admitted to me, "Well, you are right. But I'm telling you, it never happened this way before."

Somewhere from within my heart some happy feelings burst into my being like rising bubbles, making me feel quite light. I felt as if I had been in a deep sleep for ages and now suddenly I was awake once more with full consciousness. But my concern was still how I was going to communicate with my fellow inmates that I was going to be released the next day. All the women were expecting to celebrate the New Year with me. I found myself asking for an extra day in jail.

I asked the jailer, "At what time will you release me?"

"It'll be sometime in the morning."

"Let it not be in the morning," I urged him. "My friends will feel hurt. Allow me to stay with them for the party."

"That is not possible," replied the jailer formally. "I am told to get you out of the prison before seven, and I have to follow the order. And there is one other thing I want to warn you about: Please do not use your secret agents to pass the news of your release outside so that all your supporters come to welcome you chanting slogans. I don't want a great reception party waiting for you. It could create problems. I will give Shrish a call and ask him only to come to my office. Also, don't you tell any of the other inmates about this."

He called in the senior policewoman and instructed her: "Tomorrow early in the morning bring Durgaji here and do not tell this to anybody."

She saluted and acknowledged, "Yes, sir."

Then I was taken back. Everybody was waiting at the gate anxiously. As I entered, all of them started saying how worried and sad they had been, thinking that maybe I had been released. I had been out for more than two hours. Nobody was ever taken outside for that length of time except to appear in court. I heard the policewoman whispering in the *Chaukidarni*'s ear about my release, warning her not to tell anybody else. I tried to lie to everybody that I was not going to be released soon. However, I did one thing against the jailer's instructions. The two American women were still there. When I got back inside I told them I was leaving.

"Gosh! Don't go now, they'll die without you," one exclaimed, thinking of the other women.

They were happy for me, but unhappy for themselves. They would have no one to talk to after tomorrow. Because they were not able to communicate outside, I suggested they write a letter to someone that I could then take and deliver. Although it was very risky to take their letter, I thought I could hide it under the sole of my shoe. Later they slipped me a letter to be delivered to one of the girls' American boyfriend. They also gave me a gift—a Gucci handbag—and a note for the jailer asking him to give me a bottle of Joy Patou perfume that he had not allowed them to take inside. I had nothing that expensive to give them in return. I had only the Tibetan dress that I had been wearing day and night for a year. It had been sewn from very good quality satin material, so it was still in good condition. That is what I gave to them. I do not know who wore it.

The *Chaukidarni* was very sad about my release. She would not even look in my direction. Once or twice I tried to catch her eyes. I wanted to tell her several things, such as how uncomfortable my presence might have been for her for such a long time. Perhaps I had made her job difficult when I had tried to intervene? Yet, each time I approached her now, I saw water in her eyes, and so I did not dare to approach too close to her. I was becoming very emotional as well. I remembered Mahakali and how everyone had cried, including myself. I had been living here much longer, and had been trying to live as one of them. I thought, "It must be hard for her to lose one of her family members and perhaps never be with her again." I had a similar sense of separation, too. Suddenly, I realized how bonded I had become with these women, with each one without exception—criminal or lunatic. I knew all their lives. I might never again be able to belong to a family like this group at the bottom of society, even though for the rest of my life my thoughts would always be with them.

I realized that the *Chaukidarni* acted out a cruelty not of her own self. It was just the wider system of administration, the Panchayat, working through her on her other innocent fellow inmates. She and her crew played out *Pancha* over target, police over suspect, and judge over defendant, victimizing, torturing, and punishing them over again for crimes they had not committed. Once cloaked by the mantle, the *Chaukidarni* became empowered with an evil influence. Whenever that influence was active, she became cruel. Therefore I did not blame her. She was just a bit of grime rubbed off the *Panchayati* body. She herself was a victim of the system.

Because of her sad mood she pretended that she had gone to sleep and ordered everybody not to disturb her. In a way this was helpful for me. I got a chance to go around all the cells to say hello. In my mind I was telling everyone good-bye, but my lips were ordered not to say it. Some of the women were new. I noticed that they had nothing on the floor to sleep on. I observed how unhealthy all the women looked—skinny and bloodless. Some of them were very pretty, but now you could see only the skeleton of beauty, but no light. If the women had known that I was going from one room to another they might have suspected. But I moved quietly, and inmates were not supposed to watch each others' rooms. I convinced the duty women that I wanted to see the newcomers.

At around nine P.M. I returned to my room. Kripa and Susa were already snoring. Mara was still doing the homework I had given her. As I gazed at each of them I felt very sorrowful, especially for Mara. I had to leave them tomorrow morning without saying good-bye. What would they do for the New Year's party? How would Mara manage her studies? I could not talk to her much, partly through sadness and partly because if I started talking more than usual or allowed any hint to escape she would understand immediately. Therefore I decided to sleep.

I pretended to fall asleep. Now I had to detach myself from there and take myself back into my old society. It was exciting to imagine restoring my lost freedom. But as soon as I let my mind run away I started worrying about all the challenges and difficulties that I knew I would face after release. Therefore I tried to stop myself from worrying. I realized, the main thing in life was physical freedom. Once your physical self is free you can do anything you want or plan. With this thought I tried to fall to sleep, but could not. The last duty women came at four and woke up everybody in the room. Now it would be quiet for two hours until six. I heard *tang*—four-thirty A.M.—then I must have fallen asleep. At six, two policewomen came and woke me up.

As usual they said, "The jailer wants to see you."

This time I knew what it was for. I got ready quickly. My roommates were asking, "Why does Jailer *Saheb* want to see Durga *didi* today this early, police *didi?*"

One of the policewomen replied, "We don't know. Big shots can give the order any time."

I could not look into anyone's face. I was sad because I was not able to say good-bye. Somehow it was the worst negation of all. The greatest emotion there ever might have been. That, too, we were denied.

"Please come back quickly, okay?" they called to me as I left.

"I will try, but in case I am late, don't wait for me—get on with the feast," I replied.

All said, "No! We will be waiting for you, no matter how long you are away."

Everybody seemed suspicious as I crossed the yard and walked toward the gate. I wanted to say good-bye at least to the one person who knew, apart from the two foreign women. But the *Chaukidarni* was still lying on her bed.

From the door I spoke quietly, "I will come to visit you soon, take care." Then I said "Bye bye" to the Americans and quickly ran outside, their letter hidden in my shoe.

The jeep was ready. It bumped along to the jailer's office. The jailer had told me that he would inform only Shrish, and only he was there. The jailer offered me tea, and while drinking the tea he confided, "Although you are no longer my prisoner, I wish you would be. My headache was much less while you were inside."

I did not know whether to believe him, and replied, "Maybe you are just trying to be nice. After all, I was the one who was always bringing you complaints. From now on you'll be in peace."

The jailer vouched, "No, while you were here I never had a single report from the main gate police that there had been any serious fighting or torture inside. And you never made demands for yourself, your complaints were always for the other women. Other political people just complain all the time about being kept with all those murderers and lunatics."

I wondered, "If that was not torture that I saw, then what else might there have been?" But I did not want to waste much time. Therefore, I said *namaste* to him and left the jail office. Shrish, sophisticated and brand conscious, pointed at my Gucci bag and perfume. "What's this? Coming from jail, and you leave with this!"

So it was that I was released.

# 13

## Free to Go Nowhere

As soon as we left the jail complex, I immediately experienced two strong emotions. I felt a deep-seated joy at being free again. Raised from the deathbed. I did not believe it was really me alive once more. Sometimes it might amuse one to imagine such unpleasant happenings as not being real. I had read some Russian authors' accounts of imprisonment. No matter which country, the pattern of harassment, subjugation, and torture was the same under any authoritarian government—whether its name was partyless Panchayat or "one-party" communism.

"Where do you want to go?" Shrish asked, starting his motorcycle.

"To see my father first," I requested.

The second emotion played for a while. I was out, but what was next? Where should I begin? What to begin? It was all over, but now there was a certain anticlimax and the excitement muddied with the problems that began flooding my mind. I felt a sudden heaviness as an awareness dawned in me that the people who had stolen my freedom had partly succeeded. For I realized that what I was feeling was demoralization. In my past nothing had daunted me or diminished my confidence. Now, somehow, I felt that that total unboundedness had been dented, and I wondered whether I would ever return to normality. For the moment I brushed these thoughts aside and enjoyed the freshness as the same green sari flapped in the breeze from the pillion of Shrish's motorcycle as it had on that fateful day a year before.

My father had made the twelve-hour journey from Dharan to Kathmandu several months before to visit me in jail. He was still in town and it was my sacred duty to see him first. He was staying with my eldest brother, whom I had not seen since September 1975—the time when my brother had given me the choice of "family or politics." It was extremely awkward to have to visit his house again. But, compared with seeing my father again, nothing else mattered. So I went straight there. Shrish did not want to go inside, and, on this occasion, I did not insist. I entered the front lobby alone, and there, just inside the doorway, was my father. He asked me into his room, next to the lobby. His eyes were watering.

"How are you, your health?" he asked.

"Fine," I replied.

Having now lived in America, I can visualize the kind of reunion another father and daughter might have in such circumstances. Meeting like we were, they might express much emotion, and hug and kiss. But in our culture after a daughter has her first menstruation and is considered an adult, she is never again touched by her father. Not hugging or kissing does not mean there is any less love and affection. Such feelings are mute in Hindu society. You can feel the vibration of love, but there is no need to show it. Without expression, it is understood by both. A father can touch his daughter's forehead with his finger while giving her *tika* during Dasain and other religious festivals. On such occasions the father even bows down at the daughter's feet. The last time he does so is during one of the marriage rituals, the *kanyadan*, which is like giving away the bride in the West. After this, the daughter belongs to the son-in-law, and her father does not bow down anymore.

I could see that he had many questions in his eyes and face.

"Shall I ask my cook to make a cup of tea for you?" he asked me.

I said, "No." I was not sure whether it would be ethical for me to drink or eat anything there without my brother's permission, as I had not seen or spoken to him for so long. They had a non-Brahmin woman cook and a servant. When my father went to stay there, they hired a Brahmin boy because my father, my mother, and my father's widowed sister were mindful of religious codes of purity and would not eat cooked food touched by anybody else except a pure Brahmin.

Now Father was concerned with my own purity. "Durga, prison is the same as hell," he reminded me. "After you are settled, you must perform a *yagya* ritual for your purification, either at home or at Pashupatinath."

"I will," I assured him.

He wanted to talk more. But I was in a hurry to go back to my apartment to find out what was going on. He wanted to give me some money for a taxi. I told him Shrish was waiting for me outside with his motorcycle.

Looking worried, my father whispered to me, "I was told his uncle used Shrish to get you arrested. Why are you going around with him?"

"That is absolutely wrong," I replied. "If I were not Shrish's friend I would have been killed or not released for years. He was the only one who helped me until today."

My father said, "I must talk to you in detail."

I promised to visit him the next day at noon, when he would be alone at the house.

Shrish and I went on to see Meenu Koirala, a student activist. She was much younger than I, but was very mature, confident, and a good soul.

She told me, "Your apartment has been taken over by the Indian military man. You can stay with me until you find another house."

I thought to myself, "She's such a young girl, but her heart is so great." I had no alternative anyway.

The next day I sent a message through someone to the friend of the foreign girls in jail. He arrived in no time. I handed over the letter and explained the situation inside. He was really grateful, and shared with me his plan to take their cases to the Supreme Court. I provided him with the names of some reliable lawyers. Within a couple of weeks, the girls left a note at my office saying, "We came to see you and have some real tea together, but we missed you." Nothing more. No address. I had no idea whether they would come to see me again or how I could find them. Anyway, I called the jailer, who told me that the court had decided their case in their favor in the sense that they were free to leave Nepal within twenty-four hours and never return. I wished so much that I had been at the press when they had come. "Well," I thought, "who knows when we might bump into each other again?" I just put their memory in a small corner of my mind and started thinking about the immediate problems facing me.

The first problem was that our press had been invaded by someone from the Panchayat side. Although I had nothing to say against this individual personally, he was one of the prime minister's closest people, and, moreover, a *Mandale*. The prime minister had made me suffer enough. It was like another trick, a slap in the face delivered even before I was released. I did not feel like turning my other cheek to these people. Even though I knew Shrish would be in an awkward position, I gave him an ultimatum that unless that man left our press I would not set foot inside it. So until

Shrish could arrange his departure I had nothing to do, either with my newspaper or with the press.

The next thing to sort out was my apartment, from which I had been evicted. I had no idea where my belongings were. After another letter to the zonal commissioner and a petition to the king on the matter brought forth no response, I asked two policemen, three *Panchas*, and a few friends to accompany me to my apartment. The landlady did not appear in person but sent her nephew to receive us.

What we found made my heart sink. My belongings had been dumped in one small room and all my suitcases and steel trunks had been forced open. More than eighty percent of my valuables were missing. Rats had eaten holes in my wool carpets and silk saris and everything smelled of their excrement. Books were ruined.

To please me the official witnesses made a note about my missing valuables and about the condition of my other belongings. Then I transferred these things to Meenu's. It took the whole day to move, with the help of two pushcarts that I had hired along with the four men who owned and pushed them. By law I had to inventory my possessions within thirty-five days of release if I wanted to register any complaint in court. So I followed the procedure and filed a petition in the District Court for recovering my valuables. Hari Har Dahal, a private lawyer and my personal friend, volunteered to plead on my behalf. As expected, I lost the case. My landlady was experienced in such dealings and she also had all the help from the establishment.

Because I had to deal with such personal problems I could not immediately go to see my father as I had promised. I asked Meenu to call my brother's number, and when my father came on the line I explained to him what had happened. He understood. He was sensitive, too, to the problem of my going to my brother's house, and suggested that I go there again to talk in detail after midday, when he would be by himself. My sister Subhadra also came from Dharan to Kathmandu to see me. Now she told me that people linked to the government had told her I had been dropped into the Sapta Koshi River from a helicopter, and that there would be no point in petitioning to inquire where I was. Subhadra also told me how strongly she had been discouraged from filing the *habeas corpus* writ by most people she had consulted. Even one of my own cousins, who was chief of the government newspaper, warned Subhadra that, as I was unmarried, even if I were killed it would not matter. My death would mean losing one person, whereas Subhadra had a husband and four children. By becoming involved in my case she might get in trouble—be imprisoned for a long time, or even worse. He whispered to her, "Even the walls have ears. Don't mention even her name anywhere."

My father had been told a variation on the military helicopter story—that I had been dropped into the Mahakali River. Now my father told me that ever since someone had fed him that lie he had begun feeling suddenly old and had lost his life's energy. He had not wanted to believe the rumor but it had certainly affected his aging. Only after I was produced alive at the Supreme Court did he feel himself wake up again. He confided, "For me, because of my age, it was too late to return to normal. You do not have children now, so you do not understand the feeling—how much it hurts when you know your child is missing and then you hear such heartbreaking news."

He was still doubtful about Shrish. He had been told that Shrish had partnered with me in the press simply because his hard-liner uncle wanted to get information about Nepali Congress activities through me. With sadness, he also told me that my brother might mind if I visited him too often since my brother was one of the doctors of the royal family. I promised Father that this would be the last time I visited him at my brother's house. I gave him Meenu's address and said that he could come to see me there if he wanted to. Father promised to give me money to pay a year's rent if I found a house.

Meenu and I then started looking around for an apartment. Whoever we approached, the reply was negative. They would just stare at me and ask, "When did you get out of prison?" After a week of house-searching, I realized that, for average people who earn their living from renting their houses, I was a criminal, just released from jail, with the stigma of hell. Worse than that, I was the supposed attempted kidnapper of the crown prince. It seemed I had no defense.

In the meantime, Shrish managed to remove his friend from the press and I resumed my work. The press had accumulated some quite sizable debts during my absence. My father came to Meenu's and then started coming to the press to meet me. He also promised to give me some money to help me get the press going again. My joy had no limits at getting my baby back. I decided to write a prison column in the paper and Shrish agreed.

On my second day back at the press, the telephone rang. It was the minister for education and culture. "Congratulations on your release!"

I laughed and asked, "Why are you congratulating me? What made you think of me?"

He also laughed. "Honestly, I did not know about your arrest or about your release. But while you were in jail, Amnesty International kept on writing me letters about your imprisonment, requesting me to free you. They might have thought that because I am education minister and you were a former university teacher, your release was my responsibility."

"Did you write back to them?" I asked.

He hedged a little. "I don't want to tell you everything."

"Don't tell, then."

"No, I have to tell you this much because now they have sent me another letter thanking me for your release," the minister replied.

"At least now you are in Amnesty's good book, then," I joked.

He laughed, but then changed his tone. "No, what happened to you was not a joke. I am very sorry, but there was nothing I could do from my position to help you."

ॐ

I had still not given up searching for a house. Very close to our press a carpenter and his family lived in a ramshackle room above his work area. One day when he came to our press to get some bill pads printed, I asked him if he knew of any houses for rent in the area.

He said, "I have just finished building the first floor of my own new place. My plan is to build two stories. If you can give me one year's advance for both floors I can rent you the house."

I did not need the whole house and also could not afford that much rent. Shrish thought of moving our press to the ground floor with me living upstairs. It would take about another month to complete the house. I walked along the track and a couple of narrow earth footpaths that led away from the main street where we had our press into some paddy fields behind. On three sides, for about a hundred yards in each direction, the half-built house was surrounded by rice paddies. It was peaceful there, and I could scarcely hear the taxi horns and other traffic noises of Lazimpat.

I said I would take the house and gave the carpenter a year's advance for one floor. For the other apartment, we decided either to move the press or find someone to live there. We had a visitor to the press, a British lady friend teaching at the school where the crown prince was a student. I mentioned this new house to her. She said, "Oh! I have a friend staying with me at the moment who needs a place of his own." She went and sent her friend, Dan Marsh, who was involved in rural development, to meet us. I took him to show him the house. He also liked it and agreed instantly to give the necessary advance. Together we met our *sahuji,* as we called our landlord in Nepali, and gave him the money. Then we waited for his house to be completed.

Upendra also came back to the office, saying that he was still interested in working in the press. Because his appearance had not been very frequent during my imprisonment, Shrish and I had been thinking of buying him out and having the whole business to ourselves if Upendra was tired of it. It had been difficult for Shrish to run the business by himself. We did not know whether Upendra had been told to stay away from us because I was in jail. After all, he was related to the queen. We did not ask, and he did not tell. Now once more our newspaper started in full swing.

My father and sister returned to Dharan. Father was very run-down.

I had not forgotten his suggestion that I should purify myself to become free from my prison *karma*. I did not want to make a big show of this, therefore I decided to follow my father's advice quietly. I consulted a priest, who quoted some Hindu texts. "Prison is a hell," he began, "and hell is synonymous with toilet." This much I knew very well already. "Think that you have just drowned in a toilet," he continued. "When you come out you are all smelly. Other people would not like to be around you. First you have to wash. Then wash again. Apply disinfectant. Maybe a little excrement is still in your ear, or inside your nose. You have to clean yourself thoroughly, then only you can be pure if at all you can ever be the same as before."

I asked him, "Without giving me such an exhaustive sermon, just tell me what I am supposed to do. I will do it. I cannot go through a lengthy process, just a brief ritual of a couple of hours will be fine."

I hired him one morning and went to Pashupatinath. There in the temple bazaar he went around shopping for all the necessities for the rituals, and then took me inside and performed the purification rite and the chanting. Exactly as he instructed, I performed all the actions required of me. At the end he made me give a little money to each of the beggars in a line outside. That was good. All of them gave me their blessings. Then my priest suggested that on one Tuesday I visit all four main Ganesh temples in the valley, and at each one chant my Ganesh mantra and offer one hundred and eight *laddu* sweets. It was a little impractical for me to visit all four temples on one Tuesday. One of them was quite a distance away. I asked him to go to that one on my behalf. I went myself to the other three and made offerings as he had suggested.

I had always felt a deep connection with Lord Ganesh, and this time, as I surrendered myself to Him, I was aware of a deeper sense of frailty and humility than I had ever felt before. After the purification ritual, I felt overwhelmed with joy and new vital energy. I felt happy, too, that I was now ritually pure and had fulfilled the formality for my father. Personally, I had always felt that my mind was pure. While performing the rituals I could not help thinking of the prison women and seeking blessings for them. But I did not tell the priest this because he had warned me not to bring them into my mind, otherwise I might still carry some impurity.

I told some of my friends that Mara had been one of my roommates in prison. "What a sin! Is she still alive? You didn't touch her or eat food touched by her, did you?" they would cry in alarm. When I told them how I couldn't stand the smoke from all the *chula* fires, and had made Mara my cook, they all reacted in the same way. "From now on we can't eat food touched by you."

Our Hindu texts do state that, if consumed, food touched by a person who killed his or her parents transmits sufficient negative influence from the crime to cause even an innocent person to go to hell. If Kathmandu folk reacted with alarm, I wondered how other women released from jail faced their society in the remote villages. Prison stigma is something a woman can never wash away, especially the stigma of a criminal charge.

One day, a journalist friend told me that my name had been in Amnesty International's 1982 Annual Report. My first reaction was that if only I had known in jail that they had been working for my release, I would have felt more supported. Then another thought intervened: I was wrong to think only of myself. If I had known that Amnesty was helping, I might have felt as if I were someone special, and not have identified so much with the other women prisoners. Perhaps it was partly because I had felt so alone and unsupported that I had empathized so closely with my fellow inmates. Or perhaps I would have been the same regardless of knowing I had outside Amnesty support.

I had resolved inside prison after I was sure that I would be released that I wanted to work for their release also. But I had something to learn about the reality of releasing those who had been wrongfully imprisoned, and I soon became very frustrated. I found that the way the legal system operated made me powerless to help most of the innocent women. Initially, all I could do was to write a series of twelve articles in my own newspapers about cases of unlawful imprisonment, being careful not to mention specific names.

While there was no rule of law during *Panchayat raj*, unwanted people were subject to arbitrary arrest. The process of their release from prison was equally arbitrary. In my case the government had had me arrested and then extended my imprisonment, and the king had ordered my release. I never knew on what basis I was released—whether it was due to my petition, because of my father's petition, or because of Shrish's information—or as a result of the pressure from Amnesty International. Whatever the reason, this arbitrary justice eventually worked in my favor. I was happy about that. However, this same arbitrary system of justice had created a very depressed psychology in other women who were imprisoned.

All they had to look forward to were birthday "pardons" from the queen. But I discovered that pardons from the queen were not to be confused with petitions to the king. Even if women had waited five or ten years for their cases to be pushed or referred to the Supreme Court, petitions to the king, at least in theory, were petitions for legal justice. A petition to the queen was different. Questions of innocence or guilt could not enter the picture. Even to intimate that justice was at issue would be construed as contempt of court. If a victim's case had already been decided at any level, you would be interfering with a court's decision. If a case was still undecided your advocacy would be taken as trying to influence a decision, which of course it was. But that was not allowed.

I found that all I could do was to make a representation to the queen on behalf of those women in the jail who were either under or over the legal age for imprisonment, and for those who had completed three quarters of their sentence, which had become a kind of eligibility criterion for release. As I gathered data on the cases that fell into these categories, I consulted women on theft charges—who were serving shorter sentences—about whether they wanted to be included. Not one of them wanted to be released, even though they had completed three quarters of their sentences. They were all too poor.

There were sixteen women serving ten- or twenty-year sentences who qualified for pardons. Therefore, I wrote a petition to the queen on behalf of these sixteen women. A couple of months after my own release, I was at the press one day when an excited commotion broke out in the doorway. The sixteen women, my fellow inmates from prison, poured into my little front office. How happy we all were! To my delight, all, and only, those sixteen for whom I had petitioned had received the queen's birthday pardon. I went with one of them to help her to buy a plane ticket to the newly built airstrip near her daughter's home in Bhojpur. She told me, "I've never been in an airplane before!" Her last words before her departure were, "*Maiyaa!* Give me the names of your people there. I'd like to help them. Believe me! I'll be working as you are until my last breath to bring this murderous Panchayat to an end. Whatever I have to do I'm ready, and many people will be happy."

The release of the sixteen was the greatest number ever pardoned at one time. I thought, "This indicates that if facts are not misrepresented to

Their Majesties, perhaps they have ears to hear the truth, unless this was just pure coincidence." The issue of justice in the kingdom could be reduced to one question: How many people caught in the justice-seeking process could attract the king's or the queen's personal attention? The sixteen women and myself were lucky.

ఇ౧

Now telephone harassment started. Anonymous callers would phone the press and threaten, "Wait and see, you have been released on trial only for a while. You'll be arrested again and never get a chance to get out." The calls became more frequent, every day. Some of them threatened my disappearance. I did not want to discuss them with Shrish or Upendra as they might feel insecure working with me. I did not know how to deal with this situation, so I just kept quiet. There was one other worry: Although I had my own apartment I was frightened to death to live there alone. My former cook, Lama, was too scared to come back. One evening he visited and told me how badly he had been beaten by the police throughout the same eighteen days I had spent in police custody. It seemed that he was released only after I was taken to Mahakali. One of the young workers at our press offered to live at my apartment and take over Lama's housekeeping duties. Still I did not feel secure. In the daytime, while not in the office, I stayed at home. But at night in that isolated area, I could not. Therefore, I decided to sleep at Meenu's; whenever I wanted to sleep at my own place Meenu used to come with me. Police were constantly around the house watching. Some of them were acquaintances. They said it was their duty. I did not mind anything, but was haunted by the one fear of being rearrested as the unidentified callers had threatened. This time if I were arrested, the government would handle my case more cleverly and would make my release more difficult. Or it could have me sentenced for life, or have me killed.

A few days after my release, Upendra, Shrish, and I were walking from Shrish's place to the press. Our route took us around the south and west perimeter of the royal palace, shadowed all the way by towering spiked railings. Just as we were reaching the west palace driveway a blue car drew near the tree-shaded path and slowed down. A lady inside the car waved at me and laughingly shouted, "You need to see a nice movie which you can only see on video." She mentioned the name of the movie and then the car moved off. There were others also inside the car. I have absolutely no idea who she was, and by now I have forgotten the name of the movie. But Upendra's reaction was immediate.

"It seems dangerous to walk with you," worried Upendra aloud. "In that movie the king gets beheaded. Here right in front of the palace someone shouts out that remark! What is this?"

I tried to cool him down. "Don't worry, Upendraji, every dog has its day."

While we walked on I reminded myself that while I was in police custody a police officer had presented me with the book *The Day of the Jackal*, in which the head of state was the target. Now this incident. There might be much more. What message was I getting? Was it that, from the police chief to some woman in the street, people were signaling that we should get rid of the king, or were they saying that they thought I was involved? This was the irony, I thought. I was being portrayed as a revolutionary and extremist when I could not kill even a mosquito. I never liked violence. If I had had any record of violence, Amnesty International would not have adopted me as a prisoner of conscience. From my first meeting with B.P., I had made my views known to him, and he had appreciated my honesty. Nonetheless, between 1968 and 1975 it was difficult to disassociate yourself from violence and yet remain a Nepali Congress activist because throughout this period the Nepali Congress was launching the armed struggle. For many martyrs the ending of the armed struggle in 1976 came too late, and because of the party's record many more individuals involved in the party were victimized. Told that it was for my self-defense, even I had been provided a highly secret, one-week training course in throwing grenades and firing pistols with instruction by a World War II veteran colonel.

A question from Shrish suddenly took my attention. "Why are you quiet?"

"Nothing much to say," I replied. We arrived at the press. Upendra ordered tea from Ringmo's.

∞

I also heard from friends that the zonal commissioner had started some gossip that I was a lesbian. Until I came to America I did not even know what it meant to be homosexual. Back in Nepal, I used to think—like most Nepalis—that talking about man-woman relations was a sort of crime. If you are unmarried and talk about such a subject, you are viewed as very vulgar. It was out of the question for me even to be close to anybody in prison, let alone be a lesbian. I did not see any other inmates engaging in such relationships either. Jail life was not conducive to any form of human expression, positive or negative. The zonal commissioner's remark upset me briefly, but as soon as I realized that it was his purpose to hurt me, I ignored it and became stronger to face further comment. I asked my friends not to repeat to me any other comments they heard. I did not want to hear the gossip. But in Nepal, where everybody knew everything about everyone, it was difficult to live privately.

Fresh gossip started. "Look!" people began saying, "Durga must be in the palace intelligence, otherwise how could she be released by the king within a year? Other people in such cases are killed or imprisoned for life. She was not even jailed for ten years." It reminded me of a folktale that my father had told me when I was a girl. It was about a donkey, a father, and a son. The father was pulling the donkey while his son was riding on the donkey's back. People on the road rebuked him, saying, "What a silly old man to walk while his son rides the donkey." Hearing this, he thought maybe he should ride the donkey and have his son pull him. But no sooner had he done this when others commented, "Look at that old man riding a donkey while his poor son pulls it!" Therefore, both he and his son rode on the donkey. Now another group of people chided them both, "What a father and son, both riding on that poor donkey." Finally he and his son decided to carry the donkey. Seeing this, more people laughed and laughed, declaring, "It seems their brains are punctured. Look at those two carrying their donkey!" Only after this did the father and the son realize that whatever you do people are critical of you. You cannot satisfy everyone.

The lesson I learned was to stop being closely associated with anybody. My father had known my nature well and always warned me, "Your main weakness is that you trust everybody too readily." Therefore, all I now did was to move between my apartment, the press, and Meenu's house. As it happened, all three were almost in a line—it was a ten-minute walk from my apartment to Meenu's, with the press almost exactly in between. I did not keep this low profile because of fear. I had no energy to defend myself or to discuss or even listen. I was just tired of hearing other people's rubbish about who or what I had become, and I knew that I was caught in crossfire, and that it might be difficult to avoid certain problems.

ॐ

I had heard two accounts of B.P.'s reaction to my arrest. One was that it had been he who had arranged for my *habeas corpus* writ. The other was that after having made those arrangements, a friend had gone to consult B.P., who had told him, "Whatever is happening to Durga will be good for her future in politics, so do not hasten the filing of the writ." Only after my release, one of my colleagues delivered a short letter that B.P. had written to me while I was in jail. In the letter B.P. had written, "Have patience, and be strong. I am aware of your imprisonment. This imprisonment is very important for your political career."

At first I felt that several of our colleagues were given similar encouragement, but what good had it been for them? They had been killed. As a result my feelings about B.P.'s role in my case were mixed. Nonetheless, I liked him so much that I decided to go and see him. I took Meenu with me.

As I met B.P. again, I could not read his mind. His personality was always to be smiling and reassuring. He patted my back and said, "Congratulations! I was following the progress of your imprisonment and was glad that our friends saw you once in Mahakali. This imprisonment will be a boon in disguise for you."

I did not have much to say in reply. He was not in very good health. Three months later, at a little after seven in the evening on July 21, 1982, he died at his family house near the Pashupatinath temple. Meenu and I were the last people allowed to enter his room before his death was announced.

The next day on the front page of *Manas* we printed the simple headline B.P. WENT AWAY. The most striking thing about his death was the funeral procession, the largest gathering in Nepal's history. Many men shaved their heads, a ritual normally reserved for when parents die. B.P.'s body, with his face visible, was carried on the back of a truck bedecked with flowers and draped with the Nepali Congress flag. He did not look dead. Even in death, you could feel the liveliness of his presence.

B.P.'s death troubled me deeply for a long time. There was no one in the party of such stature to carry forward his quality of leadership. This was a very grave constraint for the democratic movement.

## 14
.

# Piecing Together the "Palace Matter"

Although I tried to live quietly and forget what had happened, my enemies would not leave me alone. One afternoon I went to my apartment and tried to meditate. Although I was not completely settled, the idea appeared in my mind that I must meet the king's chief secretary. My thought was that even if the king was not easily accessible, I could approach the secretary without difficulty because he knew my father very well and had visited our house in Dhankuta several times while accompanying the king on regional tours. With this idea, I went to the press and called him for an appointment. He responded instantly, "Come tomorrow evening after supper."

I was not sure how much to tell him, or where to begin. However, I told him the whole story of events both before and after my imprisonment. He listened very attentively. At the end he said, "I will convey all this to His Majesty."

After more than an hour I left his place. As I stepped outside I began partly regretting having told him so much and wondered if I was again pouring water on the sand. I questioned myself: Did he not know already what had happened and how it had happened? Would he really convey what I had said to the king? Even if he did, how would he put it? I felt a little unhappy thinking these thoughts and wondering whether I had been right to assume that this man was any different from all the others who were attached to the king for their own benefit.

As I returned, my mind became absorbed in the question: Who had been the brain behind the "palace matter" and who had made me the scapegoat? I tried repeatedly to piece the clues together.

I wondered, could those young men who had come with the grenade have been the same people as those who had come disguised as beggars in 1977? But I could not recall the faces of the group of "beggars." Neither could I imagine what the motive of the first group had been in sharing their plan with me. They had given no reason for choosing me. The second time they had said it was because I was living next to the Indian embassy, so that if necessary they could jump from my balcony for asylum there.

Before my 1981 arrest I could not even speculate who might have been behind such a great plot. Then, inside prison, being with my fellow inmates and studying their cases, a light started flickering in the darkness of my mind as I became aware of the pattern, the fabric of conspiracy, across the kingdom. My fellow inmates were almost all victims of local-level people connected with the system. Only Shagi had been a victim of a higher level *Pancha*. It was so obvious. Just as the vulnerable women around me were targeted as scapegoats for crimes they did not commit, so also was I chosen. But I was made victim by central-level people. And my case was in the political rather than the social realm.

We have a short folk story in Nepali that goes like this: Once upon a time the crown of the king was missing from the palace. The king ordered all his courtiers, the prime minister, the commander-in-chief, and the secretaries, cooks, servants, gatekeeper, room keeper, *hukka* bearer, fan waver, et cetera, to sit in a long line on a low wall with their feet dangling. The king had a soldier standing next to him with a long *khukri* sword. The king shouted at his soldier, "Eh! What are you staring at? Cut off the feet of the thief who stole the crown." Immediately the prime minister pulled up his feet, professing innocence and saying, "I didn't take it." The king replied, "Whoever is the thief, that very one's voice is the loudest."

In my case the thieves were surely speaking in the loudest voices. I thought of my cousin warning my sister Subhadra not to take initiative in my case: "If she's killed it doesn't matter about just one person. . . ." It seemed to me now that his comment definitely contained a deeper signal that the people involved were not going to let me live. My cousin must have been just a spokesperson. Then I thought of what Prime Minister Surya Bahadur Thapa himself had told my father, that it was a "palace matter" so he "could not do anything." But had the palace ordered my arrest? Had the king's brother gone to Mahakali to prevent people from visiting me in my banishment there? It was the same prime minister who had convinced my father that working with two Ranas caused my imprisonment through the influence of Shrish's hard-liner uncle, who did not want the king to give any concessions to the Nepali Congress.

One day Setha confided to Shrish that he had been embroiled in the plot by the prime minister's brother. I thought back to my meeting with the zonal commissioner the day before my release. One of the questions he had asked me was "Tell me now, why did you ask Setha to come to the Summit Hotel?" "Still they try to distort the facts," I had thought. If only we had made those military men search Setha's room it would have been exposed who had hidden the bomb and who had called whom. But then, who knows, the government people could still have arrested me if they had found me with any bomb in his room after he had made his escape from the hotel. Until the eleventh hour they had tried to frame me and convince the palace that I was the suspect. Then, after my first petition to the king, they had tried to discourage me, threatening, "You went to the wrong door." But by then I had become far stronger. All I had to do was keep dead quiet about my source of support.

Next, after my release, a cabinet minister invited himself for dinner at my place and told another story, which was a new one. I had been arrested for planning to throw a bomb at the prime minister. This story must have been based on what the police had forced me to "confess" during the concluding part of my interrogation after Kangal had been brought as their so-called witness to say that I was the brains behind the plot. I had gone along with them in that forced confession because, as a lawyer, I knew that I could easily defend myself in court on that particular bomb charge. Now he had invented another story. The minister also cautioned me, "The prime minister is 'two-tongued'—you should not trust him."

I was sure that this two-tongued prime minister was the main person plotting to kidnap the heir to the throne. By staging this plot and imprisoning the suspect he could have won the king's heart. As a reward, the king would make him premier for life—a second Jang Bahadur Rana, which was perhaps what he wanted. If I had been killed in prison, the real "brain" would have had this chance.

I still suspected that there had been a second element aligned with the main brain in this conspiracy. This might have been the faction within the extreme opposition to the king's system who were experienced in terrorism. Their purpose in aligning with the main person would be that they would gain proximity to the king. There was also the prospect that their past record of extremism would be cleared if the main person, the prime minister, helped by mending the breach between them and the king after they issued their statement condemning the action of the alleged terrorist in their effort to now prove themselves loyal.

Third, I thought that some deal must have been arranged with the high-level police. Without their involvement, an order—even from a prime minister—would not by itself have been enough for arresting the targeted suspect. In any case, some of the top police might themselves have been looking for opportunities to further tighten their bonds of solidarity with the royalty—with some of whom, so rumor had it, they were partners in crime.

So, I mused, it was another matter of trying to please the palace. The trend of Nepali history had been played out again—intrigue and conspiratorial politics about the palace. It was in the nature of the political system. An old pattern, and I had become one of their "bets." Perhaps I had been sent to die in police hands or in prison. The only reason the plotters had failed in their endeavor this time was that for some reason they had been unable to kill the framed suspect.

They could have chosen anybody as their scapegoat. All they needed for framing was an individual who had a sufficiently bad record with the police that he or she could be proved an extremist who could do anything if necessary. I qualified with all the ingredients they were looking for. I was controversial within the party, living alone, and working with opposite ideological partners. On top of everything, I had been ousted from home, so that nobody should claim me while I went missing. With luck they could make me go missing forever. All these considerations made me more vulnerable than any other target. I was an easy prey.

However, as it turned out, their calculation had gone awry. If they had killed me in custody they would have proved their point that a "known" revolutionary woman who tried to kidnap the crown prince had made a bid to escape and was killed. Obviously, within police custody there must have been division of opinion among the police about whether or not to finish me there. Not finishing me there and then was their greatest mistake. But I had not been silenced from speaking the truth. They had underestimated my strength. There were two in my family who were not cowered to put family before politics and had filed writs of *habeas corpus* on my behalf. I reappeared in Kathmandu and through one loyal friend my case reached the king's notice. Finally, my name had received international attention through Amnesty International.

I know that the whole episode of the "palace matter" might haunt me for life, and that I may have to live with it unresolved. The reason I say that the "palace matter" may never be resolved is that this episode is not a onetime occurrence in history, but an ingrained pattern of intrigue and conspiratorial politics related to the institution of the Nepalese monarchy. The palace remains a great mystery in the kingdom, and does not descend to the public level to reveal about itself either truth or untruth, or to defend itself against allegations spread usually by those who were privy to inside information. I also recall now a rumor from the late 1970s that an astrologer had seen a *khadgo,* or danger point, in the crown prince's horoscope in his ninth year—the year when his kidnapping had been plotted. There was a similar rumor about the king's own chart concerning the predictions of renowned astrologers that he would be the last Shah on the throne of Nepal. Might such rumors have been spread intentionally by high-level people interested in getting rid of the royalty, people so high that nobody could touch them except for the king himself—who was perhaps the only one not to have heard?

In those days, an illiterate palace gardener could be more powerful than a degree-holding government bureaucrat. Even a minister or prime minister who was not aligned with one of the palace secretaries would be powerless when the time came for a palace-led cabinet reshuffle. One of the original Panchayat hard-liners, Dr. Tulsi Giri, became prime minister several times and was nicknamed "Mother of Panchayat" after the way King Mahendra was known—"Father of Panchayat." Most of the newspapers used to describe him as the most notorious individual for corruption and woman hunting, a man who changed both wife and car every year. Often, this man was heard to remark, "As long as the Lord [the king] is happy, then I am safe," and on one occasion he was asked point-blank by a journalist at a press conference, "Why is there so much corruption? You have made so much money; why did you do it?"

"I might have eaten *charana,*" this prime minister replied, "but where did the *bahrana* go?" (Until the 1960s, the rupee was divided into sixteen *anas. Charana* meant four *anas,* a quarter of a rupee. *Bahrana* meant twelve *anas*—three quarters of a rupee. The prime minister's remark was an obvious allusion to the role of the palace. After all, who was above the prime minister but the king?) The same prime minister, when his weakness for women became publicized, perhaps to divert attention away from himself and toward the king, spread rumors that the king was engaged in affairs with other women. Against neither allegation did the king—or the "palace"—raise any defense.

If such allegations had been made, or such rumors spread, by the opposition to the king's system, or by any other ordinary citizen, the Panchayat government would have jailed or even executed the rumor monger. The question of this persecution still remains to be answered, either by the palace or by the palace agents, the former *Panchas*. Why did they commit such injustice toward some of us? If the palace was unaware of the incident at that time, then it should be concerned and punish those responsible even now. If it did know, then it was a coconspirator.

In 1973, Singha Durbar caught fire. Built by the people's labor and therefore national property, this was the kingdom's central secretariat, a gigantic remnant of Rana power, and even then one of Asia's vastest building complexes. At the time it caught fire, I was on a private tour of one of the remotest hill districts north of Dhankuta. Some local Nepali Congress friends had invited me for lunch, but before I reached their house some police prevented me from going any farther and forcefully escorted me a quarter of the way back to Dhankuta. Before they allowed me to continue alone, they explained, "The Nepali Congress is suspected of having set the fire, and we received a report that you were on your way to celebrate the action at a party with Nepali Congress people here. Instead of arresting you, the local administration decided to send you back home." My Nepali Congress friends were arrested, and our get-together never happened. I had to walk the three-day hike back to Dhankuta alone. Later, I came to know that the Singha Durbar fire was the criminal deed of some high-ranking *Panchas* to destroy evidence of their own corrupt dealings. The prime minister at that time was a pro-China *Pancha*, and so the Chinese ambassador had come forward quickly with an offer of assistance in extinguishing the fire. Instead of accepting it, the prime minister answered, "I have to ask the palace." But he did not communicate this with the palace. We heard that the king ordered that at least the magnificent facade of the building should be saved, but, had the Chinese ambassador's help been sought, more of the historic monument might have been recovered. As usual, a number of Nepali Congress people were arrested and tortured for this mishap.

For a long time, the king's youngest brother—whom Shrish and I used to call "Number Three"—was portrayed as a womanizer and a center of corruption in the palace. This prince was married to the queen's youngest sister (the king's younger brother is married to the queen's younger sister as well). One day in the late 1980s, he renounced his royal title as prince and left his family and his country forever. The rumor spread like wildfire that, to protect her sister and perhaps others, the queen had taken him to task about his womanizing and his illegal dealings. Clearly, his drastic step must have been precipitated by some equally virulent conditions. Again, such a rumor can only have emanated from people closely linked to the palace.

During the most recent people's movement, which restored democracy to Nepal in 1990, I read several pamphlets and articles accusing the Nepalese royal family, and particularly the queen, of amassing and transferring to foreign banks wealth on a par with Mrs. Marcos of the Philippines. Many more allegations of other royal misconduct were made. Neither the palace nor the governing *Panchas* came forward to defend her. Perhaps the reality is that even now, under a supposedly constitutional monarchy, Nepal's king and queen remain so rich, powerful, and beyond reach behind their barricades of mystery that they need no defense. After all, rumor has it that they still personally control royalties the British government has been paying Nepal for every Gurkha soldier, and that these huge reserves are used to maintain the loyalty of the Nepal army. And if they are not beyond reach, people wonder behind their backs, how it could be that the royalty allegedly still retains the option to buy confiscated, smuggled gold at a special discretionary price less than one two-hundredth of its market value? Does the silence from the palace mean consent?

"Palace matters" of a real constitutional monarchy, such as the one in the United Kingdom, inevitably become public—even the most personal of affairs. The British palace reveals the truth, particularly concerning financial dealings and matters affecting the national interest, and this provides the general public with the opportunity to form an opinion that is often sympathetic to the royalty. But in Nepal, the ancient ethic for the Hindu king, "the king can do no wrong," was applied to silence all comment while the king was doing wrong. Beyond the king's own misdeeds, everybody surrounding him was doing wrong in his name, and he remained silent. Thus, it seems that the "palace matter" became an instrument of those in power to use against others in the name of the king.

In my case, I became sure that the prime minister's "palace matter" was an excuse to empower himself to act as he wanted. Once he mentioned the word *palace* neither my father nor anyone else would dare to question anything, and the prime minister could carry on with his subterfuge as if instructed by the king himself. It might even be that some palace courtiers actually granted him a green light. In most cases, Panchayat ministers and prime ministers were eventually expelled from their positions on account of unacceptable levels of corruption and misuse of power. Perhaps expelling the ministers was the king's way of disassociating himself from corruption.

In any case, had the kidnapping conspiracy succeeded, this political episode could have turned Nepali history along a different course, at least for a while.

# 15
.

# Back to Dhankuta
# to Meet the King

The zonal commissioner had told me that the king wanted to see me and would soon be visiting Dhankuta, my home district, and that it would be best if I went there for his audience. In the early 1970s, five "development regions" were created by the present king, and Dhankuta became the headquarters of the eastern development region. Dhankuta's bazaar also serves as the local district headquarters. Because the king was fond of Dhankuta, he decided to build another palace on the hilltop at the end of the ridge. The site commanded views of the bazaar, the pine forest, and the mountains to the north, and of the Tamor River, straight below at the foot of the Dhankuta spur. The king's proposed visit was his official annual camp in one of the development regions. He toured one of the regions each winter in rotation. I always loved to visit Dhankuta, and might still have been teaching there in the private degree college had the New Education System Plan not nationalized it. I became very excited at the thought of going home. Some of my relatives were still there, and many former colleagues. And as my father was living in Dharan, I could visit him on the way up to Dhankuta and on the way back.

An American lady offered to drive me the two-day journey from Kathmandu to Dhankuta in her jeep. Knowing a little about the threats that I was getting from the people in power and that we would be two women driving alone, Shrish volunteered to accompany us. On the way, we spent a night in Dharan, where I noticed that my father's health had not improved since he'd visited me in jail. Nevertheless, he was happy that I would be able to clarify before the king what I knew about the "bad rumor"—as my father referred to the kidnapping plot. Seeming rather sad, he said, "Since I was appointed as medical officer in 1926 until the king's visit four years ago, I have always been in Dhankuta whenever Their Majesties visited there. During that last visit, when I fell ill, His Majesty provided his own helicopter to fly me to the hospital in Biratnagar. This time I do not feel physically strong enough to reach there. But you can extend my greetings to them for me." My mother was visiting my brother Krishna at the farm, an hour's drive southeast of Dharan. I promised my father that I would go to see her on our way back to Kathmandu.

I had forgotten that I had not been to Dhankuta since the construction of the motor road as part of a British foreign aid program. Now it was winter of 1982 and the fine, all-weather Dharan–Dhankuta road was complete except for some short sections of pavement, supporting gabion walls of dry stone in wire netting baskets, culverts, and bridges.

It was beautiful to see Dhankuta again. My first distant view of the Dhankuta hill was from near the pass that the new road took from Dharan. The old foot trail was too direct and therefore too steep for vehicle traffic, so the new road passed over the Mahabharat range at a different place—Dada bazaar, or "hill bazaar." Britain's Crown Prince Charles had been brought as far as this spot for a view of his country's aid project and the hills to the north—home for many of the British army's Gurkha recruits. He was said to have walked to the nearest vantage point and to have declared, "Behold glorious Gurkhaland!" After this, that vantage point came to be known as "Charlie's point." I noticed how all vehicles stopped at Dada bazaar for a beverage in one of its thriving tea stalls. We also took tea here. Breathing the exhilarating cold air, I gazed at the spectacular view. Sixty miles away, the Himalayan peak of Makalu and the Chamlang massif sparkled deep in white from recent storms and hung in the sky on the northern horizon, resting on a sea of haze. The only cloud was the plume of wind-whipped snow that marked the summit of Everest, hidden from view ten miles beyond Chamlang.

I let my eyes travel the vast space from where I stood over the hills of Dhankuta in the foreground, across to those great mountains. Dominating the landscape of the "foothills" were two great ridge systems heaving their way northward and upward, higher and higher, until they became snow-covered Himalaya themselves. The great ridge on the left became Chamlang, Lhotse, and Everest, and the ridge rising above Dhankuta to the north eventually joined the Kanchenjunga range. The ridges were like enormous snaking spines, their sides clothed in dense mixed rhododendron jungle. On either side were the ribs—ten-mile-long and five- to eight-thousand-foot-high spurs, separated by deeply cut valleys, Nepal's "mid hills." Now, the million farm terraces etched into the hillsides were a patchwork of gray and ocher, winter colors. The only splashes of green were from the countless fodder trees whose fresh bursts of leaves from crude-cut trunks offered themselves again for winter sacrifice.

These days, a gaily painted truck grinding up the familiar hills of my home replaced the quieter groans and whistles of fifty porters. The scent of *bidi* cigarettes along the footpaths from the steel-bodied porters, bent tense and dripping from their burdens, had given way to black diesel smoke. Here and there along the new road groups of laborers still quarried rock from the hillside, using picks and crowbars. They broke the rock with hammers into even-sized chips for final sections of the road surface. It was a handmade road. Women's as well as men's hands had excavated and moved millions of cubic meters of stone and soil, basket by *doko* basket. I marveled at the engineering, while wondering what all the displaced porters would do when the construction work that employed them now was over. Porters headed for destinations in the mountainous districts many days north of Dhankuta might still take the old trail, I thought. I could see some on the old trail now, wherever it intersected the bends of the new road.

The road cut a much more gradual route up the final valley beneath and beyond Dhankuta, passing near our family's rice terraces a thousand feet below our village of Kachiday. As we passed this point, I craned my head upward and saw the pine forest between Kachiday and the main bazaar. Finally, our vehicle completed a last hairpin bend and pulled up in a newly leveled gravel parking area. This was the roadhead and the "bus stop" at the lowest point of the bazaar. Vendors had set up makeshift stalls. It was now the new focal point of daily bazaar life, where all the comings and goings took place, and with them the chance to earn a few rupees. A gang of little boys, and some men and women, crowded around us to porter luggage. But we had come with only a light travel bag with just a couple of changes of clothes.

We made our way on foot up the cobbled main street of the bazaar, pausing frequently to greet people seated in the open porches of their stores and residences, facing each other across the flagstones. I noticed that the jeeps and Land Rovers of VIPs were allowed to menace their way noisily through Dhankuta's narrow, stone-paved streets, breaking the flagstones and disturbing the peace. Aside from that, I felt relieved. It was all the same, the timelessness of my beautiful hometown. Almost no "modern" straight-sided, square-cornered concrete architecture disturbed the gentler contours and natural fabrics of the traditional houses. Their dark timbers framed the white-lime and red-ocher walls. Through the intricately carved window and door frames, past the shutters, one could glimpse the fresh cow-dung-plastered floors. A few teenagers wandered about in jeans and Western dresses. But most people in this rural area were wearing the traditional national dress.

No one was expecting me in Dhankuta. I had not sent any message to arrange accommodation. Therefore, when we reached the top of the main street I called first on one of my closest friends from the days when we had worked together while I was in Dhankuta, Yogendra Shrestha, to let him and his family know I was in town. He was almost like a younger brother to me, and my welcome at their house was an emotional one. Perhaps seeing me reminded them also of Bhim Narayan, their cousin who had been executed. They were so happy to see me.

After a short reunion with Yogendra's family, we left our bags there and walked the thirty minutes through the pine forest to my family house in Kachiday. Minutes above the bazaar along the forest footpath we came to the Ayurvedic hospital where my father had worked for over thirty-five years. The wide path from there to our village had been built by my father. Every Dasain until he retired and moved to Dharan he had seen to its renovation. Mostly he would spend his own money, and other villagers would offer a little of their labor. After a while we arrived at the edge of the forest. Behind it was my village. I pointed out the large traditional family house that my father had built. It looked as beautiful as ever with its white-washed walls and the dark timbers of its balconies. I remembered how I used to lean out of Father's window upstairs and reach to pick mandarins. While I had lived with my parents, every inch of our extensive lands had been planted to maize, beans, all sorts of other crops, and medicinal herbs. Now most of the land looked empty except for the trees and around the house where some beautiful flowers were in bloom. It seemed strange to have to ask permission to enter my old home.

An American couple had been renting my family house since my parents had moved down to Dharan. Given the size of the house, we could have easily been accommodated there, but the American lady said, "We are very private people." So, although I had come back to my birthplace, I could not stay there. Feeling very emotional about the house, I asked the lady's permission to look around it. First I went up the narrow flight of wooden stairs to what had been my bedroom and the worship room. Everything was clean and lovely, yet different. Downstairs, they had built a bathroom in the room Father had used for preparing medicines, and I think his old dispensary room was now being used as a doghouse. Outside in the old cowshed a watchman was living. Then a little farther down the yard the Americans were keeping a few pigs—an enterprise in which only the lower castes engaged in Nepal. My father had already told me about this in Dharan. It was the worst thing that could ever happen at a Brahmin house, and he had been deeply disappointed to hear the news.

We returned to the bazaar to stay with Yogendra's family, and simply appeared on their doorstep to be their guests. To do that is perfectly acceptable in Nepali culture. Because of difficult communications and travel, everyone is used to the unexpected.

In the context of the events leading up to this visit of mine, our living arrangement at Yogendra's was like a stage setting for a drama. Next door, literally touching Yogendra's house, was the residence of one of the prime minister's closest people in Dhankuta. The prime minister's brother was now staying there for the king's visit. At night I found that from my room I could hear their voices through the walls. And the neighboring house on the other side was the house of Bhim Narayan Shrestha, who was executed in 1978.

Though his grandfather had ruled there as governor, Shrish had never been to Dhankuta. So it was quite exciting for him, and he did not mind being in this rural area with all its hills, mountains, and little footpaths. Moreover, to honor Their Majesty's visit and to compete for his attention, the whole town was decked out with red banners, arches, and streamers like a rich household celebrating a Hindu wedding. On such an occasion the bride's and groom's houses are decorated with everything that is bright and glittering—flowers, garlands, banners, fairy lights, and gaily patterned awnings. Dazzling kerosene pressure lamps replace light bulbs where there is no electricity. Loud music from Hindi movies blares continually, and brass bands meander through Eastern melodies with gusto and abandon.

British aid personnel trying to get their work done in Dhankuta called the royal tour "the traveling circus." To Nepalis, especially of the region, it was the once-every-five-year festival of buttering up the royalty—the occasion that crowned all other opportunities for pleasing the palace. For a month, the king had come to town, bringing his palace court with him. Behind that, he towed a good part of the central government. Every day the whirling of his white helicopter would be heard from the royal camp as he and his queen set off to hop around the fifteen or so districts of the region to tour projects.

For months before their visit *Panchas* and all other government officers had dropped virtually every normal activity in order to prepare for the great occasion. Millions of rupees had been spent on landscaping, painting buildings, and decorating every office, street, and site to be included in Their Majesties' schedule. Everyone understood that the auditors would never question the expenses. The royal visit had been good and bad news for foreign donors. The bad news had been that overseas technical advisers had become virtually redundant for several months. But the good news had been that construction projects had suddenly become invaluable political capital. Normal constraints vanished. Government offices responsible for project implementation had metamorphosed into frenzied activity. Supplies and equipment had materialized, whether begged, borrowed, or stolen. Completion dates had raced backward across bar charts. By the eve of the royal visit the hills were dotted with the scars of freshly turned soil, shining sheet metal roofs, still-damp wall plaster, wet paint, and virgin latrines. Access roads had been cut across hillsides to projects that government agency chiefs wanted inaugurated. Stakeholders had seen to it that pits were dug for foundation-stone-laying ceremonies for projects that were still on the drawing board. Whole young trees and beds of flowering plants had appeared on the grounds of new office compounds overnight. And staff who had never before occupied their posts had arrived from their homes in Kathmandu or elsewhere to put in an appearance.

Appearance was the name of the game. Office staff reengaged themselves in preparing colorful progress charts to pin over the cracks in the walls. Program targets and achievement (as far as it could be arranged) progressed relentlessly upward. Hundreds of pictures of the queen and the king, in his dark glasses, were framed and garlanded and hung on giant triumphal gates erected across the streets by *panchayats*, corporations, and government and other organizations keen to impress. Some of the arches were true feats of engineering, their wooden box frames and bright red fabric withstanding everything the windy hill weather could do for the month. Contractors had taken several *lakhs* of rupees (ten to twenty thousand American dollars) for building some of the more ambitious ones. I learned later that when judging of the gates took place midway during the royal visit, first prize for the most triumphal gate had been awarded to the prime minister's village *panchayat*. Somehow the top people always seemed to win the prize.

ဝಌ

The morning after we arrived I went up to the main gate of the camp to register my name for an audience with His Majesty. As in the past, the king's camp was situated on the crest of the Dhankuta spur, at the top of the saddle where the bazaar ended. It held a commanding view of the hills and valleys in almost every direction. From the gate, beyond some tall orange and mandarin trees heavy with fruit, I could just see the roofs of several khaki military tents farther up the hill. It was not clear which were the royal tents.

A queue of people waited outside the gate, all with some problem or other that they wanted to bring before either the king or the queen. I noticed government officials questioning each supplicant. If someone was thought to be too vocal or threatening to the administration, he or she would doubtless be dropped from the audience list. Helicopters were landing and taking off several times a day, bringing the camp supplies, and it seemed that they were taking the Kathmandu mail as well. "Well," I thought, "that is a good idea even if it is for just one month in five years." The helipad was just one terrace above and on the right of the main gate. Villagers and children alike hung around, waiting expectantly to see the helicopters lift off. Once in a while through the cloud of dust they might even see a member of the royal family.

I eventually found myself at the head of the queue at the camp main gate and registered my name. I was about to return to the bazaar when I saw a group of relatives and villagers from Kachiday, most of whom I had not seen since 1973. They were not active in any political group and received me simply as one of their relatives. It felt very natural to be with them, and we went and talked on a hillock below the entrance to the royal camp. As we were talking, we saw one of my cousins rushing toward the gate of the royal camp. Another cousin who was talking with me remarked, "There goes our chief *Pancha* of Dhankuta sweating away to show his attendance to the palace secretaries." Everybody else laughed, but I remained silent. It reminded me that I was alone, out on a limb in my family, who were otherwise aligned with Panchayat or were apolitical. My relatives all looked at me. I did not want to make any comment, and in a minute we were all at ease again.

For the whole time I was there, I allowed myself to savor the atmosphere of my hometown, watching the colorful people buying and selling mandarins, shelled peanuts, and homemade pastries and sweets. It was a balm to the wounds from my time in prison, when all of this seemed to recede into just a memory, one that might never return. After saying good-bye to my village folk, I began the steep descent down to the bazaar, following the paved steps of the main trail that skirts the edge of the pine forest. The path was cool there, deeply shaded by huge sacred banyan and pipal trees. They were planted in pairs around resting places, or *chautara*—stone-walled platforms that various religiously motivated people had built as a service to tired climbers on this steep section of the trail. It was a peaceful scene, as porters rested their loads on the edge of one platform while children climbed and jumped on the *chautaro* steps. I sat there, too, for some minutes, gazing into the quiet forest. I could see one of the paths that led through the forest to my home. Then, remembering that my father had built a beautiful *chautaro* farther down the hill at the weekly open-air marketplace, I took a different footpath. It dropped down a very steep and eroded slope of yellow-brown soil and arrived at the market area half a mile east and around the contour from the main street of the bazaar. It was not Thursday, the colorful market day, so now the area was deserted. The banyan and pipal trees my father had planted there were beautifully grown now. As I looked at the *chautaro*'s stonework I noticed an inscription of my father's that I had never noticed before. I read it. It said that he had built this *chautaro* in memory of my mother. I sat there for a while, lost in reflection. I thought, "At least my father has not totally forgotten my real mother." Then I resumed the walk back to Yogendra's.

೧೪೨

I was expecting to be called to the camp within a couple of days. A week passed with no audience. I then began to hear from the prime minister's people that there would be no audience for me, and I was warned that if I did not leave the area I was likely to be rearrested. In the meantime, Shrish received a message from his uncle, the military commander in charge of royal security, saying, "What are you doing staying with Durga Pokhrel?" It appeared that rumors were being spread around that I was going to explode a bomb somewhere. It seemed clear to me that they were trying to hatch another plot. I did not know what was best to do. If they managed to frame and arrest me here there would be no way I could escape from death or long imprisonment. I imagined the scenario: Here was the king visiting my hometown. If the government could arrest me on a bombing charge, how on earth could I escape the consequences? I began looking out consciously for planted bombs. More than anything I prayed to my Lord Ganesh that nothing like that should happen, and decided to stay a couple of days more in case circumstances might change.

Even with the prospect of having to leave suddenly, I felt impelled to go and visit some of my relatives. One morning Shrish and I set off for a walk toward my village of Kachiday. About halfway between the bazaar and Kachiday there was a temple in the pine forest called Saraswati Sthan— "place of Saraswati." It was dedicated to Ganesh and Saraswati. Near the temple there was a natural well. It was cool and silent there, deep in the forest. The only noise was the soft music of the wind breathing through the pine needles above. In the name of Saraswati, goddess of knowledge and learning, my father, supported by other villagers, had started a small primary school in our village—Saraswati Primary School. Later it was moved to this place, where there was a little temple shelter. The people from our village helped put up another building beside the shelter so that the school could offer grades one through five. While I was in my mid-teens I worked for two years as principal of this school. My own college classes ran from six A.M. to nine A.M. After finishing there, I would run home through the forest and eat my morning meal before assuming duties at the primary school at ten A.M. Every evening, for the whole time that I lived in Dhankuta, I used to visit this place of serene sanctity. Almost every Nepali student is devoted to Goddess Saraswati. As I had been a devotee of Lord Ganesh since I was a little girl, there was much reason to visit this temple regularly.

This time also we went via the temple. There was a shorter way to Kachiday, but because of its importance to me I wanted to visit this holy place. I approached the temple quietly, and before the images of these deities I chanted to myself the special Ganesh and Saraswati prayers, and bowed low, my forehead touching the floor before them. Then I rang the temple bells, first the large one, then the small ones. As I rose and turned in the direction of my village I saw a man standing on the path ahead of us. He was holding a walkie-talkie.

Shrish and I both stopped in our tracks, and I whispered to Shrish, "The king must be walking around here somewhere. If I see him, I'm going to stop him and say something."

Shrish was alarmed. "If you do that his bodyguards will just shoot at you and the king will think that you really are an aggressive woman. No one ever stops the king just like that." But before Shrish could try to dissuade me I saw the king coming down the path toward us with four other men.

"This is my final chance," I told Shrish. "I am going to stop the king. If you feel uncomfortable or embarrassed you either go on ahead or hide somewhere." Sometimes Shrish was just too polished, too genteel and formal for me.

Within a minute the distance between the king's party and us had closed and we were standing right in front of him. The thought flashed through my mind that if I were not meant to get his audience why should I be meeting him right here before the temple of Ganesh? Ganesh's blessings had led to the king's releasing me from jail. This seemed to be the hand of

Ganesh supporting me again. I knew that if I missed this chance, I would have no hope of receiving his audience and that another charge would be brought against me—this time more effectively. Steeling myself, I took the risk.

I stood in front of the king and said, "I am Durga Pokhrel. I came here for Your Majesty's audience and now other people are making unnecessary gossip about me. If Your Majesty would be kind enough to grant me some time to tell my story . . ."

As the king just stood there and listened, no one brandished a pistol. Instead, one of his bodyguards asked, "Why don't you register your name at the main gate?"

I replied, "I did that a week ago."

The king gave a faint smile and ever so slightly nodded his head. Then they proceeded on their way.

Shrish had become crimson. He closed his eyes momentarily and, releasing his tension with a long breath, said, "Now he will really believe you are a dangerous woman."

I disagreed. "I don't think so. Why did we have to meet him in front of this temple? There is some positive meaning in it. Don't worry."

We continued slowly toward Kachiday, discussing the pros and cons of my having stopped the king, but I was positive that something good would happen.

We went around the village meeting my relatives. After chatting for a short time, we turned back toward the bazaar along the same path by which we had come. By the time we reached the bazaar, rumors about what I had done were already out—both negative and positive versions. I was not in any mood to respond to anybody's questions, so for the rest of the day and the evening I stayed quietly at Yogendra's. I was acutely aware that if I failed to see the king this time I would be in a far more vulnerable position than before, as it would be a signal to the *Panchas* that the king was not willing to support me.

To my amazement, early the next morning a message came that I should be at the royal camp at eleven A.M.

"So, it worked!" I exclaimed to Shrish.

As instructed, I arrived at the appointed hour at the main gate where a week before I had queued to register my name. There I found that my audience was not with the king but with the queen. I was told that all women were given audience with the queen and that men were seen by the king. That was fine with me.

It was a fifteen-minute walk from the main gate to the queen's tent. The dusty road was wide and curving and was lined with tall trees. Every minute I was halted by sentries posted at intervals. It was similar to the time I had come eighteen years before to meet King Mahendra, although perhaps less dramatic. However, the camp was alive with the highest palace and government officials, all wearing black or gray jackets on top of their finest *daura suruwal* outfits—the formal national dress.

Outside the queen's tent was a graceful-looking elderly gentleman with a white mustache who appeared to be her secretary. He gave me the same instructions that I had been given so long ago and showed me inside. She was seated alone there, knitting.

Once I was inside I bowed my head to greet her, then stood up straight, which was a more comfortable position for me. Then I told my side of the story. Actually, I felt more comfortable with her than I would have with the king. She was my contemporary, a woman, and I had already met her on two previous occasions. She listened very carefully to everything I described. Finally she assured me that she would apprise the king of my account. Our meeting had great symbolic significance. Once a person had an audience with the king or queen, the general impression of the public was that they had received the royal blessing. I knew well how establishment people who met Their Majesties would greatly exaggerate what might have transpired in order to increase their own importance. For it was not possible for everyone to be granted an audience. Generally, applications for an audience concerning some personal request from a member of the public were directed by low- or middle-level palace staff to concerned ministries and departments, with a remark such as "Do according to the rules" or "Do whatever is necessary" attached to the request. Usually, that was as far as the application would go.

The royal camp was a place for those who were already connected and established, where the king could decorate people—first some royal family members, most probably starting with the queen, then the prime minister and other *Panchas,* and finally some of the local-level *Panchas* who might receive some insignificant cash award. From preparation until departure, everything about the royal visits was eyewash and pretension.

It was very important for me to be able to hold my head high in front of my enemies. That was all. I had no personal request.

# 16

## The Last Straw

*Raja dekhawoti vikaas mandaina*—THE KING DOES NOT AGREE TO
ARTIFICIAL DEVELOPMENT—ran the headline on the front page
of our newspaper. Usually our editorial page was on page 2, but
on returning to Kathmandu from Dhankuta, I was proud of my observations and wanted to catch the king's attention. Shrish agreed it would make
a good cover piece. It had seemed as though the whole effort of His
Majesty's government in the districts was window dressing to exaggerate
target achievements. Whether the "targets" were meaningful activities or
even existed on the ground as projects was of secondary importance. It
seemed to me that the king was being fooled as long as he could not observe the discrepancy between the window dressing and the reality in our
still economically disadvantaged countryside. Having just witnessed the extravaganza in Dhankuta, and imagining how frustrated the king must have
been with all the eyewash, I honestly anticipated that the king might give
our paper an award for the insight that my candid article gave into all that
went on behind the smoke screen of charts and gates.

Shrish wrote about the king's visit in his column also, mainly describing how the presence of the royal visitors made Dhankuta look so lively,
the regional headquarters town brimming with palace officials, ministers,
secretaries of the ministries, departmental directors, and others. You might

meet anyone there, not only from Kathmandu, but from almost anywhere in the kingdom, every individual hoping for a royal audience or to catch the eye of a courtier or a national *Pancha*. The local people really had a feel of the capital, Kathmandu. In harmony with this theme, I ended my own editorial with the Nepali saying *Behuli anmaiko ghar jasto bhayo*— "Now it has become like a house after saying farewell to the bride." This had been the Dhankuta people's comment as they had cleared their eyes and noses after the white helicopter finally left in a cloud of dust for Kathmandu. As the dust settled, the local officials who had worked hard at appearances must have been satisfied if they had personally given the king a tour of their charts or, better still, been privy to some late-night discussion at the camp. If amid all the buzz surrounding the palace secretaries they had favorably caught the attention of at least one of them, all would bode well for their prospects. The opinion of the general public counted for less.

My hope of receiving an award was quite genuine, because those newspapers that provided the best coverage of Their Majesties' tours were often given awards. It was a government tradition. How wrong I was. Before our next issue came out the following week, not an award but a summons arrived at our office. "No matter what I do, the government is always after me," I thought. A feeling of self-pity crossed my mind for a second until I became conscious of it as a sign of weakness and began to analyze the situation. The odd logic about this prosecution was that the case was brought against Durga Pokhrel personally, and not against our paper *Manas* or the publishing company, Star Publication, and not against Upendra or Shrish since they were Ranas of royal blood. It must be another plot to get rid of me, I realized. Usually such newspaper suits were filed by the local administration. But in my case the legal action was brought by the Ministry of Communication. It was the first time this had happened to a journalist.

Their first move was to summon me for interrogation at the ministry. Although I was the only one to be prosecuted, the three of us went on the first interrogation day. Obviously it was rather embarrassing for the two Ranas. During our questioning we discovered that there were two things the government considered objectionable. First, it seemed that I had used improper language for addressing the king in the headline (THE KING DOES NOT AGREE TO ARTIFICIAL DEVELOPMENT). I should have used his full title: His Majesty the King, and also the formal verb that we have in Nepali for addressing royalty. The other thing that bothered the authorities was one adjective, *ethnocentric*, which Shrish had applied to the palace in his article. When translated into Nepali it meant something like "communal." "Communal" was definitely not the meaning he had intended and it was my fault as editor not to have corrected the error. I had spotted it before publication and had meant to do so, but somehow forgot. Neither was it Shrish's fault, because while he had a strong command of English he was less accomplished in literary Nepali. As a result his objectionable line read like this: "The communal palace from Kathmandu moved to Dhankuta."

In response I defended the language of my editorial heading, saying that in literary expression you could use such informal language. But I said that if it was still objectionable, I apologized, and I promised to publish an apology for both our mistakes in our next issue. Our interrogators were not satisfied with our statement. If I was hoping that they would drop the case that was not to be. One of the government officers looked at me and announced, "Your next appearance will be in court. Your two Rana partners need not appear there—only you are required."

We left the building very disheartened. The ministry's arraignment was like cutting a bird's wing. So long as a newspaper was under a government action its publication was suspended until further notice. There was never any specific timetable for a government decision, and because this was the first time the ministry itself had brought an action it was impossible to tell what it would do or when. And the longer the decision took, the better for it and the more suppression for us. (In fact, we were allowed to publish again for a while a couple of months later pending a decision on the case.) I thought to myself, "So this is it—their first move." After my release and my audience this was the first explicit government move to harass me, even if its intentions were implicit already in the threatening calls and surveillance.

My partners knew about the harassment only at our newspaper. I had not told them about the frequent telephone threats and the intelligence people watching my house. If I had let them know everything that was going on, they might have felt too endangered to work with me. Shrish had come along up to this point, but how much further could he go in such uncertainty and insecurity? After all, they had partnered with me for commercial and professional reasons, not to save me or defend me from every threat on my life. Someone from Amnesty International's headquarters had already indicated to me that it was primarily due to Shrish that they had been able to learn the true nature of my case. In contrast, this Amnesty source told me that even some Nepali Congress people had been double-minded about whether or not I was innocent. My father and my sister Subhadra might have suffered a heart attack had anything happened to me now. But none of my other relatives would think of owning me.

One day even my former houseboy, who was underage, arrived drunk and said to me politely, "Don't just think that these are big words from a small mouth, but last year what you did was a little too much. You should never have given money to those boys. As soon as they came you should have handed them over to the police."

He would never have said anything like this to me in the past, and I sensed that something was badly wrong. I asked him to come back, but he refused and said that he didn't know whether he would ever return. He also confirmed that he had been kept in custody until I had been taken to Mahakali, and that he had been beaten badly. Later, I heard that he had been bribed by the police to reveal information about my activities, but I did not want to question him about it. I was feeling more and more isolated and doubtful about whom I could trust.

It was at about this time that I made up my mind to flee the country. I had told people at the highest levels the true story of the conspiracy, but although they had listened, I was not sure what action they were taking. The threats to my life and freedom were not diminishing. Instead, because such lawlessness prevailed in the kingdom, I felt in even greater danger. It seemed that with exposure, the conspirators' position had become more awkward. They had been hounding me—in the street, around my home, and by telephone. I was powerless against them. Cornered. They had won, at least for the time being. What use were my visions here in this paralyzed land? They were squashed. Incapable of expression. And that was what they wanted. You might be something, but there were times in the darkness when you lost sight even of what you were.

I had reached the point where I knew I had to retaliate, and that meant making my story public. My story might encourage others to come forward publicly and share their experience of fighting repressive rule in other parts of the world. But making my story public was not possible from Nepal. A bedroom window would have been opened one night, and that would have been the end of me. Or I would have been finished some other way. By now I did not want that kind of end. If there was anything I loved now, it was my life, myself. If I were going to be a martyr for some fine national cause I would not have minded, but I did not want to be a meaningless victim because some cruel and ill-motivated people wanted me to be their scapegoat. Therefore, all I could do was wish to go far from this mess—somewhere so far away that I would hear nothing from this world or from these evil people. I resolved that if I got a chance to flee the country I would, and I would not return while these autocrats were in power or even while there was still a chance for them to return in power.

But where to flee? I had no money and no passport. India was my only initial option, the only country where a Nepali can travel without a passport. I had contacted some of my journalist friends in New Delhi, and they assured me that if necessary they could help me to obtain travel documents from there. So this became one option. Another option was nearer by. A close friend offered me his wife's passport. I thought through the pros and cons of such an illegal course of action, and concluded that my life was what was most important, not the legality of my flight. And in any case, what was legal or illegal in the lawless system in which I lived? This friend's wife's passport would be my last resort. I was determined simply to leave the country, not knowing where my destination would be. Fearing that the government might invent a criminal charge and try to extradite me, I did not want to stay too long in India. I thought, "Maybe Sri Lanka?" At least there I had human rights activist friends, and an air ticket was not too expensive. I thought of giving one last try to getting my own passport back. Then I changed my mind. It might be better to apply for a new one. Perhaps the lower level people in the Foreign Ministry would not know me or know about my passport case.

I went to the Foreign Ministry, filled out a form, and left it to be processed normally. After a week, I called the person in charge. He told me, also quite normally, "Your form has been forwarded to the Home Ministry. After they send it back your passport will be ready." It sounded promising, so I waited another three days. Then I called the Home Ministry. Whoever answered the phone asked me to go there in person. I went, feeling positive. In the section of the Home Ministry that I had been asked to visit, I met a man from Dhankuta. He was the brother of one of my closest friends from school. "Great! This seems no problem," I thought.

I waited there for an hour. The man from my hometown said that he was looking for my application form to return to the Foreign Ministry. Finally, averting his look away from my face, he said, "Durga, maybe your form has already gone to the Foreign Ministry because I can't find any record of it here." I went over there. My contact person was not in his room. One of the clerks, who happened to be a sympathizer of mine, secretly showed me the House Ministry's confidential letter. It said simply, "Pending the Home Ministry's decision, do not issue any passport for Durga Pokhrel." This ended my hope of obtaining a passport from the Nepal government. For the sake of security, I did not tell this to any of my friends.

Now it had come down to far more dangerous choices: either risk leaving my country under somebody else's name, or take a chance at traveling with Indian travel documents, or, as so many of our Nepali Congress leaders had done in the past, exile myself in India.

That night I had a very unsettling dream. I woke from my sleep with feelings of grave foreboding and could not go back to sleep. In the morning I told Meenu my dream. She tried to comfort me, saying, "Don't be so sensitive about dreams, Durga *didi*." But I knew how serious it was. I went to the press and told my friends. I knew that I faced danger in several areas in my life. The feelings, intuitions of a malevolent influence, were coming so strongly that I developed an acute headache. There was a pharmacy about two minutes' walk away, so I decided to go and buy some headache medication. On the way, I spotted a small piece of gold that was lying on the road and I picked it up.

After taking the tablets at the pharmacy, I went back to the press. Before I could show what I had found to my friends, I realized that the gold had disappeared from my hand. I could not think where I might have dropped it and went out again to look for it. It was nowhere to be found. Then I remembered something my father had once told me: "If either you find or lose a piece of gold, that is not a good sign. It brings bad news."

All day I remained very disturbed by my dream of the previous night, my bad intuitions, and my father's gold story. I did not feel like eating, and stayed the whole day in our press as if waiting for bad news. Whenever any black car passed on the street outside my heart would start pounding and I would sit there too afraid to even swallow, waiting for the door to be opened by the police coming to arrest me again. I wanted to get it over with, to know what the bad omen was. At around five P.M. my sister Subhadra phoned me from Dharan. My father had become seriously ill on the previous day and was deteriorating rapidly.

So that was it. I could not stop crying because I trusted my intuition and knew from all the day's signals that the situation was going to be very serious. The problem was in finding a way to get to Dharan. I went to my apartment, took a nightdress, and then made my way straight to the bus station to see if it had anything going to Dharan. The last bus for the night was leaving Kathmandu at eight P.M. I bought my ticket and waited around the bus depot until it left. It was a noisy minibus, with very loud music. The driver drove quite fast and, as the bus took bend after hairpin bend along the grueling mountain road, a number of passengers became ill. Once we had passed over the mountain range between the Kathmandu valley and the *tarai* the bus stopped so that the passengers could have tea and urinate somewhere in the darkness. It was about two A.M. Outside in the roadside stalls one could buy very cheap tea, boiled several hours earlier, but still kept hot on top of movable charcoal stoves. The stalls were selling homemade snacks as well. I got out and stretched my legs, restless and impatient for the journey to be over. After half an hour the bus resumed its journey east along the east-west highway.

I was thinking about my father's health. He had never been seriously ill except for one time when he was a teenage boy and became sick while going up to a very high altitude without taking proper precautions. Now he was about to turn eighty-four but did not look very old. I remembered our astrologer remarking many years before about my father's horoscope. He had said that at around the age of eighty-three there was a great *khadgo*, or trouble. If he escaped from that influence then his life would last one hundred and five years. Also, my father himself had once had a dream in which he saw an old man telling him, "Wait. If you can make it until your eighty-fourth birthday, it will be one hundred and five years." My father had interpreted the "it" to mean his life span, and believed that the old man was a manifestation of Lord Shiva himself. As I sat in the bus I wished and wished for a long life for him and tried to meditate.

At eight in the morning, twelve hours after leaving the bus depot in Kathmandu, I arrived at the bus stop in the busy little center of Dharan's "new bazaar" street. Our house was another twenty minutes' walk farther up the same street, right on the main road of the bazaar. When I reached the house, the atmosphere was somber. Brother Krishna, sister Subhadra, Mother, and my aunt were all in Father's room. They were nervous and worried.

As I entered his room Father said, "Ah, I might survive—you've arrived."

I felt so emotional. He had never expressed such a personal sentiment, except once visiting me in jail, since I was a child. He began talking. Krishna told me that for the past twenty-four hours Father had not spoken at all and had been looking very serious. Krishna went to call the doctor, who immediately came from the hospital, which was just across the road from our house. The doctor thought it was pneumonia. I made some vegetable soup and gave my father the broth. It did him good, he said. I then went downstairs to his Ayurvedic clinic and brought back some of his medicines. After a few doses, he started looking a little better.

That afternoon my eldest brother, Ram, also arrived from Kathmandu. Father said, "Now I think I am better because my eldest son and youngest daughter are here," and he smiled with happiness.

I was of the opinion that we should take him to Kathmandu straightaway. Whether he received Ayurvedic or Western medical treatment, it would definitely be better there. However, I did not have the money to charter a plane and I was only the second in line to be able to make that decision. The nearest airport was in Biratnagar, an hour's drive south toward the Indian border. My brother Ram decided that we should take Father as far as Biratnagar to see how he would be and only then on to Kathmandu. Everybody knew that there was not much difference between Biratnagar and Dharan. However, as he was the main decision maker, we all went to Biratnagar, first to admit Father to the hospital, where he was immediately provided with an intravenous drip, and then to a guest house to stay. Krishna and I stayed by Father's bedside all night. It was unbearably hot there, and mosquitoes whined constantly. I could see that he was getting worse.

The next day I insisted on going to Kathmandu. Ram had heard that there was no charter plane available and no seats even for the following day's flight. I went myself to the Royal Nepal Airlines office and somehow arranged five seats for the flight the next day. I was frustrated and felt that if we had not wasted two days in Biratnagar, Father would not be as weak as he had now become. The next day we made the air journey to Kathmandu and, once there, took him straight from the airport to the intensive care unit at the government's Bir Hospital. Everything was possible and available at this hospital, perhaps because Ram was then a senior doctor there. I stayed in the hospital room with my father virtually around the clock.

For a couple of days he looked better. On the third day he talked to me at length about his anxiety for me, and he went on to share all of his other concerns for the family. About my separation from the family and about my choice for a life in politics, he said, "Although I have written you a long letter from Dharan the day before I fell ill, which you will receive soon, I will tell you briefly that I am now convinced that you will win the political game. I mean that democracy will come to Nepal sooner or later. The present *Maharaj* is more broad-minded and liberal than his father. Also people are very very angry and frustrated with Panchayat. Your struggle will not go in vain. I know you will be something in Nepal. Maybe you will be in a position from which you will have to look after your other relatives. But what I would have liked would have been to see you and your brother be together. He is a renowned doctor. Everybody knows him. I know how you felt when he gave you a choice between family and your politics. But can you not forget everything and put your ego under your right foot and talk, pretending that there is nothing?"

"I don't like pretense. You can't live in pretense with your own people," I said. "Anyway, don't worry about this now."

"I so much want to see you settled. All that worries me at the moment is seeing you without a home to live in. Where are you going to live for the rest of your life?" he asked me.

"You have educated me. I will survive somehow, don't worry," I said, trying to reassure him again.

A nurse entered and said that he should not talk so much. I repeated to him what she had said.

He said, "I wanted to tell you all these things in private. This poor nurse does not understand what is going through my mind." He smiled and continued, "If I do not tell you now I might never get the chance to tell you. Look after all my writings, and look in my trunk at home—there is something there also. Read it and act accordingly." Grief and anguish welled up within me, bringing tears to my eyes. Krishna arrived. As only one visitor was allowed to be with my father at a time, I stepped outside into the waiting room.

For six days and five nights I did not leave him. On the sixth night a friend came, insisting on taking me to her house to rest. I had had a series of very bad premonitions and was in two minds about whether to leave or stay. But I went. For a long time I could not go to sleep. Finally, I did fall asleep for a couple of hours, but then had a bad dream. In the dream, the whole family was going somewhere by bus. On the way, the bus had an accident and turned upside down. When we had recovered all of our people, only Father was missing. I woke up shocked and in tears. At six A.M. I returned to the hospital and went straight to his room. I put my hand on his forehead and he opened his eyes and whispered, "Eh! You came back. I feel like eating something."

I called a friend of mine who lived nearby and asked her if she would not mind making some mung *dal* soup for my father, and after about an hour she came with it. I told him what I had for him, but he said that he did not want to eat soup at that time. He would save it for later. He ate some jelly instead. He looked much brighter than he had the previous couple of days and I thought he was recovering. I wondered why that horrible dream had come to me.

It was about noon when I heard a noise like glass cracking. There was nothing made of glass in the room at that point, and then I remembered the thermos flask of soup. I opened it and saw that inside it had broken into pieces. That felt like a very bad sign and I started to become worried. Everybody else had left for lunch. Then my father stirred and asked me to wash his body. I sponged him gently with a washcloth and, as I was doing so, he asked again, "Where is your house; where do you live?"

"You should not talk like this now, and please don't worry at all about me," I replied, trying to comfort him.

Krishna arrived at that point, bringing food for me, so I left the two of them together and went to the waiting room to eat.

As I put food to my lips Krishna shouted, "Durga, come quickly!"

I ran back to my father's bedside and saw that his eyes were going around and around, staring at the ceiling.

Krishna panicked and shouted, "Doctor! Nurse! What is happening to my father?" He could not bear to watch and rushed out of the room crying.

I put my left hand under Father's head and massaged his face with the fingers of my right hand. As I held him, I saw a glint of life escape from his eyes with a gentle popping sound, and I knew that that was the end. But the nurses and doctors came running in and pushed me aside. They started pounding and pumping his chest. I could not stand it. Death is the supreme occasion in a person's life for meditation—when a highly evolved soul may experience all past lives and the future with perfect clarity, and even achieve union with Godhead. Any Hindu or Buddhist who has practiced forms of union, or yoga, during his or her life desires peace and prayerful support at the event of death. I knew that Father wanted to go gently, and that we needed to do our Hindu ritual of the eleventh hour as we would have done had he died at home or at peace in a *ghat* on the banks of a holy river.

I went back into the room and pleaded with the doctors, "Stop torturing him." But they would not listen to me. Only after a while did they declare that he was dead.

We had brought some sandalwood paste to the hospital, and now I made the *Om* sign and three horizontal lines across his forehead—the sign of Shiva—as he was a Shiva devotee and had always done this himself. He looked fresh, as if in deep sleep rather than death. Then the other relatives all arrived. I would have given my own life if he could have survived.

I went with the death procession. In our custom only men go to the cremation *ghat*, but I felt like doing as a son did and followed my brothers. It was painful to watch the most loved person in my life being burned. The cremation took place on the steps below the Pashupatinath temple, a most sacred place by the Holy Bagmati River, which, like all rivers in Nepal, is a tributary of the Ganges in India. "This is the way everybody has to go," I thought. The painful thought that came afterward was that he had not just gone for a little tour, or even a longer tour from which he would come back. He would never come back again in this life and in this form. His loss was overwhelming. Yet, I felt sure that his soul would find a perfect rebirth, perhaps on this earth again in another human form, and that we would meet again under happier circumstances.

I decided to go into mourning in the same way as my brothers did, which meant shaving my head. First I had to shave my mother's head, because she would not let anyone else touch her crown (the crown of the head is a sacred area). Touching the parting of her hair that was midway on her head, she said, "Your father poured *sindhur* [vermillion] over this place when I was seven years old [as part of their marriage rites]. Since then I have never let anyone touch my crown. Now I would not like to allow anybody to shave my head. You can do it because you are an unmarried daughter." And so I shaved my mother's hair first, and then mine was shaved by someone else.

As part of our tradition, we had to mourn and fast for thirteen days at the eldest son's house. Therefore I also had to go there even though it was not my preference. As Father had mentioned to me in the hospital, the letter he had written the day before he fell ill arrived on the same day he died. I left it unopened, and only opened it on the third day. Reading it made me very emotional. For the past three days my tears had not been able to break out. A great heaviness instead had been there in my chest and head. Now it broke and I wept.

He said in the letter: "Until 1978 I never thought that democracy would come in Nepal. But now I am totally confident that it will—and it will not be too long in coming. The reason I was worried by your being in the Nepali Congress was that you might be killed one day like so many others in the movement. This was simply a father's worry. I was so disappointed by your not agreeing to get married. I came to Kathmandu several times only for that purpose. Each time you disappointed me, and I was angry. I should have been a little broad-minded and thought that the time had not come for you. I thought women should marry before twenty-five—after that they are too old. But I remember now that the daughter of one of my friends married even at forty and still had children. For you there is plenty of time. Now I am fully convinced about what your aims might be and what you will do. I am sorry I did not encourage you in such things earlier on. After all, I am your father—you will not take it otherwise. . . ."

It was the longest letter he had ever written to me. As I put it down I wished that this had happened eight years before, when I had been given the choice of family or politics. Though I had no children of my own at that time, I think that at this moment I first understood how anxious he must have been all those years. During his lifetime I had been absorbed in the democratic movement, and this had worried him so much. Only when he had gone did I understand how he must have felt. Now the person I cared for most had died, and died with the realization that I was doing right—even if his message of reconciliation arrived only after his death. This made me feel even lonelier. Somebody from Tribhuvan University brought over some cassette tapes containing a recorded interview with my father made by the university. We all listened to his voice once more. It was beautiful, but my feeling for him and now my grief at his absence were heartbreaking. I wished so much that he was still alive. Our newspaper had just been permitted to operate again for a while. After reading his final letter to me I decided to write an article in our paper titled COMPROMISE WITH MY FATHER AFTER HIS DEATH.

On the thirteenth day, we had the final day of mourning. According to Hindu tradition, on this day all family members purify themselves and organize a big feast at which all the deceased person's friends, relatives, and family friends are invited. In addition, everything that the deceased person cherished is specially prepared. These might be his gold ring, certain clothes, his umbrella, his bed, and so on. They are then donated to the family priest in the hope that through his using them regularly, the soul of the loved one will receive the cherished things and be happy. Also, in the deceased person's name, the priest is given sufficient uncooked foodstuffs such as rice and beans to last for a year. If the family is rich they will donate a piece of land as well, which we did. We prepared everything for this day. Our priest, who was like one of the family, dressed in a full outfit of clothes just as my father had dressed, and his wife was dressed just like my mother. As they sat together on Father's bed for the final ritual, their resemblance to Father and Mother was deeply symbolic, and perhaps enabled Father's soul to reside for a time within the priest himself and in the blissful environment of our love and remembrance. Seeing the priest so closely resembling Father, we all wept with emotion, and even the priest cried as he sat on the bed.

I felt for Mother, but by custom she would live with her eldest son or her next son, and not with me. It is the sons who inherit parental property in our Hindu society, and whether the parties like it or not, an elderly parent has to reside with a son. So I had no role in the affair, and was all by myself. Only myself left to try to soothe both the old and now the fresh wounds within.

# 17

## Flight and Refuge

I t was the twelfth day after Father's passing, and we were all still in mourning in my brother's house. Mentally, I was at the lowest point in my life. My father, the closest person in my life, and at the last, as I now realized, the only soul who understood me, was gone. All that was left behind was the danger outside and the secret knowledge that I had to escape somewhere, though I knew not where. Strangely enough, at that moment I felt my good intuitions coming again. They flickered more and more strongly by the hour. From a kind of guilt, I tried to brush them away. How could I feel anything good at this distressing time? Yet, I had always believed in supernatural forces and felt the vibrations of power around me whenever I was in deepest trouble. The good feelings would not go away or diminish in intensity. Then someone arrived at the house bringing an envelope. It was in my name and was passed to me. Naturally, I thought it might be someone's condolence letter.

I opened the envelope and inside was a telegram. It said, "We have sent you a round-trip air ticket for Minneapolis, U.S.A. Collect it from Air India. Beverly and Earl Thompson." It was miraculous. At my hour of need—the hand of rescue! I had met these kind people from Minnesota about eight months previously, shortly after my release, when they had been in Kathmandu as tourists and I had invited them once for dinner. In return came this enormous gesture of generosity. The morning after their dinner with me they had visited me at the press. They had both said, "You must visit us in America; we mean it." "Okay," I had replied, thinking to myself, "As if it could ever be possible." Now, thinking back, I could see that they had meant to help me visit them. Suddenly I had a destination. It was almost beyond belief.

Although the rituals ended on the thirteenth day, according to custom family members were not supposed to be separated that night. So, early the next morning I left the house to go to the press. What to do? There was no point in giving up my life for Father now. I had to resume living. Sitting in the front office at the press, I thought about how best to leave for America. Within ten to fifteen minutes an idea came to me that made my whole being lighter. I thought, "I will go to see the U.S. ambassador. He will help me out." Although I had never met Ambassador Carlton Coon, Jr., before, I called his secretary and arranged an appointment to see him immediately. At the appointed hour I was at the embassy.

Naturally, knowing that a journalist was to meet him, he had called over his staff officer from the U.S. Information and Culture Agency. However, since this was not an official meeting, I requested permission to speak with him in private. The ambassador asked the other man to leave and I explained my situation in detail.

"You have put me on the spot," he responded. "But let me see what I can do."

The problem was not simply to obtain a visa to enter the United States. The major problem was to get a passport or travel document. The other complication from his side was that he was leaving the next morning for a safari camping trip.

I went back to the press and found that Shrish had already arrived. With his typical sophistication he said, "I need a vacation now."

I could not help thinking, "As if I have just had a year's vacation in jail, and now thirteen days of mourning for my father." However, I responded, "Oh, yes. You really need one, take one any time and I will take care of the press."

I was not being sarcastic. I was uncertain as to whether I would ever be able to leave Nepal. Even if I were able, I had no idea when that would be. I wondered if I would still be there after the ambassador returned from his two-week safari. Shrish could go and come back from his holiday within that time. So he left.

Two days after Shrish left I received a phone call from someone, who did not identify himself, saying that I should go and meet a person in the prime minister's office. I wondered what this was now. Another slap? At this stage, though, I was ready to do anything. So, I went as summoned to the prime minister's office in the white-colonnaded central secretariat building of Singha Durbar.

As I entered the prime minister's office, I asked somebody where I should go to find the person I had to meet there. An official showed me to a door and I saw that on it was the nameplate of the prime minister himself. I retreated several steps, thinking, "Is it the prime minister I have to see? Definitely not." Again I approached the door. There was a messenger standing on duty outside, so I asked him whether the person I was supposed to meet was in the prime minister's room. He confirmed that he was. Apprehensively, I wrote my name on a little piece of paper and gave it to the messenger to pass to the person inside the prime minister's room. Within a minute the man I was supposed to meet came out, and I introduced myself.

This man took me to another room and said just, "Wait until tomorrow."

I said, "Very well"—as if I had understood something even though I had not spent more than two minutes in his company.

On the way back to the press I pondered about what could be going on. All I could do at this point was wait for some miracle. The suspense was extreme.

The next morning at around ten o'clock another call came. This time I was asked to go to the Foreign Ministry to see the foreign secretary. I went there. I had known the foreign secretary personally before his appointment to that position. And when I arrived there, to my enormous surprise, my passport was ready and waiting. I still have no idea exactly how it had been processed. That was just a black box. I maintained absolute secrecy about the event.

The moment I arrived back at the press from the Foreign Ministry, the telephone rang. It was another unidentified caller, this time warning me, "Leave the country within forty-eight hours, otherwise you may miss your chance."

I did not have to be told a second time, and went immediately to the U.S. embassy. Obviously the ambassador must have left instructions, as my visa was prepared in no time. Now I was completely ready to flee Nepal and, to my great relief, to head toward a known destination.

Because of that anonymous call warning me to leave within forty-eight hours, I was very worried that I would be stopped by government agents at the airport. I needed some kind of symbolic support there because of this danger. Putting my ego under my right foot, as my father had admonished,

I decided to ask my brother if he would drive me to the airport. He agreed. His positive attitude to this softened me a little further, so I decided to invite all my family members, including my mother, for lunch at my house one day before my departure. None of them had even seen where I lived before, and they all came. I was so happy to have them all, and yet at the same time grieved at the absence of the principal family member, my father, who had always longed to see such a family reunion. I thought to myself, "Perhaps to gain something you have to lose something." But I was sure his spirit was with us.

Since shortly before my father died, I had been accommodating an American houseguest. He was working for the Human Rights Internet in New York at that time, and had come to Nepal for a trekking holiday. Most of the time he was out in the mountains. Some friends had written in advance of his coming to Nepal, asking if I knew somewhere for him to stay. For some reason I had formed the impression from their letter that the person I was expecting was a woman, so I had written back saying that "she" could stay with me. I had a spare bedroom anyway. Then one day here "she" came—Trip Sullivan, a man.

Looking at him, I was speechless and said, "I thought you were a woman."

"Oh! Well no, I am afraid I am not," he replied.

He looked a nice young man, and younger than me, so I said, "Well, you could be my younger brother, so you can stay." I even gave him a Nepali name, Himal, since he liked climbing mountains.

Just before I left my house for the airport, Trip returned from trekking and I told him that I was leaving. "The house is yours now, but in a few days a British man will come to live in it."

"Where are you going?"

"To America," I replied, walking away because I had little time to catch the plane.

I did not have time to explain further. He ran after me a short distance, not believing me. All I had was two vinyl shoulder bags. Nobody would believe that I was leaving for the United States.

As planned, my brother took me to the airport in his car. My heart was pounding. But one thing played in my favor—my recently shaved head. I was sure that people who were used to seeing me with long hair would have difficulty recognizing me at a glance. Also, I had taken the precaution of getting an Indian Airlines ticket for the Kathmandu–Delhi sector, so that I could keep my intercontinental sector tickets out of sight. Finally, I had no check-in baggage. Everything went without a hitch. Even the duty police constable turned out to be one of my favorite women guards from Central Women's Prison who had just been transferred to the airport. She did not check anything of mine, but just saluted and let me go through. That was a great stroke of luck.

At last, I was in the air. The plane banked steeply and circled the Kathmandu valley as it climbed through some premonsoon clouds, then after bumping a little over the deep valleys and high ridges of the Mahabharat range, it soared above the clouds into dazzling sunshine. Classical sitar music was playing in the cabin of this Indian Airlines flight. I leaned back in my seat and relaxed. Then I realized with sadness that I had not even been able to say good-bye to Shrish. I imagined that by this time he must have returned from his Indian holiday.

In New Delhi I boarded a direct flight to New York via Dubai. In the plane were one hundred and eight American Krishna Consciousness followers returning to the United States from their pilgrimage to Vrindavan, Lord Krishna's abode in India. This was more Americans than I had ever seen together before, and it felt more than a little strange to see them on a pilgrimage to my part of the world just as I was fleeing for refuge in theirs.

The plane flew low over John F. Kennedy Airport in New York, and I caught my first glimpse of America. How many millions before me had started their time of refuge from persecution in one of the ports of entry of New York?

As we disembarked, one of the airport ground staff said to me, "Your friends are already well ahead. You'd better catch up with them." Because of my shaved head he had associated me with the Hare Krishna people. I thought of telling him that women don't shave their heads in that movement, but cover their hair with their saris or scarves, and that it is only the men who shave their hair. This was my introduction to the incomprehensibly different worldview of my country of refuge. I replied only that I was not one of them.

I changed planes in New York and continued to Minneapolis. It was already dark as we left New York, and for the first time in my life, as this plane headed farther west, I saw lights spread out for miles, like a shimmering web down on the world below. I arrived in Minneapolis at almost midnight, and there waiting for me was Jolyn, the daughter of the Thompsons, with her boyfriend, Tom.

I marveled to see Jolyn driving the car, turning off one huge road and taking another in the dark night without getting lost. Minnesota was blanketed by two feet of snow. At around one A.M. we arrived at the Thompsons' farmhouse. Earl and Beverly were still up, waiting for us excitedly. Beverly's warm hugs welcomed me to my first home in America.

We all sat around a table in the kitchen. I felt very lost, and struggled to hold back a wave of emotion. I said only, "Thank you for getting me here. I needed to get out."

Beverly asked, "Why, you look so different from when we last saw you. What happened to your lovely long hair?"

For a minute, I did not know where to begin. I thought for a second, and replied, "Oh yes! My father just died, so I shaved my hair just to say to myself how much I loved him."

"Durga, I am so sorry," she responded gently. "We did not know that."

It was two A.M. They wanted me to eat something, but as I was more tired than hungry, they showed me up a flight of steps to a bedroom tucked away under the roof above the living room.

I peered out through the lattices of a small dormer window. A blizzard was blowing outside. Despite a fire in the living room below, the room was quite cold. I slipped under the quilts. For a while I lay awake staring at the ceiling and feeling so many thoughts trying to enter my mind. I determined to be neither too unhappy nor too excited about the current events whose outcome was so uncertain, and settled my active mind through a brief meditation.

It was noon, two days later, when I awoke and went downstairs.

"Are you okay?" exclaimed Beverly. "We kept coming up to check on you to see if you were all right."

I felt wonderful and assured them of this. I gazed out of the window at the snow-covered countryside. It was vast and flat—so different from my mountainous Nepal. Yet it felt comforting and safe in its openness. All I had to wear was a thin sari and blouse and a pair of sandals. I had left at the beginning of the hot premonsoon summer at home, not imagining that I should be prepared for winter. The Thompsons said, "This is the first blizzard we have had here at this time of year for twenty years." I felt blessed as I thought to myself, "Our Lord Shiva, who dwells in the snows of the Himalayas, must have brought this snow here for me as a sign of good fortune."

America! I had always imagined it as excitement, hustle and bustle, and sky-high buildings—as if everywhere was like New York or Chicago. In contrast, this place was quietness itself. Theirs was the only house to be seen anywhere around.

ॐ

When I left Nepal I had only one goal—to escape. For a month in this new quietness I could not think what to do next. I could not live with these dear people forever. But where to go? Where to get lost? Except for that first night of my arrival, I had not been able to meditate properly for more than a month—since the time of my father's passing. Earl and Beverly used to go to bed fairly early. My room was quite a distance from their private rooms upstairs in a separate part of the house, so I had plenty of solitude. Haunted by the recent past, the isolation sometimes frightened me at night, especially because my hosts never locked their house. I started locking the front door that was downstairs at my end of the house and felt a little safer. One evening I meditated again before going to bed. Afterward, I felt bathed with a feeling of serenity and peace. So I resumed the practice regularly every morning and evening. Within a week, for no particular reason that I knew, I felt lighter and happier. The snow was gone now, and it was warm.

I had the addresses of two other Americans with me. One was Leslie Klein, in Cambridge, Massachusetts, and the other was Ben Wright, who lived in Spain. Leslie was a human rights activist who had visited Nepal with her cousin Dr. Hayat Aboza after my 1982 release and had stayed in my house in Kathmandu. They had also been to my father's house in Dharan during our Dasain Festival and had received *tika* from him, and we had been to Darjeeling, India, together. Ben was a writer who had visited Nepal during the 1978 student movement. I had invited him for dinner at that time. I decided to write letters to both of them. Leslie immediately wrote back, saying, "Come and live with me as long as you want." Ben telephoned all the way from Spain, saying that he would arrange meetings for me with social democrats, lawyers, writers, and journalists there. I thought, "I must definitely make that visit." However, as my American family did not want me to leave so soon, I waited four more weeks and then set off in early June. No words can express my appreciation to Earl and Beverly.

When I arrived in Massachusetts I discovered to my amazement that Harvard University was there—right in Cambridge. Instantly the idea came to me: "I'll go to Harvard!" When I asked Leslie what she thought about my applying, she laughed. "Don't be silly! There is no use even giving it a try right now. You have to apply in December or January for admission the following September. It's just impossible. My brother went there. If you don't believe me, ask Andy when he comes."

"I may make everybody laugh, but I'm going to apply. At the worst, people will think that I am a stupid foreigner and forgive me," I told her.

"Why on earth do you want to go to Harvard anyway? Harvard people are just snobs. If you really want to study, there are many other colleges around here."

"Because our king also went there. Maybe I'll find salvation there," I said to her, joking.

"That is what I'm trying to explain to you," Leslie protested. "The people there are just snobs. What good is your king doing in your country?"

For fun I argued some more, "That's exactly what I'll tell the snobbish Harvard people—that when I go back to Nepal, I will accomplish the things that our king could have done but didn't do!"

I made her really laugh. When she found that she could not convince me not to give Harvard a try, she said, "Okay, I'll give you directions for getting there."

It was almost an hour's walk up Massachusetts Avenue. Finally, I reached the Harvard area with the help of Leslie's directions. What she had not explained was how huge Harvard was.

When I asked a woman passerby where Harvard was, she replied, "Why, this is all Harvard! What part do you want?"

I was not sure whether I wanted History, Education, Political Science, Journalism, or Law. When she saw me stuck without an answer, she suggested that I go to Harvard Information to make my inquiry.

I looked all around me, from the colorful bustle of the sidewalks and the fine shops, to the venerable old buildings, gateways, and quadrangles of America's first university. Then, alert for the busy traffic, I crossed Harvard Square and entered the Information Office. There I talked to a very sweet lady who listened to my story. She suggested that I should meet the registrar of Harvard's John F. Kennedy School of Government, so I walked down John F. Kennedy Street to the Kennedy School and into the registrar's office. She was not available then, but her assistant made an appointment for me for the following morning. I then walked back to Leslie's place near Central Square. By the time I reached her place I had been wandering around for six hours and was feeling quite hungry and tired. Just then, Leslie arrived home from work.

"I have an appointment to see the Kennedy School registrar tomorrow," I told her enthusiastically.

"Go ahead and meet her. All she will say is 'Sorry, it is not the time to apply,' and you will realize," my friend responded.

The next morning I went to see the registrar. She listened to my whole story. She was very receptive and suggested, giving me the necessary directions for how to get there, "Go and meet Dr. Nancy Pyle at HIID, the Harvard Institute for International Development. She is in charge of international student admissions for the mid-career Master's in Public Administration program."

As she suggested, I went to see Nancy without an appointment. As I entered the HIID building I noticed a display of books on political and international development and immediately felt at ease. I thought, "Here I will be able to communicate with people without hesitation." The ground-floor lobby of HIID buzzed with several groups of people engaged in conversation. Suddenly, my attention was grasped as out of one group I heard the name of Kim Dae Jung pronounced. I turned around and, in the center of one group, I thought I recognized the South Korean opposition leader who had several times escaped death at the hands of the authoritarian Korean state. During his last imprisonment, before he came to America in exile, I had worked for his release through Amnesty International's Nepal chapter. Now, just knowing that he too was here, I felt an immense sense of security and was overwhelmed with joy at finding a sanctuary where people in his and my position were understood. Six months later, on December 10, 1983, I met Kim Dae Jung personally when Amnesty International's northeastern region invited one Russian woman and myself as former prisoners of conscience and Kim as the guest of honor on the occasion of Human Rights Day.

When I reached Nancy's office, she immediately invited me inside and offered me some coffee, and once again I told my story. She listened to everything with great patience and at the end said, "You are too late for this year. But you can still apply—you never know. And anyway, you won't lose anything."

I thought to myself, "This is a positive atmosphere." I did not want any negative influence from now on. I felt that if I did not find a refuge here, there would be nowhere else where my situation would be as well understood as in this politically astute HIID/Kennedy School community.

I went back to Leslie's place straightaway and started working on the application forms. As soon as Leslie came, I asked her to please not bring up anything negative until I had submitted my application. The tide was turning and I wanted to let it move without interruption. Even a thought that was contrary to the flow could disturb it. After supper Leslie helped me with typing my personal statement and I continued working on the rest of the forms until two A.M.

At nine o'clock sharp the next morning I was back at Dr. Nancy Pyle's office to submit my application. She was not there, but her assistant checked it and said that everything was fine. Then I returned home.

As I sat and began to relax the telephone rang. Ben was calling again from Spain to remind me about his invitation. If I was accepted at the Kennedy School, then there were only two weeks before the preparatory summer program began. If I was not accepted, then I did not know how I would be able to stay on in the United States as I had only a six-month visa and no money. Anyway, I did not want to think too much. I would do one thing at a time, whatever came along first. I decided to go to Spain. I still had the return portion of my round-trip ticket, so I used that to take me as far as England, as I thought that I would stop over in England. From there, Ben arranged my flight to Spain. I left Harvard a contact address in England, as I thought that I would stop over in England on my way back from Spain to see an old friend, Lord Avebury, the chairman of the British Parliamentary Group on Human Rights.

After ten wonderful days in Spain, I felt a strong, sudden feeling. I told Ben, "There's some good news in the air. I can feel it. I'd like to call Lord Avebury in England."

"Why sure, go ahead and call him then."

I called Lord Avebury and asked if there was any news for me.

"There are two telegrams here for you, but I have not opened them," came Lord Avebury's reply.

I asked him to read them for me. The first one said, "Congratulations! You are accepted at Harvard." The second one offered me a Harvard University grant to cover tuition for the summer program. What a miracle! No one can imagine the light and relief that I felt at that moment. What a refuge I had found in my life! I had not written my personal statement this explicitly, but my situation had been one of "now or never." Where would I have gone if I had not been accepted? I had nowhere to go.

I shared my good news with Ben and his Spanish girlfriend. Now there were only four days left before I was due back at Harvard, so I shortened my visit to Spain. As Ben had already made plans for me, during the next couple of days I was able to meet and exchange views with some of Spain's social democrats. After these enjoyable last days, I went to England.

At London's Gatwick Airport the immigration authorities did not allow me to enter the country. It was midnight. I had no choice but to ask the authorities to call Lord Avebury. After talking to him, they allowed me into England.

I spent two days there, during which time Lord Avebury gave me a fine tour of Parliament and the Westminster area. Then I returned to the United States—this time with a definite goal.

ಌ

Toward the end of the summer program at Harvard, I received a letter from a friend back in Nepal. It contained news about the court case lodged against me by the Ministry of Communication. It appeared that Upendra and Shrish had been summoned to the court on my behalf. But the prosecutor had not even been interested in seeing them. He had looked at their faces and exclaimed, "What's this? We wanted Durga Pokhrel here, not you." He had then proceeded to ask them not even one serious question. It was obvious that the government's intention in this prosecution had been to target me personally and have me incarcerated again—this time perhaps forever. I thought to myself, "I escaped just in time." Later, I heard that our paper had been banned again until further notification.

After the summer program was over, Harvard helped me get a grant from the Ford Foundation toward my tuition. The Ford Foundation's representative in New Delhi, Dr. Lincoln Chen, was another good person who came to my rescue. I arranged to share Leslie's house for a year and to pay the rent by the end of the following summer. A dear supporter from Oregon, Mrs. Rydel, sent me a little money each month to help me buy food. In these ways my needs were covered—I had no extravagant habits requiring more money.

It was a forty-five-minute walk to and from Harvard every day. Often I used to almost run to my classes. My life was from apartment to department. I might have looked a poor lonely figure trudging the streets each day, especially as the New England winter set in. But compared with the past from which I had escaped, for me this was heaven.

That December, our king was invited to Harvard University as an alumnus during a state visit to the United States. Three days before the king arrived a high-level Nepal government official came and informed me that the king had told officials at Nepal's Washington embassy that he would not go to Harvard because I was there, saying, "She is a CIA agent."

I did not believe that the king could have said it, but what surprised me was that these people could still be so concerned about me as to create such gossip. I was mildly upset, but as I could not shut anybody's mouth there was nothing to do but ignore it.

Well, for me the king was the king. One day he might realize the inevitable and share his power with the people. I had nothing against him and was ready to welcome him, whether in spirit or in person. Harvard's president, Derek Bok, sent me an invitation to a dinner with the king. Naturally, I was very pleased. I fulfilled my duty as a Nepali by writing an article in support of King Birendra's current passion—his proposal to make Nepal a "Zone of Peace." In the subcontinent this had become a controversial proposal. Neither China nor India had supported it, India simultaneously arguing that the whole Indian Ocean zone should be declared one of peace. Within Nepal also, some opposition groups thought that the king was just trying to be clever, keeping India and China out of the way through the peace proposal while he continued to suppress the opposition. Others were of the opinion that Nepalis should support the proposal, rather than the alternative of militarization. For what use would our little military ever be against the big powers on either side of us? The only use for a strengthened Nepal military would have been to curb the opposition within the kingdom and further enhance the power of the autocratic regime. I was convinced by the second logic. Therefore, despite the lack of "internal peace" within our borders, I supported the king's proposal. The *Boston Globe* kindly published my article on the day the king arrived in Boston. One of its editors, Mike Kenney, was very supportive.

The Nepalese ambassador to the United States was very pleased to see my progress, and one of the king's secretaries said to me, "I think you deserve a decoration from the king."

"Don't even suggest such an insult to me. I did not write that article to please anybody. I wrote what I believed," I replied. Whether he was joking or serious, if the king had decorated me on this visit it would have been very humiliating for my political career.

After the king's visit, and on completing my first semester, I heard that the king had sacked the prime minister who had troubled me. Gambling with my life, I decided to risk a visit to Nepal. I would have to return to Harvard to complete the second semester, but I was seriously thinking of going back to Nepal after completing my master's degree in public administration. It was purely for personal reasons, and I stayed for less than a week. But while in Nepal I still did not feel secure. Friends told me of various rumors that they had heard about my departure and my position in America. Whatever I did seemed to be a topic of criticism. As usual, I ignored the gossip. There was no way of knowing where I stood as far as the palace was concerned, especially whether the king had any positive feeling for me or not. I decided to telephone another of his secretaries whom I had met at Harvard. He was very receptive and suggested I write the king a detailed petition about the real story. I agreed. Whenever anyone close to the king asked me to take any step, I did so. But still, there was no way of knowing what the petition would do for me in terms of my security.

After I returned to Cambridge I realized that once I completed my M.P.A. I would have to choose between writing the book about the conspiracy or continuing on in a doctoral program. I made the choice to continue my studies, applied to Harvard's Graduate School of Education, and was accepted with partial financial assistance from the school.

While I was in my first year at the School of Education, another Nepali man came for the Kennedy School program. I knew him. He had been the police inspector in Biratnagar when I was arrested there the first time. Now he told me that he was working as an assistant press secretary in the palace. I was very glad that there was another Nepali around Harvard, although, with the exception of various Kennedy School parties, I did not see him anywhere. After his wife came to join him, I visited them a couple of times as a courtesy and once invited them to where I was living.

I was surprised when a friend of mine wrote from Kathmandu with a warning: "I have heard that this man has been sent after you. Stay away from him. If he is not there after you, why would a middle-ranking palace policeman need a Harvard degree? He doesn't have anything to do with the academic world." I was in no position to know what to believe. I had no enmity toward this man, but nonetheless I kept a distance from him.

After starting the doctoral program I kept a very low profile. I had several pressing problems. I had to work like a dog for money. Nonetheless, I enjoyed being a full-time student once again. Like myself, my classmates were in their mid-careers. Especially during seminar-type courses, we would come to know more about one another's backgrounds and interests. I discovered that there was one other person with a background similar to my own, a political dissident from El Salvador.

However, for two years, although I enjoyed listening to the participation of my classmates, I found myself unable to experience a sense of personal academic freedom. Opinions burned within me but I rarely expressed my ideas, never sure whether even the seminar room walls might have ears. Always conscious of potential informants, I did not even mix much with other Nepalis in Cambridge. I had my own routines, problems, and struggles. Most people were simply unable to relate to my experience. It was all beyond belief for them. As I made this discovery, I no longer tried to share everything that was inside me and found myself locked up again—this time in a strange protective shell against hounding from where I had come, or disbelief from where I had arrived.

In my second year of the doctoral program, I spoke about these frustrations with Upendra Rana, who had come to Boston University as a Humphrey Fellow. He reminded me, "Wherever you go, you don't go partially, you go in totality. When your total self is here with you, it brings with it influences that are bound to affect you anywhere."

He was right. This was another dimension of my *karmic* reality. But no matter how much I continued to draw these influences, as if I was attracting the troubles that plagued me, I found Harvard provided the strong support I needed.

# 18

·

# Anthony Comes into My Life

My whole struggle with my father revolved around his desire to arrange my marriage and my rebellion against his every effort. As a result I formed the firm impression that I would never get married. My father had made me promise not to marry any man outside our matrimonial Brahmin clan. Because of this family pressure, my mind became set against it. The thought of marriage never even entered my head, so negative a concept had it become for me.

However, I believe that whatever is meant to happen happens in any case and at any cost. On the fourteenth day after my father's death, the same day that I met the U.S. ambassador, I was in the front office of the press when someone mentioned that Dan, the British man who was renting the downstairs floor of my house, was at that very moment eating next door in Ringmo's restaurant. I had still not been to my house after leaving my brother's place following the thirteen days of mourning, so I had not yet seen him.

I went to say hello. There was Dan, sitting at a table by a window. He was eating and talking with three other Westerners. I stayed in the entrance with the door onto the street half open and called to him, and he turned around and called back *"Namaste"* in his usual cheerful way. As I greeted him in Nepali and said one or two things, one of the men sitting opposite him at the table caught my attention. He was dark-haired and quite nice-looking, although I noticed he had quite a prominent, long nose. The reason that I noticed him was that he seemed to be staring at me. When I returned his gaze for a second or two, he smiled in a friendly way as if we might have known each other. I bade my housemate good-bye and returned to the press next door.

I sat down for a moment, wondering whether the other man had wanted to say something to me, or whether perhaps I had met him somewhere before. "Sometimes I am absentminded, but why be concerned?" I thought to myself. Then another distant realization flickered in my mind. It just said, "Life seems a little lonely." Even though I had not been living with my father, the only slight source of protection I had ever had was from him— even if for much of my life it had been more symbolic than real. Now Father was gone. "Well, you can't die with someone; life goes on," I thought. I had a habit of placing my left hand on my head whenever I had to think about something. I did that now and became conscious of my scalp's shaved texture. Oh! Perhaps this was what the other man had been staring at— my bald head. No wonder he smiled. I must have looked quite funny.

The next morning at around eight A.M. I saw a foreigner standing in the street just outside the press. Or perhaps he was standing outside Ringmo's. Our entrances were adjacent. I recognized him. He was the same man I had seen with Dan the previous day. Something made me get up and go outside. Once again, he was with Dan.

Dan made the introduction. "*Namaste*. Oh!—er, this is Tony. He's the agricultural adviser for KHARDEP." This was the Koshi Hill Area Rural Development Program, based in Dhankuta. It seemed that he and Dan worked together.

"Tony" greeted me in very fluent Nepali.

Before I even considered what I was saying, I asked him, "Will you look after my apartment? I'm going to America."

He looked thoughtful. "I'm not sure I need an apartment. I only come to Kathmandu for a week or ten days every couple of months. Usually I stay in the Ambassador Hotel. How long does it need looking after?"

"Oh, I'm only going for a few weeks, maybe months," I replied. "Let me show it to you, and you can see whether you like it."

I took him immediately to see my apartment. Although he worked with Dan, he had never visited the house where Dan lived.

My apartment was simple and sparely furnished. I had few belongings. I looked at him, and, as if reading my mind, he said in Nepali, "Okay, it's nice here. I'll look after it for you."

We started back to the press. "I heard that you just lost your father. I'm very sorry," he said as we walked along.

I began to get used to listening to this foreigner speaking my language. I noticed that he talked lightly and cheerily, but sensed also that for a foreigner he seemed to be unusually at ease in my country and had genuine feeling for things around him.

I invited him inside the front office and ordered some cups of tea from next door. As we drank tea we introduced ourselves to each other more. I learned that his proper name was Anthony Willett. Then I told him that where he worked, Dhankuta, was my home, and added, "I will give you the names of all my family members there and in Dharan, and at our riceland in the *tarai* not far from the junction between the east-west highway and the Dharan–Biratnagar road."

"I'd love that, and I'll definitely visit them," he promised.

"Now I have to go to the U.S. embassy for my visa. I have so many things to do before I leave the day after tomorrow," I informed him.

My future housesitter offered to take me to the embassy in his office Land Rover, and waited there while my visa was issued. I did not tell him the mystery of my passport, or that I was fleeing the country. I invited him to my house for supper the following evening—the day before I was due to leave, the same day I was inviting my family for lunch.

I was busy packing. It was not that I had much to pack, but still it took a little time. Most of all I wanted to be sure that I had my diaries and all the materials I had smuggled out of jail. My houseboy prepared the food. Anthony arrived, and we ate together sitting on Nepali wool rugs on the floor around the low plywood table in my living room.

After eating, as promised, I wrote down names of some of my closest family members together with directions for how to find them. He stayed for a while, watching me sort my belongings. Then I gave him a set of housekeys and told him, "I am leaving everything as you see it. All my things are everywhere. None of my trunks have locks. Take care of them. And, by the way, the rent is already paid for three more months. If I am away longer than that and you have to pay, I will reimburse you later."

"Don't worry about that. I'll share the rent with you."

"*Namaste,*" I said to him.

"*Namaste,* and have a good trip to America."

I did not see him again before I left Nepal the next day.

৩৩

After reaching Minnesota I wrote to him, saying I might stay longer but that I did not know for how long. Still I did not mention to him that I had fled the country. That might scare him into leaving my apartment. He replied, saying that he would look after my things as well as he did his own, or even more carefully. He also mentioned he had heard a little about my past activities, and that my friends had warned him my apartment was still being watched by the police. He was not afraid of that, and was very happy I had asked him to look after my belongings. "I admire what I have heard about you," he added. Finally he asked me to read a book by Martin Luther King Jr., *Strength to Love*, saying he thought it might be inspiring for me. The very day I received his letter in Minnesota I went to the local library and borrowed the book, and I read it overnight.

Perhaps because of my mental state, the book did not have quite the effect on me that Anthony had expected. I could not internalize its message. Instead, I found myself inspired by Anthony. I started thinking of him whenever I felt lonely in my room. Many times I would walk the quarter mile to the post office to check the mailbox for his letters. When one arrived, I would go into a small café on my way back and order coffee. Before opening the letter I would look around to make sure no one was approaching to sit next to me. Quite often people in this small country town would do so, perhaps because of my foreign-looking dress, *tika*, and nose ring. Having made sure I was on my own, I would open the letter and read it several times over. Then I would walk home, very lonely and depressed. In the evening I would start a reply. It would be free-flowing and somewhat emotional. Then the following morning I would reread what I had written and tear it up because I did not want to reveal my mental weakness. My reply would end up being more formal. But somehow I made up my mind to ask him to send his photograph. Within a very short time he sent six photos, and they were all beautiful. After that, almost every night I would gaze at them, and the more I studied them the more nice-looking I found him. I did not show his letters or photos to my hosts. They did not know of his existence.

As soon as he received my letter informing him that I was moving from Minnesota to Massachusetts, he wrote back to tell me that he had two very dear American friends who had worked in Botswana, where he had been a regional agricultural officer, and who were now living in Amesbury, Massachusetts. They were Drs. Malcolm and Marcia Odell. Mentioning their address and telephone number, he said, "They are the most warm and generous people you can find, and full of fun. They'll be lovely friends for you. Do get in touch with them. I am writing to tell them about you."

I phoned them as soon as I received Anthony's letter. The moment I said that I was from Nepal, Malcolm Odell exclaimed, "I was in the first

Peace Corps group to go to Nepal in 1962. Where in Nepal do you come from?"

"Dhankuta."

"That's where I was!" Malcolm almost shrieked through the phone. "I knew the Pokhrel village well, and I knew one gentleman from there who ran the Ayurvedic clinic."

"That was my father!" Suddenly I knew who I was talking to, and added, "You're Mac, aren't you?"

"That's right. And you were my student."

Without further ado, Mac told me to wait for just over an hour while he drove down from Amesbury to collect me. I had such a good weekend with him, Marcia, and their two children at their family home, enjoying some laughs about the time when we had known each other twenty years before. Mac brought out all his photographs of his Nepal days, and excitedly we noticed that I was in one of them. I reminded him, "Mac, you were the first white man I ever saw, and I used to think your ways were so funny. Remember how we used to watch how you ate with a fork! Never could I have imagined that I'd be here in your house!"

In addition to reminiscing, we also talked about Tony, through whom we had been reunited. They obviously felt great affection for him, and spoke with great enthusiasm about his work in Botswana. It seemed that he had worked with farmers and had pioneered a group development approach to the management of communal tribal areas. I learned that the United States Agency for International Development (USAID) had used this approach as the basis for redesigning a major national project. USAID had then hired Anthony to undertake a comprehensive study of the group development program. For a year Anthony had traveled throughout the country visiting farmers' groups of every kind and the local authorities and other agencies supporting them, and had prepared a report for USAID on this approach to rural development. He had been asked to return to Botswana from Nepal for two weeks in 1982 to lead a series of seminars on his findings.

Mac showed me Anthony's report, which had been published in four volumes. I felt even closer to him in his absence because of his published work. I always admired people who could write. I also learned that he had been to Cambridge University in England. I was very impressed. I almost wrote to him to tell him so, but did not.

However, we kept up our correspondence. He was the only person writing to me regularly from Nepal because no one from my family wrote to me. Gradually I grew to look forward to his letters, which brought me news of Nepal and sometimes of my friends. However, his two most frequent themes were his frustration at working in a Nepal government rural development program and his ill health. He used to compare the closed political environment and bureaucratic inertia in Nepal with the openness and vitality of the government in democratic Botswana, where he had lived for over seven years. And in Nepal, not a single month passed without his falling sick with some intestinal parasitic complaint. In my replies I told him to be patient until democracy came to Nepal too, and to be more careful about drinking only filtered and boiled water. After I started my program at Harvard, I also encouraged him to think about taking a break from his fieldwork, and I described the flexibility and international flavor of the Kennedy School's M.P.A. program and recommended it to him. I told him, "This program teaches you how to work within the public sector and how you can achieve success in development work. It's so interesting attending seminars with people from many different countries and discussing different policies and management methods. You will find all your field experience starts falling into place, and you'll gain more skills and confidence to deal with the kind of problems you have been facing." Then, for some reason, I added, "Later, when I am in power, you can be my adviser."

In several of his letters he used a few terms to refer to me in Nepali that one only uses to address one's closest person. To begin with, I did not respond like this in writing, but in my heart I did.

ॐ

As I mentioned earlier, after the king sacked the former prime minister— toward the end of my first semester at Harvard—I decided to gamble on a return trip to Nepal. I thought it was important for me to show that I had not disappeared.

At the time, Anthony was in Dhankuta. I asked Dan to send him a radio message from the KHARDEP office in Kathmandu. He came four days later, and had to go back after two days. We spent one day traveling around and visiting some friends I wanted him to meet. We had little time alone. Anthony went back to Dhankuta, and I took my flight back to America.

On the plane, I realized that perhaps being in Nepal had made it difficult for me to express the emotion I felt for him. My culture prevented me from being expressive. I could feel his love for me, but for me it felt very awkward to say "I love you." "Well," I thought, "if something is meant to be, it will surely happen." For some reason at that time, I found myself feeling more excited thinking about him in his absence than being with him in person.

Within a couple of weeks of my return to Cambridge, he wrote about his decision to take a mid-career academic break from his work. After many years working for the U.K. aid program he would have been eligible for British government funding for this if he had studied in England. But I suggested that he do it in the United States.

One day the letter from him arrived that perhaps I had been longing to receive—the one with the most exciting news, that he would visit the United States to see me and find out more about Harvard's international development program. I wrote back, "Do come, and come quickly."

At this time I had started my doctoral program and did not have enough money to support myself. Therefore I was living with an American lady, Regina Towne, and her two children, Jason and Anyah Lee. Once in a while Regina would go dancing in the evenings and I would baby-sit, so she did not charge me any rent. I told her about Anthony's coming.

She said, "Oh! It will be fun for you. You must have been feeling so lonely. It must be hard being separated for so long. Let him come, it's okay with me." I did not explain to her that Anthony was not my boyfriend. I just thought to myself, "These Americans—they really take these things so easy."

We three females in the house—Regina, her daughter, and myself—used to sleep on the third floor, while Jason had his room on the second floor. We had no extra bed, so I asked Regina if Anthony could sleep on the couch in the living room next to Jason's room.

She laughed, "Don't be so ridiculous! Let him sleep in your room."

This time I protested, "No, really—we are not close."

She insisted, "Well then, silly, that's how you will be close. It's common here. A boyfriend sleeping in the living room? What a joke!" And she just laughed at me.

She was a very nice, kind, jolly lady. I had the most wonderful time with her and her children.

It was December 1984. Regina had gone away for a week for Christmas with her children. Anthony called me from England, where he was spending Christmas with his mother, saying that he would be coming in the New Year. I told him, "Come quickly, before Regina comes back. We have some problem here."

"If there's some problem, then I'd better not come."

"No, it's not like that. It's not a serious problem, but you must arrive before they come back," I urged.

"Okay then, I'll just jump on a plane and come," Anthony reassured me.

This meant that he would be arriving on New Year's Eve.

The night before the evening of his arrival I worked almost the whole night for an elderly and sick lady who used to pay me for keeping her company and nursing her. Also I was a little excited and could not sleep. Early in the morning I returned to Regina's and took a shower, meditated, and fed Jason and Anyah Lee's two cats. Anthony's plane was supposed to arrive at Boston's Logan Airport at one P.M. I left home at eleven A.M. I did not have a car, so I walked to Harvard Square and took the subway. During the whole journey to the airport I felt very nervous about his coming. Until then I had been very, very excited and happy about it. Now something inside me changed, and my excitement changed to fear. I reached the airport at noon. Still an hour to go. With every passing moment my nervousness increased. I went to a restaurant and drank a cup of coffee. While drinking the coffee my mind started entertaining the thought that he would not come—"Maybe he missed the flight, and will not come."

At twelve forty-five P.M. I went downstairs and looked at the arrivals board. His plane was delayed by two hours. I felt a little better, and relaxed. "Maybe the plane will never come," I thought again. There were so many people crowding the airport, and all the noise and movement made me feel dizzy. I went to a less crowded area and sat on a chair. Ignoring all the hubbub, I tried to meditate and to think. After a while the thought popped into my mind, "I hope he won't come in those short pants everybody wears in America. Oh no, of course he won't, it's winter. Still, I do wish that he will arrive wearing a nice suit." I had never seen him dressed in anything but very casual clothes in Nepal.

It was five minutes to three, and with this thought I went down again to the arrivals lounge. I waited and waited there. Everybody else from the flight appeared, meeting their loved ones and friends, but there was no sign of him. Maybe he had really missed the plane after all. Oh! Why had I allowed myself to think that? I began to feel very sad, and was about to go away when I saw him coming—the last passenger off the flight—and wearing a very nice smart suit. I felt immensely relieved. I was still one hundred percent Nepali. I could not give him a hug or a kiss. Perhaps, just arriving from Nepal, he too was conscious of our cultural decencies, for he did not approach me for anything like that. We just looked at each other happily and I told him how pleased I was that he had come wearing a suit.

He replied, "It's the first one I ever bought myself."

I helped him with his luggage. I asked if we should go by taxi, and explained the alternative. He said he was happy to take the subway and to take a taxi from there. So we took the airport shuttle to the subway's blue line, changed in Boston to the red line, and arrived at Harvard Square. At this point, when I noticed his tiredness from the flight as he hauled his luggage, I thought, "I should have insisted on taking a taxi from the airport." Anyway, we took a taxi from Harvard Square. It was dark by the time we arrived.

While drinking tea at Regina's he asked, "Why did you want me to come before the first of January?"

I explained to him what Regina had thought—that he was my boyfriend—and that we did not have a spare room. "In her presence it would not be nice to create complications, so what shall we do?"

Anthony gazed at me as he replied, "She's right. The moment I first saw you with your shaved head I fell in love with you."

I smiled. "I'm sure I did then too."

ཙ༅ཙ

The next morning I felt a little awkward. I knew nothing about him really, except for his name and what he had written and told me about his work. There had been almost no context for finding out more about who he was. He knew something about my family background from working in Dhankuta, and a little about my past activities from some of my friends. I thought, "After all, we are both human beings. We can be sensitive to each other." In this way, we immediately decided that we would get married and grow together. It would be almost like an arranged marriage in our culture, where you know nothing about one another to begin with.

When we told Regina she was absolutely thrilled. "What did I tell you?" she teased me.

We wanted to tell some close people besides Regina, so Anthony phoned Mac and Marcia in Amesbury. He told Mac, "I'm over here on a visit. Can we come and see you?"

Without hesitation Mac responded, "Why sure! Come straightaway, and bring Durga with you."

So we took a bus to Amesbury. On the way all we could talk about was how we were going to break our happy news to our old friends. Mac met us at the bus stop and drove us to their lovely, two-century-old home. It faces the Merrimac River, where their family still runs Lowell's Boatshop, the oldest boatbuilding operation in North America and home of the dory, created by the Lowells in 1793. After an ebullient welcome, we announced that we were going to get married. Everybody was delighted. Within minutes Mac appeared with a bottle of champagne to toast us, saying, "This is my Nepali sister, and Tony, my best friend. I gladly accept their marriage." Then he announced that there would be an engagement party that very evening. Our engagement party was the happiest of occasions. I thought to myself, "Destiny is so unexpected. Here in America, on the other side of the world from my country, I am going to get married to a foreigner. It was a very radical step from my side, but Mac was there to play the role of my guardian. It reminded me of our Sanskrit verse *Vashudaiva kutumbakam*, meaning, "The whole universe is your family."

After a couple of enjoyable days staying with Mac and Marcia, we returned to Regina's. Regina had already made plans for us to go for a holiday in New Hampshire. She drove us there to stay with her close friends Mike Lombard and Anne Aasgaard and their two children. They were also very, very dear people and immediately made us feel as at home as if we had always known one another. I thought, "After all, America was my favorite country politically. Now, coming here has given me the opportunity to feel the warmth of America's good people." They had built a bright cozy house in a large plot of forest with a separate guest house complete with a wood stove above a large garage. It was surrounded on all sides by trees. The forests of New England were in deep mid-winter during our stay. Anthony and I took long, long walks through the snow, enjoying the crisp stillness. I loved watching him skillfully cut the firewood and do a little skiing. I had never experienced this kind of joyful and fulfilling holiday in my life.

Three weeks flew by, and it was time for Anthony to return to Nepal. During his stay he had gone to meet various professors at Harvard. He confided in me that as he felt himself to be a "field" person, he had found the academic environment very strange and forbidding. Nonetheless, he decided that he would definitely apply for the M.P.A. program. If he was accepted, he would come back to Cambridge for the summer program, which would start in August.

I went to see him off at the airport. I felt as if I had always been with Anthony, even in my previous lives. I returned by the same subway route we had traveled together from the airport, but without him. I felt a great heaviness. This was the first experience in my life of having so much feeling and caring for another person. I stepped out of the subway onto the street at Harvard Square. It was snowing heavily. I decided to walk home. As I walked alone for an hour, I felt a sweet sense of romantic separation.

As soon as he arrived in England the following morning, he called me. He told me how much he loved me—and my cooking. Then he confirmed that he was departing for Nepal the next day. Because I had spent so much time with him, I had a huge backlog of term papers and other assignments. I turned all my attention to finishing them.

Until his first letter came from Nepal I had almost forgotten about him.

I had also started wondering whether I had made the right decision. Marrying a foreigner would be a blot on my political career, I thought. But morally there was no going back now that we were engaged. I made up my mind, even if I am in politics, it is not a crime to marry the person I like. With this new resolve, for the first time I also wrote him a romantic letter. Now I addressed him as "my dearest love," and told him how deeply I missed him and longed to be with him forever, even in lives to come.

Now I started feeling the separation in an awful way. He did not have a telephone in Nepal. For him to phone from Dhankuta involved walking twenty minutes from his house to the town's telecommunications office and often waiting a couple of hours before the local operator managed to get through to a Kathmandu operator to place the call. Sometimes, the call could not be made and he would return hours later in vain. But to my great joy he succeeded a few times. Fortunately, his work qualified him to send and receive mail via London through the British Foreign Office's "diplomatic bag." So, despite the remoteness of my hometown, to send a letter and receive a reply took only one month.

In the meantime, Anthony received his admission to Harvard. It was so exciting to send a congratulations telegram to him in Dhankuta. Soon afterward, he phoned me from Kathmandu, saying that he had completed his assignment in KHARDEP and describing the emotional farewell from his Nepali neighbors in Dhankuta. He asked me what he should do with all his household stuff. I suggested he store everything there, because we would be returning soon. He told me he had taken Upendra's and Shrish's families on a picnic, and felt my absence there. Although he would be coming to the United States in July to start the Kennedy School program in August, we decided to meet in England in June. The day before leaving for England I moved from Regina's to a one-bedroom apartment in one of the nicest Harvard housing areas, Shaler Lane. This was a small, quiet street of English cottage-style terraced houses by the Charles River, a short walk from anywhere we needed to go at Harvard. I took the whole morning to carry my things to the new house, and arranged the rooms as nicely as I could. I looked at my arrangement. It felt cozy and romantic, and I imagined how lonely it would be to live there all by myself. Then I quickly packed a bag and left for the airport, very excited this time.

I boarded a plane bound for Gatwick Airport, and he was there to meet me. It was cold and drizzling. Anthony had hurt his back gardening and had been lying flat for three days. He had gotten up from bed to come to collect me and looked very poorly and unshaven. I longed to take care of him. He drove me to his mother's home in nearby Reigate—a picturesque town in the lap of the North Downs countryside, yet only twenty miles from central London. There, I gave his back a tender massage. His mother was very touched.

Unlike my very large family, his was very small. It was easy for me to learn the names of all his relatives. I just had to get to know his mother, two unmarried aunts on his late father's side, an uncle and aunt on his mother's side, and three cousins, two of whom were married. There was only one child in the entire family. In my family, from my two uncles and one aunt on my father's side alone I had ninety-six relatives at this time. In addition, one of my uncles on my mother's side had six sons, two daughters, and so many grandchildren and great-grandchildren that there was no point in even trying to keep track of them all. Anthony constantly got muddled trying to figure out the relationships among my cousins, nephews, and nieces, and said that until I drew him a family tree he would never be able to understand who was who.

In England that July, Anthony and his mother took me on a delightful tour of historic places, including Oxford and Shakespeare's birthplace, as well as rural counties like Herefordshire and Shropshire, where his mother's family had been landowners and farmers, and to Gloucestershire and the Midlands, where his cousins live now. I loved meeting them all. We also visited Canterbury, where he had attended "the King's School," and his college, Pembroke, at Cambridge University.

We spent a month in England, then boarded a transatlantic flight together for the first time. For a while we lived with Professor Edward S. Mason, the eminent development economist. He had recently suffered a stroke, and his son had approached the Kennedy School to find a graduate student or couple to help care for him. The school had phoned us in Reigate to inquire whether we had any interest, perhaps knowing that I had been caring for an elderly Harvard woman. As I had been a Mason Fellow at the Kennedy School the previous year, I considered the invitation a great honor.

As scheduled, Anthony started his preparatory "summer program" in August, and I had a month to get organized before the fall semester began. Within even this short time, I discovered how different our perspectives were on social and cultural issues in developing countries. I did not care as much about his understanding of other countries, but I was very concerned about his knowledge about Nepali society and Hindu culture. Sometimes he would mention the close friendship he had developed with certain families, and that he had eaten in their homes. But from their surnames I would discover that they were from lower and even untouchable castes. He had even had an untouchable woman as his cook. I never entertained any hatred toward so-called lower castes, and would always do all I could to support their upliftment in our society. Yet I did not believe that by identifying myself as one of them I placed myself in the best position to help them. This did not mean that I believed in the caste system. But its existence was the reality in Nepal. I had warned Anthony in a letter that even though I was a believer in democratic socialism, he might still find me somewhat "feudal," though perhaps not to such an extent as some members of my family. He said he would try to understand.

Worse still, I found him not to be an inward, private person, whereas by culture and from political necessity I had grown up as an intensely private person who had retained almost all my feelings and opinions within myself all my life. In contrast, Anthony, like many Westerners, revealed things about himself or about me readily to almost anyone. As I grew conscious of this, I began to feel increasingly restless and uncertain about our future together. I found it very difficult to discuss these things with him. Nevertheless, no matter how much anxiety I expressed, he kept on saying that had it not been for me he would have never come to America.

One night at around the peak of my anxiety, I had a strange dream in which I was looking in a mirror and seeing an old, wrinkled woman with gray hair. I became frightened and as I shouted out "Aaah!" the woman became my present self. Hearing my scream, another Nepali woman entered the room and said softly, "One day you will be like that woman in the mirror. Don't wait for anything. Time will keep running along. Marry the man." When I awoke, I felt very disturbed, but never told Anthony until much later, after we had children. The following night my father appeared in a dream smiling with happiness. I thought, "No longer should I hold any doubts about Anthony," and shared this dream with him.

While we were living with Professor Mason, we decided to arrange a small civil marriage ceremony for ourselves and then move to our Shaler Lane apartment. Living on our own and doing everything together, I began to open up about my anxieties about him. But I told him that even though he was not how I would have liked him to be, I was the last person on earth to interfere with another's personal qualities. With characteristic simplicity he replied, "I'm sorry I am not living up to your expectations. I'll do anything you want me to do to change myself. I don't want to live in my past. You teach me your values." He became very emotional, and recalled a dream that he had had years before in which he was walking along the right-hand sidewalk of a bridge over a wide river in a city at night. The road was deserted. Running toward him was a dark-haired woman seeking refuge from danger. He had sheltered her in his arms and taken her into his life. "That woman was you," he said with certainty. Increasingly, we found that we could discuss with frankness any doubt, misunderstanding, or cultural taboo that came between us. Each time we resolved some new issue we felt the bond of our love deepen further. We were growing together.

My classes also began. It was quite romantic being Harvard graduate students together. Although we were studying in different schools, our fields were closely related and we selected some courses in common. Friends would always see us arriving at classes and at the libraries together on one bicycle, with me balanced on a cushion on the crossbar. We even did our weekly shopping this way, and found that we could haul over a hundred dollars' worth of foodstuffs home by carefully loading the bicycle's front and rear baskets. We never bought a car because, like most graduate students, we had little money. Anthony used up his savings to finance his degree. I worked in the mail room of the Education School. As a result I got to know all the faculty and administrative staff and every corner of the school, and I surprised some old hands when I won the school's Trivial Pursuit competition.

We also became friends with Edward Bernays, known in America as "the Father of Public Relations." He was then ninety-four years old. Mr. Bernays, who lived just around the corner from us, wanted to arrange our wedding party in his house. Our wedding had been a small private affair, and we did not want Mr. Bernays to go to the trouble of a reception, so we accepted his next offer of a small dinner party for us to which Upendra Rana was also invited. As usual, Upendra was a little late to arrive, but as soon as he was seated, Mr. Bernays directed at him the following question: "So, when are you going to overthrow your king?" Upendra laughed heartily. We spent a memorable evening listening to Mr. Bernays discussing the prospects for democracy in Nepal. Mr. Bernays concluded that there was no hope for this until Nepal's present government was overthrown and the king's power was curtailed.

In the meantime, I asked Anthony to apply for a Ph.D. program. He was very reluctant. The field was his love, and the one year of academic life he had come for had been enough of a struggle for him. Finally, he agreed after I convinced him that it would be a prestige issue back home if I was a "Dr." and he wasn't. He gained admission at MIT and at Cornell, where a professor even arranged a USAID fellowship for him. Anthony much preferred Cornell, and we visited and loved it. However, although I could finish my dissertation easily enough there, something held me back. I still lacked full trust in him, and found myself clinging to my Harvard sanctuary, where I thought I would be safer. When I shared my anxiety with him, he agreed to accept the MIT offer. I was very happy that we would be living in America longer as students.

Anthony now joined me whenever I was invited to functions by Amnesty International or other groups around New England. We gave talks together, illustrated by his color slides of Nepal. I had become enrolled in Amnesty's northeastern region's speakers' bureau after I found out that Amnesty's California chapter had worked for my release (I had contacted the group's leader, Sally Parker, to thank them). Perhaps subconsciously I felt protected while I was with the groups in New England, because it must have been a group like this in California that had adopted me. I found it so rewarding to talk to these sincere people. Many group members had little international exposure and little conception of the political, economic, social, cultural, and legal conditions that lead to human rights violations in developing countries. I was able to illumine many things for them, and in return I found audiences who were able to believe my story.

# 19
.

# Marriage
# and Reconciliation

fter Anthony's graduation from the Kennedy School in June 1986, and before he started at MIT, we went for three months to New Delhi, where Anthony was involved in a Ford Foundation review of its support to Indian nongovernment organizations. For two months I accompanied him on his tour of six Indian states and a dozen or so Ford Foundation grantee organizations. His assignment took us to meet some of India's most innovative development professionals and social reformers. We were struck by the dynamism of the voluntary agency sector in India's democratic, open political system. Here we saw what people's indigenous organizations and social change agents could achieve where there was freedom of organization and social movement. It was not that poverty and injustice were absent from Indian society. The difference was that the Indian government imposed fewer restrictions than did Nepal on foreign donors, allowing them more discretion in their funding of local voluntary agencies. As a result, the Indian agencies were being supported for advocacy and empowering activities that enabled the poorest groups to demand their legal rights and a fair share of services from the government. Encouraged by this more liberal climate, voluntary agencies in India were listening more closely to their clients and were responding directly to the realities of disadvantaged people's lives. I reflected that this environment and these kinds of organizations were what was missing in Nepal, where the law prevented people from organizing freely. The very theme of Panchayat was "no organization" unless you were tied up with the system.

One of the spiritually oriented organizations we visited was the Self-Employed Women's Association (SEWA) of Mithila, in the state of Bihar. Here we were received with love by SEWA Mithila's inspired organizer, Mrs. Gauri Mishra, who was known and adored locally as Maaji—"respected mother." Maaji had gathered destitute and battered women from that part of rural Bihar, Brahmin child-widows and untouchables alike. In doing so, she had to face severe censure and opposition from conservative social groups opposed to this mixing of castes and to her perceived intrusion into the lives of families. To combat the basic affliction of poverty, the movement's cultural and economic core was the revival of indigenous local Mithila art. Traditionally, art forms—depicting glorious scenes from the Vedic epics—had decorated temples, homes, external walls of houses, and ritual objects. Now the formerly destitute Maithili women were adapting the traditional designs and themes to today's uses, producing exquisitely hand-painted silk saris as well as calendars, decorative bangles, and baskets. Some of the paintings deviated from traditional Vedic themes, telling instead the stories of these women's struggles in present-day feudal Bihar society. In this women's movement, activities in the economic and social fields reinforced each other. As the women gained economic independence their voice against outdated social practices like child marriage and the dowry system grew stronger. Faced with women's protest marches and popular theater campaigns in the villages, former male critics were quieted and even brought around to a realization of the distortions in their society.

I saw here an example of what I would have liked to have done for Nepal's prison women and similar destitute groups. These women were also skilled. All they needed was someone to help them organize so that they could use their skills to earn a livelihood and overcome their social stigma.

Our days with Maaji were very moving, and it felt so comfortable being among the women. On our last day Gauriji and her women surprised us with an extraordinary, spontaneous gesture. They told us that our marriage perfectly symbolized the bonding of Eastern and Western cultures and that therefore they wanted to formalize our marriage right there in their office according to their Mithila traditions. They presented me with a traditional wedding sari. Anthony was already wearing white Indian dress. Gauriji performed the role of the priest and married us, guiding Anthony through such rituals as the pouring of the vermillion *sindhur* marriage mark into my hair parting. Then all the women sang the traditional wedding songs that accompany the moment when a bride is given away to the groom. I thought to myself that although my father did not live to arrange my marriage, perhaps this Brahmin lady and her family of destitute women sensed what needed to be done. This was the way it had to be.

I was not thinking of going home to seek my family's approval of my marriage. I still considered my relationship with my family as a story of "once upon a time." But I wanted to see my mother. I remembered how lost and grieved she had been when I had left her after my father's death. For three years she had been much in my mind. When I had visited Kathmandu for a week after my first semester at Harvard, she had been at my brother Krishna's farm far away in the *tarai* and I had not been able to go there. Now that we were close by in India, I decided to visit Nepal to see her.

Except for her, my widowed aunt, and my sister Subhadra, there had been almost no one else to think about. I knew that my mother would be living with my eldest brother. Once again, swallowing my feelings, I went to his house. Seeing my mother brought tears to my eyes. I could not believe how much her physiology had deteriorated. Her attention seemed to be no longer in this world. From the age of seven, when she had married my father, she had never been separated from him except for the period when he was studying in Banaras. Even then, she had lived with his parents. Now, I wished so much that I could live with her and nurture her for the rest of her life. "Well," I thought, "here at her son's she has a young housegirl to look after her."

After being with my mother for a while, I was about to say farewell when my brother asked me to go upstairs to see him. In the past also, whenever he welcomed me I went to him, and whenever he discarded me I went away. I bore no ill will against him anyway. I went up to meet him, my sister-in-law, and their daughter Pooja, whom, since her birth, I had seen only during my father's illness and mourning. She was a big girl now.

I do not know what might have been in my brother's mind after eleven years without communicating with me except for what had been necessary at my father's end. The reason he wanted to see me was to propose that my marriage be formalized according to traditional Vedic rituals. At this moment I felt neither excitement nor objection. My sister-in-law added her support for my brother's proposal: "Now that your father is not alive, your eldest brother has his duty to arrange your marriage. Also the question of social integration is there. Once you are accepted by the family through our rituals, then society cannot ignore you."

I thought to myself, "As if I care for society." By having married a casteless Westerner, I had already violated social conventions in the extreme. My family might have no comprehension of how much I had suffered trying to keep "society" satisfied for so many years. I wished that I could feel more grateful for my brother's proposal and wipe out the past, but the reality was so bitter that I thought I could never forget it.

Perhaps I had been sunk in this thought for a few seconds when I heard them propose a date for the ceremonies, August 15, which was in three days' time. August was not one of our usual marriage months, but it did not matter because we were already married anyway. However, our great day would coincide with India's Independence Day. I supposed that might be auspicious for us.

I considered for a minute, then said, "I want to ask Anthony." I put a call through to New Delhi and explained the situation. He reacted instantly, "There's nothing that I would love more." He had not been planning to come to Kathmandu, but was clearly overjoyed at the prospect of a real Hindu wedding. Forty-eight hours later he was in Kathmandu.

The evening he arrived, which was the eve of our wedding, my sister-in-law and others led us around the busy market streets of the city shopping for certain essential items of clothing and jewelry for both of us. Then Anthony and I went to Upendra and Sushila Rana's house to stay the night.

My Pandit uncle, one of the greatest Veda scholars in the kingdom, came forward with the formula for making Anthony socially eligible in my caste so that he could marry me in accordance with Vedic tradition. My uncle was living in Dharan and could not come in person, but he briefed my brother and his priest over the telephone. Accordingly, early in the morning of our marriage day, Anthony was required to go through several hours of Vedic rituals that invested him with the sacred thread and mantra of a Brahmin and the title of the Kafle Brahmin family, which was our matrimonial clan.

The rituals were performed in one of the temples in the precincts of Pashupatinath. It was a Krishna temple where *bhajan* prayers are chanted continually—twenty-four hours a day, seven days a week, all year long—creating a pure, most sublime atmosphere. Some of the devotees lived there.

The same cousin who had once discouraged my sister from filing a writ of *habeas corpus* while I was in prison now helped my British husband dress in a pure white vest and *dhoti*, and arranged a ritual shawl around his shoulders. I could not help thinking about what he had said to my father and sister while I was a missing prisoner, but, after a great effort, the thought came that perhaps his actions now represented reconciliation.

Both he and his wife, who had made the arrangements for the rituals, were very kind to us this time. There was great sweetness in the air this day, and Anthony absorbed every element of it and looked, felt, and behaved as if he had always been a Nepali Brahmin. I felt that the spirit of my father was with us.

The marriage rituals began at my brother's house as soon as we arrived from the temple. They too lasted several hours. We dressed in the traditional way for a Hindu wedding. I suppose our Hindu marriage was a kind of reconciliation, something like the compromise with my father after his death. I wanted at least two of my party leaders, K.P. Bhattarai and Ganesh Man Singh, to be invited, but my brother said, "It will become political, and it is not appropriate for them to be invited to my house." I felt that there was no point in arguing since the wedding was not my initiative. Nonetheless, Upendra and Shrish were among the invitees to the evening reception.

I thought that I had broken all tradition by not marrying a Nepali through a family arrangement. By not marrying a Brahmin, I had done the very thing that my father had most feared. Worse than that, I had chosen a man with no caste at all. But my marriage ended up being arranged properly, and was performed according to Vedic rituals. More than that, my family made Anthony a Brahmin! Upendra Rana summed it up, "Here am I, a Kshatriya [someone of the warrior caste], unable to take Brahmin caste. And Anthony, an Englishman with *no caste*, comes along and becomes a highest-caste Brahmin just like that! What is this?" The conversion of a foreigner into a Brahmin is almost unknown in our country. Thus my life-long struggle with my father about not marrying ended in a marriage that would have been acceptable to him. I was sure that from wherever he was watching he was happy for us and gave us his blessing.

Our marriage ceremonies were not over yet. On our way home to America we stopped over in England to see Anthony's mother. She wanted to arrange a blessing for us in her own Anglican church. I wore a white sari with red designs—a kind of compromise between the red that Hindu women wear for marriage and the white that is worn in the West. It was a nice little ceremony. Unlike our Hindu marriage, it was very brief and very quiet—just Anthony and myself, his mother, a neighbor and close family friend, Sir Norman Statham, and the vicar. We joked afterward that including our legal ceremony and a private temple ritual that Anthony and I had performed for ourselves in New Delhi, we had now been married to each other five times. Especially for me, it was indeed an irony.

Our first son was born on February 4, 1987, in Cambridge, Massachusetts. We named him Samyog, which in Nepali means "destiny"—or, more completely, "the good outcome of a destined coming together." For my mother-in-law, because Anthony was her only child, Samyog was the crown prince and should therefore have a proper English name. Before she had the chance to propose names that might sound harsh to me, such as Frederick, we selected the milder-sounding name of Julian. At home we began to call him Baba—"loved one" or "yogi."

ಞಞ

As my personal life had now been blessed with happiness, for a time I kept wondering how, where, and when I would return to political life. I did not want to vanish from the Nepali scene. Since the age of twelve I had been engaged in the democratic struggle in our country with my thoughts, words, and actions. Now, once in a while, my impatience would explode and I would discuss my anxiety with Anthony. He used to pacify me: "Don't worry. The time will come in Nepal when a social movement will overthrow the Panchayat regime. Then we can go back and do the sort of things we believe in."

"Isn't that a bit opportunistic?" I would ask him.

"I don't think so. You did all you could in those conditions and it may still be dangerous there. Besides, we both have so much to learn here about how to design and implement sound policies and projects. You need 'polishing,' as you yourself say. Then you can go and help your leaders by sharing what you have learned."

In the summer of 1987 we wanted to go back to Nepal, so Anthony arranged a job in Nepal consulting for a British private voluntary organization—Action Aid. We stayed with Upendra and Sushila Rana again while Anthony's work took him to some remote hill areas.

After completing his assignment he said to me, "My love, there's just no *end* of work to be done in Nepal to help people have a better life." Except for the *Panchas*, everybody in the villages was waiting for the day when revolution would break and bring a government that would put the livelihoods of the people first. People were joining the Action Aid–supported Village Development Committees in open defiance of the Panchayat, knowing that when they participated in those committees their opinions counted and that Action Aid delivered on its promises. But Action Aid's target area was only one ninth of one district. In much of the rest of the country people were deprived of their most basic needs, such as clean drinking water and a health service. "It'll never be too late for us to come back with some good plans and ideas. I'll help you when it's safe for us to return," declared Anthony.

Well, his love for Nepal was one of the main reasons I had married him. We had nothing to argue about.

Always, we felt that we were preparing ourselves to go back. The question was when to return. How quickly I tended to forget the terror of the past.

In February 1989, exactly two years after Samyog, Shristi was born. The name we chose for him proved no coincidence. It means "new life," "new creation," "new beginning." He changed us. We were already devoted parents, and Samyog had been the center of our lives. We all slept together in one bed and did everything together. But with Shristi's arrival came an even deeper realization of the centrality of family. We had both completed our doctoral coursework, but we needed some family income. The position we had as residential tutors at one of the Harvard undergraduate houses provided a nice apartment and meals, but only a small stipend. Anthony had a number of job offers in Asia, but all would have involved extensive travel, and we could not tolerate family separation. We thought seriously about returning to Nepal, but only a job for Anthony would make that possible. I had no job and no chance of one there. In any case, I wanted to be a full-time mother while my children were small. So Anthony wrote a few letters to say that he was in the market for international assignments. A couple of prospects almost came to fruition in Nepal—one of them through Cornell University—but we learned through a back door that because of me Anthony was also controversial there.

It was not just my political record. Now a rumor had spread that I had a land dispute with the royal family. While working with Action Aid two years earlier, we had bought a beautiful flat hilltop piece of land in the Kathmandu valley. A few months afterward, my brother called me to say that we had to surrender our land to the royal family. We came to know that the king's second brother, together with the queen's youngest sister—and wife of the third prince—had decided that they wanted the entire hill for some development. Traditionally, the royal family could do as they pleased. In our case, they offered to buy us an equivalent size plot behind theirs. To resolve our problem we had visited Kathmandu again for a week the following year, and found that the site they were offering us involved too much steeply terraced hillside. No longer would we have the view and the seclusion that we had loved in our original site. We could not meet them face-to-face, so we left our lawyer with a proposed site plan acceptable to us and instructions to bargain with their aides for more hilltop and less hillside, and we returned to the United States. We heard through friends that they started building their perimeter wall with our plot in the middle somewhere.

Thus I was alleged to be having a confrontation with the royal family. It hurt me deeply. Anthony had brought over his savings from England to buy the land. I told him, "Let's not go to Nepal now, but to wherever you find an assignment."

# 20

.

# Return of Democracy

Just as we realized that the time had not yet come for us to return to Nepal, we heard through my good old friend Syd that a British consulting firm was looking for a project manager in Zanzibar, Tanzania. We thought a project on a small island would be an ideal assignment from a family perspective, and I imagined that Zanzibar might be a little like Sri Lanka, a beautiful island I had visited and loved.

Anthony sent his curriculum vitae to this firm and, within a week, was on a plane to meet a Zanzibari delegation in Rome that included Zanzibar's chief minister. He was selected for the job. Six weeks later we were on a Kenya Airways flight to Zanzibar. The island looked idyllic from the air—coconut palms and coral reefs. However, the moment I stepped out into the heat and breathed the languid air I felt physically and mentally suffocated. I found the island decadent and claustrophobic.

For me, it was another kind of imprisonment. Hour after hour, day after day, the children and I found ourselves confined inside, in one or another air-conditioned room. The telephone never rang unless it was Anthony calling from his office, not far away. Letters rarely reached us, except, for some reason, Harvard tuition bills. Exhausted each night, I was making no progress with my dissertation.

There was nowhere very pleasant to go. To escape we could make the twenty-minute boat trip across the harbor to Zanzibar's most celebrated recreation spot—Prison Island. The alternative was Grave Island. For tourists, two or three days were regarded as sufficient for savoring what Zanzibar had to offer. I felt that, faced with the falling price of Zanzibar's almost sole export of cloves, twenty-five years of African socialism had done nothing for this Moslem former slave island.

After eight months, we discussed Anthony's resignation when his boss visited from England. He begged us to stay on, offering to fly someone from Nepal to Zanzibar to help me if that was necessary so that Anthony could maintain progress with the project. We tried without success to find a Nepali who was willing to come to Africa.

In the meantime Samyog became ill. He lost all control over toilet activities and became intensely upset each time the inevitable happened. We consulted a missionary doctor. His wife took us aside and warned us that children were born as Satan and only became "good" through discipline. This was the absolute reverse of our Hindu belief, which is that children are little gods and should receive nothing but love until reason develops after five years of age. We ignored the missionaries. Luckily, there was a Romanian lady doctor, a United Nations volunteer, on the island too. She advised that Samyog needed only much more attention. It was purely a psychological disturbance, a transferal of my own mental tension aggravated by the accumulated months of relative neglect while I had to attend to his baby brother and the heavy burden of housekeeping and food preparation in a very unclean environment. Anthony took this doctor's advice and began taking Samyog to the office with him and coming home from work earlier. But it was an arrangement that Anthony clearly could not sustain from a work perspective, and we knew that for the sake of family we would have to leave.

We had virtually no communication with the outside world on Zanzibar except—thank God—for the BBC.

On February 18, 1990, I had tuned in as usual to the BBC while I was in the kitchen. Suddenly over the crackling of the radio I heard the word *Nepal*. A people's movement had begun. It had been launched on "Democracy Day," the day Nepal celebrated the 1950 ousting of the Ranas. I tuned in anxiously to the BBC almost every hour for the next fifty days, listening for more news about the movement that the Nepali Congress was organizing with leftist groups.

As pieces of information came over the radio, often my mind became irrational and I would long to go home. I knew that I was missing the climax of years of struggle for the restoration of democracy. But though I would have been thrilled to participate, I had to endure following the events from an isolated African island. The very kind Indian consul general on Zanzibar was sympathetic. He lent us the Indian papers, which we devoured even though they were always about ten days out of date. Piecing together the information we got from these papers, the BBC, the Voice of America, and, once in a while, All India Radio, we gradually gained a fuller understanding of what was taking place. Even from Zanzibar we could sense the seriousness of the situation.

The prodemocracy movement, or the opposition camp against the partyless Panchayat system, had been formed from the Nepali Congress party and an alliance of seven communist groups, the United Left Front (ULF), chaired by Sahana Pradhan—the other woman lecturer who was expelled from Tribhuvan University with me in 1975. The compact between the Nepali Congress and the communist groups was a breakthrough in the history of opposition to the Panchayat regime.

Personally, I was not sure whether the compact was an entirely sound strategy for restoring democracy in the Nepali context. In the past, the communists had never supported the Nepali Congress in any movement, but either joined the Panchayat camp or criticized Nepali Congress policies harshly. In fact, throughout the Panchayat era the Nepali Congress was uniformly opposed, whether by *Panchas*, communists, neocommunists, or royal communists. The odd alliance between communists and the king's absolute monarchical system had always intrigued me. Presumably, communists felt comfortable infiltrating the Panchayat system because its "partyless" character bore an ideological resemblance to the communist one-party system. But most strange was the apparent trust that the king and his followers had in the communists' intentions, when certain communist factions had systematically murdered rich people in parts of the country. Would it not be logical, if the communists came to power, for the prime target of such people to be the richest family in the kingdom—the royal family? Surely the Nepali Congress should be the king's preferred alternative, as it avowedly supported a constitutional monarchical system. I thought that if B.P. were still alive he would never have built a coalition with the communists to restore democracy in Nepal.

In any case, the situation now was that leaders of Nepal's different opposition groups had started planning the Movement for Restoration of Democracy in January 1990. First of all, the Nepali Congress held a packed three-day assembly at Ganesh Man Singh's residence beginning on January 18. More than four thousand party workers had participated. It was at the end of this assembly that the date for the movement was set: February

18. The assembly also resolved that the minimum demands of the movement would be the formation of an interim government and the holding of free and fair elections within a multiparty system. To counter the Nepali Congress's meeting, the Panchayat prime minister funded *Pancha* rallies around the country and introduced tougher censorship on the press.

On January 30, the Nepali Congress and the ULF formed a coordinating committee, with secret membership, to conduct the movement. The committee announced an action plan on February 1. The movement was to start with the February 18 demonstration, then continue with a national strike on the nineteenth, and, later, a "Black Day." If the king did not meet the movement's demands through these demonstrations, strikes would continue to be called until he did. Professional groups of lawyers, teachers, students, doctors, and ex-servicemen added their endorsement to this declaration of the opposition. In response, the government started its arrests. By February 10, over five hundred people were in police custody.

On February 12 events caught up with the king in Pokhara. Students were celebrating the release of Nelson Mandela in South Africa. Government-paid *Mandale* agents clashed with them, and the police arrested about five hundred of the celebrating students. Some of the women were stripped, and about six people were killed.

Before the scheduled start of the movement, in typical fashion the government, as in the past, closed down schools and colleges across the kingdom. It reminded me of my student days, and of how this government move would favor the movement as the closures freed students from their classes. I thought, "Great! All the politically motivated students will be very happy about this first tactic of the government."

Then came the first demonstration, the one we followed on the BBC on February 18. By this time some five thousand people had been arrested. As usual, the king's message to the people on Democracy Day defended his father's authoritarian Panchayat system as being in accordance with national interests, values, and norms. But the Nepali people were no longer content to listen to the king's usual pronouncements. On this Democracy Day another thousand people were arrested as prodemocracy demonstrators clashed with government-organized rallies of *Panchas* whose monthly allowances had by now been as much as doubled.

As planned, the program of strikes and demonstrations escalated and spread nationwide. The February 19 national strike was a resounding success. Almost all transport and trade shut down. Buses that were moving were set on fire. Police tried to force some shopkeepers to open their shops, but were met with stone-throwing crowds. On February 19 and 20, about twenty demonstrators were shot dead. In Biratnagar, B.P.'s hometown, hundreds of women walked the streets during the day of February 21 with gags over their mouths and lit lanterns, protesting against violations of human rights.

On February 23, doctors and other medical staff at the Teaching Hospital went on strike. They were protesting against police dumdum bullets and other forms of brutality. This day was one of the most sacred days for Hindus, the night of which is celebrated as the night of Shiva, *MahaShivaratri*. Normally thousands of pilgrims come from all over Nepal and India to the Pashupatinath temple and the king pays his own homage. But not this year.

Not seeing any sign of compromise from the king, the opposition carried out its Black Day on February 25. People carried black flags and wore black armbands. About another thousand people were arrested, including some party leaders. Reports came of disappearances and of torture in the prisons. Medical staff at Bir Hospital went on strike. Finally, on February 26, school and university teachers formally joined the movement. At this point, the U.S.-based human rights organization Asia Watch demanded the release of political prisoners and called on the Nepalese government to respect freedom of expression and association.

Still, the government gave no positive response. The opposition organized a second national closure on March 2. On March 5, about five hundred advocates observed a one-hour silence, wearing black badges, to demonstrate against the government's arrest of their colleagues and other violations of human rights. Then, on March 8, International Women's Day, more women came out in solidarity with the movement in various parts of the country. In Biratnagar they were beaten up by the police and arrested.

At this point the leaders of the movement altered tactics away from the large demonstrations that were attracting massive police repression. Smaller groups here and there started burning effigies of *Pancha* leaders and other symbols of Panchayat. In reply, more activists were imprisoned and killed. Some corpses were found decapitated, as in the aftermath of King Mahendra's 1960 coup. But this time the party people were defiant, and only increased the pace of peaceful resistance, distributing their party flags to places across the country.

On March 14, the third national strike was organized. Paid *Mandales* were mobilized by the government to attack students of the engineering campus. Two days later artists and writers at the Tri Chandra campus protested peacefully, with their mouths symbolically gagged. All were arrested. On this day, the king returned from Pokhara and, in a speech, used the 1980 Referendum outcome to justify the view that fundamental changes to the Panchayat system were unnecessary. I could tell that the situation had become very serious and that, if the king showed no sign of negotiating, the government could become more brutal. Yet, equally, the Nepali people were also showing no sign of stepping down. Contrary to whatever expectation the king might have had, even Nepal's intellectuals came out in open defiance of the repression of the king's system. Hundreds of intellectuals participated in a symposium at the university in Kathmandu to discuss their role in the current political crisis. All were taken into police custody. By March 23, more than twenty thousand people across the country had been arrested by the police, and five thousand were being held in prisons and temporary jails.

One evening at about this time I told Anthony, "This time it's for real. Take leave from here, and let's go for a while."

He responded, "Calm down! Even if we go, what can you do while we have two little children?"

"You look after them. I'll take part in the movement. Maybe I can write pamphlets. I'm sure I can do something even from home."

Anthony reminded me that he could not take leave just like that and asked me if there was any other way in which I could contribute.

I reminded him about the book I had always wanted to write to expose the Panchayat government's cruelty. Along with our doctoral theses, writing this book had been one of our personal objectives in coming to Zanzibar. But lacking dependable people to help in the house and with the children, we had made no progress at all with any of our writing.

Anthony was as gripped by the movement as I was. He immediately came up with an idea. He would help me prepare an outline, and then, if necessary, we could leave Zanzibar and start writing.

We started work on the outline that night, and continued every night for three weeks. With every day we felt the urgency of the book increase. Or perhaps our sense of urgency reflected my frustration at being stuck at home during the day, able only to listen to radio reports. We finished the book outline, but the very moment that we did so, we knew that we would never be able to write it in time to warn the king to make room for genuine opposition in Nepali politics before it was too late.

"Why don't you write to the king and tell him about your latest dreams?" Anthony suggested.

I had just had a series of dreams foretelling the imminent collapse of Panchayat rule and grave danger for Nepal's king. In the first dream I had seen Queen Mother Ratna on a stage, diminutive in size, tiny like a puppet, crying for help. No one had come to help her until the tiny spirit of her late husband, King Mahendra, appeared and took her away. In several other dreams the present king and his queen were stuck, unable to go "up" while roads and ground around them collapsed, or people massed to attack them. In one final dream the present queen and many Nepali women closely associated with her were suspended in the sky upside down.

I did draft a letter to the king. Actually, I wrote to one of his closest secretaries, whom I knew well. I almost mailed it. Then I thought again. Most of our correspondence in and out of Zanzibar was opened and censored by the island's politically suspicious authorities. In Nepal, too, mail would be interfered with. The Indian consul general offered his offices. But I did not want to use his help. I decided not to send the letter, fearing that it might fall into the wrong hands. If it did, then the same kind of people who had framed me before could do so again by misinterpreting my letter.

In the meantime, we heard over the Voice of America that the U.S. State Department was siding with the people and urging the king to stop the bloodshed and negotiate with the leaders of the prodemocracy movement. At this stage I decided to write a letter to President Bush thanking him for his State Department's message to the king and requesting that his administration not lose interest in Nepal's democratic struggle. Therefore, instead of sending the letter to the king, I wrote to the president on March 26. Basically, I repeated to him the message I had intended to give the king. I wrote:

> Our constitution should be re-drafted by a constituent assembly so that it: provides for universally accepted fundamental rights and duties; contains a bill of rights; and gives genuine power to a legislative assembly. I am not against some royal prerogative which can be reserved in case there is need to settle disputes between political groups. At present the problem is not with the King but with the wrong way in which certain high-level individuals interpret, implement, and re-interpret the constitution. . . .
>
> It will be important that the new constitution guarantees societal and professional pluralism, allowing groups to organize according to their own respective interests. A major provision in a new constitution should be national elections on the basis of individual candidates' chosen issues, policies, and programs. Candidates with similar programs and policy positions could then group to form official opposition benches within the house. . . .
>
> In terms of political process, once the constitution allows people to organize freely, official opposition to legislation could be created as above

within the house. In this respect I even do not see that much significance in declaring a multi-party system at once in the constitution. Although communism/socialism is declining in the West and even in Eastern Europe, it is still very rigid in our northern neighbor, and it will still be an influencing force in an underdeveloped, poor country like Nepal. By declaring a multi-party system in Nepal, I visualize that parties will become organized according to their respective ideological backing. By doing this, in some ways we will encourage more communist organization and influence in the country. Although democratic parties could be organized likewise, events are not hidden in a democracy, and if any party tries to take undue advantage through foreign intervention it would be quickly exposed. However, the nature of maintaining secrecy in communist regimes, whether in the backing or the recipient country, discourages exposure. Therefore, multi-party political processes in Nepal should be evolutionary. . . .

I genuinely believed that if the king considered these questions carefully, he might take the appropriate steps to democratize politics in Nepal through a more stable process. If he only sought to protect his father's system, then the opposition leaders might have no alternative but to harden their demands.

In due course, I received an appreciative reply from the State Department.

ଓଌ

Back in Nepal, seeing no sign of compromise from the king, people began raising slogans against the royal family. On March 29, student demonstrators burned copies of the constitution. Another two hundred arrests were made. Citizens began a new nonviolent form of protest that night, switching off all lights in response to an opposition call for a blackout.

The next day, in Patan, across the river and half a mile south of Kathmandu, the people began several days of open rebellion and resistance. The Panchayat office and district court were attacked. Barricades were built and trenches were dug across roads into the town to hinder the access of police vehicles. There were a number of serious clashes with the police, and several citizens were reportedly killed.

On April 1, the king reshuffled the cabinet, bringing in more hard-liners. At this point the public lost patience. Slogans were raised demanding that the king be overthrown. Tens of thousands of people massed in Patan, Bhaktapur, and Kirtipur. A march on Kathmandu was quashed by the police, but in these and other cities and villages around the kingdom demonstrators set Panchayat buildings and vehicles on fire. Police, backed up in Kirtipur by army helicopters, responded using truncheons, tear gas, and automatic rifles. There were more deaths. During the next two days all shops in the Kathmandu valley closed in protest at police atrocities, Royal Nepal Airlines Corporation (RNAC) staff staged a sit-in strike, and two marches of around thirty thousand people each were held in Kirtipur and Patan to honor martyrs and maintain defiance. On April 4, the government sent tanks into the streets of Kathmandu. Fears grew that the army might attempt to recapture Patan.

On April 6, the king dismissed the government and formed a new one under a different prime minister. However, the members of the new government were still the same old *Panchas*. The Nepali people were only more angered by this. Lawyers were arrested as they marched on the Supreme Court. In the afternoon, more than a hundred thousand people attended a mass meeting to demand the full restoration of multiparty democracy. Then the crowd began a march on the royal palace. Just at the time when, inside the palace, the king was swearing in the new *Pancha* prime minister, tens of thousands of people outside were converging on the palace from the surrounding streets. The police opened fire, killing between fifty and one hundred people, including one British tourist, and injuring many more. Bodies not brought to the government's Bir Hospital were removed by truck to a mass grave. Once more, the king seemed decided on taking a hard line. The military took control of Kathmandu, and a strict curfew was imposed on Kathmandu and Patan and some other cities. Troops recaptured the people's "liberated zone" of Patan.

Far away in Zanzibar, Anthony and I remained riveted to our radio as reports of this massacre came over the air. Part of the world outside, we waited and wondered. Was the movement to end in a communist-style crackdown against the people? I knew that this was a real possibility, because the king was supreme military commander and controlled Nepal's army of world-renowned Gurkhas in a real sense.

However, instead of using his army, the king ordered his government to begin a dialogue with opposition leaders on April 7. Some of the key leaders were released, and members of the new government tried to see them. But when the king's new prime minister tried to meet the Nepali Congress leader, Ganesh Man Singh, who was ill and in a hospital, he refused to see him. The situation in the big cities remained very tense, and large demonstrations took place in Bhaktapur and Biratnagar against the suppression of the previous days. In response the curfew was extended to Bhaktapur the next day. Hundreds of tourists, who had been trapped in their hotels, were evacuated on special RNAC flights to New Delhi.

Finally, the king appealed to the party's leaders to come to the palace with their demands. During the afternoon of April 8, the leaders gathered at Ganesh Man's bedside to discuss the king's offer of a dialogue. Later that evening, the Nepali Congress president, K. P. Bhattarai, and secretary, Girija Prasad Koirala, together with the ULF leaders, went to the royal palace with the uncompromising demand of the Nepali people—nothing less than a full multiparty democracy. Thus, the king was forced by the people's power to restore his lost *dharma,* and late that night the news was broadcast that the king had agreed to lift the ban on political parties. Multiparty politics had arrived in Nepal overnight.

I interpret the king's eleventh-hour concession as his restoring of *dharma* because the alternative of using force and killing thousands was always there. After all, he was the supreme commander of the army. Also, he faced the same intensity of pressure to resist the movement from the nexus of hard-liner royal relatives and vested interests that had led his father, King Mahendra, to abandon democracy and kingly *dharma* thirty years before. But, finally, King Birendra was compelled to go with the tide of global movement for democracy. Still, I remained doubtful that the Nepali Congress and the communists could share power.

In the final analysis, I felt that my thinking about an evolutionary restoration of multiparty politics was not overcautious. I felt strongly about three things. One was that the king must be kept as a symbolic head of state. The second was that there was a real lack of administrative experience in the people leading the multiparty movement. Third, I feared that if a multiparty system came at once and communists were voted into power, then their political principles would not favor a continued democratic process. In other words, in the name of multiparty politics, there was a real danger of a mere transfer of power from partyless Panchayat rule to one-party communist rule. That would have been the very end of both democracy and monarchy that B. P. Koirala had foreseen. Although the communists, too, are Nepali freedom fighters, I was always cautious about the gap between their grass-roots-level political propaganda and the central-level implementation of their ideology. I still believe that if the king had delayed even a week in negotiating with the democratic leaders, communists could well have stormed his palace and taken over Nepal.

After K. P. Bhattarai became prime minister of the interim coalition government, I somehow managed to get through to him over the phone and congratulated him. After the people's triumph my mind left Zanzibar forever. I only wanted to go back to Nepal. We had already talked with Anthony's boss about leaving. Then, a few weeks later, *karma* haunted me again.

It was about eleven P.M. The air conditioners were vibrating noisily as always. Anthony was sleeping with Samyog in an adjoining bedroom. I was lying with little Shristi, who was awake, clinging to my breast. Suddenly I heard a rasping sound that appeared to come from the next room. It went on and on for many minutes. At last Shristi let go of me and slept, and I climbed out of the mosquito net and parted a curtain to peep outside. I froze as goose pimples rose all over my body. Just outside in the bushes were three African men, one of them armed with a long *panga* knife. One of them had just finished sawing his way through the screen to our little study room, next to my bedroom, and was pulling the wires out of the way. A bigger man was removing a window louver and was just about to ease his head and shoulders through a gap in the security bars. For several moments I could not even move. Speech would not come. Then, as I saw the bigger man start to move as if to enter the window, my voice returned.

I screamed, "Anthony! Anthony! Thieves!"

He woke up and was there in an instant, opening the study door. The three Africans vanished into the darkness. We called our night watchman—an old tribesman from Mozambique. He arrived with his bow and arrow, pretending to be surprised. Now we did not know what to do. It seemed an inside job. What protection was there? At last Anthony managed to get armed police to the house who guarded us for the rest of that night. But we did not feel secure even with them. I never slept properly again in that house, and still get nightmares even now thinking of what might have happened had that armed man entered the house. Anthony resigned the next day, and three weeks later we boarded the little Kenya Airways plane for Nairobi and left Zanzibar behind. Somehow we had endured eleven months in Zanzibar, although I never overcame the culture shock that I experienced on our arrival.

In the excitement of the revolution, we nearly returned to Nepal. But, at last, I realized that the struggle was already over. There was nothing further that I could contribute. If we returned to Nepal, I would become distracted from writing. Besides, with my little children, I was not in a position to be swept into political life immediately. Therefore, we decided to return to the United States. On the way, we spent a month in England where we met one of my close political colleagues, Sher Bahadur Deuba, who was completing a program at the London School of Economics. He brought me up to date on events back home.

Obviously, *Mandale* agents, ousted *Panchas*, and other like-minded reactionaries were busy creating disorder and confusion around the kingdom in an effort to undermine the democratic transition. Sher Bahadur was hurrying back to Nepal and to his constituency to begin his campaign for the general election planned for May 1991. He encouraged me to do the same. I wished that I could. But I knew that to return to Nepal would involve personal risks to which I could not consider exposing my children. Furthermore, if I did contest the election, my constituency would be my birthplace, Dhankuta, and I was sure that I would be standing against the former Panchayat prime minister who had imprisoned me in 1981. The thought of encountering him in an election brought back the bitter memory of my arrest and imprisonment. I felt strongly that before I returned home people should know that he had framed me as the scapegoat for the conspiracy that he had staged. I told Sher Bahadur briefly about the planned book. He encouraged me, "If you write the book, that will be your contribution."

I felt reassured by this. We had a few meetings and meals together. Before he left for Nepal, he told us that he had wanted to visit the United States for a couple of weeks en route home, but that the U.S. embassy in London had denied him an entry visa.

I told him, "Democracy may have been restored, but the democrats are still seen as antinationals by the Nepal government, and it seems that's where the American Embassy takes its cue as in the past. In their weak foreign policy they don't have a clue about who is who." I joked with him, "Don't worry, before very long you'll be visiting America as their state guest!"

He went back home via France instead.

Strictly speaking, we should have returned to Cambridge for me to complete work on my dissertation, but Harvard housing would be far too expensive for us. Also, to recover from Zanzibar I wanted to live in a quiet, like-minded community. We knew some people in the meditating community in Fairfield, Iowa, and thought that might be a good choice. When we called them, they were so warm and welcoming that we decided instantly to move there. So it was that we rented a trailer in rural Iowa. Fairfield was a small, peaceful, midwestern university town, and to live there was heavenly for me after what I had gone through in Zanzibar. As expected, the meditating community was most loving and helpful.

# 21
.
# Revisiting the Past

One day in early January 1991, a firm from Washington, D.C., asked Anthony to go to Kathmandu on a two-week mission. The day after his arrival Anthony called me with the news that he had been to visit the prime minister, K. P. Bhattarai, early that morning at his residence. It was the week the Nepali Congress was holding its national convention, and several hundred party leaders from all over the country had been gathered in the prime minister's compound. With characteristic friendliness and spontaneity, Bhattaraiji took Anthony by the hand and walked him into the center of the crowd to announce, "Listen everybody. This is Durga Pokhrel's husband!" Anthony felt greatly honored and delighted to receive this warm welcome and introduction.

Anthony also met another of the veteran Nepali Congress leaders, Ganesh Man Singh, and had breakfast with him at his house. He called Sahana Pradhan, the leader of the United Left Front, as well, and gave her our news. Whenever Anthony called me from Kathmandu, he would mention the names of more people he had met. I would be thrilled to hear what one after another of my old colleagues and friends were now doing. Anthony's introductions to my political friends in my absence were as exciting as our long-distance romance had been seven years earlier. I thought to myself, "Even if I could not go to Nepal myself, at least my husband is able to be there and meet my people." I was happy about that.

While Anthony was in Kathmandu, I asked him to inquire about a missionary lady who had redeemed my jewelry—the last of my family heirlooms—from a bank after I had fled the country. I was hoping that Anthony could rescue them, because after he had joined me at Harvard we had arranged to repay her.

Anthony reported back that her husband had retired and the couple was back in the United States. I obtained the telephone number where they were living, and called her to give her my news. To my shock, she informed me bluntly that she had sold all my jewelry and then she hung up the phone.

For a long time after this incident I could not believe that it had happened. For several years in the past, this missionary lady had shown much concern for me while I was a politically and socially unprotected "destitute woman." Now, I felt she had looted me. The jewelry, some fifteen items of twenty-four-karat gold and precious stones, was all that had remained after most of my valuables had been stolen during my imprisonment, and their emotional value was unforgettable.

After a while I thought to myself, "Maybe all my past *karma* washed away with those last remnants of my past."

I picked up a letter that she had sent me at Harvard. She had written, "I am glad I don't have to pray to little stone elephants who can neither hear, nor see, nor think." She was referring to my personal deity, Ganesh, who had always blessed me and faithfully protected me from grave danger. Just recently, on September 26 and 27, 1995, my wonderful Ganesh astounded the world and captured media attention as he blessed millions of his devotees with his live presence, causing images of himself to drink their offerings of milk. In devoutly religious India, his images accepted milk on such a scale as to create a milk shortage in parts of the country. I thought to myself that after nearly thirty years in the subcontinent trying to spread her gospel, the missionary woman had understood nothing about the culture and spirituality of those she set out to convert.

Toward the end of Anthony's fortnight in Kathmandu he called me with some emotional news. "Early yesterday morning I had tea with Bhattaraiji at his residence. The home minister was also there. We talked about our book and about prison reform. They were both very receptive and suggested that I met the chairman of the Jail Reform Commission. When I went to meet him, I also met the new superintendent of police in charge of jail administration. They were both extremely friendly and cooperative. From their office, they took me in a police jeep to the Central Prison. I was taken to the jailer's office. He welcomed me and then accompanied us down the lane to the women's prison. I stepped through the little half door in the main gate and met the present *Chaukidarni*. Immediately, I was surrounded by the other inmates. I told them that I was your husband. Some clapped and danced for joy. Many of them remembered you. I had half a dozen photographs with me of Samyog and Shristi, and one of you. I gave them all away to the women. They kissed the photographs and wept thinking of you. The *Chaukidarni* showed me your room. I walked all around the yard. I saw the tap, the *pagal* shed, the *tulsi* bush, the wasteland, every corner of the jail as you had described it."

My eyes were watering as I held the phone and listened to Anthony describing his visit and mentioning the names of some of the inmates with whom I had lived closely. I was so glad, too, that Bhattaraiji and other leaders had received Anthony so warmly. The day after his visit to the jail, he returned to the jailer with gifts for the women. This time, the jailer called some police guards and the *Chaukidar* from the men's prison to accompany Anthony as far as the main gate. At the gate, Anthony gave the *Chaukidarni* loaves of bread, a bag of mandarin oranges, sugar, tea, and some money to distribute among the women who had been there with me. He also took two pastries from a cake shop for two foreign women who were inside—one Iranian and a Nigerian.

Part of me was amazed that Anthony, a foreigner, had been allowed inside the prison. It was unheard of. Visiting the prison was as difficult as visiting the palace. The two extremes in the kingdom. Then I reminded myself, "Of course, there is a democratic government now." Everything was different. One of the first actions of the democratic government had been to reinstate all of the professors, myself included, who had been expelled from Tribhuvan University. Sahana Pradhan, the only other woman who had been expelled with me in 1975, had been serving as a cabinet minister in the coalition government and was now a Member of Parliament representing the capital, Kathmandu. And B. C. Malla, the seniormost professor who had also been expelled, had been appointed vice chancellor of the university. I thought excitedly that if I returned, I could resume my old teaching profession and become fully involved in the changed political environment of Nepal's new democracy.

Three months after Anthony's return, in May 1991, Nepal conducted its first democratic general election in thirty-two years. The Nepali Congress won a simple majority of seats, but the communists finished the contest a close second. During the election I called some of my friends to follow the results. They said that the former Panchayat prime minister had not even been able to put a foot into his Dhankuta constituency. The people had threatened to lynch him. He contested the seat in absentia and lost heavily—to a young communist, one of my students from when I was teaching in the Dhankuta Degree College.

Following its victory, the Nepali Congress formed the government. Girija Prasad Koirala, the leader of the party's militant wing during the days of armed struggle against the Panchayat regime, became Nepal's new prime minister. In 1959, the Nepali people had chosen B. P. Koirala as their country's first democratically elected prime minister. Now they had voted his younger brother into the same office. It was my view that this can happen only if a family remains intact in the same *dharma*. It was no coincidence.

Sher Bahadur Deuba—my good friend, whom we had met in London after leaving Zanzibar, and who had been denied a visa to visit the United States—was given the position of home minister, the very ministry responsible for the prisons and the police. I called to congratulate him, and reminded him not to neglect the jails.

ॐ

As we settled down in Iowa to write this book, I remained conscious of the challenges my colleagues at home were facing in government. On the one hand it was exciting, and a source of pride, to know that after their years of political imprisonment, torture, and daily harassment, the tables were turned and they were now leading the nation. On the other hand, I knew that thirty years of authoritarian rule had left a bankrupt society. Our little-known story was similar to the one the new democracies of eastern Europe were facing. Whether it was totalitarianism of the left or of the right, both systems left the same legacy.

Now the freedom fighters had to turn around and become society builders, administrators, and legislators. Theirs was not an easy task. Where would they begin? By reforming the police? Or the prison system? With the economy? With education? Or with the environment? Anthony and I imagined the donor agencies debating the development strategy for this third-poorest nation in the world. What would the new government's priorities be? The development jargon played in our minds. Should the economy go for "growth" or "equity" or "growth with equity"? "Growth" in what? Would "basic needs" still be in favor? What was meant by "sustainable development"? Or "progress"? Or "quality of life"?

As I pondered Nepal's conspiratorial political reality and reflected on its present poverty and uncertain future, I felt a sense of loss, a conviction that something fundamental was missing amid all the slogans of change and in the political ideologies and guiding theories that purported to explain such processes as democratization and sustainable development. It seemed that none of the current "development wisdom" could explain *why* some countries, or cultures, were able to implement a vision and prosper, while others remained in poverty and disorder. Already there were signs of growing support in Nepali cities for the discredited claims of communism. How could livelihoods be secured fast enough to reassure these lost people? What kind of livelihoods would satisfy them? How would Nepalis learn to trust again in the sincerity of politicians? I heard rumors that even some of the new ministers had lapsed into corruption just as in Panchayat times. The habits and patterns of error in our society would die hard. If patience ran out, the old problem of "peace and order" might return. The same pressures and the same conspirators lurked behind the scenes to urge the king once again to abolish our vulnerable democracy. Alternatively, this time the king himself might be swept away, to be replaced by another reactionary group.

This view of mine might seem overly skeptical given that multiparty democracy had finally been restored in Nepal, with the social democratic Nepali Congress party indeed in power. However, the news I was receiving about the new government's performance was not very encouraging. Corruption and nepotism were being widely alleged, and even politically less conscious people were commenting on the absence of substantive Nepali Congress policies for uplifting the lives of ordinary Nepalis. I knew the Nepali Congress had no magic wand to wave; yet public expectations were such that the conduct—indeed, sacrifice—of Nepal's new leaders should have been self-evident. I knew that if the leaders' dedication did not become evident, the general tendency of the people would be to revolt against them, especially now that there was freedom of expression.

ཀྱི

It was with this kind of pragmatic warning to my colleagues—not to allow power to obscure consciousness—that I ended the first draft of this book's manuscript in 1992. Since then, over two years have elapsed before I could complete this work, during which time several significant events occurred in my personal life and in Nepal that only served to reinforce the essential message of this book.

During the earlier part of the two years we sketched out the manuscript for a second book I had been longing to write for the sake of my inmates in jail; we provisionally titled the book *Rape of Dharma: Stories of Women in Prison in Nepal*. After drafting this book, at last I was able to turn my attention back to Harvard and complete my dissertation before the Graduate School of Education became too cross with me. Then, after helping me with all these writing projects, Anthony's turn came, and he found a wonderful group of faculty at Iowa State University who helped him complete his Ph.D. research in the field of indigenous knowledge—specifically, the Vedic tradition and agriculture in Nepal.

Meanwhile, I began making plans to return home. After all, I had married him for his love of Nepal, and he wanted to work there—if necessary, forever. Initially, Anthony had come to America only for the one-year M.P.A. program at Harvard, and it was I who had pushed him to continue with a Ph.D. program, perhaps from a cultural instinct that told me a husband should be at least as, if not more, educated than a wife. I was very proud of him for completing his doctoral program, and we were both equally excited about going back to live and work in my country.

But whenever I went to sleep having spent the day or the evening discussing our return to Nepal, without fail I would receive the most frightening dreams and intuitions during the night. Had Anthony not understood my past and my intuitive nature as well as he did, I might have driven him crazy over this period, because one day I would decide "From tomorrow let's start hunting for jobs in Nepal," only to say on the following day, "We should absolutely not return there for at least three to five years as there is great danger occurring there." For me to be so afraid of danger now seemed the greatest irony, but I felt deeply the reality of being a mother and being protective of my children. There were times of frustration when I must admit I wondered if I should not have married so I could have decided on a course of action without hindering others. But now any decision I made would affect all four of us. So I continued trying to meditate upon my dreams and interpret them for Anthony, and although I could not tell exactly how much he was able to internalize them, he would still agree to do whatever seemed good for the family in light of my interpretations.

Anthony's belief in the significance of my dreams had been reinforced already in 1992 and 1993, when for several weeks I had the darkest, most disturbing succession of dreams, along with incessant bad intuitions, since the times of my father's and mother's deaths. At the time of these disturbing omens, I warned Anthony, "Just wait and see; very soon we will hear that some of our relatives have died." I tried hard to meditate upon the dreams in order to become prepared for who was to die, but perhaps I was thinking too consciously of the older members of my family, because the visions that came to me were ones I could not interpret. The truth came tragically over the course of a year when, one after another, three of my cousins, my youngest paternal uncle's daughters, all died of ovarian cancer. Two of them had been very close to me—except in politics—since we had grown up together in Dhankuta. Now, far away from home, I felt deeply emotional about their suffering and my inability to help them, and I had many nightmares. During the mourning period for their deaths, my youngest aunt, Father's youngest sister, also died. I telephoned my only other surviving paternal aunt, the one widowed in childhood, to comfort her. Since my father's death she had been living with my sister Subhadra. She said to me, "I'm now next in line. I don't know when you will ever come—I might never see your family." I tried to assure her that because she had always lived such a pure, healthy life, she should live for many more years and that when we finally came I wanted her to live with us.

Then, in England, the elder of Anthony's two paternal aunts died. As she and her sister had never married and had no other relatives, Anthony went to England in May 1992 for her funeral.

It was late September 1992, and we had still not overcome our sorrow. The "first deposit" date for Anthony's dissertation was four weeks away, and he was writing solidly when his mother called from England with the unexpected news that she wanted to visit us early the following month. Anthony suggested that she wait until his dissertation was in and that she stay with us through the New Year, but she was insistent. It was "now or never." I could not understand why she did not want to stay with us for longer; in our culture, one can expect anyone to arrive at any time and stay indefinitely. And in the case of a mother and an only son it goes without saying that she should be living with the son's family. Therefore, I was more than prepared to receive her, even if for a short visit, and the boys were equally excited about Nana's coming.

Just eighty years old, and small and neat in appearance, she arrived a little weary from her long journey and from cleaning and tidying up her house "because the neighbors would be looking in to take care of the mail during her absence." For five days she had a lovely time, especially with the boys. She was an accomplished artist, and taught them some drawing and painting. She had brought us some of her original watercolors, which we framed and kept saying that she mustn't forget to sign them. On the sixth day, she thought she felt a cold developing and spent the day in bed, eating almost nothing. Then, very early in the morning of the following day, a Friday, she awoke with mild chest pain. We wanted to take her to the hospital to see a doctor, but she did not want to go. Instead, she rested in bed again the whole day, but began craving all sorts of specialty foods and drinks such as rose-flavored mineral water. Several times I went on errands to the nearby stores to purchase what she desired, and then fed her.

Her chest pain subsided, but at times during the day the gaze from her eyes became remote and distant.

After the evening meal, we told stories and cuddled the boys to sleep, and then went to Nana. She was so frail, she could hardly stand or raise her head. We helped her to the bathroom. She did not want to wash "until tomorrow." Again in bed, she lay back, her eyes barely open, and apologized to Anthony that her illness was disturbing his work, then faded into sleep. Anthony returned to his study, where he was working on the penultimate chapter of his dissertation, which was due on Monday. I did not feel like sleeping. I felt again as though news of death was in the air, and although I could not bear to think about it, I was very worried about her. I went downstairs to Anthony and said, "Sorry to worry you, but I must tell you someone else is going to die in our family. I hope it will not be your mother." Anthony did not think it could be her because her appetite had improved and she seemed a little better. He asked me to meditate and then sleep. I followed his suggestion and did not know at what time he came to bed. That night Anthony had a dream about taking his mother for cremation in Des Moines.

At around four A.M., I awoke from a disturbing dream, the flickering around my left eye as bad as ever. Very restless, I could not go back to sleep. We had left the door to Nana's bedroom half open, and at a quarter to five I heard a strange, mild snoring sound. I went to turn on the bathroom light so that I could see into her bedroom without disturbing her. She appeared in deep sleep. Then, suddenly the snoring sound stopped. Something made me run to wake up Anthony. Quietly, I urged him to go to his mother's room to see if she was all right.

Anthony entered her room. She was lying still, her mouth open and her eyes staring upward. Anthony called her gently, but received no reply.

It was not yet five A.M., but we called some close Nepali friends who kindly came in the eerie predawn and took Samyog and Shristi to their house for an early breakfast just as the funeral home car parked in our driveway. A doctor was called, and he verified that Nana had passed away after heart failure.

I had always been scared of seeing the dead, and now two of the people closest to me had died right in front of me, and I had touched them after they stopped breathing. I consoled myself, knowing that it must be very comforting for the dying one to know that his or her closest people were present, giving love and compassion even after death. My mother-in-law was a very spiritual and compassionate lady herself, and went almost effortlessly with her loved ones.

Anthony and I performed some purifying rituals for her together, and arranged for her cremation that day in Des Moines. Later that day we collected the children and told them what had happened. Four-year-old Shristi thought that Nana must have been reborn as a butterfly, because he said that on her last day she had looked at the flowers in her room and told him she wanted to be a butterfly in her next life. I was a little surprised to hear this because she had been a devout Christian, and I had not imagined that she would believe in reincarnation. "Yet," I thought, "there are so many cosmic influences surrounding us at all times that one can never tell what element might influence one's vision at the end of life." In any case, her end was peaceful and glorious, and it occurred without trouble to herself or, for that matter, anybody—exactly as she would have wanted. Although Anthony felt heartbroken that she had come and died in his house while he had been so busy as to be almost unaware of what was taking place, he too recognized the spirituality of the event, and within two days he was able to finish his dissertation on schedule.

We could only visit England six months later for her memorial, burying her ashes next to her husband's in her natal family church in Herefordshire and holding a thanksgiving service at the local Anglican church, where she had been very active. She had many devoted friends and few relatives. Just as all my relatives had gathered in my brother's house after my father died, so her friends and relatives met at Anthony's home. Several times, I felt the presence of her spirit in the house. We had planned a six-week visit to England to take care of her affairs and for me to make a brief trip from there to Nepal. But on the very day of her memorial service, Anthony's last surviving relative from his father's side, his other aunt, suffered a stroke that left her almost blind. For two weeks, Anthony visited her daily in the hospital, where she suffered another massive stroke. By now, Anthony had studied some Tibetan Buddhist literature about death, and he calmly spoke to his dying aunt to help her prepare, and even remained comforting her alone for a long time after she stopped breathing. Then we arranged her funeral before returning to Iowa.

In the meantime, we discovered that I was pregnant with a third child. This was a little more than Anthony could easily handle, but I was overjoyed—I had been longing to have another. Shristi reasoned, "Now that Nana and Auntie have died, and Mummy is going to have a baby, Mummy is recycling them," which I thought was a profound statement. But, as Anthony was feeling, our future was very uncertain and now we were about to be a family of five; and he had no job. To him, it seemed at this time that all travail was behind us and that this was the time to return to international development work, ideally in Nepal.

I tried to meditate on what might be best for our family. I did not want to leave the United States until after December 1994, when the baby was due, and if we went overseas I felt again that it should be to Nepal, where we both could contribute. In another country, it would only be possible for Anthony to work, because I would not want to abandon my children to baby-sitters in order to work. Only in Nepal could I also be active, because my children could be with my family members whenever I went away. Therefore I told Anthony that because of our circumstances and our conviction about raising children in a closely bonded way, I saw only two options at the present—either Nepal or America, where I could manage to work a little at home. I also said that we had spent a long time in rural areas and that perhaps this was a time to be nearer a center of power. If we were to live for longer in America, that meant Washington, D.C. If nothing developed there, we should wait in Iowa until the baby was born and then go to Kathmandu.

But at this time, whenever I slept after thinking about Nepal, I would experience the most disturbing dreams, which I interpreted as omens of more political trouble there. In one of the dreams I saw our three veteran Nepali Congress leaders being stoned and almost killed in Dhankuta—and then chased by hordes of teenagers through many crowded places. And in several dreams I was chased myself by a buffalo, the animal we understand in Hinduism to be the vehicle of Yama Raj, the God of Death, and I knew from my past experience that if I were to go to Nepal I would face severe danger.

We were left with the choice of Washington, D.C. At just this time Anthony happened to make one phone call to a contact in Washington and was asked immediately to send his résumé because interviews were already in progress for a research position in a conservation organization. Although new to the field of conservation, and by preference a field manager, within weeks Anthony found himself selected as this program's senior conservation analyst. For him it was like caging a free jungle bird. I, too, did not like big cities. Yet some force seemed to be directing us to the D.C. area, and so we moved there in the late fall. Just over a month later, on December 21, we had our third baby boy in Washington. We tried to think of the meaning of his birth, and concluded that seemingly against all odds, and in contrast to our material preference for quiet and simplicity, we had come to Washington partly through his influence for some purpose that might only become manifest in times to come. It was as though we were performing *tapasya*, or austerities. Therefore, we chose the name *Tapasya* for this little boy.

Some six months earlier, in Iowa, I had done some library research into publishing houses for this book. From hundreds of listed publishers I had made a short list of six likely ones. One day in early 1995, I reopened this file and began sorting through the notes I had made. To my amazement, I found that the publisher that, from some intuition, I had placed at the top of my list had an address just a quarter of a mile down the road from the house we had bought in Virginia. With excitement, I called Anthony at his office and asked him to phone this publisher. Summoning all his consciousness, he called and was immediately asked to write a synopsis of the book concept he had described. He did so, and within days we were asked for this manuscript, which was accepted.

Our life seemed to be falling into place. But Nepal seemed to many people to be falling apart. Around the D.C. area, we began meeting Nepalis, most of whom were disenchanted with the Nepali Congress government back home and were in favor of the communists' coming into power. I knew that people without ideological conviction would always be reactionary. How could democracy lead logically to communism? For these Nepalis living in America and enjoying all kinds of materialistic values it might be easy to declare support for communists, but I knew that in reality a communist takeover of power in Nepal would simply push our poor country further backward. It was the previous Panchayat regime that had created these neocommunists during the days when all doors to join the ruling system were closed for Nepali Congress supporters but open for neocommunists. Once inside the system, those who joined could take advantage of opportunities for jobs and sponsored education in America. Much foreign aid was spent providing education for such reactionaries. There were a few individuals who had managed to reach the United States on their own, and I found them more neutral in opinion than the others.

Just as from Zanzibar I had wanted to warn the king—that if a multiparty system came all at once it might be difficult to sustain democracy in Nepal, and that he should be both compromising and cautious about democratization—exactly what I had feared did happen after just over three years of Nepali Congress government. The old-style reactionaries, the communists, and Nepali Congress 1991 election losers all acted to undermine the vulnerable Nepali Congress government, which, in any case, was not proving competent enough at the difficult task of capturing the momentum the Nepali people had created in the 1990 revolution. In particular, the three veteran leaders of the Nepali Congress—Koirala, Bhattarai, and Singh—failed to provide united leadership; Nepalis joked that these three combined respectively only their weaknesses—no brain, no toughness, and no education. In the process, they neglected and hurt many of those Nepali Congress activists who had suffered most in the past for the cause of overthrowing the Panchayat system, picking up instead a bunch of former Panchayat reactionaries. Neither was the Nepali Congress government experienced in development and public administration. Nor did it provide systematic training of administrators for running a democratic government. Finally, there were charges of corruption that Prime Minister Koirala would not answer to Parliament's satisfaction, and perhaps overconfident in his power, he preferred to dissolve Parliament and called for fresh elections rather than resign and give his leadership to others.

In the costly November 1994 mid-term election, Nepali Congress 1991 election losers, communists, and other reactionaries fought against the Nepali Congress in power. Thus, Nepali Congress voters became divided between the official candidates and others. Finally, the counting of votes revealed that the communists had won five more seats in Parliament than the Nepali Congress. But the allegedly corrupt strongman many Nepalis wanted to get rid of—Prime Minister Koirala—won the election from two constituencies.

As the world's only communist government in a Hindu monarchy came into office, the comment in the American press was surprisingly sympathetic. Apparently, with the end of the Cold War, Westerners have been quick to forget the essential character of communism, even though they see its legacy playing out in current events around the margins of the former Soviet Union. For the Nepali communists were described in these U.S. newspapers as "democratic socialists," and the writers, even if perplexed, seemed unworried by the prospect of their rise to power. But this viewpoint worried and angered me. How was it that a communist government could be bad news elsewhere, but all right in Nepal?

Nevertheless, the communists were unable to command sufficient support in the new Parliament to have their own speaker, and the minority Nepali Congress retained that position. In this way—with the communists in power, the democrats in the minority but controlling the house, and the king still on the throne—the most improbable mishmash of power began ruling the kingdom.

I told Anthony that I gave the communists six months to rule. Six months into their government, in April 1995, Anthony made a work-related trip to Nepal for four weeks and spent several evenings and weekends with the Nepali Congress party president, Bhattaraiji; the house minority leader, Sher Bahadur Deuba; and other sympathizers of both parties. Some of them suggested the name of the person they suspected in the kidnapping conspiracy, but I did not agree with their theory because this suspect had not been among those who had come to me before my arrest seeking my cooperation. In any case, in my reckoning this suspect, even if involved, would only have been a small fry used by those in power, and I still feel that the real brain should be tracked down and brought to justice.

The impression Anthony gained from ordinary Nepalis about the communist government was not entirely negative. Nonetheless, the sheer scale of the challenges facing any Nepali government seemed formidable. In particular, the environment in the Kathmandu valley—even over the four years since his previous visit—had deteriorated unimaginably. Now, many pedestrians and cyclists wear face masks to protect themselves from the black fumes and dust that fills the city air. After just an hour or so outside, Anthony reported, one becomes weary, one's eyes, nose, and lungs smarting from the excursion. The whole valley seems to be becoming an untidy building site, with piles of rubble, bricks, and other building supplies along every street and narrow pathway. On any plot, no matter how small, to which access is feasible, ugly concrete-frame houses are being erected. Seeing the desecration of the valley, Anthony's heart sank. With few exceptions, nowhere did he see anything aesthetically pleasing to the senses. None of the beauty, loveliness, or charm that once made Kathmandu renowned. Just filth, roughness, and noise. It appears as though development and population growth in the valley have gotten completely out of control, with small, polluting industrial activity totally unregulated and brick factories swallowing up more and more acres of fertile farmland.

Equally disturbing to me were his reports of social and cultural changes. Gone are the days, it seems, when it was safe to walk around the quiet Kathmandu streets late at night. Now, the littered streets appear eerie, with groups of rough-looking youths loitering in the shadows and motorcycles ripping aggressively through the darkness. A decade ago, the "in" place to hang out was an ice-cream bar. Now, a dozen or more new-style restaurants have opened where popular musicians play at loud volume. The atmosphere inside is thick with cigarette smoke. Young Nepali boys with long hair, dark glasses, colorful scarves tied around their heads, jeans, and T-shirts, dance and shout with wild abandon, drawing deeply on their cigarettes and drinking heavily.

These (what I call "lost") Nepali youth presumably represent the communists' constituency in the cities. No doubt a novel authoritarian system is equally able to control the news and make believe that no misdeeds are happening in the country. But I heard through other friends that whatever chaos reigned during the Nepali Congress's three years occurred within three months of communist rule. Predictably, the communists began sup-

pressing, arresting, and even killing Nepali Congress activists, and impos-
ing censorship on the media. And in the economic field, naturally they
started introducing their ideological policies, reversing the Nepali Congress's privatization initiatives.

As I predicted, their rule lasted barely six months and, by June 1995,
Nepal had a dissolved parliament again. This time it was the communists
who were calling for a midterm national election to be held on November
23, 1995. The cost of this trend of annual midterm elections, both financial and in terms of political instability, chaos, and confusion, was clearly
undesirable. Even worse, it became clear that the communist government
intended to gain an absolute majority in parliament by means of this
midterm election *by hook or by crook*. I heard that our northern neighbor
was actively backing its ideological groups in Nepal, and that there was
every indication that the communists were organizing to establish all the
classic features of their ideology in Nepal, presumably to the point of its
logical conclusion in a monarchical context.

Whereas the Nepali Congress was the villain for communists, the other
reactionary groups would blame the multiparty system for the inevitable
instability. Thus, the great danger arose again in 1995 of the king becoming compelled to use his father's techniques of restoring "peace and order"
by snatching away the democratic process from the kingdom. Democracy
was tottering between the frying pan and the fire. As this reality dawned
on the Nepali Congress leaders, the three formerly divided and egocentric
veterans finally came together and decided to forge an odd alliance with
the various groupings of former Panchayat system politicians who together
occupied twenty of the elected seats in the House. In this way, in September
1995 the Nepali Congress formed a new government, with its noncom-
munist partners holding a 25 percent share in the cabinet.

In terms of political ideology, these Panchayat partners might pose a less
harmful threat for the Nepali Congress than the communists. Yet we should
not forget that for thirty years communists were integrated into the king's
Panchayat system intentionally to undermine the democratic Nepali Congress. They figuratively blindfolded and deceived the king together. As I
heard of the new alliance into which the Nepali Congress had entered, I
thought to myself that B.P. would never have made any compact with either group, and would have put his energies into healing his party's internal conflicts long before they threatened the party's disintegration. I find
it interesting that the former *Panchas* who are now included in influential
cabinet posts are royal loyalists rather than the criminals who joined Panchayat to shield their crimes. I cannot help wondering whether the palace

is into another intrigue. Are these loyalists there to protect the king from the communists? In the past, the palace used communists to keep the Nepali Congress away. Is the palace this time using the Nepali Congress against the communists? If, rather than to protect democracy, the king's intention is only to be clever, then no one will trust him, and the end result will be very disturbing.

There is another most disquieting aspect to the present alliance. Behind the cabinet as "advisers" are four former prime ministers from both the Nepali Congress and Panchayat sides. One of these advisers is the very Panchayat prime minister who, my evidence suggests, staged the kidnapping plot and framed me as the suspect. If indeed he did, then the possibility exists that he could do something similar again, particularly if, as I suspect, the other element from the former terrorist group that may have been involved again offers support. The pattern of conspiracy in Nepali politics is ingrained. Moreover, the actual pattern repeats itself. The very same conspiratorial elements born of the 1980 referendum outcome—whose victim I became in 1981—appear poised now, as if waiting in the wings for an opportunity to deceive the king again.

Whether or not this former prime minister had any role in the kidnapping plot should be established through a legal process. If he is found not guilty, then he should bear some responsibility for identifying the culprit. As long as the real culprit remains officially unidentified, as I have said earlier, a painful part of my own life will forever remain unresolved—a condition that should not persist with the restoration of democracy.

ဘယ

In the new government, my good old friend Sher Bahadur Deuba—whom the U.S. embassy in London had denied a visa to visit America, and who had later become Home Minister and then opposition leader during the communists' six-month rule—now became Prime Minister. After he formed his government, I called and congratulated him, but I added, "When we were recruited into the Nepali Congress long ago, our leaders always told us that it was not the king but his stooges who were our enemies. What have you done now by bringing them into your cabinet?"

He replied, "I realize now that in politics there does not seem to be any permanent enemy or friend."

He might be right given Nepal's present political situation. But I feel deeply sad that this political chaos was created simply by the Nepali Congress's incompetent leadership. It seems to me that there remains, more than ever, a real possibility of an end to Nepali democracy at this time, with the prospect of dictatorship lasting for another generation, either of the king or of the communists. In either case, the issue is not only Nepal's backwardness but the question of Nepal's surviving as an independent state. The only factor historically protecting Nepal from an Indian takeover has been Nepal's status as the world's only Hindu state. However, India, the world's largest democracy, might no longer tolerate a small country on its northern border that is ruled by an autocratic king, even if he keeps the constitutional provision of a Hindu state. If the communists take over power in Nepal and overthrow the Hindu king, India will definitely act; it will not want to have a communist country between it and its old enemy China. And if India moves toward Nepal, China will not stay quiet. Thus, I can foresee Nepal's becoming a battleground between our two giant neighbors if specific steps are not taken soon to stabilize Nepal's internal democratic process.

I still believe that there is only one individual in a position to keep the political balance, and that is the king. His father resorted to military insurgency in 1960, but I admonish this king to adopt a spiritual path to lead Nepal forward to another golden age of social and cultural harmony, stable democracy, and holistic economic prosperity. In this state, it would not matter whether leftist or rightist individuals formed a government, because all would be committed to a national framework of action suiting a Hindu kingdom.

༄༅

There are times when I find it hard not to be impatient to return home. But my circumstances have changed, and I have young children. It is not that I have changed or become somehow diminished in commitment, having married a non-Nepali. I remind Anthony, "For me, it has to be either all or nothing." People who do not know me well might not believe that I could become a devoted mother. But, to me, motherhood, no less than Nepal's democratic struggle, is a cause that demands my all, at least until my children become less vulnerable.

I have resolved that, until that time, I will concentrate on writing and planning the work I will eventually do in my country. I have begun to see the culmination of the events of my past as the dawn of my deepest realization of my *dharma*. In hindsight, every loss I experienced, every paradox of my existence, was in fact preparation: loss of family; loss of friends; loss of role, of freedom, of peace; and ultimately the loss, for a time, of my country itself. It was a process of being forced to learn things that otherwise I would never encounter. The struggle and loss were the means through which a fresh vision and purpose were forged. For, during my exile, I have come to realize two general things: that political democracy and individual rights are not ends in themselves and that development— political, economic, and social—in any society is best grounded in the indigenous worldview and spirituality of its culture.

Similarly, I have come to realize that the most important thing in life is life itself—and the right to live. Reflecting on the whole episode of my struggle and imprisonment, I recall that whenever I was threatened by death, it was that spark, that energy of life—my soul—that would cheer and comfort and, ultimately, protect me from being killed. Based on this personal experience, I can imagine that all those who are being killed around the world—even as I write—must feel the same most personal, precious desire, as I did, of life. Unfortunately, they have gone—some for something, and many for nothing.

I feel sad to think of the uselessness of many human lives. And I wonder now whether the mere restoration of democracy will guarantee the human right to life in my homeland. For me, life has evolved beyond the political paradigm and beyond the national boundary.

# Epilogue: A Future

It was only in jail that I realized that victimization in our society was pervasive beyond the political realm. In prison, I used to see myself as one among many victims, with myself a political victim while others were social and economic victims. Later, I came to perceive a deeper explanation of the phenomenon of social victimization. The victims came from the most vulnerable categories in our society. They were not just women, but the most vulnerable among women—child-widows with no male heir, women deserted by husbands or lovers, young women living alone. I might have been politically targeted, but I began to realize that I was chosen because I fell into a preexisting cultural stereotype. I was victimized because I was seen in the context of our society as a vulnerable, unprotected woman.

Now, far away in exile in America and with the passage of time and recent events, I recognize that I should no longer lay the blame for victimization only on Panchayat. The evils in our society ran deep. Ours was a society in which victimization was a pervasive pathology, and it seems that this pathology was compounded, rather than caused, by the political system. It was a story of disempowerment and the abuse of the vulnerable in a society where the protected preyed on the unprotected. It was the collapse—indeed, the reverse—of the noble ideals of a true Vedic Hindu society. It was also a women's story.

The traditional Hindu attitude honors and protects women for their motherliness, care and prudence, cleanliness and purity, piety, and creativity. But the collapse of societal *dharma* in contemporary Nepal turned women from a protected group into a vulnerable one. If a woman was found unprotected for any reason, she became an easy object for any predator, and in my own case, without knowing it, when I left family for politics I walked straight into the cultural stereotype of a "prey," declaring myself a candidate for victimization. I acted out a cultural drama, even though abuse of political power was the motive for making the drama play out in my case.

In prison I found that, almost without exception, as each victimized woman pondered her fate, *dharma* was the familiar cultural concept that she kept repeating in her effort to find meaning. There is no word for "rape" in Nepali. It is an unmentionable subject in our culture. If she could ever bring herself to speak of her shame, the nearest a woman might venture would be an indirect reference: "He forcibly did" or, more commonly, "He looted my *dharma*." The woman would then say that the man who "forcibly did" had "lost" his *dharma*. Similarly, each woman so polluted, or cornered into abortion, would say that she had lost hers. The *Pancha* who framed her had turned from his *dharma*. The police who forced her confession had lost their *dharma*. The bribed judge who never asked her a question and sentenced her had neglected his *dharma*. At every turn and at every level, *dharma* was lost. It was as if the whole kingdom was upturned and disconnected from its bond with nature. These women were holding the mirror up to society.

*Dharma* is fundamental to Hindu thought and is ingrained in the Hindu way of life. It is the most abstract concept of eternal truth and, at the same time, a most concrete set of guidelines that governs even precise rituals and other daily observances. In the abstract, *dharma* means the ultimate law of all things, the pure consciousness that interacts with matter to govern creation. *Dharma* also means religion, how people express their belief in, and reverence for, this sacred energy that governs and creates the universe. In this sense *dharma* embraces all ritual and all paths toward God-realization and enlightenment. Finally, Hindus understand *dharma* in terms of right conduct in conformity to the ultimate law. In this sense of righteous duty also, *dharma* is a wide-ranging concept, because for harmony and coherence to prevail, every individual, every relation, every caste or profession, every ethnic group, every office, and every institution, including society itself and the king himself, has its own *dharma*.

Nepal remains the world's only Hindu state, with *dharma* as a central concept of Hinduism, Hindu society, and Hindu monarchy. But, particularly during the Panchayat period, *dharma* became abandoned as the governing principle of our society, and the king became surrounded by advisers without traditional Hindu wisdom.

We have another concept, *dharmasankat*, which occurs when the king's ability to uphold his *dharma* is endangered and chaos in the kingdom results. It happens when some enemy or vested interest group disallows a king to perform his right duty. The Rana oligarchy did this for a century by physically locking the kings away in their palace and keeping them in a darkness of ignorance about their kingdom's affairs. Similarly, during *Panchayat Raj*, the king was blindfolded through the systematic deception of his courtiers. What made the Panchayat king so vulnerable was the centralization of power that the king allowed in his palace and his sole patronage of a political system that protected a narrow, self-seeking minority. With their fawning smiles, they would assure the king, "Everything is fine, Your Majesty. There is peace and order in the kingdom." But as dissent periodically burst through the cracks, and those cracks were sealed more strongly, preventing yet more people from participating, the ramparts that separated *Pancha* from non-*Pancha* in Nepali society were raised higher and higher. Inside the *Pancha* community, life became increasingly fractured. Even prime ministers were dumped as the system failed to contain the pressures, and expelled *Panchas* became as critical as the banned opposition. Knowing the home truths, their disloyalty became a dangerous force as the system narrowed, shielding fewer and fewer, until finally only the power brokers and lawmakers of the palace were left.

The supreme danger for the king, in identifying himself so directly with his political creation, was that no one could speak truth to power. Under Panchayat laws, to criticize royalty was treason, the only offense in the land that carried the death penalty. So came the rule of thumb: "*Mai chup, tai chup, sabai chup*"—"I quiet, you quiet, everyone quiet." Most Nepalis were non-*Pancha* and could have given the king plenty of advice. But because the system was closed, their views could not be heard. There was no shortage of either priests or astrologers around the palace, and no way they could have been unaware of the *adharma* [converse of *dharma*] of his rule. Were all the king's religious advisers too political to speak the truth? Did the hardliner relatives of the king whisper in the priestly Brahmin's ear, "Say it like this, not like that"?

How lonely the king might have felt. How exposed. How falsely protected he was from the time of his coronation, when unsightly beggars were rounded up and trucked out of Kathmandu to the *tarai* (only to return later on foot), to the pantomimes of his development region camps, when, again, the unsightly and unwanted would be screened away. It might be difficult not to believe what everyone surrounding you tells you. If every-body says a tree is crooked then even a straight tree might appear crooked. If everyone tells the emperor that his new suit of nothingness looks won-derful and that only a fool cannot see it, then the emperor might parade naked before his subjects. A person maintains his right image only if his consciousness is established in right action.

I believe it is this lack of consciousness that is our national problem. Nepal's human rights problem, the vulnerability of the weak groups in our society, was only partly the product of undemocratic, unaccountable rule. More than that, it was a spiritual problem. Our society was steeped in big-otry and mutual disrespect. The so-called high exploited the so-called low. Also, high-caste males, basically, were the lawmakers who made and in-terpreted the laws that were unjust to disadvantaged groups. Our human rights problem was one of neglected consciousness and the abandoning of our social *dharma* by these people. This is still what needs correcting.

The structure of our Hindu society has become rigid and distorted. Caste, with its linguistic root of *kes* (to cut), means "chaste," "pure," "cut free from faults." Higher caste should equate with higher consciousness and righ-teous dutifulness. We devotees of Shiva believe that, by closing the two eyes of flesh and quieting the mind through a mantra, you open the third, spiritual, eye—through which you see the eternal knowledge within you and perceive good, bad, right, wrong, truth, falsehood, past, and present. What did I do today? Did I cause anyone any harm? Did anyone seem un-easy in my presence? Was everyone happy to see me? Why might some-body have hurt me? Might I have once done something to cause that? What can I do to lift away that cause, that unhappiness? As I see people, can I tell how they are feeling, what they are thinking? Whoever is able to an-swer all these questions positively, this is a conscious person. Highly con-scious people live with this degree of perception, from the smallest detail of life to the largest affair of leading a nation. People of goodness and vi-sion, they always think constructively. We say they are *vivekshil*, having those balanced qualities of compassion, discernment, and impartiality. Consciousness and *dharma* are almost synonymous in Hinduism. If people do not focus on eternal knowledge, they lose consciousness and, accord-ing to the Vedic view, open themselves to negative social influences and even those of the cosmos as a whole. As a result, they become incapable of performing their rightful duty.

*Bramhagyan*, the highest level of human potential, can be lost by anyone who is not constantly in tune with the field of pure knowledge. When totally "out of tune," people become dull, blind, directionless, out of control, and lost amid the jumbled thoughts of the mind, unable to discern the real from the delusion, subject to mindlessness and whim. Inevitably, unable to perceive the result of brutality, they will be cruel. Unfeeling for others' security and livelihood, they will be greedy and corrupt. Unconscious of truth, they will falsify. Being untrustworthy, they will mistrust and conspire. When people holding power are themselves thus governed, the nation suffers these consequences: irritation, fighting, disrespect, conspiracy, insecurity, fear, famine, injustice, and poverty.

Increasingly, I have become conscious of the shallow quality of freedom in Nepali society. We were and are a nation without a cultural vision. Half-dressed tourists have been permitted to come and get stoned, or gamble in the plush hotel casino owned by the royalty. In the Panchayat times I knew, business meant bribes, smuggling drugs and antiquities to the West and imported gold and electronic goods into India. Industry that flourished was in liquor, bottled soda, and tobacco. Even the sacred Himalayan Mountains became littered with garbage as each expedition brought in its multithousand-dollar price tag to the government. And as state elites became more in tune with the temptations of international culture, foreign aid meant fresh project funds for syphoning off, foreign travel, and Western education for their children, who would in all likelihood not return and share their acquired knowledge for the benefit of other Nepalis. By many accounts, it appears that some of these trends have only accelerated in the virtual anarchy that has overtaken Nepal under multiparty democracy.

The more I think about the deep-seated problems facing Nepal the more my conviction grows that conventional international development approaches are powerless to lift our society out of its ingrained cultural habits and establish a fresh positive pattern for each negative trait. Can a prime minister restore this degree of harmony in our society by relying only on the tools of Western science and technology delivered in packages of assistance from donor agencies? The alternative vision I see is of a Nepali society grounded in a revival of our own culture.

Perhaps it is strange that this fresh insight came to me as I mused on the fate of my fellow inmates in prison. Nevertheless, this new insight stunned me when it first came, as it forced me to question what difference a political transformation of power would make when human rights violation was such a deeply ingrained pattern in society. Mere enacting of rules might have little impact on the pathology of abuse. Even when democracy is won, political leaders seem too absorbed with votes, and their struggle to hold on to power, to be concerned about the abuse and wrongful incarceration of women and other vulnerable groups that is societally condoned. I am aware that in a democracy at least there should be freedom of speech, and that the abuse of the vulnerable can be raised as an issue. But do political leaders struggle to enact and implement the necessary social, legal, and institutional reforms? Surely, a transformation of consciousness at a more profound level in society must occur first. It is my belief now that at the level of the ordinary Nepali in every village, a sense of conscience must be restored that no longer tolerates the abuse of the vulnerable but demands the restraint and punishment of the predator. This mission amounts to much more than a political challenge. It means enlivening a realization in Nepali society of the deeper level of life—*dharma*. We must enliven the pure, sacred traditions of our culture, our indigenous worldview.

Nepal needs a vision.

My vision is of a heavenly kingdom flourishing in the Himalayan foothills. Intermingling Hinduism and Buddhism, Nepal can be a society of religious tolerance and a supremely culture-centered nation. If Nepalis rededicate themselves, instead of turning the Kathmandu valley into an ugly semiindustrialized urban sprawl suffocated by pollution and inevitable power and water shortages, we can make the valley beautiful by restoring its—and the rest of the nation's—palaces and temples to their original splendor. Our Hindu king, instead of sponsoring a political system and clinging to executive, legislative, and judicial power—or acting as a mere constitutional head—can protect *dharma* and maintain the consciousness of his kingdom. If he does this, he will become a respected and loved role model for the Nepali people, guiding them impartially along a unique right path suited to Nepali culture.

A Hindu democracy is the unique political path for Nepal. Nothing else will provide remotely the same positive uniting force. The moment Nepal leaves its binding Hindu *dharma* behind, it will invite communal and religious conflict into Nepali society just as these forces try to tear India apart. What secularism does in inherently religious societies like Nepal and India is to politicize religion, and the last spectacle I wish to see is a Hindu resurgent movement mobilizing against other groups in society. Indeed, missionaries are doing their best to steal people away from their traditional *dharma* within our society even though Nepal outlaws proselytizing. Their converts are almost entirely the most oppressed lower-caste groups, or others influenced by Western materialistic culture. I feel sickened to see missionaries capitalizing on the current collapse of our social *dharma* and seeking to substitute their religion.

At the same time, some communist Nepalis have already been advocating secularism and anti-Hindu feeling in Nepal. To me, this extends and misdirects what was a justifiable revolt against Panchayat misrule and *adharmic* practices into one against Nepali culture and *dharma* itself—an action that is as antinational on a cultural and spiritual level as was the *Pancha* looting of the country on a political and economic level. My fear about a communist regime installed in Kathmandu has always been that it might abolish the institution of Hindu monarchy and replace it with some faceless alternative totalitarianism. Nepal's misled youth and uneducated masses might have voted for communists out of frustration and sheer poverty, but once implemented, true communism cannot possibly merge with Nepali cultural values. A communist cadre trying to whip up collective action on a commune will hold no more appeal to a simple *dharma*-following villager than a *Pancha*. In any case, where will communism take Nepali society? The communist world's revolutionary struggles to establish classless societies have been distinctly disappointing in accomplishment and, notably, in the field of human rights.

Nepal needs a form of government that protects the Nepali people from misrule and guides Nepali society along a development path that harmonizes with Nepali culture, preserves Hindu and Buddhist thought and practice, and at the same time permits evolutionary social change. In my view, this should be a uniquely Nepali sociopolitical vision that blends what is relevant and good from the Vedic and other indigenous traditions with good elements of modern democratic political development. Therefore, my vision is of a spiritually proactive Hindu monarchical state with democratic political rights tempered by a Hindu-Buddhist social compact that would continue to moderate individual rights within the boundaries of a progressive interpretation of Hindu *dharma*.

I believe that our constitution should continue to bestow upon the king the traditional reverence and protection reserved for the Hindu king who strives to perform his *dharma* of impartially protecting his subjects. He should become, in a true sense, the spiritual protector of the Nepali people—a benevolent figurehead, pious as in ancient times, while yet progressive. He should surround himself with strong, religious, spiritual advisers from Nepal's traditional religions who can propound *dharma*. The *dharmic* advisers of the future should be respected spiritual leaders of any indigenous religious tradition in Nepal. The king should consult the world's greatest Vedic seers.

If the king focuses on the spiritual level, his relationship with the elected prime minister and the government and the people should contain no ambiguity. The king and the prime minister would be working at two different but complementary tasks. The role of our king would be to preserve

Hindu culture and values that embrace all indigenous traditions, and to reestablish consciousness in Nepali society. The prime minister would meet the people through the election. His *dharma* would be to reconstruct and develop the country, manage its economy, and maintain law and order. That duty of his would be less endangered if the king worked alongside him, protecting it at its source. Through this orientation the king's role need not collide with that of the government elected by the people. We need democratic revival and spiritual revival, and they should be simultaneous and complementary. Everything should be vested in the people, with the king guiding, the prime minister providing, the people participating, and no one undermining.

If the king can rebuild his share of these relationships, he can become powerful and influence policy. He should not impose ideas, even Vedic or other indigenous ones. But he can champion them. If the people support them, they can be implemented either by the state or by organizations of the private or nongovernment sectors. For inclusion in government programs, elected representatives would have to include the king's ideals in their manifesto. He might initiate a movement for revitalizing the Hindu-Buddhist tradition in schools and other institutions. He might approach this by campaigning around his kingdom and using the Nepali media to reawaken and remind his people that Vedic knowledge and other indigenous traditions are their heritage, to be practiced to help solve today's ills. He might sponsor a revival of Ayurvedic and other traditional systems of health as the indigenous basis for a national primary health care system, and promote Nepal as market leader in the emerging medicinal plant field in the West. Or he might patronize organizations conserving Nepal's antiquities and temples that provide cultural meaning to Nepalis, as well as drawing in income from tourism. Applying the Vedic science of architecture, *sthapatya veda*, to guide housing policy and the replanning of Nepal's polluted urban environments might be another royal cause, as might investment in reviving *gandharva veda*—sublime harmony-creating music. His Majesty and the queen might renew their interest in patronizing freely operating social sector organizations to help them fight social problems such as drug abuse, excessive drinking, gambling, prostitution, vagrancy, and mental illness. In all these and many other areas the king's serious support could contribute immeasurably to rebuilding a coherent Nepal nation. If the people sanction them, then they can be legislated.

When I think of Nepal's present dependence on foreign aid, an alternative vision comes to me of Vedic pandits and other indigenous specialists engaged as consultants in different fields. Astrologers should work alongside modern planners to combine classical wisdom on appropriate timing and placement with modern insights on technology and implementation. Education policy should encourage learning, research, and development of all branches of Vedic knowledge, using modern science and technology wherever it helps explain or develop our own indigenous sciences. Approaches to education that promote consciousness should be emphasized. Meditation and yoga teaching, practice, and research would be encouraged at all levels, and to maximize access to education, schooling should be free and compulsory through high school. Those unable to attend regular schools can be reached in alternative ways, including private education.

In my vision, I see the Himalayan kingdom of Nepal as the Shangri-la of legend. From healthy minds spring healthy ideas and actions. Through renewed will and a revival of indigenous science, her people can rediscover prosperity in a sustainable, ecologically sound development path. The kingdom's development plan should harmonize developments in agriculture and health to produce a population of healthy minds and healthy physiology. Ayurvedic and other traditional health systems can integrate conservation, food production, nutrition, and preventive and curative medicine into a comprehensive policy framework. Instead of relying only on introduced Western-style health care programs, which have had little impact throughout the hills, we should train local people in affordable traditional practices for primary health care in every small village where farmers can produce the herbal ingredients locally for most of the tonics and medicines. Only serious cases needing surgery or other specialized treatment would need referring to modern hospitals in district or regional centers. In complementary fashion, our agricultural and nutritional programs should encourage production of the components of a pure, balanced diet in each season, relying as far as possible on organic methods rather than on foreign chemicals. It is my belief that, if the nation invests in research to revive knowledge of herbal products and treatments, our plan for keeping our own population healthy will complement our new export orientation. If we aim to establish an international institute in this emerging field, we can become the global market leader.

Instead of exporting millions of tons of soil erosion, which contribute to Bangladeshi flood disasters, Nepal can be a purer, better neighbor, providing high-quality off-season produce for markets in northern India and beyond. Forests can regenerate or be replanted and serve as the protective canopy for medicinal and aromatic plants. Trade policies can be strengthened to control illegal overharvesting and export of these plants to India and Europe and additional conservation areas established with local communities in order to protect these and other natural resources for sustainable use. In the hills, the downward spiral in fodder supply, livestock numbers, manure, soil fertility, and crop yields can be reversed through a revival of indigenous farming systems attuned to local agroecology.

The kingdom should export essential oils, the finest silks, exquisite carpets and art, disease-free seeds and other planting materials of high purity, and Nepal's aromatic rices such as Krishnabhog ("to offer Krishna") and Jeerasari ("small as cumin seed"), which are far superior to any Basmati—all produced in appropriate locations outside the Kathmandu valley. It should produce what the world increasingly demands—organic produce for health food stores and Ayurvedic and other traditional remedies for the ills of Western civilization—heart disease, cancer, and immune disorders.

As for tourism, in my view it should build upon the uniqueness of Nepali culture rather than package standard international vacation technology. The world already knows of Nepal's scenic beauty and of the peace in her remote hills; of the birthplace of Lord Buddha; of Buddhist monasteries fourteen thousand feet up, nestling within amphitheaters of Himalayan peaks; of river rafting and jungle safaris. Adventure and exhilaration have always been available. What Nepal needs is high-quality organization to transform the average tourist experience from one of stomach illness and mild frustration—and now lungfuls of pollution—to one of radiant health, coherence, absorbing learning, and spiritual upliftment. Tourists and "seekers" should come to Nepal to explore its antiquities, follow its paths and trails, breathe in its natural beauty, learn its knowledge, receive its cures, and deepen their self-awareness.

We can turn the street children from pickpockets into conscientious young tour guides. Mountainside learning centers, clinics, and hospices can be staffed with Nepalis highly trained in Ayurvedic and Tibetan mind/body healing techniques and nutritious Vedic cuisine. If the government ensures the highest standards of purity, an affluent Western clientele can be ferried by a helicopter service into Himalayan settings for the mountains' restorative treatment. As these people rejuvenate, they can wander through protected areas to study the healing plants of the Himalayas. The government might even recommend codes of dress for foreign visitors, as scantily clothed foreigners look unsightly and offend Nepali sensibilities.

Physically, Nepal can become a Himalayan Switzerland. Rivers should be harnessed. The barren east-west valleys between the Mahabharat and Chure mountain ranges can be flooded, providing irrigated land for settlement, recreational lakes, and cottage industries in brasswork, jewelry, stone and wood carving, sericulture, weaving, floriculture, and horticultural and herbal-based agroindustries. I envision industry directed toward meeting basic needs as in housing, organic farming, and small-scale solar and hydro energy. Large-scale hydroelectricity-generating projects planned and implemented with diligent attention to environmental and social issues can earn national income from sales to neighboring countries and enable food processing of seasonal horticultural surpluses at different altitudes. It will be necessary, also, to expand the road and communications network to facilitate transport and trade.

To slow migration to the plains and the towns, we must raise living standards on the hillsides and in the valleys in the hills. The hill people are strong and enterprising. For long they have guided trekkers, woven carpets, carried goods, and farmed with no government support. If the government provides them with a little training, basic services, resources, and markets, their local trades can flourish.

Our ex-Gurkha servicemen can also provide an enduring security role. The hill people who left to join foreign armies to serve in Gurkha regiments have been returning to little more than collecting their British pensions. Perhaps controversially, I see them settling with their families in irrigated reintegration communities along the Indian border. With their military and other practical skills these people would make productive settlers and at the same time help secure our borders.

Finally, I see a solution for Nepal's prisons. If their inmates and staff all meditate and practice yoga daily they can become models for a correctional process based on our indigenous principle of *danda*, that system of rehabilitation that restores a person's realization of *dharma*, right duty, and thereby social harmony. Meditation and yoga clear the fears and prejudice we carry around with us. Realization returns. Each individual can contribute and be satisfied, knowing that what he or she does is respected because others too live in that state of realization. Quickly, prisons will empty and a healing process will spread throughout society. Even a Pode might have a vision for doing her job better, or she might envision another calling.

In a conscious Nepali society established in right action, there will be less rape, fewer unwanted pregnancies, and fewer pressures to abort. Society will sympathize more with the single mother. And even if social acceptance is slow to come, the lawgiver can be liberal in interpreting antiabortion laws, careful to consider the health of the mother. In a coherent society we will not need "women's organizations." In Hindu thought male and female are created equal and inseparable. Women's "issues" are not some infection in society's body that has to be treated in isolation. Society will not need separate pressure groups and lobbyists who will swamp the legislators and endanger democracy.

In time Nepal may become a society of equal opportunity. An untouchable may become a Brahmin. Caste in Nepal is inextricably linked with human rights violation. It has become ingrained for "higher" to disrespect "lower." Choice of caste and restructuring of the caste system are not unknown concepts in Nepal. Historically, people were given freedom of choice to decide their caste professions. It is not that once born a shoemaker, or Sarki, all generations thereafter have to remain Sarki. In the Veda there are precedents for conversion from one born caste to another according to a person's actions, or *karma,* in this current life.

In my vision of a tolerant, pluralistic Hindu kingdom, new social and religious organizations will be spawned. People will be free to perform their *karma yoga* or any form of devotion. But, to stimulate mobility—to free the Nepali nation from its paralysis—more than "passive" freedom of religion, and more even than caste conversion, will be needed. A progressive path of consciousness attainment should be one that is acceptable both to the performer and to all groups in our Hindu-Buddhist society, no matter what their form of religious expression.

A Vedic formula can be revived that enunciates such a path and reinterprets the meaning of caste according to attributes and the changing texture of Nepali society as it modernizes. People wishing to progress along this path can learn a similar consciousness-enhancing technique and contribute together to restoring their society's collective mind. If all groups in society grow together in this path, caste will take on its originally intended symbolic meaning, reflecting an individual's freely chosen *dharma,* the state at any moment in time of his or her vision, will, conduct, and profession. People may start remarking, "He's so Brahminic, the way he can discern the truth in any situation," or "What a Chhetrini she is in her fight against drug abuse," or "He's a great Vaisya, so clever at business," and "She works away with the humility and devotion of a Shudra." This would be a casteless Hindu society.

As society becomes Westernized, the distinctive values of castes break down, but in a disorderly, negative way that creates victims. Instead of this, we need leadership to guide social change positively while staying within the boundaries of culture. Every caste and ethnic group should have an equal right to live in the light of any branch of Vedic or other indigenous knowledge. Anyone may become enlightened. A Nepali may be pure in thought, word, and action, and still not hesitate to clean the street. Beyond a political revolution, freedom to choose *dharma* within a spiritually inspired society should restore realization and human rights to each and every Nepali.

# Glossary

| | |
|---|---|
| Abala | Literally a- (no) bala (strength), or weak. It is used to indicate the feminine (weaker) sex, though not in a negative sense. Also powerless. |
| Aila | (Newari language) Highly intoxicating liquor home-brewed from finger millet or rice. |
| Aiyaa | Expression of pain. |
| Ama | Mother. Also, any elderly lady may be called ama by younger people. |
| Anchaladhish | Zonal Commissioner. From Sanskrit, Anchal, zone + adhish, chief. |
| Arya | Aryan. |
| Ayurveda | Ayu (life) + veda (science). The r is a joining consonant common in Sanskrit. Ayurveda was the only formal health care system in Nepal until the early 1900s. Its emphasis is on balance and the complete integration of spirit, mind, and body to prevent as well as cure illness. |
| Bahini | Younger sister. Often people in Nepal do not call one another by their names but use relational forms of address. A younger woman is addressed as bahini, an older woman as didi (older sister). |
| Bahula | Lunatic. The Nepali equivalent of the Hindi pagal. |
| Bakhu | Traditional Tibetan dress worn by women. |
| Bandha | Closed. |
| Bar-pipal | Male and female trees (banyan and pipal) believed to possess sacred qualities, planted and used for religious purposes. |

| | |
|---|---|
| Behuli | Bride. |
| Bhai | Younger brother. Used in a similar way to *bahini*. |
| Bhajan | Devotional Hindu psalm sung in praise of a deity. Many are well established and well-known, with more or less unvarying form. But, with thirty-three million forms of deity distinguished in Hinduism, there is plenty of room for fresh compositions. |
| Bidi | Indigenous cigarette of Nepal and India. Small, cone-shaped cigarette of raw tobacco and molasses mix wrapped usually with a leaf of the Sal tree. |
| Bindi | Ready-made liquid red *tika* in a small bottle with applicator. |
| Birta | Inheritable, tax-free land grant. Land gifted by the ruler in recognition of bravery, loyalty, services. |
| Brahmagyana | Eternal truth. *Brahmagyani*, one who is enlightened; literally, with eternal knowledge of God. |
| Brahmin | (Sanskrit; Nepali, Bahun) Highest rank in the Vedic social order and Hindu caste system. Literally, the possessor of knowledge. Mythological origin—those who sprang from Bramha's head. |
| Bramha | God, the creator aspect of Godhead. |
| Chaukidarni | Literally, watchperson (the *-ni* suffix denotes a female). Term adapted in prison to denote the head of the inside-prison criminal organization. |
| Chautaro/chautara | (Singular/plural) Platform made around bar-pipal trees for travelers to use to rest. |
| Chhetri | Nepali for Kshatriya, the second social rank in the caste system. Female, Chhetrini. |
| Chhori | Daughter. |
| Chita | Funeral pyre on which a Hindu is cremated. In prison there was just a symbolic *chita* where dead bodies were laid until a Pode-caste person came to remove them. |
| Chulo/chula | (Singular/plural) Indigenous floor-level mud stove. |
| Dada | Hills. |
| Dai | Older brother. |
| Daju | Older brother (more formal). |
| Dal | Pulses, particularly of the lentil species. |
| Damini | An untouchable (Shudra) caste group whose women are traditionally tailors. |
| Danda | Punishment. The obverse of *dharma*; a traditional system of correction whose result was to restore a person's realization and consciousness of *dharma*, right duty, and thereby social harmony. |

| | |
|---|---|
| Darshan | Audience, vision. Reverent word for a vision of a deity or for a saint or a king's sharing of his presence with disciples or subjects. |
| Dasain | The biggest Hindu festival of Durga Puja, fifteen days' celebration of the goddess Durga's slaying of a devil (nine days of struggle, the tenth-day victory, and five days of celebration). The same festival is known as Dashera in India. The rituals are slightly different. |
| Daura-suruwal | Nepali men's national dress. The *daura* shirt is similar to the women's *kurta*. Worn with *suruwal*, a matching pair of pants. *Suruwal* pants are tight around the legs and very wide and baggy around the hips and backside. Women's dress is the *kurta suruwal* (see *kurta*). |
| Dera | A rented room or house. |
| Devanagari | The ancient script of written Sanskrit. Nepali and Hindi use the same script today. |
| Dharma | Eternal truth or natural law governing creation; religion, the sacred law; righteous duty or way of living. Thus *Raj dharma*, the king's rightful duty; *nyayadhish dharma*, the rightful duty of a judge; or the *dharma* of caring for the poor. The adjective is *dharmic*, as in "a *dharmic* person or place," meaning righteous, religious, or attuned to truth. *Adharma* is the negative or opposite of *dharma*. *Kuldharma* is ancestral religion or customary law. |
| Dharmasankat | The state of *dharma* in danger or in trouble. |
| Dhoti | A loincloth worn by Hindu men. |
| Didi/dijyu | Older sister. *Dijyu* is the more respectful form. |
| Doko | A three-foot-deep basket woven from bamboo and carried on the back and held by a strap across the forehead. Used throughout the Nepal hills for transport of materials by porters and farm families. |
| Durbar | Palace. |
| Durga | Goddess of strength, with eighteen arms, indicating the personality and power of nine people. Durga is called *Durgati nashini*, "destroyer of bad conditions." In Hinduism the female has the most significant role in society, therefore many people become *Devi bhakta*, devotees of female deities or aspects of God. Durga Puja, the biggest Hindu festival, is an example of such following and celebrates the victory of knowledge over ignorance. |
| Ganesh | Elephant-headed deity, son of Shiva and Parvati, who personifies all endearing qualities such as cheerfulness, naïveté, obedience, and dutifulness; worshipped as the god of good |

|  |  |
|---|---|
| | fortune. To worship any other deity, or undertake any activity, a Hindu should first perform *puja* of Lord Ganesh. *Shree Ganesh* means "to begin with." Then any door will open. |
| Ghee | Clarified butter, used especially for preparing religious offerings. |
| Gorkha | One of the seventy-five districts of Nepal and the original seat of power of the Shah kings. In the late eighteenth century, the then-king of Gorkha, Prithvi Narayan Shah, unified what is now Nepal. He was a skillful and reputedly just ruler. There was a saying—"*Nyaya na paya Gorkha janu*"— meaning "If you don't receive justice, go to Gorkha." The British first recruited Gurung tribesmen, noted for their dogged loyalty, from the hills of the Gorkha area and called them Gurkhas. Later, Limbus and other hill ethnic groups were recruited. |
| Gurkhas | British depiction of Nepali warrior class (see *Gorkha*). |
| Guru | Teacher. Connotes a spiritual master, a spiritual teacher, or a guide who undertakes to lead his or her disciples to God-realization. Female, *gurumaa*. |
| Guyashowri | Shiva's consort. |
| Gyan | Knowledge. |
| Hakkim | A senior officer, especially a chief of an organization or government office. |
| Haldar/Hawaldar | Sergeant, the rank above constable in the Nepali police force. |
| Himal | Snowy mountain. |
| HMG | His Majesty's Government of Nepal. |
| Jaya | Victory, glory. *Ki jaya* means "of victory." |
| -ji/-jyu | Suffix added at end of a person's name, title, or rank; expresses love or respect. When used after a deity's name it indicates reverence. |
| Jogi/jogini | Male/female person who has renounced family life to live in a temple *dharmasala* or hermitage (see also *yogi*). |
| Jyotish | Astrology. One of the systems of Vedic science. |
| Kalopani | Black water. |
| Kamdar | Worker. |
| Kanchhi | Youngest female. |
| Karma | Fortune or luck; action or work; the law of causation; the reaction, reward, or fruit of past actions in this and previous lifetimes. |
| Kaviraj | Ayurvedic physician. |
| Khadgo | Grave obstacle. Usually refers to an astrological event visi- |

|   |   |
|---|---|
| | ble in an astrological chart. Vedic formulas may be used to avert their influence. |
| Khukri | The Nepali national weapon, a slightly curved heavy field knife (a little thicker and shorter than a sword), often with embossed decorations on its handle and leather case. Used for farm and domestic work, as well as for defense. |
| Korra | A cruel instrument of torture used routinely by the Nepali police during Panchayat rule. It was a beating stick with a sharp iron spike at a right angle to the end of the stick that could gouge deep wounds in a victim's body. |
| Krishna | The supreme personality of Godhead. Hero of the *Mahabharata* epic and a divine being who takes different incarnations to punish evildoers and protect the good, as He explained to Arjuna in the Bhagavad Gita. The Krishna cult is one of the most devotional spiritual paths in Hinduism. |
| Kshatriya | (Sanskrit) Ruling or warrior caste, second in rank in caste system after Brahmin. |
| Kukhurikaa | The sound of a cock crowing. |
| Kurta | Women's *punjabi*-style below-the-knee-length shirt, worn with baggy-topped tight-legged *suruwal* trousers. |
| Laash | Corpse. |
| Lakh | One hundred thousand. |
| Lakshmi | Goddess of wealth, worshipped at Lakshmi Puja. People become devotees of Lakshmi, and worship her daily, if they desire her blessings so that they may become rich. Lakshmi Puja is celebrated by all Hindus in Nepal and India in what Westerners call the Festival of Lights. |
| Lokadalat | Literally, people's court. *Lok adalat* in pre-Panchayat Nepal was an informal, generally local-level, court mediated by respected village elders. In contemporary India nongovernmental organizations and social activists have helped strengthen such indigenous institutions, enabling village people to solve disputes and sometimes serious cases locally, avoiding the hassle and expense of the official judiciary. |
| Lungi | A two-meter-long sarong-type waist wrap of cloth, worn informally. |
| Maaji | Respectful way of saying "mother" in Hindi. |
| Mahakali | The farthest west of Nepal's fourteen zones, named after the Mahakali River, which forms the western border with India. Mahakali (Sanskrit: *maha* [great], *kali* [black]) is a terrifying black form that the goddess Durga takes in the struggle to punish evildoers. |

| | |
|---|---|
| Maharaja | *Maha* (great) + *raja* (king). The formal designation of a Hindu king who remains pious. By tradition, Nepalese kings are still addressed as Maharaja. |
| Maithili | A rich, literary Indian language spoken in north-central India, bordering south-central Nepal. It is the language of old Mithila, an ancient culture and one of India's prosperous former kingdoms. |
| Maiya | Loved one. Affectionate form of address for females in Nepal. Alone, or as *nani maiya*, it may also be a girl's name. |
| Manas | Mind, conscience. The title we gave to our weekly newspaper. |
| Mandale | *Mandal* (group of people). *Mandal* became the name of the Panchayat government-backed student union. Members of the *Mandal* student union became known as *Mandales;* the government used them as spies and thugs for disrupting opposition activity. |
| Mano | Volume unit of grain measurement, equivalent to less than a pound weight of rice. |
| Mantra | A sacred syllable, word, or set of words that produces a sound vibration believed to embody the deity or transcendental influence invoked and that, when repeated and reflected upon, helps a person quiet and deliver the mind from illusion. *Sri Ganeshaya Namaha* is an example of a mantra, meaning "I bow down to, or take refuge in, Lord Ganesh." |
| Mathi | Above. *Mathi bata* (from above). |
| Mukhiya | Third rank from the bottom in HMG bureaucracy. |
| Mulnaike | *Mul* (main) + *naike* (foreman). A position in the inside-prison criminal organization. |
| Munti | Most abusive Nepali, meaning "come here." |
| Naike | Chief, or foreman. Outside prison, *naike* is the term used for forest nursery keepers; water *naikes* have the duty of turning the piped water supply on and off. In jail, *Chaukidarni* was like commander-in-chief, *Mulnaike* the commanding officer, and *naikes* like company commanders. |
| Namaste/namaskar | Nepali greeting used any time you meet or bid farewell to someone. At the same time you must press your hands together in front of or just below your face. The greeting means, "I salute your soul, or God in you." *Namaste* is more common and informal. *Namaskar* is more polite. |
| Netaji | Politician, leader. The *-ji* suffix denotes respect. |
| Newar | Tibeto-Burmese ethnic group in Nepal. Newars are mainly traders and skilled artisans who have established tight communities across most of Nepal as centers of trade. They are |

|  | the dominant inhabitants of the Kathmandu valley. Newari is their language. |
|---|---|
| Pagal | Hindi equivalent of *bahula* (lunatic). Most Nepalis are unaware that *pagal* is Hindi, therefore the terms are used interchangeably. |
| Paisa | Money (generic term), *pai* for short. It is also Nepali currency, one *paisa* being one hundredth of a *rupiya*, the Nepali rupee. |
| Pancha | Member of a *panchayat*. *Pradhan pancha* was the chief *pancha* in a town or village *panchayat*. |
| Panchayat | Name of the political system that ruled Nepal for thirty years, 1960–1990. The name was derived from *panch* (five) + *ayat* (house)—the name for the groups of five elders who used to govern villages and maintain local-level law and order in the past. King Mahendra borrowed this name in 1960 for his partyless political system. The *Rastriya Panchayat* became the national assembly. Below this level were *jilla*, *nagar*, and *gaun panchayats*—at district, town, and village levels, respectively. |
| Paper | Colloquial term for a *bidi* (cigarette) that is wrapped in paper instead of leaf. |
| Parkote | Unexposed to city civilization, rustic. |
| Parvati | The consort of Lord Shiva, understood in Hinduism also as Shakti, the female energy or aspect of creation. |
| Pashupatinath | *Pashu* (animal) + *pati* (lord) + *nath* (lord). Another name for Lord Shiva. The Pashupatinath temple in Kathmandu is one of the holiest temples and places of pilgrimage for Hindus in the world. |
| Peon | The lowest-rank worker in any formal office. Messenger, tea maker. |
| Pode | A Shudra (untouchable) caste whose profession is street and toilet cleaning and disposal of dead bodies of vagrants and the homeless. |
| Pranayama | Yogic practice of controlling breathing as an aid to meditation. |
| Prasad | Offerings of food, drink, or flowers blessed by the deity for ritual consumption by devotees. |
| Puja | Hindu worship ritual performed with elaborate offerings. |
| Raj | Rule. *Panchayat(i) Raj*, Panchayat rule. |
| Raja | King or sovereign ruler. Any male member of the royal family is addressed as Raja by his servants. |
| Rana | The Kshatriya (Chhetri) clan that ruled Nepal as its fiefdom for 104 years, 1846–1950. |

Rishi     A Vedic sage or seer, especially one who propounded early Hindu concepts and scripture.

Rupiya, rupiah     Unit of currency. Rupee, the Nepali currency. The current exchange rate is fifty-two *rupiya* to the U.S. dollar.

Sagarmatha     Literally, "head of the mountain." The Nepali term for Mount Everest.

Saheb     Nepali for the Hindi *sahib*. Originally a title of respect equivalent to "sir" that the British borrowed from Hindi for their subjects to use when addressing their colonial masters. The Hindi word meant "master," "lord." Nowadays in Nepal almost anyone can be a *saheb*—"Jailor *Saheb*," "Doctor *Saheb*," "Police *Saheb*."

Saraswati     Goddess of learning. Symbolized by a very beautiful goddess dressed in white, playing the *bina* (a stringed instrument similar to a sitar), and holding a book.

Sarkar     Government. The Nepali king is also addressed as Sarkar, meaning "Your Majesty."

Sarki     Shoemaker caste, a Shudra group.

Sati     A widow who goes to be burned alive on her dead husband's funeral pyre. The word is also used for a woman who lives utterly chastely in her husband's name for life, whether he is alive or dead.

Satwo, sattva     Purity, truthfulness. The element or quality of *satya* (truth).

Satya     Truth, truthfulness. *Satwic:* evolutionary, possessing the attributes of *satya*.

Shaash     Breath.

Shiva     God of destruction and purification of creation. Shiva (or Maheshwara) is one of the Hindu trinity of gods—Bramha, Vishnu, and Shiva. Shiva is also worshipped as the Absolute God and Creator, the male partner for creation, by Shiva followers. Shivaratri, "night of Shiva," is the annual festival, fast, and nighttime *puja* of Shiva.

Shudra     Laborer. The fourth category of the Hindu social order, its members perform tasks involving uncleanliness and are therefore regarded as untouchable. Believed to have sprung during creation from Bramha's feet.

Siddhi     Extraordinary power or mastery (equivalent to "miracles") gained through certain religious practices and austerities. Enlightenment.

Sindhur     Vermillion. Also the vermillion mark of marriage a Hindu woman places in her hair parting.

Sri     A term of respect or reverence. Ordinary usage translates as "Mr." For God the address is spelled with a longer *i*, making *Shree*.

| | |
|---|---|
| Sthan | Place. |
| Sthapatya veda | Science of architecture. A branch of the six-thousand-year-old knowledge system of the *Vedas*. |
| Sunya | Empty, quiet. |
| Tapas, tapasya | Austerity, acceptance of voluntary inconvenience or sacrifice for a higher purpose. |
| Tarai | The fertile southern belt of lowland in Nepal bordering the Gangetic plains of India. |
| Tika | A symbolic or decorative dot, star, or other shaped mark on a woman's forehead, traditionally compulsory for married women and now commonly used in makeup. *Tika* also refers to any religious ceremonial marking of the forehead, in which case its meaning is nearer to "blessing." |
| Topi | The national cap of Nepal, worn by men as part of national dress. The hand-weaving of *topi* is a traditional skill of some of the hill ethnic groups, who produce multicolored patterned fabric specially for *topi* making. Alternatively, a *topi* may be black. |
| Trikaladarshi | *Tri* (three) + *kal* (period) + *darshi* (one who sees or visualizes). |
| Tulsi | A plant of the basil family, planted in a sacred raised bed, or *math*, in every Hindu family yard. It is believed that Vishnu resides in this plant. A leaf from this plant is placed in the mouth of a dying person so that it will be easier for him or her to give up breath. |
| Vaisya | Merchant, farmer. Third rank in the Vedic social order. |
| Veda | Original revealed scriptures. Literally, "science" or "knowledge," referring to complete knowledge of manifest and unmanifest creation. Vedic texts span every imaginable area of knowledge of life. |
| Vishnu | The first expansion of Godhead for the creation and protection of the material universes. |
| Vivekshil | Kindly, benevolent. |
| Yagya | Sacrifice; a major religious ritual performed to divert negativity, purify, or to supplicate God for something (e.g., to conceive a child). *Yagya* includes the sacred fire ceremony in which the worshipper offers back to the Divine portions of the five elements that sustain creation. |
| Yamaraj | The death god, symbolized by a fierce-looking figure carried by a wild black buffalo. |
| Yoga | Literally, "union" (Sanskrit). Vedic knowledge or discipline for attaining union with the Divine or transcendent. The branch of yoga involving physical postures is properly called Hatha Yoga. |

Yogi  Practitioner of yoga. A transcendentalist, hermit, or ascetic who has renounced family life and is devoted to a spiritual path of union with the Supreme. Some remain for years in caves and temples, others (called *jogi* in Nepali) wander around from house to house for *bhikshya*, a handful of uncooked rice and a few *paisa*. Great yogis are *trikaladarshi*, meaning they can see past, present, and future.

# Index

## About the Authors

In Nepal, DURGA POKHREL was a university lecturer, a journalist, and a pro-democracy and human rights activist. Jailed often from 1974 to 1982, she was adopted by Amnesty International as a Prisoner of Conscience. She was forced to flee Nepal in 1983 and came to the United States, where she attended Harvard University's Kennedy School of Government as a Mason Fellow. In addition to receiving a master's degree in public administration and a doctorate in education from Harvard, she holds a bachelor's degree in history and literature, a master's in modern history, and a law degree.

Born in England, her husband and coauthor, ANTHONY WILLETT, is a specialist in international rural development and conservation, with advanced degrees from Cambridge, Reading, Iowa State, and Harvard universities, including a doctorate in agricultural education. The parents of three boys, Samyog, Shristi, and Tapasya, they live in McLean, Virginia.